DUBLIN RISING 1916

POBLACHT NA H-EIREANN

THE PROVISIONAL GOVERNMENT

OF THE

IRISH REPUBLIC

TO THE PEOPLE OF IRELAND

IRISHMEN AND IRISHWOMEN. In the name of God and of the dead generations from which she receives her old tradition of nationhood, Ireland, through us, summons her children to her flag and strikes for her freedom.

Having organised and trained her manhood through her secret revolutionary organisation, the Irish Republican Brotherhood, and through her open military organisations, the Irish Volunteers and the Irish Citizen Army having patiently perfected her discipline, having resolutely waited for the right moment to reveal itself, she now seizes that moment, and, supported by her exiled children in America and by gallant allies in Europe, but relying in the first on her own strength, she strikes in full confidence of victory.

We declare the right of the people of Ireland to the ownership of Ireland and to the unfettered control of Irish destinies, to be sovereign and indefeasible. The long usurpation of that right by a foreign people and government has not extinguished the right, nor can it ever be extinguished except by the destruction of the Irish people. In every generation the Irish people have asserted their right to national freedom and sovereignty: six times during the past three hundred years they have asserted it in arms. Standing on that fundamental right and again asserting it in arms in the face of the world, we hereby proclaim the Irish Republic as a Sovereign Independent State, and we pledge our lives and the lives of our comrades-in-arms to the cause of its freedom, of its welfare, and of its exaltation among the nations.

The Irish Republic is entitled to, and hereby claims, the allegiance of every Irishman and Irishwoman. The Republic guarantees religious and civil liberty, equal rights and equal opportunities to all its citizens, and declares its resolve to pursue the happiness and prosperity of the whole nation and of all its parts, cherishing all the children of the nation equally, and oblivious of the differences carefully fostered by an alien government which have divided a minority from the majority in the past.

Until our arms have brought the opportune moment for the establishment of a permanent National Government, representative of the whole people of Ireland and elected by the suffrages of all her men and women, the Provisional Government hereby constituted, will administer the civil and military affairs of the Republic in trust for the people.

We place the cause of the Irish Republic under the protection of the Most High God, Whose blessing we invoke upon our arms, and we pray that no one who serves that cause will dishonour it by cowardice, inhumanity, or rapine. In this supreme hour the Irish nation must, by its valour and discipline and by the readiness of its children to sacrifice themselves for the common good, prove itself worthy of the august destiny to which it is called.

Signed on Behalf of the Provisional Government,

THOMAS J. CLARKE,

SEAN Mac DIARMADA,   THOMAS MacDONAGH,
P. H. PEARSE,   EAMONN CEANNT,
JAMES CONNOLLY,   JOSEPH PLUNKETT,

Paramount, Cork.

Dublin Rising 1916

Joseph E.A. Connell, Jnr

Wordwell

To Pam
Mo cheann gra fior

First published in 2015
Wordwell Ltd
Unit 9, 78 Furze Road, Sandyford Industrial Estate, Dublin 18
www.wordwellbooks.com

Cover image—Destroyed buildings on Henry Street, looking east towards Lord Nelson's Pillar. © National Library of Ireland.
Back cover—Abbey Street corner and ruins of Dublin Bread Company. © National Library of Ireland.

ISBN 1 905569 90 8

British Library Cataloguing-in-Publication Data.
A catalogue record for this book is available from the British Library.

All images © National Library of Ireland except where indicated.

Typeset in Ireland by Wordwell Ltd
Copy-editor: Emer Condit
Cover design: Ger Garland
Printed by Castle Print, Galway

Contents

Acknowledgements

I must thank my parents for everything; without them I would have had no such love for Ireland. And, of course, my brothers and sister and their families supported me at all times.

I am most grateful to Wordwell Ltd, and it has been a pleasure to work with Nick Maxwell, Una MacConville, Helen Dunne and everyone at the publishing house. They have given polish to my efforts and all their assistance was wonderful.

My raw text was beautifully edited by Emer Condit. She corrected my errors and I cannot thank her enough. Tommy Graham of *History Ireland* has been most encouraging and helpful at all times. I am indebted to him for allowing me to write a column, *Countdown to 2016*, in *History Ireland*.

Mary Mackey of the Irish National Archives has always been most helpful and has given me wonderful direction, as well as being very generous with her time.

Tom Duffy has been unstinting with his time and support, and his knowledge of Dublin, its history and its people is unequalled. Without his encouragement this book would not have been contemplated; without his advice it would not have been completed.

I am grateful to Anthony Tierney for his continuing advice and suggestions.

Dr Patrick Geoghehan and Susan Cahill have given me the privilege of a recurring spot on their NewsTalk radio show, *Talking History*. It has been a joy to work with them over the years and I am most grateful.

Mícheál Ó Doibhilín, the editor of www.kilmainhamtales.ie, has let me submit articles for his site and has published a small book of mine, *Rebels' priests*, under his imprint. I am always pleased with his editing and guidance.

Lorcan Collins kindly lets me lead his 1916 Easter Rising Tour on occasion and I particularly thank him for the opportunity.

I am extremely thankful to Lou Yovin for his kind and most patient assistance, as I am technologically illiterate as far as computers are concerned. His help was invaluable.

I have always been welcomed throughout Ireland with the greatest kindness and hospitality, and I thank everyone with whom I've spoken. I assure you that those feelings are returned with the deepest and most lasting affection.

Those individuals who have helped and encouraged me are too numerous to mention and I thank them all. Everyone I asked always gave me assistance, reassurance and direction. All heartened me when I needed that most, and from time to time most fed me when I needed that most, too. At the risk of offending someone I omit, I must especially mention Pam Boyd, Áine Broy, Dr Mary Clark, Bob Clarke, Finbar Collins, C.B. Connell, Briny M. Connell, Revd Paul Connell, Clare Cowley, Kerry Edwards,

Bob Fuquea, Col. David Fuquea, James Connolly Heron, Barbara Hollandsworth, Grainne Áine Hollandsworth, Lar Joye, Peggy Keating, David Kilmartin, Desmond Long, Sinead McCoole, Jim McIlmurray, Barbara and Dominic Montaldi, Gregory O'Connor, Donal Ó hUallachain, Maeve O'Leary, Pól Ó Murchú, Detta and Seán Spellissy, John and Judy Wohlford and Pádraig Yeates.

And, always, Pam Brewster for all things.

Preface

I have become so accustomed to thinking of Rutland Square, Sackville Street and Great Brunswick Street that I have to remind myself that those names are long gone. But whenever I walked Sackville Street (O'Connell Street) or any of Dublin's streets I wondered just what secrets were held within the buildings, rooms and halls that lined them. In those buildings I found the ghosts of men and women who lived in the years of rebellion. Walking in their steps humanised those who participated in the Rising, and this book attempts to unlock the places that are in plain sight yet remain secret to many passers-by. These streets and buildings make the characters real by associating them with what is still visible before us. This is a book about backstage Dublin as well as 'front-stage' Dublin—not just the high streets but also the byways and boreens.

It is not intended that the book should be read from cover to cover. It was not written that way and I wish it to be an awakening for the reader, as it has been for me. This makes for a book that one can read for just a few minutes or into which one can delve for hours. Any time spent will allow the reader to begin a process of getting to know those whose dedication, industry and life's blood made modern Ireland. A fundamental question is whether the Rising advanced or hindered Irish independence; I believe Charles Townsend stated it most simply when he said that it 'quickened the pulse of the separatist movement'. Knowledge of the places that played a part in the lives of those who led and participated helps us to understand them better.

Navigation throughout the postal codes is easy using the maps provided. One should freely use the Index and referral notes to move from one location to another. Each section of the book is arranged alphabetically to allow the easiest access to the information, which then appears chronologically within an address.

Like all revolutionary endeavours, the Rising was a gamble. It was launched by dedicated men and women who believed that any effort was better than none, but their plans of operations had not been, and could not have been, fully worked out. All revolutionaries extemporise—it is only their determination to be revolutionaries that is fixed. The participants left few notes and still fewer 'minutes' of meetings. Only afterwards did some write down their thoughts and try to memorialise events. Nevertheless, although there are many primary source documents and they are readily available, the recollections of those who took part differ markedly.

A good illustration is the question of exactly *when* Padraic Pearse joined the Irish Republican Brotherhood. The most probable date is shortly *after* the foundation of the Volunteers. It was said that 'In December [1913], Bulmer Hobson took a further decisive step—he swore Pearse into the IRB'. Others, however, have written that 'He joined the IRB in 1913, five months before the Irish Volunteers began'. And some note that Pearse was also said to have been refused membership in an IRB circle in the ordinary way and was 'co-opted' into the IRB at the end of 1913.

The history of the period is replete with such stories, and this book is an attempt to give the reader the fullest information possible by noting where such events took place, the circumstances, and the most comprehensive lists of individuals involved. Use was made of as many primary sources as possible, particularly official records and correspondence of the participants, as well as newspapers and journal articles that appeared very shortly after the events.

The Bureau of Military History's Witness Statements and collection of contemporaneous documents were invaluable. Whenever possible, the statements were cross-checked with other sources to provide an accurate record, and contrasts are made between contemporary accounts of events and those that appeared later. As with all oral histories, however, there are caveats. A reader must exercise caution in relation to the witness who may have had lapses in memory, either intentionally or unintentionally, or through exaggeration. Anyone working with oral sources and retrospective testimony needs to familiarise himself/herself with the methodologies of oral history and memory studies to assess and interpret them well. There are two generally agreed principles when working with oral sources: (1) they should be used in conjunction with surviving contemporary evidence; (2) recollections of events that an interviewee actually witnessed or experienced are generally more accurate than information heard second-hand. Moreover, one must consider the fact that these statements were recorded after the witnesses had knowledge of subsequent events, and decades after the events occurred. Still, the statements are a veritable gold mine of information, and one can tell how vivid the memories were for all who frankly recorded them.

A list of those who applied for pensions for service in the Rising was released in 2014. Applicants were required to supply a great deal of supporting documentation and to provide very detailed accounts of their activities; their testimony needed to be verified and clarified, sometimes through oral examinations.

I also wanted to include as many women and their stories as I could find. Prior to the Rising, women worked a 90-hour week (men worked 70 hours) and received an average wage of five shillings (men averaged fourteen shillings). Life was terribly hard for all in Dublin in those years, but especially so for women. James Connolly aptly described them as 'slaves to the slaves'. Early in the twentieth century women's efforts were primarily social and for universal suffrage. But owing in part to the labour shortage caused by World War I, many women entered the salaried workforce for the first time. Moving into the paid workforce had a consciousness-raising effect on women—they became much more politicised.

The commitment of women before, during and after the Rising helped to bring the Irish nation to support the separatist movement. The widows of those executed in Kilmainham Gaol after the Rising did more to draw attention to the independence movement than any other group. The widows and female relatives of the captives filled the voids in leadership and ensured that Irish independence did not die with their loved ones. In the aftermath of the Rising, women were primarily responsible for the propaganda that helped mould opinion to respect the martyrdom of the 1916 leaders. Women created a revolutionary fervour throughout the countryside.

One hundred and forty-six witness statements were taken from women, and many women also provided collections of original documents and photographs. Those are the documents and recollections of women's history, 'grounded on first-hand testimony, grounded on observations at the critical level of the ordinary and commonplace'.

During the early twentieth century women became increasingly important in the pursuit of Irish independence and political and civil rights for all. They came from every walk of life, asserting their rightful claim in shaping the nation. They joined the male-dominated organisations of the period—particularly the Home Rule Party, Sinn Féin and the Gaelic League—but also started their own organisations. Often they had to do so in order to have a role in their operation and influence on their policies. Inghínidhe na hÉireann, the Women's Social and Political Union, the Irish Women's Workers' Union, Cumann na mBan, the Irish Women's Franchise League and many others all contributed greatly to the independence, labour and franchise movements of the time.

Yet women were far removed from the decision-making levels of the Dáil elected in 1918 and other organisations. They were not put forward for Cabinet or other high offices, though there were many qualified candidates (Countess Markievicz was the only exception). They were judges, educators, writers, social and labour activists, freedom fighters, spies, county council officials, but seldom major politicians. Women were often intentionally sidelined by the male-dominated nationalist groups; such wonderful leaders as Áine Ceannt, Helena Molony, Marie Perolz, Winifred Carney and so many others were ignored or relegated to lesser political roles, or were later appointed to the Seanad, bypassing election to the Dáil. The ability to make decisions and to implement them is not a gender-specific trait—it is a common human one.

Discussion of the women of the period usually focuses on the influence and activities of Countess Markievicz and Hanna Sheehy-Skeffington, as well as Kathleen Clarke and other widows of the executed Rising leaders. But as Mary Cullen so aptly wrote, 'A woman like Markievicz may be seen as a part of Irish history when she is participating in nationalist or labour political or military activity. But she and other women are not seen as part of Irish history when they campaign in support of women's claims for civil and political rights.' While these women were the most noted activists of the time, tens of thousands of mothers and wives who did not achieve public or celebrity status played an enormous role in changing popular opinion—they irrevocably changed the role for Irishwomen, albeit a role that is still to be completely achieved. *They* converted the nation. *They* pushed their families towards nationalist beliefs and equal rights and opportunities for all.

Heroes, every one.

Abbreviations

Ancient Order of Hibernians	AOH
Baronet	Bt
Criminal Investigation Division	CID
Defence of the Realm Act	DORA
Dublin Metropolitan Police	DMP
Dublin United Tram Company	DUTC
Gaelic Athletic Association	GAA
General Post Office	GPO
Honourable	Hon.
Irish Citizen Army	ICA
Irish Trade Union Congress	ITUC
Irish National Aid and Volunteers' Dependants' Fund	INAVDF
Irish Republican Army	IRA

> During the Rising, James Connolly declared the amalgamation of the Volunteers and the Irish Citizen Army the 'Army of the Irish Republic', and it was frequently called the Irish Republican Army thereafter. In Irish it is called 'Óglaigh na hÉireann'. An individual member was usually called a 'Volunteer'.

Irish Republican Brotherhood	IRB
Irish Socialist Republican Party	ISRP
Irish Transport and General Workers Union	ITGWU
Irish Women's Workers' Union	IWWU
King's Counsel	KC
Member of Parliament	MP
Monsignor	Msgr
Queen's Counsel	QC
Reverend	Revd
Royal Irish Constabulary	RIC
Services, Industrial, Professional and Technical Union	SIPTU
Teachta Dála	TD
Trinity College Dublin	TCD
Ulster Volunteer Force	UVF
University College Dublin (formerly National University)	UCD
Voluntary Aid Detachment (of nurses)	VAD

Military/rank abbreviations

Adjutant	Adj.
Aide-de-camp	ADC
Brigadier	Brig.
Captain	Capt.
Chief of Staff	C/S
Colonel	Col.
Commandant	Cmdt
Corporal	Cpl
First Lieutenant	1Lt
General	Gen.
General Officer Commanding	GOC
General Headquarters	GHQ
Headquarters	HQ
His Majesty's Ship	HMS
Lieutenant	Lt
Lieutenant Colonel	Lt Col.
Lieutenant General	Lt Gen.
Major General	Major Gen.
Non-Commissioned Officer	NCO
Officer Commanding	O/C
Officer Training Corps	OTC
Private	Pvt.
Quartermaster	QM
Second Lieutenant	2Lt
Sergeant	Sgt

British award/decoration abbreviations

Companion of the Most Honourable Order of the Bath	CB
Companion of the Most Eminent Order of the Indian Empire	CIE
Companion of the Most Distinguished Order of St Michael and St George	CMG
Distinguished Service Order	DSO
Grand Cross of the Bath	GCB
Grand Cross of the Most Distinguished Order of St Michael and St George	GCMG
Grand Cross of the Royal Victorian Order	GCVO
Knight Commander of the Most Excellent Order of the British Empire	KBE
Knight Commander of the Most Honourable Order of the Bath	KCB
Knight of the Most Noble Order of the Garter	KG
Knight Commander of the Most Distinguished Order of St Michael and St George	KCMG
Member of the Most Excellent Order of the British Empire	MBE
Military Cross	MC
Order of Merit	OM

Name changes/area alterations

Following the revolutionary period (1913–23), many streets, barracks, bridges and other areas were renamed, many of them in honour of those who had been leaders or had served in the Rising, the War of Independence or the Civil War.

For street names containing 'Upper', 'Middle' or 'Lower', the position may be determined as follows: the 'Lower' part of a street is that part nearest to the mouth of the Liffey.

The following is a list of street/area names in italics, with their contemporary names in non-italics.

Amiens Street: Eastern end of Seán MacDermott Street.

Amiens Street Railway Station: Connolly Station.

Ancient Order of Hibernians Meeting Rooms: Kevin Barry Memorial Hall.

Broadstone Railway Station: Constitution Hill, Phibsborough, now a bus terminal.

Clarence Street (Great Clarence Street): Macken Street.

Clarence Street South: Macken Street.

Constabulary Barracks: Garda Síochána HQ in Phoenix Park.

Davy's Pub: Portobello Pub (at Portobello Bridge).

Densil or *Denzille Street*: Fenian Street.

Drogheda Street: First name of the street that became *Sackville* and then O'Connell Street.

Findlater Place: Cathal Brugha Street (the first block off O'Connell Street).

Gloucester Street: Cathal Brugha Street (the continuation east from O'Connell Street).

Gloucester Street North (see *Great Martin's Lane*): Upper Seán MacDermott → Lower Seán MacDermott Street.

Great Britain Street: Parnell Street.

Great Brunswick Street: Pearse Street.

Great Clarence Street: Macken Street.

Harcourt Street Railway Station: Demolished, now housing.

Islandbridge Barracks: Partially demolished, it was renamed Peadar Clancy Barracks. Clancy Barracks was sold to developers in early 2004.

King's County: County Offaly.

Kingsbridge Railway Station: Seán Heuston Station.

Kingstown Harbour: Dún Laoghaire Harbour (seven miles south-east of Dublin).

Linen Hall Barracks: Linenhall Street; demolished, now housing.

Marlborough Barracks: McKee Barracks in Phoenix Park.

North Dublin Union: St Lawrence's Hospital.

Portobello Barracks: Cathal Brugha Barracks.

Queen's County: County Laois.

Queenstown: Cobh, Co. Cork.

Richmond Barracks: Originally on Bulfin Road, Inchicore, it became Keogh Barracks, then was taken over by the Christian Brothers and became St Michael's Primary School, and then Keogh Square.

Rotunda Picture House: The Ambassador Theatre.

Royal Barracks: Collins Barracks, part of the National Museum of Ireland.

Royal University: National University.

Rutland Square: Parnell Square. The surrounding streets were once known as *Charlemont Row* (Parnell Square West), *Cavendish Row* (Parnell Square East), *Palace Row* (Parnell Square North) and *Great Britain Street* (Parnell Street).

Sackville Place (Lane): O'Rahilly Parade.

Sackville Street: O'Connell Street (before *Sackville Street* it was *Drogheda Street*).

Ship Street Barracks: Government Buildings next to Dublin Castle.

South Dublin Union: St James's Hospital.

Wellington Barracks: Griffith Barracks (now a college).

Westland Row Railway Station: Pearse Station.

Overview

In the 1880s Archbishop Thomas W. Croke of Cashel maintained that 'ball-playing, hurling, football kicking according to Irish rules . . . may now be said to be not only dead and buried, but in several localities to be entirely forgotten. What the country needed was an Irish organisation to bring order and unity to sport on a nation-wide basis.'[1] In August 1884 Michael Cusack outlined to a group of local athletic enthusiasts his plans to establish a national organisation for Irish athletes and to revive hurling, and on 1 November 1884 the Gaelic Athletic Association (GAA) was founded.[2]

Similarly, the Gaelic League was founded by Douglas Hyde, Fr Eugene O'Growney, Fr Michael Hickey and Eoin MacNeill on 31 July 1893 as a non-political, non-sectarian organisation dedicated to the preservation and revival of the Irish language, and the 'celebration of, and if possible the resuscitation of, traditional dress, dances and customs'.[3] Hyde began his crusade with his lecture 'The necessity for de-Anglicising Ireland':

> Just when we should be starting to build up anew the Irish race and the Gaelic nation—as within our own recollection Greece has been built up anew—we find ourselves despoiled of the bricks of nationality. The old bricks that lasted eighteen hundred years are destroyed; we must now set to, to bake new ones, if we can, on other ground and of other clay.[4]

To Hyde and the other founders, that birthright cast aside must be recovered. The Gaelic League quickly had a major impact on the social life of Ireland.[5] It was responsible for giving the Irish language a prominent position in the national school system, it revived Irish poetry, drama and literature, and after 1903 St Patrick's Day became a national holiday. And to the Gaelic League is due the credit of 'having established the first Irish national society which accepted women as members on the same terms as men'.[6]

Irish people began to recognise, and take pride in, their Irish culture. 'Celtic Dawn' is the term used to describe all these trends and it was an accurate description of the changes at many levels of Irish society. As injustices were rectified and some educational and economic opportunities created, there was a recommencement of some of the growth and cultural expansion that had been halted by the Act of Union.[7] This Irish cultural renaissance, advanced by both the GAA and the Gaelic League, led to an increased desire for Home Rule. Irish separatists at this time still primarily promoted a 'constitutional' solution to their aspirations, not the 'physical force' solution fostered by the Irish Republican Brotherhood (IRB). The IRB, however, utilised the

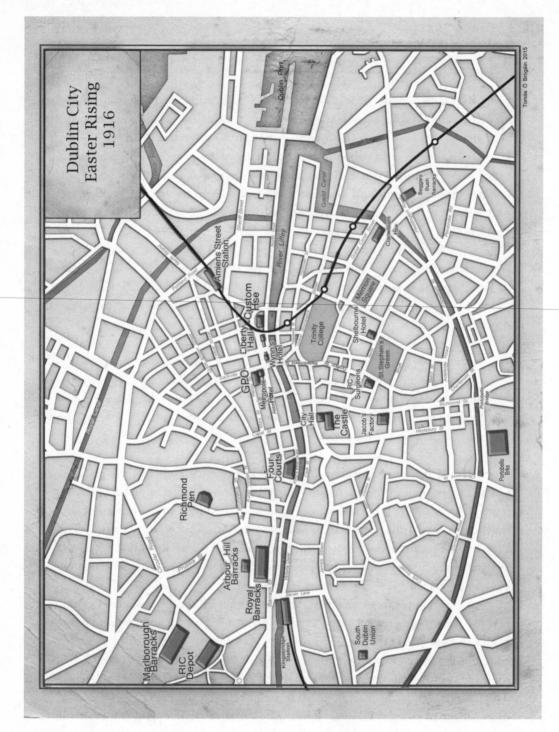

Principal sites associated with the 1916 Rising.

meetings of the Gaelic League and the GAA as prime opportunities for recruitment. It was not the last time that the Brotherhood would exploit other organisations to further its separatist aims.[8]

These movements in Ireland reflected other contemporary European social, economic and cultural revolutions. Nineteenth-century Europe was the crucible for many of the ideas and institutions that now shape life in Ireland, including the industrial revolution (particularly in Ulster at that time), capitalism, demands for a more democratic government, socialism, unions, bureaucracy and nationalism. The tinder that fed the fire was an economy that left many of the poor starving. The city was a miserable place in the early 1900s, with overcrowded and dilapidated housing, acute poverty and tens of thousands unemployed. 'Every house should have a bathroom so that a man's shirt need not be taken out of the pot for his dinner to be put into it.'[9]

> We knew that Dublin has a far larger percentage of single-room tenements than any other city in the Kingdom. We did not know that nearly twenty-eight thousand of our fellow-citizens live in dwellings that even the [Dublin] Corporation admits to be unfit for human habitation.[10]

In these circumstances the appearance of three men in Dublin provided the catalyst for the changes that were to come.[11]

James ('Big Jim') Larkin arrived in Ireland in 1907 to begin work as an organiser for the English National Union of Dock Labourers.[12] In 1908 that union suspended Larkin from his post because of his concentration on specifically Irish problems. But Larkin's personality immediately drew all working people to him and his particular devotion to Ireland induced him to invest the labour movement in Dublin with a definitely nationalist character.[13] Soon he founded his own union, the Irish Transport Workers' Union, and the first members were enrolled and union cards issued on 20 January 1909 under that name, though the union was thereafter known as the Irish Transport and General Workers' Union (ITGWU).[14] Dublin's employers were horrified as they saw his new union tackle firm after firm, raising wages and improving conditions.[15]

The philosophy of the union was expanded under the influence of James Connolly, who returned from the United States and began his syndicalist teaching in 1910, especially his 'One Big Union' concept and the promotion of his socialist ideals.[16] After leaving the British army in 1889,[17] Connolly became a wandering union agitator, a pamphleteer, a voracious reader and a self-taught intellectual. He wanted a union with 'one card, one badge, one executive, and one common enemy'.[18]

In 1873 Thomas Clarke, a young man who was born on the Isle of Wight on 11 March 1857 as the son of an English soldier, travelled to Dublin to be sworn into the

IRB. He then travelled north to Dungannon, but after coming to the attention of the police he left for America in 1880. In the United States he was inculcated with Irish separatism as a member of Clan na Gael. When he returned to Ireland in 1907, Clarke set out to bring the IRB's 'physical force' ideals to the fore in the minds of younger nationalists. The IRB was revitalised in the early twentieth century, led by this new generation of Irish patriots. Clarke deserves the credit for reviving the IRB, establishing its newspaper, *Irish Freedom* (a militant anti-English paper), and bringing new blood into the IRB leadership, especially mentoring his protégé, Seán MacDermott.[19] Clarke became the trusted link between Clan na Gael in the US and the IRB in Ireland, and his contribution to the national revival and the events of the time was crucial:

> Clarke can truthfully be described as the man, above all others, who made the Easter Rising. He, it was, who inspired it originally, and he, it was, who, in broad outline, laid the plans.[20]

With these three highly influential men—Larkin, Connolly and Clarke—in place, the stage was set for both economic and nationalist upheaval to begin.

On 25 August 1913, trams all over Dublin stopped in their tracks. Larkin's intent was not only to shut down the tram system but also to mobilise all Dublin's workers, and thus began the Great Lockout of 1913. Under the leadership of Larkin and Connolly, the Dublin workers made their first concerted effort to raise their living standards and improve their lives.[21] Larkin said that the Dublin worker is not a 'natural revolutionary, but he is a natural soldier'.[22] In 1914 a review of tenement conditions in Dublin declared that 'Larkinism, in so far as it is a revolt of intolerable conditions of life, is one of the by-products of our civic administration'.[23]

Larkin left for the United States in October 1914 on a fund-raising tour, and thus Connolly became the central figure in the workers' opposition to the Employers' Federation. He assumed leadership of the ITGWU and pressed forward with the Irish Citizen Army (ICA) following the Lockout. The ICA was created to protect the workers from any groups that might be used by the employers, including the Dublin Metropolitan Police, whose assaults on workers had killed three and injured hundreds during the Lockout.[24] Connolly vowed that the workers would protect themselves in the future. He saw the ICA not only as a defence force but also as a revolutionary army, dedicated to the overthrow of capitalism and imperialism.

Besides the ICA, two other armed militias were established in Ireland in 1913: the Ulster Volunteer Force (UVF) and the Irish Volunteers. In a direct reaction to the possibility of Home Rule for Ireland, Edward Carson, leader of the Irish Unionist Alliance in parliament, and James Craig, head of the Ulster Unionist Council, founded the UVF as a unionist militia. Their intention was that Protestant unionists in the north would resist the enactment of Home Rule.[25] At the start of 1912 unionists and members of the Orange Order began drilling, and on 9 April 1912 Carson and Andrew Bonar Law, leader of the British Conservative Party, reviewed 100,000 men marching in columns. Carson and Craig, supported by some Conservative politicians, threatened to establish a provisional government in Ulster should the province be included in any Home Rule settlement. On 13 January 1913 the Ulster Volunteer Force was formally established by the Ulster Unionist Council. Recruitment was to be limited to 100,000 men aged from seventeen to 65 who had signed the Ulster Covenant, under the command of George Richardson.[26] During this time the UVF enjoyed the wholehearted support of the Conservative Party, even though it threatened rebellion against the government.

As so often happened during the period, the perception grew that, with armed men in Ulster threatening force to counter Home Rule, a similar organisation was necessary to pressure Britain in the other direction. To this end Eoin MacNeill, co-founder of the Gaelic League and a professor at University College Dublin, published an article in the Gaelic League newspaper *An Claidheamh Soluis* on 1 November 1913, 'The North Began', arguing for the necessity of such a force. MacNeill called on Irish nationalists to form a paramilitary body to reinforce their demand for Home Rule, just as Ulster unionists had established the Ulster Volunteer Force in 1913 to resist it more effectively. Paradoxically, the nationalist Irish Volunteers were sworn to uphold an act of the British parliament—Home Rule—whilst the unionist Ulster Volunteers were preparing to fight parliament to prevent the enactment of this same act. Unknown to MacNeill, the IRB surreptitiously infiltrated the Irish Volunteers, intending to use the organisation for further physical-force efforts. That IRB involvement made John Redmond, the moderate nationalist leader and head of the Irish Parliamentary Party, reluctant to give the Volunteers his support. Only after he was permitted to nominate half the seats on its Provisional Committee in June 1914 did he gave his approval for the Volunteer movement. At its peak in mid-1914 Irish Volunteer membership reached approximately 160,000.

As soon as they were organised, both the Volunteers and the Citizen Army began extensive military training. Though their numbers were smaller, the equipment and training of the Citizen Army were superior to that of most of the Volunteers because the ICA had trade union money behind them and, consequently, full uniforms and a full-time, well-trained professional soldier, Capt. Jack White, to instruct them.[27] White's goal was a well-trained ICA and he was intolerant of the conflicts between the ICA and the Volunteers. Ultimately he resigned from the ICA in May 1914 as a result of that conflict and joined the Volunteers.[28] From that time onward the ICA was primarily under Connolly's overall command, and Cmdt Michael Mallin, a member of the ICA and a former soldier in the British army who had served in India, became chief of staff and directed training.

Soon the need for arms led the UVF to procure 25,000 rifles and two million rounds of ammunition from Benny Spiro, an arms dealer in Hamburg. They acquired the transport steamers SS *Clydevalley*[29] and SS *Fanny* and brought the weapons back to Ulster. The gunrunning was planned secretly and was meticulously accomplished under the command of Major Fred Crawford.[30] On 24 April 1914 the port of Larne was taken over by the UVF while the *Clydevalley* docked there and unloaded. Arms were also landed at Bangor and Donaghadee.[31]

Though the British government prohibited the importation of arms thereafter, the landing of arms at Larne prompted the Irish Volunteers to purchase and bring ashore their own arms shipment. The Ó Rahilly, director of arms for the Volunteers, sent two nationalist supporters, Darrell Figgis and Erskine Childers, to a firm in Hamburg, where they purchased 1,500 rifles and 45,000 rounds of ammunition. Childers's yacht, the *Asgard*, landed 900 rifles and approximately 26,000 rounds of ammunition in the small port of Howth, just north of Dublin, on 26 July 1914, and the remainder were landed in Kilcoole.[32] The Howth landing was deliberately organised in a spectacular way to win the utmost publicity for the Volunteers and to wake up the country. Conversely, the Kilcoole landing was deliberately organised as a secret operation.[33] While the 'Howth Mausers' were obsolete, they were the basis of arms for the Irish Volunteers,[34] and about 800 Volunteers mustered and marched from Dublin out to Howth on the day of the landing. The British sent contingents of the Dublin Metropolitan Police and the army to prevent the distribution of arms. When the soldiers returned to Dublin there was a confrontation with civilians at Bachelor's Walk.[35] Four civilians were killed and more than 35 seriously injured during firing by the soldiers.

This landing of the Howth Mausers was a continuation of the training and arming that had been promulgated by the IRB for several years.[36] Many of the Volunteers bought their own rifles; there was a collection at each meeting and at that time the price of one rifle and 100 rounds of ammunition was £7.[37] So, too, many of the ICA members bought their own weapons through a subscription paid to their rifle club, at a rate of one shilling per week toward the purchase of a rifle and sixpence per week toward the purchase of a revolver.[38] There were also purchases from British soldiers, thefts of British ordnance and occasional smuggling.[39] Ammunition and explosives were stolen from the Arklow munitions factory, and from railway cars and collieries in Scotland. Still, the Volunteers and ICA were desperately short of weapons, with only an estimated 3,700 rifles and handguns in their hands prior to the Rising.[40]

The Volunteer and Citizen Army training may have been elementary, but they had been training since 1913; indeed, they had received more training than many of the British soldiers they were to face. Many of the British troops, both those already stationed in Ireland and those who came from England, had only completed their most basic training; though they were much better armed, well organised and disciplined with good morale, they were not front–line, battle–tested troops. In fact, many of the South Staffordshire and Sherwood Forester Regiment troops who came to Ireland to fight in the Rising were disembarked in Kingstown and immediately marched out onto the piers to load and fire their weapons—for many, that was the only live–fire training they had before going into battle in Dublin.[41] The British noted that some of their troops were 'untrained, undersized products of the English slums . . . The young Sherwoods that I had [at Beggars Bush Barracks] had never fired a service rifle before. They were not even able to load them. We had to show them how to load them.'[42] While the Rising was their introduction to war for almost all of the Volunteers/Citizen Army, this was also the case for the majority of the British troops.

Within a fortnight of the Howth arms landing events in Europe began to run out of control. Archduke Franz Ferdinand had been assassinated in Sarajevo on 28 June, Russia mobilised its army on 30 July, Germany invaded France on 3 August and Britain declared war on Germany on 4 August. World War I erupted across the Continent, Home Rule was shelved and the time the IRB had been anticipating was at hand. World War I provided the impetus that allowed the IRB to pursue a change in nationalist thought.[43]

But the Volunteer force split in September 1914 when Redmond, in the hope of ensuring the enactment of the Home Rule Act, encouraged the Volunteers to support the British war commitment and to join Irish regiments of the British army. Redmond made a political calculation that in time would backfire. He encouraged Irishmen to join the British army in the belief that Irish solidarity would prevent England from reneging on its Home Rule commitments. His action was strongly but unsuccessfully opposed by the Volunteers' founding members. Following the split, his supporters and most of the Volunteers broke away and formed the National Volunteers, of whom approximately 35,000 enlisted.[44] A militant Irish Volunteer organisation remained, but was reduced to fewer than 14,000 members at the time of the split. They retained the name 'Irish Volunteers', were led by MacNeill and called for Irish neutrality. Yet the longer the war lasted, the weaker Redmond's position became.[45] Many of his National Volunteers joined the British army but recruitment of new National Volunteers eroded, while recruitment for the Irish Volunteers did not. By the time of the Rising, the Irish Volunteers' rolls held a nominal 16,000 men nationwide.

On 1 August 1915 Jeremiah O'Donovan Rossa was buried in Dublin's Glasnevin Cemetery after a great Fenian funeral. He had been the founder of the Phoenix Society in 1856. ICA member Seán McGarry, a great friend of Tom Clarke, approached James Connolly to write an article for the programme and was taken aback when Connolly replied: 'When are you fellows going to stop blathering about *dead* Fenians? Why don't you get a few *live* ones for a change?'[46] Later Clarke talked to Connolly, and Connolly wrote an article in which he managed to turn a dead Fenian into a live incitement to revolution:

The Irish Citizen Army in its constitution pledges its members to fight for a Republican Freedom for Ireland . . . We are, therefore, present to honour O'Donovan Rossa by right of our faith in the separate destiny of our country and our faith in the ability of the Irish Workers to achieve that destiny.[47]

It was at this funeral that Padraic Pearse[48] made his most famous speech:

They [the British] think that they have pacified Ireland . . . They think that they have foreseen everything, think that they have provided against everything; but the fools, the fools, the fools!—they have left us our Fenian dead, and while Ireland holds these graves, Ireland unfree shall never be at peace.[49]

By 1915, the Supreme Council determined that a small group of members of the IRB who had 'devoted special attention to military study' should plan a rising. Pearse, Joseph Plunkett and Éamonn Ceannt were appointed as the Military *Committee*. The Committee determined to use the Irish Volunteers' organisation, training and equipment without the knowledge of the Volunteer Executive. Some months later, when Seán MacDermott was released from prison, he and Thomas Clarke acted as ex officio members of the Military Committee. After the meeting of the Supreme Council on 16 January 1916, it was decided that all additions to the renamed Military *Council* were to be at the discretion of the Executive, but in reality the Council added members solely on their own initiative.

The date of the projected rising had already been selected, but the prime consideration of the Military Council was how to get the entire Volunteer organisation involved without exposing their secret purpose. They were very mindful of the 1914 capitulation to Redmond by Volunteer leaders—especially MacNeill and Bulmer Hobson—and they did not feel that their plans could safely be left to a vote of the Volunteers or the Supreme Council. Thereafter, the Military Council directed Pearse, in his role as director of organisation, to plan and order exercises and manoeuvres throughout the country that would most benefit the plans of the Military Council. It was the Council's intent that the Volunteers' plans would be determined by and subservient to those of that select group of the IRB. By Easter 1916 a Pearse order for a general exercise would not sound any alarms and would ensure a general mobilisation at the Military Council's direction.[50]

Early in 1916 MacNeill had suspicions that he was not being told the purpose and intent of Volunteer manoeuvres. In February he issued a Memorandum conveying what he felt were the objectives of the Volunteers at that time:

. . . I wish it then to be clearly understood that under present conditions I am definitely opposed to any proposal that may come forward involving insurrection.

If any feasible proposal is brought forward to increase the arming of the Volunteers, I will support it—and those who are impatient of inaction should find scope enough for their activity in that direction.[51]

At times it seemed that the Military Council was making attempts to bring MacNeill, Hobson, The Ó Rahilly *et al.*, as well as members of the public, over to their way of thinking—that a rising was necessary—but there was little hope of this being successful. In April they tried a different approach and published the 'Castle Document'. This document, printed on 13 April 1916, alleged that the Castle authorities proposed to arrest many important and well-known public figures and to raid their homes and residences along with those of several other persons, including the residence of Archbishop William Walsh of Dublin. The most likely and current view of the document is that '. . . it was not (as has usually been said) a forgery, but it was "sexed up" (by Joseph Plunkett) to make the plans appear imminent, to try to get MacNeill to support immediate action'.[52]

At first MacNeill was convinced that this document relayed the true intentions of Dublin Castle. In response, he issued the following order to the Volunteers:

> Your object will be to preserve the arms and organisation of the Irish Volunteers . . . In general, you will arrange that your men defend themselves and each other in small groups . . .[53]

Only after he had been informed of the loss of the arms ship *Aud* did MacNeill question and disbelieve the document, and upon hearing that Roger Casement had been captured in Tralee and that no other German aid would be forthcoming he issued his famous countermanding order.[54]

The Military Council had scheduled the Rising for 6.00 p.m. on Easter Sunday, 23 April, and Pearse issued an order on 8 April for a general mobilisation on that day.[55] This order was issued publicly and with the full authorisation of the Volunteer Executive in order to deceive the Dublin Castle authorities.

On Holy Saturday the Military Council knew that their plans had been severely compromised by the loss of a ship from Germany, the *Aud*.[56] It was loaded with weapons but its arrival at Fenit was foiled owing to failures in communications.[57] Because of the war there was no direct communication between Germany and Ireland. German communications regarding the arms shipment and the plans for German aid had to be transmitted through the German embassy in New York and given to John Devoy, the exiled Fenian and head of Clan na Gael in America. Devoy asked the Germans for 100,000 rifles, artillery pieces and German officers. The

Germans offered 20,000 rifles and 1,000,000 rounds of ammunition, but no artillery and certainly no military advisers.[58] It was decided that Devoy would communicate with the IRB leaders in Dublin via couriers, owing to the likelihood that the British might intercept any electronic communication, and then pass along all messages to the German High Command. Devoy contacted Berlin and gave them the date of the Rising as Holy Saturday.[59] But the Volunteers changed the date of shipment, deeming a Holy Thursday delivery too early, and Devoy himself decided to ask that the arms be landed a single day ahead of the start of the Rising.[60]

The *Aud* arrived on schedule and its captain, Lt Karl Spindler, had been instructed to look for two green lanterns from the shore in reply to his signal.[61] Upon this signal a pilot boat would arrive and guide them into the harbour where the *Aud*'s cargo of guns and ammunition would be landed. Unknown to Spindler, the Volunteers on shore, acting according to the revised schedule, had been told to look for the ship's signal on the evening between Holy Saturday and Easter Sunday.[62]

On Good Friday night, Spindler weighed anchor to flee the Irish coast but was soon overtaken by the Royal Navy. The armed British sloops HMS *Zinnia* and HMS *Bluebell* joined the HMS *Lord Hennage* in pursuit. The *Zinnia* stopped the *Aud* and for a while it looked as though Spindler would talk his way out of capture. Finally the British decided to escort the *Aud* to Queenstown (Cobh) Harbour, where she would be searched. But Spindler knew the ruse had failed and scuttled her.[63]

The importance of the arms on the *Aud* was underscored by the inspector general of the RIC, Neville Chamberlain, who later argued that if the *Aud*'s arms and ammunition had been landed, the Volunteers outside Dublin would not have held back.[64] Nevertheless, the Volunteers' plan does raise some questions beyond the lack of communication with the *Aud*. Even if the Volunteers were able to get all the arms and ammunition ashore, could they have been distributed into the hands of Volunteers efficiently and in time to make a difference? According to his biographer, the Volunteer O/C in Kerry, Austin Stack, had a 'detailed plan prepared for the landing of arms at Fenit and their distribution', but no plan was communicated to the Volunteers there and no plan has been found.[65] There is no other evidence of a specific plan to move the weapons from the quayside at Fenit, and that quantity of weapons and ammunition would have required a well-coordinated effort to make them available to Volunteer units.[66] In contrast, when the weapons and ammunition were landed by the Ulster Volunteers in Larne in 1914 members of the UVF manned pickets and patrols along the length of the coast road between Belfast and Larne.[67] The men at these pickets were to give directions to any who needed them and were provided with reserve supplies of petrol and tools for repairing any vehicle that had problems. In Larne itself, UVF members wearing armlets stood 'in line silent as soldiers on parade' and manned cordons that blocked the roads, preventing vehicles without a special permit from entering or leaving Larne. Owing to the quantity of weapons, temporary arms dumps had been set up in the surrounding districts so that the vehicles could return as quickly as possible to receive another load.

> . . . There was no rush or bustle in the doing of it. It was accomplished with celerity, yet without fuss or splutter, because it was done in pursuance of a well-formed plan, executed as perfectly as it had been preconceived . . . So exactly had this mobilisation been arranged that these hundreds of motors reached the assembly point at an identical moment. It was an amazing sight to see this huge procession of cars nearly three miles in length descending upon the town with all their headlights ablaze . . .[68]

The Larne consignment was slightly larger than that on the *Aud* (25,000 weapons to 20,000), but no fleet of 'hundreds of motors' was laid on by the Irish Volunteers for this landing. Moreover, the highly efficient mobilisation of the force around Larne prevented the police and customs officers from interfering, and a 'blind eye' on the part of the authorities greatly benefited the landing, whereas no such advantage would have existed for the Volunteers.[69] Vehicles or railway cars carrying weapons would certainly have attracted the attention of the civilian and military authorities around County Kerry, and no comprehensive plans seem to have been made for distribution after offloading from the *Aud*.

Further, would the Volunteers have been able to expertly use weapons they had never seen?[70] During the Rising, when the British troops were landed at Kingstown, many were marched out onto the piers and told to fire their weapons. They had had no weapons training up to that point. Their inexperience was apparently such that one of the first British soldiers to fire a volley fell to the ground crying out 'I've been shot'. His company commander, Capt. Frank Pragnell, examined the boy and exclaimed angrily, 'Good God, man! You're not hit—it's only the recoil'.[71] As regards the Volunteers, when the Swords Company fell in on Easter Monday, Capt. Richard Coleman paraded the 65 men for inspection and found one shouldering his cocked rifle. To demonstrate the danger of this, Coleman pressed the trigger and the rifle went off.[72] Fatal accidents involving carelessness, horseplay and poor discipline were relatively common during the Rising and the subsequent War of Independence.[73] It is estimated that at the time of the Rising the Volunteers and Citizen Army had only 3,700 weapons and no machine-guns, so weapons (especially the ten machine-guns on the *Aud*) were desperately needed. But to put 20,000 rifles into the hands of the untrained Irish would have been a military mistake.

When MacNeill found that he had been deceived about the Rising and the 'Castle Document', and heard the news of Roger Casement's capture in Tralee[74] and the loss of the *Aud*, he cancelled the manoeuvres scheduled for Easter. He issued an order on Saturday night, published in the next day's *Sunday Independent*:

Owing to the very critical position, all orders given to Irish Volunteers for tomorrow, Easter Sunday, are hereby rescinded, and no parades, marches, or other movements of Irish Volunteers will take place. Each individual Volunteer will obey this order strictly in every particular.[75]

The members of the IRB's Military Council angrily decided to call a meeting in Liberty Hall on Easter Sunday morning.

I saw Eoin MacNeill's countermanding order in the paper and heard the discussion in Liberty Hall. Connolly was there. They were all heartbroken and when they were not crying they were cursing. I kept thinking 'does this mean that we are not going to go out?' There were thousands like us. It was foolish of MacNeill and those to think they could call it off. They could not. Many of us thought we would go out single-handed, if necessary.[76]

At that meeting, the Rising's leaders determined that to delay further would be fatal for their plans and so the Rising was rescheduled for Monday at noon. The Military Council made two equally important decisions: first, they sent dispatches immediately to the various commands *confirming* MacNeill's cancellation of that day's manoeuvres; second, they decided that the Rising would commence the next day at noon, and that dispatches to that effect would be sent out on Sunday night. The first decision was intended to remove the possibility that units outside Dublin might start their operations before the Dublin battalions could revise their plans and occupy their allotted positions on Easter Monday. Moreover, Pearse intended that this would obviate any further action by MacNeill. In addition, it was thought that if the British became aware of this follow-up to MacNeill's order their suspicions would be allayed. Messages confirming the MacNeill order were therefore sent out from Liberty Hall from 1.00 p.m. on Easter Sunday. The second decision, to commence the Rising on Monday, was the vital one. At that point the Military Council would not be swayed from their plan to rise.[77]

MacNeill's order did convince Under-Secretary Matthew Nathan and the Dublin Castle authorities that, whatever the purpose of the original manoeuvres, there was no longer any threat of immediate trouble.[78] Nathan, a former governor of Hong Kong and a career administrator, was a cautious, methodical man to whom reports came every night in Dublin Castle.[79] He kept close watch on the activities of all the Irish 'rebels' and was convinced that there was no trouble immediately brewing. Still, he told Chief Secretary Augustine Birrell that the Castle was unable to get precise inside information on what the rebels were planning in Dublin.[80] As a result, the British *were* taken by surprise, because they had not prepared adequately for any conflict in Dublin:

> Generally, a rising either in the country or in Dublin, except in support of any enemy that had landed, was looked upon as most improbable. Neither the strength, armament nor training of the Volunteers was of a nature that seemed likely to promise to them a measure of success as would lead them to make the attempt.[81]

On Friday morning, toward the end of the Rising, Pearse issued a War Bulletin from the GPO that included the following:

> Of the fatal countermanding order which prevented those plans being carried out, I shall not speak further. Both Eoin MacNeill and we have acted in the best interests of Ireland.[82]

But the views of the members of the Military Council were well known and were not so ambiguous. Plunkett was reported to have spoken to Pearse of 'how much bigger an event it would have been had the original plans gone forward unchecked'.[83] Clarke told his wife, Kathleen, of MacNeill: 'I want you to see to it that our people know of his [MacNeill's] treachery to us. He must never be allowed back into the national life of the country, for sure as he is, so sure he will act treacherously in a crisis. He is a weak man, but I know every effort will be made to whitewash him.'[84] Seán MacDermott said 'We have been betrayed again'.[85] Éamonn Ceannt told his wife, Áine, that 'MacNeill has ruined us, he has stopped the Rising'.[86] While Ceannt had planned to sleep away from home on Saturday, he later remarked to her: 'I may thank MacNeill that I can sleep in my own home—the cancelling of manoeuvres will lead the British to think everything is all right'.[87]

MacNeill later addressed his decision:

> . . . all that was actually counted upon was shipments of sufficient arms and ammunition . . . Of course, without those German arms and ammunition they must have failed in any event . . . The seven martyrs went to martyrs' deaths. Their fondest dreams were exceeded. Ireland's freedom was at last in sight! . . . This explanation, I trust, will establish once and for all my motive in issuing those orders.[88]

At noon on Easter Monday, 24 April 1916, approximately 800 Volunteers and 200 ICA members stormed buildings in central Dublin and declared an independent Irish Republic. Under the command of Pearse and Connolly, the Volunteers and ICA members were combined into what Connolly termed the Irish Republican Army

(IRA). Utmost secrecy was maintained in planning—only three copies of the plan were drafted and no original is known to exist.[89] The Volunteers' plan had two elements: first, to prevent British access to the city centre from the major British military barracks or from Kingstown; second, to keep open a line of communication between Dublin and the country in order to have a line of retreat if it became necessary to fall back into guerrilla war. Hopefully, a corridor was to be kept open out of Dublin. They chose their positions carefully, forcing the British to attack, as the rebels were holding the capital city of Ireland, and to ensure that they could hold out for long enough that the Rising would attract international attention as a rebellion, not just a mere riot.

Orders for the 'Rising to proceed' were sent to Cork and the other southern and western commands on Easter Sunday, but the confusion sowed by MacNeill's countermanding orders and the subsequent new orders relegated the efforts of those outlying commands to an afterthought. Commandants throughout the country received a series of conflicting orders during the weekend, not all delivered everywhere and not always received in the sequence in which they had been issued. The result was a state of immobilising confusion, uncertainty and frustration, particularly outside Dublin. With three exceptions—the mobilisations at Enniscorthy, the action at Galway led by Liam Mellows and the fight outside Dublin at Ashbourne—the entire Volunteer force in the country was rendered ineffective by the confusion.[90]

Joseph Plunkett was the primary planner of the military actions, along with James Connolly; to a lesser extent, Padraic Pearse and Éamonn Ceannt also contributed.[91] After his inclusion on the Military Council in January 1916, Connolly was authorised to plan detailed operations for the Dublin area within the overall Plunkett plan, including some few operations outside Dublin.[92] Neither Plunkett nor Connolly was a trained military strategist, and since 1916 most have challenged the military soundness of the plan. In particular, it has been questioned whether the Volunteers and Citizen Army should have taken the buildings they did, whether a static defensive plan could have been successful, and whether their intent to engage in urban warfare could have achieved their aims. But Plunkett was a student of military history and no doubt knew of Clauswitz's principle that 'the side which is surrounded by the enemy is better off than the side which surrounds its opponent'.

An examination of the strategy, tactics and results of the Rising leads to several conclusions. Militarily, strategy is the concept, plan and formulation of the battle, the primary objective to be achieved by the operation. Tactics are the implementation of the plan and the follow-through result of the strategy. For any military operation, soldiers must focus their efforts on achieving the main aim of their strategy. A realistic examination of the Irish 'aim' would conclude that the Irish merely hoped to attract sufficient international attention to provoke intervention on their behalf. While there was little hope of defeating the British army, the planners of the Rising felt that international opinion would soon force the British to come to terms with the rebels and to give independence to the country. Éamonn Ceannt told his wife: 'If we last a month they—the British—will come to terms. We have sent out messages throughout the country, but as the men have already received at least two other orders, it is hard to know what may happen. However, we will put our trust in God.'[93] The Irish strategy, therefore, must be considered a failure. Nevertheless, although the overall strategy of the Volunteers was suspect, even mad, the urban tactics employed by the Irish were quite advanced for their time, and their general tactics showed considerable skill. The British commanders made some tactical errors, particularly pressing on at Mount Street Bridge and approaching the Mendicity Institute without adequate reconnaissance, but their overall strategy and tactics were sound. Both Irish and British were well led in the field and mostly effective offensively and defensively on a tactical level.

The overwhelming strength of the British troops tends to overshadow the skill of the Volunteers, but they were quite effective in choosing some positions and then defending them well. The Irish choice of positions on the brigade level has been criticised, but the deployment of troops on the battalion and company levels deserves more credit than has been given. Their ability to fight in those positions took more training and military ability than have been granted to the Volunteers. Moreover, the defensive nature of these plans indicated the Volunteers' recognition of their limitations, primarily because of a dearth of arms. They had not a single machine-gun, only home-made grenades and no heavy weapons at all. The weapons lost on the *Aud* could have greatly increased the firepower in Dublin, as well as arming many in the west, and the inability to import sufficient weapons to supplement the inadequate arms of the Volunteers was devastating to their plans.

Their plan also contained many tactical weaknesses. Illustrating German Gen. Erich von Moltke's maxim that 'no battle plan survives contact with the enemy', the Rising started to go wrong within the first few hours. The lack of weapons (particularly machine-guns) and manpower greatly hindered the implementation of the overall plan. The operation was spread over too large an urban area. As a result, the fighting was disjointed after the initial capture of the buildings, and isolated locations could not be reinforced. There was no provision to take Dublin Castle or Trinity College.[94] The rebels' inept attempt at taking Dublin Castle and their lack of an attempt to take Beggar's Bush Barracks (which they believed was heavily manned but which was almost undefended) showed that their intelligence concerning the current British troop strength was non-existent.[95] Moreover, the insurgents' digging of trenches in St Stephen's Green was a military disaster, and one that should have been easily foreseen. Further, the rebels took positions on both sides of the River Liffey, splitting their forces. It is a military axiom that the side that controls the bridges controls the battlefield. By taking positions on both sides of the river without controlling all the major bridges, the Volunteers made communication and reinforcement between garrisons difficult, and as the Rising progressed impossible. The Irish intended to cut communications from Dublin to the country, as well as to England, but their efforts were incomplete or ineffective. In consequence, the British were able to summon aid quickly. In addition, the rebels simply did not have the manpower to take either of Dublin's ports, at Dublin Port or Kingstown. It was hoped that at least one German submarine would be deployed to deny those ports to the British but the Germans never acquiesced in this.[96] The Irish attempted to take the train stations, but except for Westland Row Station were not successful in holding them. As a result, during the following week the British were able to bring in thousands of reinforcements from England and from their garrisons at the Curragh, troops from Belfast and artillery from Athlone.[97]

In planning for war in Dublin, Connolly took his lead from the ancient Chinese general Sun Tzu, who wrote that 'the worst course to have forced on a general is to have to fight his way into a defended city'. When the British forces tried to advance against the defences of the Volunteers, they must have realised that war hadn't changed in that regard in 3,000 years. A city offers cover and concealment for troops and weapons, and the attacker is forced to proceed along defined and defended routes chosen by those occupying the buildings, usually under the fire of the defender. The attacker has difficulty finding the defender's concealed positions, while the defender funnels the attacking troops into fields of fire previously chosen and usually in sight of several well-defended positions. Street fighting is most effective when the units are placed in positions that are mutually supportive; while the Volunteers' positions within battalions or companies were so sited, there was little mutual support between the battalions. The Volunteers and the ICA were to seize strongholds in Dublin's city centre sufficiently close together to form an inner defensive cordon. It was intended that they would take positions that would threaten rail and highway communications, impeding British forces travelling to the city centre. But their plan did not contain adequate provisions for mobility between these strongholds. Gaps between battalions became larger as the fighting went on, as rebels in outlying positions were withdrawn into the battalion HQ position and contact with other battalions was lost. Because that kind of urban fighting separated each unit, the Volunteers were not able to send much support from one garrison to another. In any case, all the battalions were seriously under strength, mostly owing to the cancellation order, and to send adequate reinforcements from one position to another would have required a far larger number of men and women than was available. Generally, too, the men in forward positions were not in direct communication with their battalion headquarters.

The greatest use of cover in urban and street fighting is to enter a building and then tunnel from that building to the next until the troops are able to flank the enemy, as well as to confuse an attacker as to just where the defensive force is. Especially at Mount Street Bridge and the South Dublin Union, the principles of enfilading the British columns (bringing the British under fire along the whole column, as at the Bridge) and defilading (by moving from one concealed position to another, as in the Union) were very effectively used by the Irish and were hallmarks of the choice and preparation of positions.

Such urban fighting was also new to the British and caused them great difficulties. Under-Secretary Nathan later testified that by occupying buildings the 'insurgents avoided any attack involving concentration or movements under fire'.[98] The lord lieutenant, Lord Wimborne, noted that such tactics made it possible for the Irish to carry out their revolt. 'There was no conflict in the streets. The ordinary tactics of revolution, which I imagine to be barricades and so on, were not resorted to . . . At the very start they took to the houses and house-tops.'[99] The British troops had no training in urban warfare and disliked the house-to-house fighting that it entailed. The British War Office had observed combat in built-up areas, but both the British government and military failed to see the threat of a conflict in cities and in 1916 the British army lacked proper planning and equipment. What little training they had received was in the field/trench warfare they expected to encounter in France, and they found close-quarter fighting both physically and psychologically disorienting.

Historians have always debated the concept of the Rising as a 'blood sacrifice' led by men who felt that a rising, even though precipitate and probably futile, was necessary.

> It was the British decision to declare war on Germany that allowed the Irish Republican Brotherhood to think seriously in terms of a rising by getting enough guns to challenge superior British firepower. This would have been irrelevant if the sole purpose of the Rising was simply a blood sacrifice. That was a purpose of the Rising for several of the leaders, but it was not the sole purpose of any one of them.[100]

There is little doubt, however, that for Pearse the Rising as a blood sacrifice was necessary to bring the Irish people to revolt.[101] He stated as much in his writings,[102] and especially in his play *The Singer* and his poem *Renunciation* in 1915.[103] Other leaders, too, indicated their acceptance and even their wish for such a sacrifice.[104] Nevertheless, few of the 'rank-and-file' members of the Volunteers and the ICA knew that the manoeuvres scheduled for Easter Sunday were to precipitate an actual revolt, and there certainly was no feeling of a need for a 'blood sacrifice' among them.

In the end the British had to use artillery (and the resulting fires) to remove most defenders from their entrenched positions; this destroyed much of the centre of Dublin and inflicted significant losses on civilians.[105] It should be emphasised that the incendiary shells that the British used were of greater effect in ending the Rising than were high-explosive shells. Fire is the quickest and best way to get insurgents out of buildings, and it was the fires throughout the centre of Dublin that brought the Volunteers to ruin.[106] While the Volunteers did consider the danger of fire, and many means were taken to douse fires as they occurred, it was the flammability of the oils and chemicals in shops and stores around the centre of Dublin, as well as the flammability of the buildings themselves and their fixtures, which made their defensive positions so vulnerable.[107] Ultimately, the fires succeeded in forcing the evacuation of buildings and were the primary cause of the surrender.[108]

Certainly the military plan was doomed once the *Aud* was scuttled, and arguably was ill conceived. From the outset many questioned the strategy of sitting within a tightening ring in Dublin waiting for the English to attack, and it is axiomatic that bad strategy cannot be overcome with good tactics. But the original plan for the Volunteers called for substantially larger garrisons than reported on Easter Monday. Although no exact numbers of men in the Dublin battalions are known, the best estimate is that there were approximately 5,000 on the Dublin rosters and as many as 10,000 on rosters throughout the rest of Ireland. Many of those were not always active, and many may not have reported to a real battle order, but after the cancellation order the Volunteers' ranks in Dublin were severely depleted. (Since they were under the command of Connolly, the Citizen Army was not greatly affected by MacNeill's order.) It is accepted that only about 800 Volunteers and 200 Citizen Army members reported on Monday. Though those numbers were considerably augmented as the week progressed, had each garrison had its full complement of assigned Volunteers and Citizen Army members the positions would have been much better manned. There was, however, no chance for the rebels to have taken on an offensive plan of action—they simply did not have the necessary men, had no machine-guns or heavy weapons, and had no means to support units on the run. The Volunteers *were* amateurs, but they showed greater organisational and military skills than those with which they are usually credited. The Military Council had been planning a rising for several years; knowing that their resources were limited, they planned to use natural terrain and concealment well, and their initial plan of deployment was sound. Even the British grudgingly praised their planning: 'Apart from its general ultimate futility, the conduct of the insurrection showed great organisational ability and more military skill than had been attributed to the Volunteers'.[109]

After capturing the General Post Office (GPO) on Sackville Street, Pearse read the *Proclamation of the Provisional Government of the Irish Republic* at the front of that landmark building, although the few people assembled were more wary and confused than enthusiastic.

The British military reacted quickly at the outset.[110] Their immediate objectives were to recapture the Magazine Fort in Phoenix Park, to secure the Viceregal Lodge in the Park, to relieve and strengthen the garrison in Dublin Castle, and to get reinforcements from garrisons and from England.[111] The first reinforcements from the 3rd Reserve Cavalry Brigade, billeted at their camp at the Curragh, arrived at Kingsbridge Station at 4.15 p.m., and troops continued to arrive there and at Amiens Street Station on Tuesday. By later that day, trains were arriving at twenty-minute intervals until about 2,500 troops were encamped in Dublin that night. The British initiated actions to relieve Dublin Castle, made certain of the security of the barracks throughout Dublin as well as other positions on the perimeter of the rebellion, and summoned reinforcements from every barracks in Ireland and from Britain.[112] Orders were given at once to send reinforcements to Ireland; by Monday night a scheme for the transport of troops from Liverpool[113] had been drawn up and the troops who were to be deployed were notified.[114] The eighteen-pounder artillery battery was called from Athlone and more artillery units were prepared to go to Dublin; the 4th Battalion of Dublin Fusiliers from Templemore and available troops from Belfast arrived at Amiens Street Station on Monday evening.[115] Then the British put their efforts into securing the approaches to their administrative headquarters at Dublin Castle and isolating the rebel headquarters in the GPO. By early Tuesday morning the British had taken the steps necessary to safeguard the Castle, secured the other barracks in Dublin, summoned additional reinforcements, and provided the basis for the offensive actions to follow which would lead to the defeat of the rebels.[116]

The Crown forces greatly outnumbered the rebels, marshalling almost 20,000 troops by the week's end in opposition to about 2,100 insurgents. The British immediately began their counter-attacks, specifically directed towards the centre of the rebel positions in the GPO, and isolating each of the other garrisons at the same time. On Tuesday they began to control the area south of the Liffey, opening a corridor from Richmond Barracks to the Castle and then eastward to Trinity College. In effect, once it was established that the GPO was the rebel headquarters, all of their other positions were attacked or bypassed, but actually isolating each of them.

After eliminating the threat to the Castle, the British attacked City Hall, and that garrison, along with its outlying positions, was taken by Tuesday evening.[117] The Shelbourne Hotel was occupied in the pre-dawn hours of Tuesday, and when the hotel and the adjacent United Services Club were taken the Citizen Army position in St Stephen's Green was untenable.[118] Cmdt Mallin's garrison awoke on Tuesday morning to machine-gun fire from the buildings surrounding the north side of the Green, and withdrew to the College of Surgeons. Though they held that position until the end, they were effectively isolated from the fighting. Also on Tuesday, the British established their headquarters in Trinity College, cutting the rebel positions, divided by the Liffey, in two.[119] After the machine-gunning of St Stephen's Green and the surrounding of Jacob's Biscuit Factory on Tuesday, there was little need to proceed against those garrisons, with the British plan of separation and isolation working.[120]

On Tuesday evening the Mendicity Institute was still held south of the Liffey. It was originally occupied to obstruct military movement from west to east along the quays.[121] Some contend that Heuston's men were not supposed to have been sent there in the original plan, but that Ceannt and Connolly, realising that they could not occupy the Guinness buildings and Kingsbridge Station because of the restricted turnout on Monday, sent the Fianna there as an alternative.[122] In any case, Heuston's detachment was intended only to hold the Institute for a few hours but was able to hold out until Wednesday.[123]

On Wednesday morning the British commander, Brig. Gen. Lowe, turned his attention to rebel strongholds north of the River Liffey.[124] Liberty Hall had long been considered the centre of all rebel activity in Dublin, not just that of the Citizen Army. Because of the activities that originated in Liberty Hall, officials at Dublin Castle considered it the centre of nationalist sentiment, though it had little connection with the Volunteers. The newspapers described it as 'the centre of social anarchy in Ireland, the brain of every riot and disturbance'.[125] But the Citizen Army left it deserted on Monday. Nevertheless, Lowe decided to attack and, apparently following Western Front policy, first laid down an artillery barrage.[126] Two eighteen-pounder guns were brought from Trinity College and opened fire across Butt Bridge.[127] A small gunboat, HMY *Helga*, sailed up the Liffey and augmented the artillery pieces, firing 24 rounds at Liberty Hall.[128] There are stories that the *Helga* 'lobbed shells' over the Loopline Bridge, but the flat trajectory of her guns would have made this next to impossible; she fired under the bridge into Liberty Hall.[129] Just to make sure that the Hall was destroyed, fire was also opened from machine-guns in the Custom House, the tower of the Tara Street fire station and the Tivoli Music Hall on Burgh Quay across the Liffey. The interior of Liberty Hall was gutted but the outside walls remained. The British troops had their foothold on the north side of the Liffey at the eastern end of the rebel positions.

Also on Wednesday the British made their greatest error, and suffered their largest number of casualties, in the advance up Northumberland Road towards Mount Street Bridge. The Sherwood Foresters arrived in Kingstown from Liverpool on Wednesday morning, tired, seasick and disoriented. One column headed to the Royal Hospital in Kilmainham and reached it without incident. The other column was ordered to head to Trinity College and marched into a massacre.[130] The seventeen Volunteers of the 3rd Battalion at 25 Northumberland Road, Clanwilliam House and the parochial hall and schoolhouse at the bridge were perfectly situated and were excellent marksmen with plenty of ammunition. The British were raw troops,[131] many of whom had never fired a live cartridge, had had training only in trench fighting, had no grenades at first, and were completely overwhelmed by urban/street fighting.[132] The British charged the house at 25 Northumberland Road and then charged the bridge, making only one small attempt at a flanking movement, which was uninspired and unsuccessful. Finally the British obtained some grenades, which they used to destroy the door of the house; they killed one of the rebels there, while the other escaped. The British field commander, Col. Maconchy,[133] relayed his dire position, but inexplicably Gen. Lowe commanded the Sherwoods to continue through the bridge to Trinity College.[134] As a result, all of the Sherwood officers were either killed or wounded and there were 242 casualties among other ranks. The seventeen Volunteers had disabled a whole regiment.

By Wednesday the British began to tighten their pincers around the rebel positions on the north side of the Liffey. The results of the fighting to come would seem predictable even at that stage, but there was much that was unpredictable, as the fighting up Northumberland Road and across Mount Street Bridge showed. At this point Gen. Lowe became more cautious and took no chances.[135] He began the assault on the GPO by sending troops westward from Amiens Street Station, and down Sackville Street from the Parnell Monument.[136] Machine-guns fired on the Imperial Hotel from Westmoreland Street, and on the GPO from Amiens Street and the Rotunda. Snipers were sent to fire down Sackville Street, Talbot Street and Lower Abbey Street.[137] Then Lowe brought his artillery into play and set up eighteen-pounders at the junction of College Green and D'Olier Street, starting by firing into Kelly's Fort at the corner of Sackville Street and Bachelor's Walk,[138] followed by a 'walking barrage' north up Sackville Street,[139] setting fire to the buildings and isolating the Volunteers. This was the first artillery barrage in the area, and the firing continued until Friday. While the Volunteers stood up well to the artillery, they began retreating into the GPO from their outlying positions. By late Wednesday there were no rebel positions held north of the GPO, and its Henry Street side was being bombarded by fire from Capel Street.[140] The GPO was surrounded and cut off from the 1st Battalion garrison in the Four Courts area, thus completing the isolation of both.[141]

On Thursday that same column of Sherwood Foresters, having camped overnight around Mount Street Bridge, was finally on its way to the Royal Hospital, Kilmainham. As they approached the Rialto Bridge, they were attacked by the Volunteer 4th Battalion in Marrowbone Lane and the South Dublin Union. They were reinforced by British troops from Portobello Barracks led by Major Sir Francis Vane, and some of them broke into the Union and some of its buildings.[142] Late on Thursday the column finally passed by the Union and reached the Royal Hospital. This was the last major fighting in the Union; the 4th Battalion Volunteers were isolated and they surrendered on Sunday.[143]

The location of the GPO made it difficult for the British to direct either machine-gun fire or artillery on the building from either end of Sackville Street, and buildings completely blocked it from east and west, but that also meant that the rebels had narrowed fields of defensive fire. Thus by Thursday the GPO was completely cut off, and only forays by single couriers were possible.[144] In an attempt to determine the viability of an escape or the reallocation of troops, Connolly was very seriously wounded on a reconnaissance patrol on Thursday afternoon.[145] After that, the command in the GPO began to withdraw all outlying posts to the GPO, and all had been withdrawn by Friday morning.

By Friday the GPO was in flames. When Gen. Maxwell arrived on Friday morning to take over command, the British had, to all intents and purposes, defeated the Rising.[146] On Friday night the GPO garrison made a breakout, but only to Moore Street, where they passed the night. On Saturday afternoon they surrendered. The British plan to outflank and isolate the rebel defences had been successful, and the shelling and fires rendered virtually all the rebel positions untenable. On Saturday 29 April, 'in order to prevent the further slaughter of Dublin citizens, and in the hope of saving the lives of our followers, now surrounded and hopelessly outnumbered', Pearse gave the order to surrender, and shortly afterwards all the rebel positions around the GPO were turned over to the British.

Battalion Commandants Daly (1st), MacDonagh (2nd), de Valera (3rd), Ceannt (4th), Ashe (5th) and Mallin (St Stephen's Green) did not surrender until Sunday, but there was no further organised action after Pearse surrendered to Gen. Lowe at the northern end of Moore Street.

There was very little public support for the rebels during the Rising.[147] For the most part, the Irish people supported the British war effort. Moreover, many Dublin civilians were killed or lost their property in the fires.[148] Nothing these men and women had done during the week led the public to take their side, though the bitterness of the people was tinged with a little admiration—they had fought well against the regular troops.

During the Rising several Capuchin priests from the Church Street Friary ministered to the Irish in their garrisons, and afterward the friars were asked to assist in communicating the surrender orders. To clarify the situation for those Volunteers still fighting and who had not received proper notice of the Irish surrender, Fr Columbus went to Dublin Castle, where he met a British officer and explained to him that he needed a document to convince the Volunteers in the North King Street area that the Rising was over. The officer suggested that he should go in person to Pearse at Arbour Hill Detention Barracks and ask him to rewrite the surrender note. Gen. Maxwell, the British commanding officer, received him courteously, and when Fr Columbus asked to be allowed to see Pearse and the others held there his request was granted. Fr Columbus wrote that Maxwell expressed his horror at the loss of life and destruction of property but said, 'Oh, but we will make those beggars pay for it'. Fr Columbus replied, 'The blood of martyrs is the seed of martyrs'. 'Are you backing them up, then?' asked Maxwell. Concluding that prudence was the better part of valour, Columbus said nothing.[149]

British General Staff policy held that it was inadvisable to carry out death sentences on rebels, because the rebel groups thrived on those executed as martyrs.[150]

Nevertheless, reporting to Prime Minister Herbert Asquith regarding the executions, Maxwell wrote:

> In view of the gravity of the Rebellion and its connection with German intrigue and propaganda and in view of the great loss of life and destruction of property resulting therefrom, the General Officer Commanding in Chief Irish Command [Maxwell] has found it imperative to inflict the most severe sentences on the organisers of this detestable Rising and on the Commanders who took an actual part in the actual fighting . . .[151]

Gen. Maxwell ordained that all seven signatories of the *Proclamation* should be executed in Kilmainham Gaol, along with several other prominent commanders of rebel positions—a total of fourteen in Dublin. James Connolly, so badly wounded that he lay in a hospital bed in Dublin Castle from the time of his surrender, was taken from the hospital, seated on a rough wooden box and shot. Later, when Maxwell refused to hand over the bodies for burial, he wrote:

> Irish sentimentality will turn these graves into martyrs' shrines to which annual processions, etc. will be made which will cause constant irritation in this country.[152]

The executions created a wave of protest and outrage in Ireland.[153]

The Rising had hardly been the work of a massive conspiracy, but the British acted as if it were.[154] Britain, profoundly engaged in World War I, determined that the Rising was an act of 'treason' and that the participants and leaders should suffer the fate of traitors in wartime. In addition, the rebels had enlisted German support, a move that prompted outright vilification.[155] Over 3,000 men and women were imprisoned after the rebellion, many in jails in England and Wales. These mass arrests and increased military presence portrayed Ireland as a country in the control of an oppressive and alien government that could only rule the country by force. Many in Ireland began to feel a communion with past fighting generations, and the words of James Fintan Lalor were often quoted: 'Somewhere, somehow, and by someone, a beginning must be made'. Pearse, the idealist, and Connolly, the Lalor disciple, had begun the rebellion in Lalor's words: 'even if [it was] called premature, imprudent or dangerous—if made so soon as tomorrow—even if offered by ten men only—even if offered by men armed with stones take their side'.

The Rising was not an intellectual landmark but an event of enormous political power. The leaders did not regard themselves as great thinkers, and their political and social thoughts on Ireland could not have stood up to the veneration that followed. The statement that 'Pearse was more than a patriot; he was a virtuous man. He possessed all the qualities which go to the making of a saint . . . it would not be astonishing if Pearse were canonised some day . . .' seems embarrassingly preposterous today.[156] Their political and social ideas were fairly limited and naïve, even by the standards of the day. Few of their ideas, even those of Connolly, could stand the test of time.[157] But it was a culmination of centuries of grievances against British rule, and of the efforts of generations of nationalists. Liam Ó Briain wrote: 'It was a unique experience to feel that, once again, after a hundred years or more, the foreign yoke had been cast off, and that men in their own capital, with their own flag above them, should be standing at bay before their own race'.[158]

The Rising was planned by a few men who feared that without a dramatic gesture of this kind the sense of national identity that had survived all the hazards of the centuries would flicker out within their lifetimes. Its necessity arose from the need to reawaken a spirit of nationalism that seemed to them to have died in the hearts of a majority of the Irish.[159] Before the Rising, most of Ireland's nationalist population did not subscribe to Fenian belief in physical force. Immediately after the Rising this view did not change. Soon, however, that adverse opinion of the rebels would begin to evolve and the public would increasingly support their position and objectives, if still disapproving of their means. The admiration of the people for the rebels' having fought well and honourably against the British began to move closer to approval.

Throughout Ireland, the executions began to revive the Irish spirit and alter the people's opinions as the Rising had not done. While the executions were ongoing, George Bernard Shaw, who described the Rising as a 'collision between a pram and a Pickford's van', wrote:

> The shot Irishmen will now take their places beside Emmet and the Manchester Martyrs in Ireland, and beside the heroes of Poland and Serbia and Belgium in Europe; and nothing in heaven or earth can prevent it . . .[160]

The Catholic Church traditionally held that there were five conditions required for a lawful revolt:

- a tyrannical government, without legitimacy in the country;
- the impossibility of removing that government except by force;
- the evil caused by the revolt to be far less than that to be removed by the revolt;
- serious possibility of success;
- approval of the community as a whole.

The Church's hierarchy, under the leadership of Michael Cardinal Logue, archbishop of Armagh and primate of all Ireland, held that the Rising was unjustified because none of these required conditions was met. On 7 May 1916 the archbishop of Cashel,

Dr John Mary Harty, told a large congregation at St Michael's Church in Tipperary:

> The history of the past has shown that all revolutionary measures are doomed to failure. The people of this Archdiocese and of this town of Tipperary realise that to the fullest extent, and hence during the last sorrowful fortnight they kept calm and showed that now, as always, they are true, patriotic Irishmen.[161]

Later, however, the same influences that inspired many of the rebels—the GAA, the Gaelic League and Irish nationalism/separatism—also appealed to the younger members of the clergy. As the dying words of the executed leaders were reported in a religious vein, the attitudes of the clergy began a very slow change.[162] Soon some support for the nationalist ideals appeared among younger priests, who came forward at nationalist rallies and on Sinn Féin platforms. The conversion of some priests into more outspoken nationalists was vital to the growth of the movement after the Rising.

The actions of the British in executing the leaders and imprisoning so many had adverse effects outside Ireland as well. Particularly in the United States, with its active and powerful Irish population, there were outcries and protests. The same Irish separatist organisations that contributed so heavily to the Rising brought pressure to bear on the American government to intervene on behalf of the thousands of Irish prisoners in English jails. By the end of 1916 the British authorities determined to release most of the rebels, and these were home in Ireland by Christmas. They returned to a riotous welcome, a complete turn-around from the send-off they had been given by the populace eight months earlier on the way to prison. The tide of public opinion had clearly changed.

The Rising was a battle, not a war. From battles, the combatants must learn the lessons to enable them to fight the next battle and win the war. The republican forces learned that public opinion is essential to a guerrilla campaign. The Irish learned the effectiveness of an ambush and that one can be used just as productively on city streets as on country roads. Their leaders learned the necessity for holding forces in reserve and ready to counter-attack. The Volunteers who returned from captivity learned that they could not train a large group to fight in a city, and so turned their training and strategising to small parties of well-trained, disciplined troops that they deemed 'active service units' and 'flying columns'. They learned the absolute necessity of intelligence, and that it had to be kept current.

The Irish learned how to fight the War of Independence. Whether they could have learned all those lessons without the Rising is another question. They also achieved Clauswitz's third aim of war: 'to gain public opinion'.

On 5 May 1916, the headline on the front page of the *Daily Sketch* read: 'Out of the ashes of tragedy spring Ireland's hopes'.

Notes

1   Ó Dubghaill 1966, 17.

2   Garnham 2004.

3   Garvin 1986, 79. A precursor to the Gaelic League was the Society for the Preservation of the Irish Language, founded in 1877 by Archbishop John MacHale of Tuam, Archbishop Thomas Croke and Dr William Walsh, president of St Patrick's Institute in Maynooth.

4   Delivered to the Irish National and Literary Society in Dublin, 25 November 1892. The Society was the precursor of the dramatic movement which led to the founding of the Abbey Theatre.

5   Clery 1919.

6   Jennie Wyse-Power, 'The political influence of women in modern Ireland', in W. FitzGerald (n.d.), 159.

7   Coogan 2001, 29.

8   Owen McGee, 'The politics of the IRB and its role in the Irish Revolution, 1916–1923' (lecture given at a conference entitled 'The Long Revolution: 1916 in Context' at University College Cork, 27 January 2006).

9   Statement of Walter Carpenter to the Local Government Board Inquiry into the Housing Conditions of the Working Classes (1913).

10   *Irish Times* editorial, 4 February 1914.

11   Kennedy 2003.

12   Moran 1978; McDermott 2005.

13   Wells and Marlowe 1916, 30.

14   Edward MacLysaght, 'Larkin, Connolly and the Labour Movement', in Martin 1967, 124.

15   Charles McCarthy, 'Larkin and the working class, 1907–1913' (a paper read to the Irish Labour History Society in September 1980).

16   Syndicalism originated in France as a response to the failure of existing socialist parties and labour unions to represent the economic interests of the unskilled worker. At that time most labour unions were composed of skilled workers and were more like guilds. Syndicalism emphasised direct action, militancy and strikes to build workers' consciousness, culminating in general strikes where workers could take control of industry and organise for the benefit of all.

17   Most sources indicate that Connolly was in the British army in his youth, though there is no direct evidence. Little information is available on Connolly's time in the army owing to the fact that he was reticent about this later and because he used a false name when he enlisted. See Collins 2012, 28ff.

18   MacLysaght, 'Larkin, Connolly and the Labour Movement', in Martin 1967, 123ff.

19   Kevin B. Nowlan, 'Tom Clarke, MacDermott and the I.R.B.', in Martin 1967, 109ff.

20   Seán T. O'Kelly in *An Phoblacht*, 30 April 1926.

21   Newsinger 1993.

22   Wells and Marlowe 1916, 33.

23   Fox 1944, 17.

24   O'Connor Lysaght 2006.

25   J.C. Beckett, 'Carson—unionist and rebel', in Martin 1967, 81ff. See also A.T.Q. Stewart, 'Craig and the Ulster Volunteer Force', in Martin 1967, 67ff. For the UVF, see Bowman 2002.

26   Lt General Sir George Richardson, KCB, CIE, CB, was a former British commander in India.

27   Capt. Jack White, DSO, the chair of the Army Council, was the son of Gen. Sir George White, the British commander of the defence of Ladysmith in the Boer War, and was himself a professional soldier.

28   White 1930 [2005], 202ff.

29   The *Clydevalley* was briefly renamed *Mountjoy II*, after the *Mountjoy* which broke the boom across the Foyle in 1689—thought a more appropriate historic name of good omen to the Ulster Volunteers. This conversion was achieved by using strips of canvas 6ft long, which were cut and painted with white letters on a black background and affixed to her bows and stern.

30   Frederick H. Crawford, CBE, JP. Crawford was a former officer with the Mid Ulster Artillery regiment of the British army before being transferred to the Donegal Artillery, with which he served during the Boer War, in which he earned the rank of major. See Crawford 1947.

31   Jackson 1993.

32   Martin 1964. See also Nixon and Healy 2000. For a statement of a participant, see Rosney,

Joseph, Witness Statement 112.

33   Fitzgibbon, Seán, Witness Statement 130.

34   The rifles were I.G. (Infanterie-Gewehr) Mod 71 German Mausers. The M71 was a long-barrelled, single-shot, bolt-action rifle that fired an 11mm black powder cartridge, roughly .45 calibre, and they were obsolete. There are contradictory accounts about the exact amount of ammunition that was landed, varying between 25,000 and 29,000 rounds. In any case, it was less than 40 rounds per rifle. The Volunteers would have to learn to shoot without pulling the trigger. The rifles were too long to be carried between the tunnelled buildings. Furthermore, the black powder they used gave their positions away on firing and made sniping difficult. During the Rising the British were mainly equipped with Lee Enfield .303s, which were much shorter, known both for rapidity of fire and for accuracy, and they used smokeless cartridges, which was a great asset. Moreover, the same .303 cartridge was used for the rifles and the British machine-guns, which made resupply much easier.

35   Jackson 2004, 136.

36   Curiously, the RIC and the DMP often encouraged and even assisted in this military training at first. Golden, Gerry, Witness Statement 521: 'We used to form up in columns of four and march out on the Market Square with our Captain in front and about twelve ex-British Army Sergeants to drill us. This went on until the 29th July when all the Reserve men and Militia men were called up, as they thought, for a month's training'. Most of the rank-and-file RIC were in favour of Home Rule, though it was generally accepted that most of the officers were opposed to it. As a result, especially after their initial foundation, the other ranks often assisted in drilling and training the Volunteers, but not for long. See Bratton, Constable Eugene, Witness Statement 467.

37   Holohan, Garry, Witness Statements 328 and 336.

38   Robbins, Frank, Witness Statement 585.

39   Handley, Sgt Edward, Witness Statement 625.

40   British PRO, Kew, WO 904/99.

41   McHugh 1966, 69ff.

42   Gerrard, Capt. E., Witness Statement 348.

43   Diarmuid Lynch, 'Recollections and comments on the IRB', NLI MS 11128.

44   There is no agreement on the total number of Irishmen who served in the British army and/or navy in the First World War. There appears to be a consensus on the figure of 210,000, of whom at least 35,000 died, though the figure on the National War Memorial is 49,400. David Fitzpatrick, 'Militarism in Ireland, 1900–1922', in Bartlett and Jeffrey 1966, 397. See Denman 1994. See also Callan 1987.

45   Ó Clerigh 2008.

46   McGarry, Seán, Witness Statement 368.

47   Diarmuid Ó Donnabhain Rossa, 1831–1915: Souvenir of Public Funeral, 1915.

48   Pearse was the founder of St Enda's school, a poet and an active IRB member.

49   Many newspapers carried copies of the address, most completely in *The Irish Volunteer*. The original handwritten script is on display in the Pearse Museum, St Enda's, Rathfarnham, Dublin.

50   Lynch 1957, 48ff.

51   Martin 1961, 234ff.

52   Townshend 2006.

53   Eoin MacNeill, *Memorandum to Volunteers*, 19 April 1916.

54   Martin 1961. See Dillon 1936a.

55   There is evidence that the Rising was first scheduled for Good Friday, 21 April 1916, but was changed to Easter Sunday because 'a mobilization on Good Friday was a departure from the usual rule that mobilizations were ordered only for Sundays and Holidays when the majority of men were not at work, and any change would cause comment and might also be a dangerous signal to the British'. See O'Brien 1936; Dillon 1936b; Béaslaí 1952b.

56   Duggan 1970.

57   O'Donoghue 1966.

58   Chatterton 1934, 242. Chatterton summarises the British Admiralty's attempt to survey the *Aud*, and found that the weapons were captured from the Russians. The cargo was an estimated 20,000 rifles, 1,000,000 rounds of ammunition, ten machine-guns and explosives. The majority of the rifles were the Russian Mosin-Nagant 1891. The Germans captured these rifles from the Russian army at the Battle of Tannenberg. Chatterton wrote that the

rifles also bore the 'butt stamp of the Orleans small arms factory, 1902. The barrels were marked with the Russian War Office and overstamped with the name "Deutschland".'

[59] Golway 1998, 212–16.

[60] Devoy 1929, 458.

[61] Spindler 1931. Spindler skilfully navigated the *Aud* on a circuitous course that took the vessel north, nearly to the Arctic circle, then south and west, in an effort to avoid vessels of the British navy. The *Aud*'s greatest lack was a wireless, so it was incommunicado from the time it left Lübeck.

[62] O'Leary, Mortimer, Witness Statement 107. O'Leary was the pilot designated to take the *Aud* in to Fenit Pier. 'On that (Holy Thursday) evening when I got back to Leary's Island I saw a two-masted Steamer of about 3000 tons . . . I watched her from the back window from nightfall until 12 midnight. I did not see her make any signal during that time. She was so much larger than the size of boat which Tadg Brosnan's description had suggested to me that I did not connect her with the arms ship. It did not enter my mind at the time that she was the expected arms ship . . . He [Brosnan] did not, at any time, either on Thursday or Saturday, say anything to me about green lights for signals, or any other kind of signals. I doubt if he knew anything about them then.'

[63] O'Donoghue 1966; Ireland 1966, 9–26. See also Reilly, RIC Constable Bernard, Witness Statement 349.

[64] Inspector general's confidential report for 1 April–31 May, dated 15 June 1916, PRO CO 904/99.

[65] Stack's biographer, J. Anthony Gaughan, claims that there was a 'detailed plan' but gives no further details or evidence for a plan in his book; Gaughan 1977, 45–8. 'In March 1916 during a parade of the Company in Ballymacelligott, Austin Stack discussed with the other two officers and myself the possibility of securing at short notice, forty horses and carts from Ballymacelligott which may be used for the transport of military equipment. We were able to assure him that the transport could be provided by our Company at short notice. That was all any of us knew and we were told nothing or given any details': McEllistrom, Thomas, Witness Statement 275.

[66] 'I was one of the few members of the company who was aware that this special mobilisation had been called for the purpose of marching to Tralee to take over the arms about to be landed on the south coast of Kerry. On this particular night we waited all through the night for final instructions which never came. The same position obtained during Easter Week. We received no instructions and were completely in the dark as to what was doing': McElligott, Patrick, Witness Statement 1013.

[67] Jackson 1993.

[68] *Belfast Evening Telegraph*, 25 April 1914.

[69] Kee 1972, 490.

[70] 'Both of us were members of the Cycle Corps attached to the Tralee Battalion . . . He told us we were to go to Banna and try and get in touch with Austin Stack who had already gone in that direction . . . Switzer and a man named Brennan, whose Christian name I cannot recall . . . gave each of us a loaded revolver . . . We continued on until we reached the strand . . . We looked all round but there was no sign of anyone on the strand. Neither of us had ever fired a shot from a revolver, and we were not too sure of how they worked': McGaley, Jack, Witness Statement 126.

[71] Ó hUid 1966.

[72] Lawless, Joseph, Witness Statement 1043.

[73] 'We were mobilised on Friday night at the Rink [in Tralee]. We were told to carry only empty rifles. Cahill gave an order before leaving the Rink that if any rifles were loaded they were to be unloaded. We marched up towards Rook Street. We got an order to double. Some Volunteer dropped a loaded revolver; it went off and I got the bullet in the leg. That put me out of action for the remainder of the period': O'Connor, Éamon, Witness Statement 114. He was a Volunteer in County Kerry just prior to the Rising.

[74] Roger McHugh, 'Casement and German help', in Martin 1967, 177ff.

[75] *Sunday Independent*, 23 April 1916.

[76] Molony, Helena, Witness Statement 391.

[77] Lynch 1966.

[78] Lt Col. Sir Matthew Nathan, GCMG, PC, was under-secretary for Ireland from 1914 to 1916. Ryan 1949 [1957], 96.

79   See Haydon 1976.

80   Letter from Sir Mathew Nathan to Augustine Birrell, 18 December 1915.

81   Sir Matthew Nathan to Royal Commission of Inquiry, London, 18 May 1916, p. 10. To some degree, the Castle authorities had anticipated a rising but were misled into delaying action by MacNeill's order. See Ó Broin 1966, 81–8. For Birrell's own account see Birrell 1937, 193–236.

82   Pearse statement from the GPO, Friday 28 April 1916. Original's whereabouts are unknown. Printed by the *Irish War News* from O'Keefe's Printers on Halston Street by Joe Stanley at Pearse's direction. Later printed in the *Sinn Féin Rebellion Handbook* published by the *Irish Times* (1916, 47). A copy is in the Irish Volunteer papers, University College Dublin.

83   D. FitzGerald 1966, 1.

84   Clarke 1997, 94.

85   Joyce 1966, 353.

86   Ó Conluain 1963, 165–6.

87   Ceannt, Áine B.E., Witness Statement 264.

88   Talbot 1923, chapter 3, 'Eoin MacNeill, Ulsterman'.

89   Florence O'Donoghue, 'Ceannt, Devoy, Ó Rahilly and the military plan', in Martin 1967, 192; O'Donoghue 1963. Commenting on the fact that the IRB's and Military Council's plans were kept so closely held, see Lynch 1957, 54: 'Herein we have splendid testimony to the extreme care in recruiting exercised by the men responsible for the IRB over a generation (coupled with propitious circumstances), and in particular to the methods followed by the Military Council who guarded their secrets so jealously that the insurrectionary forces were enabled to march unopposed into their several strategic positions on Easter Monday'. But see Cmdt William Brennan-Whitmore, letter to the *Evening Herald*, 8 January 1966: 'The plans were no more elaborate than the surprise seizure of previously selected buildings, fortifying them as best we could, and holding them as long as possible'.

90   Brennan-Whitmore 1966, 47.

91   Seán MacDermott to O'Hegarty: 'The plans were Plunkett's and he had already worked them out when we got in touch with him, and they were adopted practically without alteration' (O'Hegarty 1952, 700ff).

92   'Revolutionary warfare', *Workers' Republic*, 29 May, 5, 12 and 19 June, 3, 10, 17 and 24 July 1915. (This series of articles was unattributed but almost certainly written by James Connolly.)

93   Ceannt, Áine B.E., Witness Statement 264.

94   Fox 1944 [2014], 149: 'There was never any question of taking the Castle. The forces were too small for the Castle to be taken and held. It was hoped, however, that by holding the Guardroom and commanding the entrance from adjacent posts, the effectiveness of the Castle as an attacking base would be destroyed. Here, again, the plan was crippled by the small number taking part. But the success achieved by the audacious attack created panic on the other side.' Regarding Trinity College see Slator, Thomas, Witness Statement 263: 'He [MacDonagh] told us one of the places which we were to occupy was Trinity College, and an officer named Paddy Walsh of "D" Company was detailed for this job. As, however, the numbers which could be spared from the main body at Stephen's Green were so small, Tom MacDonagh decided to call off the taking of Trinity College as it would have meant a heavy loss of life with no hope of getting in. All that we could have spared for this job would be about twenty men'. As further evidence that the rebels could have taken Trinity, 'by 7.00p.m. [Monday evening] the garrison there stood at 44': Brennan-Whitmore 1996, footnote on p. 153.

95   'The Beggar's Bush Garrison consisted of no more than 10 men at the start of the Rising'— statement of 'one who was present at the Mount Street action', *Irish Times*, 4 July 1966.

96   Caulfield 1995, 48–9.

97   A secret Operations Circular issued by Major Gen. F.C. Shaw (General Staff, Home Forces) at 4.20 p.m. on 25 April reported that four eighteen-pound guns left Athlone in the early hours of that day (Asquith Papers, Bodleian Library, MS 42, f. 11).

98   Sir Matthew Nathan to Royal Commission of Inquiry, London, 18 May 1916, p. 10.

99   Lord Lieutenant Ivor Churchill, Baron Wimborne, to Royal Commission of Inquiry, London, 18 May 1916, p. 39.

100 Lee 2006.

101 Gilley 1986.

102 'Ireland will not find Christ's peace until she has taken Christ's sword.' Lyons 1971, 336.

103 'I have turned my face
To this road before me,
To the deed that I see
And the death I shall die'
—*Renunciation*. See *Collected works of Patrick H. Pearse. Plays, stories, and poems* (5th edn, Dublin, 1922).

104 The nature of the Rising as a 'blood sacrifice' has been addressed by many. 'The insurrection of 1916 was a forlorn hope and a *deliberate blood sacrifice*. The men who planned it and led it did not expect to win. They knew they could not win . . . But *they counted upon being executed afterwards* and they knew that *that* would save Ireland's soul' (emphasis added): O'Hegarty 1924 [1998], 3. Terence MacSwiney wrote in 1914: 'We want to set Ireland on fire: and we think our personal sacrifice not too high a price to pay . . . Let Irish blood be the first to fall on Irish earth—there will be kindled a crusade for the restoration of liberty that not all the fires of hell can defeat . . . Our Volunteers are not as yet fully alert . . . A sacrifice will do it: like a breath from Heaven it will blow upon their souls and kindle the divine fire; and they shall be purified, strengthened, and made constant, and the destiny of Ireland will be safe in their hands' (*Cork Weekly Fianna Fáil*, 7 November 1914). See Shaw 1972, 117, 125–6; Martin 1966a; 1968; Greaves 1991; Neeson 2007.

105 In his lectures and articles on street fighting, and in his discussions on the plans for the Rising, Connolly naïvely pronounced that the British would never use artillery, as 'A capitalist Government would never destroy capitalist property' (Brennan-Whitmore 1996, 22). At the first sound of artillery, Connolly realised that 'any Government, capitalist or otherwise, threatened from within and possibly from without, would not hesitate to utilize every weapon at its command, property or no property' (Caulfield 1995, 145).

106 For the effect of the fires and the difficulty in extinguishing them see the report by Capt. Purcell, chief of the Dublin Fire Brigade, in *1916 Rebellion Handbook* (*Irish Times* 1917 [1998 edn]), 29–32. See also Hally 1966.

107 Saurin 1926: 'When Hoyte's [on Sackville Street] first caught fire it was a terrific spectacle, as it burst into one huge flame the moment it was hit. It was a roaring inferno in less than a minute. Stored as it was with chemicals of all sorts and with oils and colours it spouted rockets and stars of every hue and was the most wonderful fireworks show I ever saw.'

108 Hally 1966–7, Part 2, 52.

109 Sir Matthew Nathan to Royal Commission of Inquiry, London, 18 May 1916, p. 10.

110 At the start of the Rising, British troops in Dublin consisted of squadrons of the 5th and 12th Lancers of the 6th Cavalry at Marlborough Barracks (approximate strength 885), the 3rd Royal Irish Regiment at Richmond Barracks (approximate strength 405: eighteen officers, 385 other ranks), the 3rd Royal Irish Rifles at Portobello Barracks (approximate strength 670: 21 officers, 650 other ranks) and the 10th Royal Dublin Fusiliers at Royal Barracks (approximate strength 470: 37 officers, 430 other ranks). Each of these units had an 'inlying picket' of 100 officers and other ranks which was kept in readiness to 'aid the civil power in the enforcement of the law'. Normally there were approximately 300 troops assigned to Ship Street Barracks adjacent to Dublin Castle. The assigned Dublin garrison strength was approximately 120 officers and 2,260 other ranks. There were an additional 3,000 British troops in the Curragh. In addition, in Ireland there were 9,500 armed policemen and in Dublin the DMP numbered about 1,100.

111 Hally 1966–7, Part 2, 51.

112 G.A. Hayes-McCoy, 'A military history of the 1916 Rising', in Nowlan 1969, 275.

113 French 1931, 338.

114 G.C. Duggan, employed in the Transport Department of the Admiralty, made this statement in the *Sunday Press*, 29 March 1964.

115 P.A. Foley, a railway man on duty in Amiens Street Station, made this statement in the *Sunday Independent Easter Rising Commemorative Supplement* (1966).

116 Hayes-McCoy, 'Military history of the Rising', in Nowlan 1969, 275.

117 Emily Norgrove Hanratty, a member of the City Hall garrison, gave her statement to the *Irish Press Supplement*, 9 April 1966, p. 13.

118 Brennan-Whitmore 1996, 46.

119 McHugh 1966, 165.

120 Margaret Skinnider, statement in the *Irish Press Supplement*, 9 April 1966, p. 12.

121 Paddy Holohan, statement in *The Capuchin Annual* (1942), 232.
122 Heuston 1966, 34ff.
123 P.J. Stephenson 1966; J. Stephenson 2005.
124 William Henry Muir (W.H.M.) Lowe, CB, was a British general who had served in India, Burma and the Boer War.
125 *Weekly Irish Times*, 29 April 1916.
126 Ó Broin 1955, 116ff.
127 McHugh 1966, 190.
128 Joye 2010.
129 Ireland 1966, 38–45.
130 'The Robin Hoods', 1/7th, 2/7th and 3/7th Battalions. Oates 1920, 282.
131 Caulfield 1995, 228ff.
132 McCann 1946, 46ff; Caulfield 1995, 208–28.
133 Col. E.W.S.K. Maconchy, CB, CIE, DSO, was regimental commander of the Sherwood Foresters.
134 British National Army Museum, Brig. Gen. E.W.S.K. Maconchy memoirs.
135 Hayes-McCoy, 'Military history of the Rising', in Nowlan 1969, 284.
136 E. McDermott, statement in the *Daily Chronicle*, 29 April 1916.
137 MacEntee 1966, 133ff.
138 Humphreys 1966, 161.
139 Callender 1939, 90.
140 Lynch 1957, 170.
141 Callender 1939, 94.
142 Vane 1929, 270.
143 O'Brennan 1947 [2006].
144 McLoughlin, Seán, Witness Statement 290. See McGuire 2006.
145 Ryan 1942, 223.
146 Gen. Sir John Grenville Maxwell, GCB, KCMG, CVO, DSO, PV, had served in the Sudan, Egypt, the Boer War and France.
147 Ironically, Pearse's play *The Singer*, written in autumn 1915, foretold this 'quietness' in the country:
'Cuimin: We've no one to lead us.
Colm: Didn't you elect me your captain?
Cuimin: We did; but not to bid us rise out when the whole country is quiet.'
See *Collected works of Patrick H. Pearse. Plays, stories, and poems* (5th edn, Dublin, 1922).
148 Duffy 2013.
149 His manuscript was discovered in the Capuchin Archives in Church Street. Fr Columbus, OFM Cap. See Benedict Cullen, 'Echoes of the Rising's final shots', *The Irish Times* (*http://www.aohdiv7.org/hist_easter_aftermath.htm*).
150 It should be noted that Maxwell had previously ordered the execution of several Egyptian rebel leaders at Khartoum in 1898, declaring that 'a dead fanatic is the only one to extend sympathy to' (James 1994, 283).
151 Coogan 2001, 135–6.
152 Hally 1966–7, Part 2, 53.
153 Toby 1997.
154 Cyril Falls, 'Maxwell, 1916, and Britain at war', in Martin 1967, 203ff.
155 Curran 1966, 22.
156 LeRoux 1932, x.
157 G. Fitzgerald 1966, 32.
158 Ó Briain 1923.
159 G. Fitzgerald 1966, 29.
160 *Daily News*, 10 May 1916.
161 Cronin 1966, 74.
162 One prayer card for the executed leaders read: 'O Gentlest Heart of Jesus, have mercy on the souls of Thy servants, our Irish heroes; bring them from the shadows of exile to the bright home of Heaven, where, we trust, Thou and Thy Blessed Mother have woven for them a crown of unending bliss'. (Prayer cards for the repose of the souls of the following Irishmen who were executed by English law, 1916, TCD MS 2074.)

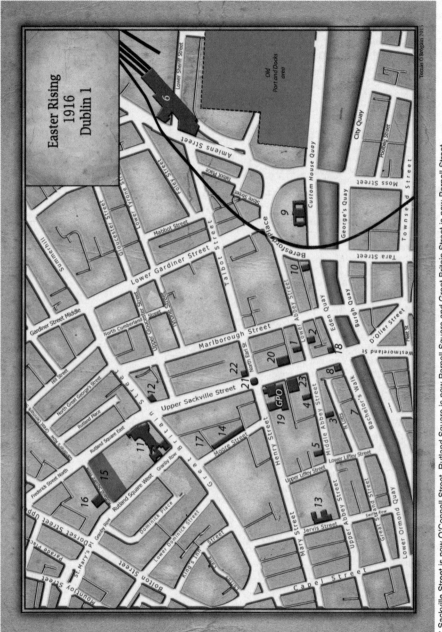

Easter Rising
1916
Dublin 1

Tomás O Brogáin 2015

* Sackville Street is now O'Connell Street, Rutland Square is now Parnell Square and Great Britain Street is now Parnell Street.

1 4 Abbey St. Lwr, The *Irish Times*

2 37 Abbey St. Lwr, Wynn's Hotel

3 55 Abbey St. Middle, The *Irish Catholic*

4 84 Abbey St. Middle, *Freeman's Journal*

5 111 Abbey St. Middle, Independent House

6 Amiens St.

7 Bachelor's Walk

8 56 Bachelor's Walk, at corner of Sackville St.,* Kelly's Fort

9 Custom House Quay

10 18 Beresford Place, Liberty Hall

11 Great Britain St., Rotunda Hospital

12 75A Great Britain St.,* Clarke's tobacconist

13 Jervis St. Hospital

14 Moore St.

15 Rutland Square*

16 25 Rutland Square, Gaelic League Meeting House

17 Sackville Lane

18 1 Sackville St. Lwr, Hopkins & Hopkins

19 Sackville St. Lwr, GPO

20 20 Sackville St. Lwr, Clery's

21 Sackville St. Lwr, Nelson's Pillar

22 33 Sackville St. Lwr, at the corner of North Earl St.

Dublin 1

Key locations

Abbey Street
Amiens Street
Beresford Place
Capel Street
Dorset Street
Henry Street
Marlboro Street
Moore Street

Mountjoy Square
Mountjoy Street
North Wall
Rutland Square (now Parnell Square)
Sackville Street (now O'Connell Street)
Summerhill
Talbot Street

I n the late forenoon of Easter Monday, 24 April 1916, men and women of the Irish Volunteers and the Irish Citizen Army began to assemble in front of Liberty Hall on Beresford Place.

'COME 484, PAT, AND FORGET THIS FOOLISHNESS.'
Mary Brigid Pearse
(Patrick Pearse's sister)

It was not an auspicious start for Padraic Pearse on that Monday, the day he was to be named Commandant General of the fighting forces and the first President of the Provisional Government of Ireland. The Easter Rising began from the steps of Liberty Hall, the side of the Hall where the James Connolly statue now stands. Did you know that in 1916 Liberty Hall fronted Beresford Place, not the quays?

Ever wait for a Luas in front of Wynn's Hotel on Lower Abbey Street? Did you know that ladies watched the 'attack' on the GPO from the windows of Wynn's as if it were a play? If you stand outside Wynn's Hotel, you're standing on the spot where the first barricade was raised. Look across to Madigan's Pub, as it is today: it was an *Irish Times* office in 1916. It was from this *Irish Times* office that the Volunteers commandeered rolls of newsprint to make the barricade, and it provided fuel for the oils and spirits that led to the fires that ravaged Dublin's centre.

The streets of Dublin are paved with stories, and a good way to build one's knowledge of the Rising is to walk in the very steps of the men and women of 1916.

Dublin 1 includes many of the central sites of the Rising and was part of the geographical area for the residences and training of the 1st and 2nd Battalions of Volunteers prior to the Rising. Ordinarily, those who resided north of the Liffey and west of Sackville (O'Connell) Street were assigned to the 1st Battalion, while those who resided north of the Liffey and east of Sackville Street were assigned to the 2nd Battalion. Members of the Irish Citizen Army came from all areas of Dublin, but the majority resided north of the Liffey.

Dublin 1 includes the actual route by which Pearse marched up Abbey Street Lower after his sister embarrassed him. Pearse and the others walked alongside James

Connolly, who had been asked by Bill O'Brien, as he left Liberty Hall, 'Is there any hope?' Connolly replied: 'None whatsoever . . . we're going out to be slaughtered'.

Follow the route of The Ó Rahilly as he led a party of 30 Volunteers from the burning GPO out into Henry Street, intending to make a dash up Moore Street on Friday evening. See just how far The Ó Rahilly crawled after he was wounded to the spot where he died. Then take a look up and see his heart-rending note to his wife, as it is immortalised on the plaque on the wall of what was then Sackville Place and is now Ó Rahilly Parade.

Walk from 16 Moore Street alongside Connolly on his stretcher. Walk with Willie Pearse, who headed the main body waving his white flag and who was to be executed only for being Padraic's brother. Close behind him came Tom Clarke, and towards the rear walked Seán MacDiarmada—crippled by polio, he was leaning on his cane—and Joseph Plunkett, who needed to be supported by Julia Grenan and Winifred Carney because he was near death from tuberculosis.

Because of its centrality in the city, Dublin 1 contains many of the iconic locations of the Rising, and Liberty Hall and the GPO top the list.

Liberty Hall was the headquarters of both the Irish Transport and General Workers' Union and the Irish Citizen Army. The *Irish Worker* and the *Worker* newspapers were printed in its print shop, as was the *Proclamation of the Irish Republic* on Easter Sunday. It was the focus for the Lockout of 1913, and the locus of the food distribution that followed. Since that time it had been under constant surveillance by Dublin Castle authorities and the DMP, as it was considered the centre of all revolutionary activity in Dublin. When Connolly hung his famous banner—*We Serve Neither King Nor Kaiser*—across its front, it was confirmation to the authorities that all persons moving into and out of the Hall must be scrutinised and their actions analysed.

The General Post Office on Sackville Street, which opened in 1818, is 200ft long and 150ft wide, with a height of 50ft in three storeys. Its architect was Francis Johnston. The portico is 50ft long, an Ionic portico of six fluted columns, a pediment surmounted with statues by John Smyth of Hibernia, Fidelity and Mercury, and a tympanum decorated with the royal coat of arms. Pearse read the *Proclamation of the Irish Republic* outside at 12.45 p.m. on Monday 24 April 1916. The GPO was probably the one official building in Dublin that would be frequented by many of the general populace. Its location on Sackville Street, as well as its imposing appearance, made it a prime spot for the Rising's headquarters but would ultimately entrap its defenders.

The many newspapers (*Irish Independent, Irish Times, The Leader, Sinn Féin, Freeman's Journal, Evening Telegraph, Irish Catholic*) and printers (Irish Industrial Printing and Publishing, Devereaux Neuth and Co., William H. West, Maunsel and Co.) in the area attest to its being a centre for the media of the time. Likewise, the shops along Sackville Street and Henry Street, and especially the food shops in Moore Street, show that it was the commercial and marketing centre for northside Dubliners of the period.

The theatres in the Rotunda, the Coliseum Variety Theatre and the Abbey Theatre demonstrated the area's cultural importance. Its abundance of hotels (Wynn's, the Gresham, Hammam, Vaughan's, the North Star), halls and meeting rooms (the Irish National Foresters' Hall, the Celtic Literary Society rooms, the Gaelic League rooms and offices, Grocers' Hall) were in constant use as meeting places for those who planned the Rising.

And there was no more important place for rallies (and riots) than the expanse of Sackville Street.

Abbey Street Lower: Forty-five buildings were burned during the Rising, including Mooney's Pub, the *Daily Express* office, Union Chapel, Methodist Chapel and the Peacock Theatre.

3 Abbey Street Lower: Keating's cycle shop; the bicycles were used for barricades during the Rising.

4 Abbey Street Lower: Reserve printing offices of the *Irish Times*, a very Unionist paper. During the Rising, George Plunkett led the Volunteers who took newsprint rolls for barricades, which greatly contributed to fires started on Thursday afternoon.

On the Tuesday morning of Easter Week, the *Irish Times* described the Rising:

This newspaper has never been published in stranger circumstances than those that obtain today, an attempt to overthrow the government of Ireland . . . At this critical moment our language must be moderate, unsensational, and free from any tendency to alarm. As soon as peace and order have been restored the responsibility for the intended revolution will be fixed in the right quarter . . .

. . . During the last twenty-four hours an effort has been made to set up an independent Irish Republic in Dublin. It was well organised; a large number of armed men are taking part in it and to the general public, at any rate, the outbreak came as a complete surprise. An attempt was made to seize Dublin Castle but this failed. The Rebels then took possession of the City Hall and the *Dublin Daily Express* office. During these operations a soldier and policeman were shot dead. The General Post Office was seized and a green flag was raised over its roof. Several shops in this quarter of Sackville Street were smashed and looted . . .

. . . In the very centre of the city a party of rebel Volunteers took possession of St Stephen's Green where they are, as we write, still entrenched. Fierce fighting has taken place between the rebels and the soldiers and there is reason to fear many lives have been lost . . .

Of course this desperate episode in Irish history can have only one outcome and the loyal public will await it as calmly and confidently as may be. Nothing in yesterday's remarkable scenes was more remarkable than the quietness and courage with which the people of Dublin accepted the sudden and widespread danger in the very neighbourhood of the fiercest fighting and the streets were full of cheerful and indifferent spectators. Such courage is excellent, but it may degenerate into recklessness.

Perhaps the most useful thing we can do now is to remember that quietness and confidence shall be our strength and to trust firmly in the speedy triumph of the forces of law and order. Those loyal citizens of Dublin who cannot help their country's cause at this moment may help it indirectly by refusing to give way to panic and by maintaining in their household a healthy spirit of hope.

The ordeal is not over but it will be short.[1]

On 1 May, in its first edition after the Rising, it opined:

The State has struck, but its work is not yet finished. The surgeon's knife has been put to the corruption in the body of Ireland and its course must not be stayed until the whole malignant growth has been removed. In the verdict of history weakness to-day would be even more criminal than the indifference of the last few months. Sedition must be rooted out of Ireland once for all. The rapine and bloodshed of the past week must be punished with a severity which will make any repetition of them impossible for generations to come. The loyal people of Ireland, Unionists and Nationalists, call to-day with an imperious voice for the strength and firmness which have so long been strangers to the conduct of Irish affairs . . .

Where our politicians failed and failed badly, the British Army has filled the breach and won the day. The Dublin insurrection will pass into history with the equally unsuccessful insurrections of the past.[2]

A week later its editorial stated:

Much nonsense is likely to be written in newspapers and talked about in Parliament about the restrictions of Martial Law in Ireland. The fact is Martial Law has come as a blessing to us all . . .

For the first time in many months Dublin was 'enjoying real security of life and property'.

We have learned that the sword of the soldier is a far better guarantee of justice and liberty than the presence of politicians.[3]

(Now Madigan's Pub)

5 Abbey Street Lower: Ship Hotel and Tavern. Occupied by Frank Thornton's and George Plunkett's men during the Rising.

33, 34 Abbey Street Lower: Royal Hibernian Academy. Burned during the Rising, with the loss of many great works of art. At the time of the Rising Dermot O'Brien was the president.

35–37 Abbey Street Lower: Wynn's Hotel (often written 'Wynne's' but photos clearly show the name without an 'e'). The Irish Volunteers first met here as a group on 11 November 1913. The following attended, according to both The Ó Rahilly and Bulmer Hobson: Piaras Béaslaí,[*] Joseph Campbell, Éamonn Ceannt,[*] James Deakin, Seán Fitzgibbon,[*][4] Bulmer Hobson, Eoin MacNeill,[*] Seán MacDermott,[*] The Ó Rahilly,[*] Padraic Pearse[*] and W.J. Ryan ([*]became members of the Provisional Committee). The Ó Rahilly noted that D.P. Moran was invited but did not attend,[5] but Hobson did not recall this. Hobson noted that Séamus O'Connor,[6] Colm Ó Lochlainn[7] and Robert Page *could* have attended.[8] Others noted that Michael Judge, Éamon Martin[9] and Col. Maurice Moore[10] attended.[11]

Abbey Street Lower at Sackville Street (now O'Connell Street): Hibernian Bank. Capt. Thomas Weafer was in command of the Volunteers who took this position, and he was killed here.[12] His body was consumed in the fire that burned the entire corner.[13]

55 Abbey Street Middle: The *Irish Catholic* newspaper office, owned by William Martin Murphy. The newspaper was violently opposed to the ICA and the Volunteers, as was Murphy's *Irish Independent*. In early May 1916, it wrote of the Rising and the leaders:

> Pearse was a man of ill-balanced mind, if not actually insane, and the idea of selecting him as chief magistrate of the Irish Republic is quite enough to create serious doubts as to the sanity of those who approved of it . . . Only the other day when the so-called Republic of Ireland was proclaimed . . . no better President could be proposed . . . than a crazy and insolent schoolmaster. This extraordinary combination of rogues and fools . . . to find anything like a parallel for what has occurred it is necessary to have recourse to the bloodstained annals of the Paris Commune.[14]

On 20 May it opined:

> What was attempted was an act of brigandage pure and simple, and there is no

reason to lament that its perpetrators have met the fate which from the very dawn of history has been universally reserved for traitors ... We need say no more, but to say less would be traitorous to the highest and holiest interests of Ireland.[15]

(See 177 King Street North [Dublin 7].)

84 Abbey Street Middle: The *Freeman's Journal* newspaper office.[16] This was the most conservative, Catholic and anti-Parnellite of popular newspapers.

The *Freeman's Journal* was also the voice of John Redmond's Nationalist Party. It opposed true Irish independence and accepted Home Rule as it was proposed in parliament. Its circulation dropped greatly and it became a weekly after Redmond's recruiting speech to parliament. Redmond's party subsidised the paper at the time of the Rising.

The building also housed the office of *Sport*.

96 Abbey Street Middle: Maunsel and Co. Ltd, publishers; burned during the Rising.

111 Abbey Street Middle: Independent House. The newspaper offices of the *Irish Independent*, owned by William Martin Murphy, were situated here and at 3–4 Liffey Street. A major newspaper, anti-mainstream Irish Parliamentary Party, it tried to break up the ITGWU strike of 1913 and the Union itself, and its editorial stance advocated full dominion status for Ireland following the Rising.

On Thursday afternoon James Connolly suffered a serious leg/ankle wound while emerging from the back entrance of this building on his way back to the GPO (he had been wounded in the arm earlier that afternoon). He crawled down Prince's Street and was carried into the GPO.

The *Irish Independent* called for the execution of the leaders of the Rising and was especially hard on Connolly. The following appeared in its editorials:

4 May: 'No terms of denunciation that pen would indict would be too strong to apply to those responsible for the criminal and insane rising of last week.'

10 May: It published a photo of Connolly with the caption: 'Still lies in Dublin Castle slowly recovering from his wounds'.

10 May: 'If these men are treated with too great leniency they will take it as an indication of weakness on the part of the government and the consequences may not be satisfactory. They may be more truculent than ever, and it is therefore necessary that society should be protected against their activity.

Some of the leaders are more guilty and played a more sinister part in the campaign than those who have already been punished severely, and it would be hardly fair to treat these leniently because the cry for clemency has been raised, while those no more guilty than they have been severely punished. Weakness to such men at this stage would be fatal.

Let the worst of the ringleaders be singled out and dealt with as they deserve.'

12 May: After Connolly was executed, but before it was known: 'Certain of the leaders remain undealt with, and the part they played was worse than that of some of those who have paid the extreme penalty ... We think in a word that no special leniency should be extended to some of the worst of the leaders whose cases have not yet been disposed of.'

111 Abbey Street Middle: The *Sunday Independent* newspaper offices. The editor was Paddy J. Little. It was in this paper that Eoin MacNeill placed his notice 'cancelling' the Rising on Easter Saturday night. MacNeill gave the notice to Mr Cogley, the night editor, at midnight:

NO PARADES

Irish Volunteer Marches Cancelled

A SUDDEN ORDER

Owing to the very critical position, all orders given to the Irish Volunteers for tomorrow, Easter Sunday, are hereby rescinded, and no parades, marches or other movements of the Irish Volunteers will take place. Each individual Volunteer will obey this order strictly in every particular.[17]

The editor during the time of the War of Independence was Tim Harrington and the sports sub-editor at the same time was George Gormby. The *Irish Independent*'s offices became overcrowded, so some of the staff moved to Carlisle House on Westmoreland Street.

The building also housed some offices for the *Evening Herald*.

Amiens Street: Amiens Street Railway Station (now Connolly Station). The terminus for the Drogheda and Dublin Railway, also known as the Great Northern Railway, built between 1844 and 1846.

The Volunteers did not take it and it remained an open terminus for British troops coming from the north.

It was renamed Connolly Station in 1966.

26–30 Amiens Street: North Star Hotel. Michael P. Colivet, commandant of the Limerick Brigade, met Padraic Pearse here on Spy Wednesday. The meeting took place in the restaurant and they 'disguised' their conversation by pretending to be a buyer (Pearse) and seller (Colivet) of farmers' goods. Colivet asked about the Rising and Pearse confirmed that it was on for Sunday.[18] This was to cause problems when the news got back to Eoin MacNeill.

41 Amiens Street: J.M. Butler, newsagent. He was prosecuted and fined £20 in June 1916 for publishing a statement purporting to be that of Thomas MacDonagh in the dock. Four hundred and seventy copies of the publication were seized. (See 9 Temple Bar [Dublin 2] for the complete statement.)

Bachelor's Walk: On 26 July 1914 at 6.30 p.m., following retrieval of the Howth rifles, four civilians were killed and more than 35 were seriously injured when fired on by the King's Own Scottish Borderers (quickly nicknamed the 'King's Own Scottish Murderers' by Dubliners).

About 100 of the Borderers under the command of Capt. Cobden had marched towards Howth to the Malahide Road, where there was a confrontation with the Volunteers. Negotiations took place between the Volunteers and William Vesey Harrel, the Assistant Commissioner of the Dublin Metropolitan Police (DMP), who had originally called in the military.[19] The troops continued towards the city and were met along the way by a further 60 men under the command of Major Coke. They were harassed by civilians along the route and when they turned from Sackville Street onto Bachelor's Walk the command was turned over to Major Haig.[20]

The Borderers were returning to their barracks at Royal Barracks (now Collins Barracks) when they were met by a hostile crowd as they marched along Bachelor's Walk. At the inquiry into the shooting the senior officer gave evidence that Major Haig, at about 6.15 p.m., returned to barracks and was told that a portion of his men had been called out to assist the civil authority. He got into uniform and proceeded in the direction of Clontarf. He met up with the rear of the column of his men at Talbot Street; Major Coke was in charge and the column consisted of about 150 men with eight officers. Haig received a report of what had happened. There was a very large crowd and many of his men had been knocked about. Haig ordered all rear guards to be recalled and the column to proceed in force to barracks by way of Sackville Street, then along the Quays to Royal Barracks. As the column proceeded along their chosen route they were followed by the hostile crowd, who continued to hurl stones at them; the crowd grew in number, as every side street they passed appeared to hold more rioters, who joined the body of the mob pursuing them.

Major Haig told the inquiry: 'The crowd was composed of roughs—men and a few what people might call boys up to 18 years of age. The men were up to 30 or 40 years of age, and one or two women. They were throwing a constant shower of stones of all sizes.' He endeavoured to get on as quickly as he could. The crowd were pursuing them and gaining on them and finally were about fifteen yards behind their rear flank. When the column got to within 100 yards of the metal bridge (Ha'penny Bridge) the crowd were right up behind them. Major Haig was hit four or five times with stones— four times about the head and face and once with a rather large stone on the elbow.

As the attack intensified, Major Haig gave the order at Liffey Street that enough men should align themselves across the street to cover its width, the intention being that this line should halt the progress of the pursuing crowd and allow the rest of the column to proceed to Royal Barracks. Between 20 and 30 men were used to block the street; they formed two lines, some kneeling. Haig told the inquiry that he felt that his men would not get safely back to barracks if he did not threaten the crowd with more than bayonets. At this stage about 30 or 40 rioters joined the attack from Liffey Street, and the crowd on Bachelor's Walk numbered between 500 and 600. Haig claimed that he was not aware that the soldiers' rifles were loaded. Later, however, he told the tribunal that 'first his intention was to warn the crowd, and, secondly, in the event of the threatening and stone throwing by the crowd continuing, he would have asked that those men so spoken to should shoot two particular ring leaders to be pointed out by himself'.

The soldiers blocking the street fired on the crowd. They had been lined up across the street when Major Haig attempted to address the crowd. Haig claimed that he raised his sword to attract the attention of the crowd before he attempted to speak, but as he lowered his sword the soldiers interpreted this as the order to fire.

The tribunal concluded that Haig 'plainly disapproved . . . of the action and notion of an order given to troops to fire indiscriminately upon a crowd. This, however, is what occurred. We are satisfied that neither Major Haig nor any of his fellow officers did give an order to fire.' The military claimed that a total of 21 men discharged their rifles into the crowd and that 29 shots were fired.[21]

The British inquiry found that Harrel illegally decided to seize the arms from the Volunteers, and that everything that happened afterwards was illegal. Col. Sir Walter Edgeworth-Johnstone, the Chief Commissioner, and Sir Neville Chamberlain, the Inspector General of the DMP, were exonerated.[22] (See Howth, Dublin 13.)

Four people were killed:

(1) James Brennan (18) of 7 Lower Buckingham Street, who was employed as a messenger. A bullet wound to his leg severed the femoral artery, causing his death. He died an hour after admission to Jervis Street Hospital.

(2) Mrs Mary Duffy (50) of 20 Lower Liffey Street, Dublin, was both bayoneted and shot. Her son from her first marriage, Thomas Tight, was serving in the 5th Battalion, Royal Dublin Fusiliers. She was admitted to Jervis Street Hospital on the evening of the 26th but was dead on arrival.

(3) Patrick Quinn (46) of 1 Gardiner's Lane, who was employed as a coal porter and was married with six children, ranging in age from nine to nineteen. A bullet wound to his leg severed the femoral artery, causing his death.[23]

(4) Sylvester Pidgeon died on 24 September 1914 from wounds received. He was employed as a printer and was married with five children, ranging in age from three months to eleven years old.

No one was ever charged in relation to the gunrunning or the Bachelor's Walk massacre. Harrel was sacked the following day. The Borderers left for France and by October they had suffered 85% casualties.[24]

32 Bachelor's Walk: Second office of the Irish National Aid and Volunteers' Dependants' Fund, primarily run by Kathleen Clarke and Sorcha MacMahon. (See 10 Exchequer Street [Dublin 2].)

56 Bachelor's Walk (corner of Lower Sackville Street): Kelly and Sons, Guns and Ammunition.

'Kelly's Fort'. The sign on the building's side announced 'Fishing Tackle and Gunpowder Office'. Peadar Bracken commanded the garrison here; Joe Good was a member.[25] Bracken came to Dublin because 'they needed experienced fighting men there'; he was appointed captain by Pearse and then was sent to O'Connell Bridge by Connolly. He had been in charge of three others at O'Connell Bridge at the outset of the Rising; then he led the men in 'Kelly's Fort', ultimately having about 35 under his command.[26]

7 Belvedere Place: Home of William (Bill) O'Brien, a member of the IRB. James Connolly sent his son Rauri (Roddy) here for safety after the GPO caught fire on Thursday. Nora Connolly and Lillie Connolly stayed here when James was in Dublin Castle.[27] O'Brien succeeded James Connolly as head of the ITGWU.

In 1916 the Military Council of the IRB appointed William to a civilian 'Provisional Government', along with Arthur Griffith,[28] Tom Kelly, Seán T. O'Kelly[29] and Hanna Sheehy-Skeffington, for the purpose of maintaining food supplies during the Rising. It was never able to function.

18 Beresford Place (at Eden Quay): Liberty Hall. In the early nineteenth century the building had been a chop-house. Later in the century it was the site of the Northumberland Commercial and Family Hotel, the meeting place for members of the Young Ireland movement. Still later, the Northumberland became the meeting place for members of the Land League. By 1911 the hotel had become almost derelict. In 1912 it became the headquarters of the Irish Transport and General Workers' Union (ITGWU).

Because of the activities originating in Liberty Hall, officials at Dublin Castle considered it the centre of nationalist sentiment, though it had little connection with the Volunteers. The newspapers described it as 'the centre of social anarchy in Ireland, the brain of every riot and disturbance'.[30]

In early 1914 Connolly announced the reorganisation of the Irish Citizen Army 'to protect workers' meetings' and 'to prevent the brutalities of armed thugs occurring in the future'.[31] On 22 March 1914 Larkin presided at a meeting reconstituting the ICA. The new constitution was drawn up primarily by James Larkin, Seán O'Casey, Countess Markievicz and other militarily minded members of the ITGWU. It provided for an Army Council and included explicitly nationalist aims:

Article One: The first and last principle of the Irish Citizen Army is the avowal that the ownership of Ireland, moral and material, is vested of right in the people of Ireland.

Article Two: That its principal objects should be:

a. To arm and train all Irishmen capable of bearing arms to enforce and defend its first principle.

b. To sink all differences of birth, privilege and creed under the common name of the Irish people.

Article Three: The Irish Citizen Army shall stand for the absolute unity of Irish nationhood, and recognition of the rights and liberties of the democracies of all nations.

Article Four: That the Citizen Army shall be open to all who are prepared to accept the principles of equal rights and opportunities for the People of Ireland and to work in harmony with organised labour towards that end.

Article Five: Every enrolled member must be, if possible, a member of a Trade Union recognized by the Irish Trades Union Congress.

Captain Jack White, DSO, chaired the Army Council. (White originally proposed the name 'The Civic League' to Larkin and Connolly.) Ironically, although the Citizen Army had been formed as a force to protect the workers, the ICA was never called into action in any major way during the Lockout.

Though their numbers were small, the equipment and training of the Irish Citizen Army were superior to those of most of the Irish Volunteers, because the ICA had trade union money behind them and, consequently, full uniforms and a full-time, well-trained professional soldier to instruct them. Capt. White was the son of Gen. Sir George White, the British commander of the defence of Ladysmith in the Boer War, and was himself a professional soldier.[32]

White's goal was a well-trained ICA and he was intolerant of the conflicts between the ICA and the Volunteers.[33] He resigned from the ICA in May 1914, offering the following reasons:

Dear Sir,

With reference to a paragraph which appeared in some of this morning's papers connecting my name with a challenge issued by the Citizen Army council to the provisional committee of the National Volunteers, I wish to state that I had nothing to do with it; in fact I resigned from the chairmanship of the said council a week ago, doubtful of my power to prevent and determined not to become involved in such policy. In my opinion the all-important point is the speedy formation and equipment of a volunteer army implicitly or explicitly determined to achieve the independence and maintain the unity of Ireland . . .

For an 'army council' which has not yet created an appreciable 'army' to issue a challenge to the organisers of a strong and growing movement seems to me to be little short of the absurd . . . [34]

Of White's resignation, Seán O'Casey wrote:

It is only fair that a quiet reflection of past events convinces the writer that Captain White did not obtain the ready and affectionate co-operation his nature craved for.

His efforts to understand the mysterious natures of working-men were earnest and constant, and were never fully appreciated by those amongst whom he spent his time and a great deal of his money.[35]

After 1914 Liberty Hall was the headquarters of the Irish Citizen Army, of which Connolly became O/C. Officers included Major Michael Mallin (second in command), Capt. Walter Carpenter,[36] Capt. Seán Connolly, Capt. Richard MacCormack, Capt. Séamus McGowan,[37] Capt. John O'Neill, Countess Constance Markievicz, Capt. William Partridge, Capt. Christopher Poole, Lt Michael Kelly, Sgt Joseph Doyle and Sgt Frank Robbins.[38] Under Connolly's leadership an appreciable change began to appear in the posture of the Citizen Army Council towards the Volunteers. Passive sympathy was gradually replaced by an attitude of active unity and cooperation.[39] (Robbins was imprisoned after the Rising and upon his return felt that the spirit of the ICA had changed greatly. He wrote: 'There was a new atmosphere, a new outlook entirely from that which had been moulded by Connolly and Mallin. The kernel of the problem was that the majority of the new members, strange as it might seem, did not hold or advocate the social and political views that had motivated those who fought in 1916'.[40])

The *Irish Worker* was published here and was suppressed in 1914. *The Worker*, which James Connolly also edited, was subsequently founded and was suppressed after six issues. On 24 March 1916 the print shop attached to Liberty Hall was raided. Much of the type was taken, so the printers had to 'borrow' type from William H. West of

Capel Street to set the *Proclamation* later in April 1916. They were only able to obtain about half the type needed for the job and so the *Proclamation* was printed in two parts: the first three paragraphs were set, and then the type was broken down and 'reused' to set the final three paragraphs.

On 16 April 1916 the 'Irish Republic' flag, with the harp but without the crown, was first raised over the Hall. Connolly wrote:

> The council of the Irish Citizen Army has resolved, after grave and earnest deliberation, to hoist the green flag of Ireland over Liberty Hall, as over a fortress held for Ireland by the arms of Irishmen. This is a momentous decision in the most serious crisis Ireland has witnessed in our day and generation.[41]

Molly O'Reilly, aged sixteen, unfurled the flag. Connolly handed the flag to her, saying: 'I hand you this flag as the sacred emblem of Ireland's unconquered soul'.[42] Connolly chose Molly to hoist the flag in place of Countess Markievicz, as he feared that Markievicz would be the target of a British assassination attempt. On the weekend prior to Palm Sunday Molly had been at a dance in Liberty Hall; swinging around, she had broken a window. When Connolly sent for her to raise the flag, Molly thought that she was in trouble for breaking the window and was relieved when he asked her about the flag instead.

Rather than going to Irish dancing classes in Liberty Hall, Molly would go and hear Connolly speak. Despite her youth, she was very aware that her family enjoyed better conditions than those who lived in abject poverty all around her. She went to work in the food kitchens during the Lockout and collected money for the families. Molly's father was a stonemason and pro-British. Her mother was outside their family home one day when Molly appeared with two young men and a cart with sacks on top. Inside the sacks were the unassembled guns from the *Asgard* that had been landed at Howth. Her mother asked what was in them and Molly replied, 'That is of no concern, Mother; Mr Connolly would like you to mind these for him for a while'. Her mother asked her where she would put them and Molly said that she would put them under her father's bed, and that is where they remained. When British soldiers searched the house Molly's father was in his bed, but they considered him a pro-British sympathiser, wished him good evening and never searched under his bed. (Molly's parents were so opposed to her republican activities that she finally left home.) Molly was at Liberty Hall on Easter Monday, standing in line with the Citizen Army, when her mother ran up to her and tried to drag her home. Molly told her to go home and mind the children, that she had work to do for Mr Connolly. She was assigned as a dispatch runner, carrying messages between City Hall and the GPO.[43]

Mary Shannon, a machinist at the Liberty Hall shirt-making cooperative, made the flag. Massed in front of the Hall for the flag-raising were the Irish Citizen Army, the ICA

Women's Section, the ICA Boy Scouts under Capt. Carpenter, and the Fintan Lalor Pipe Band. Capt. Christopher Poole led a colour guard of sixteen to escort the Colour Bearer, who was also accompanied by three young girl dancers known as the Liberty Trio: Veronica Connolly (sister of Seán), Louise Holloway and Margaret Green.[44]

> So closely had the crowds been packed that many thousands had been unable to see the ceremony on the square, but the eyes of all were now riveted upon the flag pole awaiting the re-appearance of the Colour Bearer. All Beresford Square was packed, Butt Bridge and Tara Street were as a sea of upturned faces. All the North Side of the Quays up to O'Connell Street was thronged, and O'Connell Bridge itself was impassable owing to the vast multitude of eager, sympathetic onlookers . . . At last the young Colour Bearer, radiant with excitement and glowing with colour in face and form, mounted beside the parapet of the roof, and with a quick graceful movement of her hand unloosed the lanyard, and
> ### THE FLAG OF IRELAND
> fluttered out upon the breeze.
> Those who witnessed that scene will never forget it. Over the Square, across Butt Bridge, in all the adjoining streets, along the quays, amid the dense mass upon O'Connell Bridge, Westmoreland Street and D'Olier Street corners, everywhere the people burst out in one joyous delirious shout of welcome and triumph, hats and handkerchiefs fiercely waved, tears of emotion coursed freely down the cheeks of strong rough men, and women became hysterical with excitement . . . As the first burst of cheering subsided Commandant Connolly gave the command, 'Battalion, Present Arms', the bugles sounded the General Salute, and the concourse was caught up in a delirium of joy and passion.
> In a few short words at the close Commandant Connolly pledged his hearers to give their lives if necessary to keep the Irish flag flying, and the ever memorable scene was ended.[45]

From 26 March to 16 April, only a week before the Rising, Seán Connolly, an actor at the Abbey Theatre, played the lead role in the first performance of James Connolly's new play, *Under Which Flag*. The play was about an Irishman torn between serving in the Irish or the British army, and ended with Connolly raising a green flag and uttering the words, 'Under this flag only will I serve. Under this flag, if need be, will I die'. Seán Connolly was killed in City Hall on Monday afternoon, 24 April, the first rebel casualty of the Rising.[46] At the play's last performance, Molly O'Reilly was asked to sing *Signal Fires* during the interval of the production. Michael Mallin had taught her the song. She would be in the City Hall with Seán Connolly, and one of her last dispatches was to take the news of his death to James Connolly in the GPO.

On 19 April, Spy Wednesday, Connolly informed Citizen Army officers Richard

MacCormack, Joseph Doyle and Frank Robbins[47] that the Rising was scheduled for Easter Sunday: it would begin at 6.30 p.m. in Dublin and 7 p.m. in the provinces.

On 23 April, in his final lecture on tactics, Connolly warned:

> The odds against us are a thousand to one. If we win, we'll be great heroes; but if we lose we'll be the greatest scoundrels the country has ever produced. In the event of victory, hold onto your rifles because the Volunteers may have a different goal, and may stop before our goal is reached. Remember, we're out not only for political liberty, but for economic liberty as well. So hold onto your rifles.[48]

Also on 23 April the *Proclamation of the Irish Republic* was printed in the Liberty Hall print shop. Thomas MacDonagh gave the manuscript to three men and one woman to compose the type and print the sheets. Christopher Brady (who worked in the printing department of the Bank of Ireland) was the primary printer;[49] Michael Molloy (a printer at the *Independent* newspaper[50]) and Liam F. O'Brien (who worked at O'Reilly's Printing Works[51]) assisted.[52] When they presented themselves at Liberty Hall on Sunday, Connolly immediately had them 'arrested', so that if they were questioned afterward they could honestly claim that they had printed the *Proclamation* 'under duress'.[53] The men had previously been printers for James Connolly's *Workers' Republic*. Rosana Hackett, a former Jacob's Factory worker who had not been re-employed after the 1913 Lockout, assisted the men.[54] They knew that they did not have enough type for the *Proclamation*, so they borrowed type from William West, a printer in nearby Capel Street. Even so, there was still not enough type, so the *Proclamation* had to be printed in two 'halves'. They finally finished late on Sunday night, after borrowing the type and coping with problems with the press. They had intended to print 2,500 copies but only about 1,000 were completed. The machine used was a 'Wharfedale Double-Crown' of a very old pattern and in poor condition. The paper was of poor quality, similar to that used in the printing of the *Workers' Republic*, white with a greyish tinge to it, and had been procured from the Saggart Paper Mills in Dublin. When the printing was completed, the *Proclamation* was given to Helena Molony, who supervised its distribution.[55] (See 21 Henry Street.)

After hearing of Eoin MacNeill's countermanding order on Holy Saturday night (22 April), the members of the IRB's Military Council (Pearse, Clarke, Connolly, Ceannt, MacDonagh, Plunkett and MacDermott) angrily decided to call a meeting in Liberty Hall on Easter Sunday morning.

> I saw Eoin MacNeill's countermanding order in the paper and heard the discussion in Liberty Hall. Connolly was there. They were all heartbroken and when they were not crying they were cursing. I kept thinking 'does this mean that we are not going to go out?' There were thousands like us. It was foolish of

MacNeill and those to think they could call it off. They could not. Many of us thought we would go out single-handed, if necessary.[56]

In that meeting, the Rising's leaders determined that to delay further would be fatal for their plans: the Rising was rescheduled for Monday at noon. The Military Council made two equally important decisions: (1) to send dispatches immediately to the various commands *confirming* MacNeill's cancellation of that day's manoeuvres; (2) that the Rising would commence the next day at noon, and that dispatches to that effect would be sent out on Sunday night. The first decision was intended to remove the possibility that units outside Dublin might start their operations before the Dublin battalions could revise their plans and occupy their allotted positions on Easter Monday. Moreover, Pearse intended that this would obviate any further action by MacNeill. Alternatively, it was thought that if the British became aware of this follow-up to MacNeill's order their suspicions would be allayed. (See 7 Belgrave Road, Rathmines; 53 Rathgar Road, [Dublin 6].)

William Oman was the bugler who sounded the 'fall in' for the ICA on Easter Monday, 24 April.[57] Originally the 2nd Battalion of Volunteers was to muster here and march to St Stephen's Green. Frank Thornton and Séamus McGowan[58] commanded the unit guarding the munitions that were transferred to the GPO on Monday afternoon in fifteen commandeered lorries and cabs. Thereafter the Hall was deserted, except for Peter Ennis, the caretaker.

On 26 April Liberty Hall was fired upon by the HMY *Helga* (24 rounds). There are stories that the *Helga* 'lobbed shells' over the Loopline Bridge, but the flat trajectory of the *Helga*'s guns would have made this next to impossible. She fired under the bridge into Liberty Hall.[59]

Standing 195ft high, the present-day Liberty Hall rises sixteen storeys. Construction began in 1961 and finished in 1965. It is the headquarters of the Services, Industrial, Professional and Technical Union (SIPTU).

Beresford Place: The **James Connolly statue** stands across from Liberty Hall. Sculpted by Éamonn O'Doherty, the work was unveiled by President Mary Robinson on 12 May 1996, the 80th anniversary of Connolly's execution. The flag that forms the background is the Starry Plough, the plough and the stars symbolising respectively the present and the future of the working classes.

Buckingham Buildings: Home of Patrick Kelly (12), who was shot in the back of the neck on 28 April and died from the gunshot wounds.[60] He was first treated at the TCD VAD hospital on Mountjoy Square.[61]

12–13 Burgh Quay: Tivoli Music Hall, occupied by British soldiers firing machine-

Padraic Pearse had been a Home Ruler, but in a speech at a Home Rule rally in March 1912 he made his position clear: 'If we are tricked this time, there is a party in Ireland, and I am one of them, that will advise the Gael to have no counsel or dealing with the Gall but to answer henceforward with the strong arm and the sword's edge … If we are cheated once more there will be red war in Ireland.'

Seán MacDermott was 32 when he was executed on 12 May. His fiancée, Mary Josephine (Min) Ryan, saw him in Kilmainham Gaol: 'He preferred to talk of casual matters, asking about different people we knew, enjoying little jokes almost as though we were in Bewley's. He had worked and planned for Irish independence since boyhood. His last words, save for his prayers, were "God Save Ireland".'

Thomas MacDonagh was O/C of the 2nd Battalion and was the last man to be invited onto the Military Council of the IRB. He was a schoolmaster, a poet, a theatre manager, a literary critic, a supporter of women's rights and the Gaelic League.

Thomas Clarke spent fifteen years in British prisons and moved to the US upon his release, returning to Ireland in 1907. He set out to bring the IRB's 'physical force' ideals to the fore in the minds of younger nationalists. Clarke revived the IRB, bringing new blood into the leadership.

James Connolly was a socialist and one of the founders of the Irish Socialist Republican Party. He spent 1903–10 in the US as a labour organiser before returning to Ireland to continue this work. The leader of the Irish Citizen Army, he was executed on 12 May.

Joseph Plunkett was the primary planner of the military actions, and had undergone surgery for glandular tuberculosis just before the Rising. Plunkett said just before his execution: '... I am dying for the glory of God and the honour of Ireland'. (Image: Caoimhghin Ó Croidheáin)

Éamonn Ceannt was the O/C of the Volunteer 4th Battalion. Standing about 6ft tall, he was an excellent musician and played the uilleann pipes before Pope Pius X in Rome in 1908. Ceannt was executed in Kilmainham Gaol on 8 May.

Pearse surrenders to General Lowe at the northern end of Moore Street, on Saturday 29 April. Nurse Elizabeth O'Farrell acted as go-between and she can just be discerned on the right side of Pearse in the photograph.

Abbey Street corner and ruins of Dublin Bread Company. The glass roof of the DBC was described as a 'Chinese-like pagoda'. When it caught fire it was described as follows: 'The flames kissing the ball on the dome's summit are singularly impressive. A scene of greater splendour I have never witnessed . . .'

Amiens Street Railway Station. The Volunteers did not take it and it remained an open terminus for British troops coming from the north. It was renamed Connolly Station in 1966.

Prior to the Rising, Lord Nelson's Pillar stood in the middle of Sackville Street, almost opposite the GPO. Located between Henry Street and North Earl Street, it distinguished Sackville Street Lower from Sackville Street Upper. The original stone was laid on 15 February 1808 and the monument was completed in 1809.

O'Connell Bridge and Sackville Street Lower before the Rising. The pagoda-like roof of the Dublin Bread Company can be seen, and at the corner is Hopkins and Hopkins, Jewellers, which became 'Hopkins Fort'. That entire corner was destroyed.

At the time of the Rising Clery's Department Store and the Imperial Hotel shared a building on Sackville Street. The building was completely destroyed by the fires that followed the artillery bombardment: '. . . the plate-glass windows of Clery's run molten into the channel from the terrific heat'.

Prince's Street ran between the Hotel Metropole and the GPO—the artillery shelling and the resulting fires ruined them both. On Easter Monday morning, Michael Collins came here to escort Joseph Plunkett to the GPO.

Volunteers who had bored through walls from the GPO to get there held the Coliseum Theatre on Henry Street until the fires that resulted from the artillery shelling forced the garrison out. Completely destroyed, it never reopened as a theatre.

On 26 April Liberty Hall was fired upon by HMY *Helga* in the River Liffey—she fired 24 rounds. There are stories that the *Helga* 'lobbed shells' over the Loopline Bridge, but the flat trajectory of the *Helga*'s guns would have made this next to impossible. She fired under the bridge into Liberty Hall.

British soldiers in Henry Street after the Rising. The Volunteers fleeing the burning GPO left by the side door into Henry Street. A post office van was dragged across the street to screen them from the British, who had set up a machine-gun position further to the west on Henry Street.

33–37 Abbey Street Lower were the premises occupied by the Royal Hibernian Academy and Wynn's Hotel. The fires that followed the artillery barrage gutted both. The Hibernian Academy was filled with many works of art, and all were lost.

The artillery shelling and subsequent fires destroyed buildings on Henry Street, which runs north of the GPO. The Volunteers crossed this street in their retreat from the GPO. Here the ruins can be seen, looking east towards Lord Nelson's Pillar.

The Dublin Bread Company building was a landmark on Sackville Street with its glass-domed roof. It was taken by the Volunteers on Monday and held through the week until destroyed by fire. Witnesses described '. . . the avalanche of flame and smoke that crashed to the ground when the dome collapsed at 5 o'clock'.

The destruction on Sackville Street can clearly be seen weeks after the Rising, as workers removed the rubble from the destroyed Hotel Metropole and the gutted GPO. Despite 'pot-shots' from Volunteers in the GPO, Nelson's Pillar suffered little damage.

guns on Liberty Hall during the Rising.

2 Capel Street: Home of Seán and Noel Lemass. On 29 January 1916 Herbert Phelan Lemass, the youngest brother, was shot by mistake by Seán. The coroner's verdict held that it was an accident, but said that 'it was a result of young men playing with guns'.[62] Both Seán and Noel were in the GPO during the Rising. Seán was taoiseach from June 1959 until 1966.

45A Capel Street: Premises of William Henry West, printer, who provided the type for the *Proclamation*. (See Beresford Place, Liberty Hall.) He was prosecuted under the Defence of the Realm Act (DORA) in June 1916 for printing a statement purportedly made by Thomas MacDonagh in the dock, and was fined £5. (See 9 Temple Bar [Dublin 2] for the complete statement.)

Coleraine Street: John Beirnes was killed here by South Staffordshire Regiment troops during the Rising. (See North King Street [Dublin 7].)

15 Cumberland Street North: Home of Patrick Ivors (14), who was killed during the Rising.[63]

Dorset Street, 1 Long Lane: Home of Patrick Featherstone (Featherston?) (12), who was hit in the thigh by a bullet on Easter Monday. He died in Jervis Street Hospital and is buried in Glasnevin Cemetery.[64] In 1911 two Featherstone families lived in North Brunswick Street with four other families. In that three-roomed house there were six families, totalling 30 people.[65]

68 Dorset Street Lower: Birthplace of Peadar Kearney (Peadar Ó Cearnaigh) in 1883. A well-known poet and writer, he wrote the words to *A Soldier's Song/Amhrán na bhFiann* (1907) and is usually given 'credit'. Paddy Heaney wrote the music (although there is some evidence that Seán Rogan may have assisted). According to Kearney's nephew, Séamus de Burca, Heaney 'worked on the melody for a week and gave up in despair when half way through the chorus—his inspiration had failed. When Kearney called round to see him on a Sunday morning, Heaney was dejected. Kearney asked him anxiously how the music was coming along and for a reply Heaney threw the manuscript in the fire. Kearney snatched it out, smoothed it on the table. The tune was all right, but the chorus was all wrong. They went over the words and Kearney suggested they go back on the melody of the verse. So Heaney toned out the tune and Kearney lilted the words. And thus *A Soldier's Song* was born.'[66]

It was not until the Rising that the song became a commonly sung anthem, but afterwards it was a favourite among separatists. Bulmer Hobson published the lyrics in

Irish Freedom in 1912. The song was first published in sheet form in 1916, with the image of a rifle entwined with lettering of Celtic design: 'Words by Peadar Kearney, Music by Patrick Heaney, arranged by Cathal MacDubhghaill and published by Whelan and Son, 17 Ormond Quay Upper, Dublin' (see Dublin 7). Following the Rising, the music was arranged and published by Victor Herbert in New York in December 1916, with the proceeds going to Ireland. The song was written in English and translated into Irish by Liam O'Rinn.[67] (See 101 Mecklenburgh Street.)

Kearney was a house-painter by trade, but preferred to work as a stage-hand at the Abbey Theatre.

75 Dorset Street Lower: Keogh Bros Ltd, photographers, who produced several postcards showing ruined buildings and Dublin streetscapes after the Rising.

North Earl Street: Thirty-two buildings were burned here during the Rising, and many were looted.[68]

29–31 North Earl Street: Tyler's shoe shop, looted during the Rising.

Eden Quay: Fourteen buildings were burned here during the Rising, including Hopkins and Hopkins, jewellers and silversmiths, now the Irish National Building Society (Eden Quay and Lower Sackville Street); Barry, O'Moore and Co., accountants and auditors (1, 2); Gerald Mooney, wine and spirit merchant (3); the London and North-Western Railway Co. (4); G.R. Mesias, military tailor (5); the Globe Parcel Express (8); J. Henry Smith, ironmonger (9); Joseph M'Greevy, wine and spirit merchant (10); the Douglas Hotel and Restaurant (11); the Mission to Seamen Institute (13); and Moore's Pub (14).

1 Foster Place: Wm Montgomery and Son, assessors for property destroyed in the Rising.[69]

18 Frederick Street North: Keating Branch of the Gaelic League. Cathal Brugha was branch president and members included Conor Collins, Richard Mulcahy, Diarmuid O'Hegarty, Gearóid O'Sullivan and Rory O'Connor.

The plans for the Rising included an intention to take control of Dublin's telegraph and telephone systems, and to control British communication with England. Capt. Dermot Lynch was given the task of obtaining information about the telephone and telegraph systems in Dublin, and to determine how to disable them so that the British could not use them to call for reinforcements in Ireland or from England. Richard Mulcahy was an employee in the Post Office Department and was assigned to assist Lynch.

On Wednesday of Holy Week I attended a meeting in Keating Branch Gaelic League Hall, North Frederick Street, presided over by Dermot Lynch. Others attending were Andy Fitzpatrick, J. Tyrrell, J. Twamley, Martin and George King, all employees of the Engineering Branch Post Office. We were told that a special squad was being formed to deal with communications and that specific tasks would be allotted to those present. Plans were to be prepared immediately for cutting communications so as to isolate the city. We were not told at this meeting that action had been decided upon but that we were to have plans prepared immediately. After some discussion the meeting adjourned until the following evening. On Thursday evening at the same place, the meeting reassembled and was attended by Thomas McDonagh [sic], who informed us that we were going into action on the following Sunday at 6 p.m. and that we were to submit our plans for the isolation of the city. A plan was then hurriedly prepared and the following decided on: Andy Fitzpatrick to cut cross-channel cable from G.P.O. at point in Talbot Street; J. Tyrrell to cut cables at Dunlaoghaire and Blackrock; J. Twamley to cut cables and wires at Bray and Shankhill. Martin and George King to cut cables in Westland Row area. We were informed that the Telephone Exchange, Crown Alley, was being attended to by G.H.Q. staff. I was detailed to cut the trunk telephone and telegraph lines at 7th Lock Bridge between Inchicore and Clondalkin. On Good Friday I surveyed the position at 7th Lock and made notes of equipment required for the job. We met at Liberty Hall that night and submitted our reports to James Connolly; we were supplied with such tools as pliers, hacksaws, axes, sledges and ropes which we brought to our homes to be kept in readiness. We made a further survey on Saturday and noted all police wires which were to be cut to isolate all barracks. F. Byrne was to do this job. We met again on Saturday night in Liberty Hall and completed arrangements. On Sunday morning, on seeing the parade cancellation notice in the paper, I proceeded to Liberty Hall and there met members of the Executive Council. I waited until the Executive Council meeting was over. I was then informed by Seán McDermott [sic] that the Rising had been postponed and that I was to cancel all 'action orders' until further notice. I proceeded to Blackrock, Dunlaoghaire and Bray and contacted M. Tobin, J. Tyrrell, M. Higgins (Loughlin's town) and J. Kenny (Bray) and gave instructions not to proceed with demolition work. I returned to Dunlaoghaire at about midnight. On Monday morning I received an order from Dermot Hegarty to mobilise company at Blackhall Place. I went to Summerhill and left instructions for J. Costelloe, company mobiliser, to carry out the mobilization. I then went to Liberty Hall and met James Connolly, who told me to join my battalion at Blackhall Place, and that the battalion officers there would decide on whatever demolition was to be carried out in the area. I was instructed by Comdt. E. Daly to select a Point near Liffey Junction for the cutting the western trunks (Athlone, Sligo, Galway).

I proceeded to Broome Bridge via Royal Canal and, with the help of a bridge demolition party in the area, cut down the pole and wires.[70]

At 8 p.m. on Easter Sunday night, Padraic Pearse arrived here with dispatches that couriers were to take throughout the country: 'We start operations at noon today, Monday. Carry out your instructions.'

It should be noted that women carried most of these dispatches, as they did for many of the important communications throughout the period. Men chose women for many of these missions because they could move about the country more easily than the men, providing that they dressed conventionally in long skirts or dresses. Even Margaret Skinnider, who often dressed as a boy, dressed as a woman when doing dispatch work and when running weapons.[71] British soldiers generally refused to strip-search women unless a lady searcher was available. Since women were less conspicuous and less likely to be searched, they also ran other important errands. Marie Perolz obtained extra revolvers from an arms dealer in Dublin.[72] In one case, the Volunteers sent a group of Cumann na mBan women to save a batch of guns shortly before the Rising: they asked Brighid Foley, Effie Taaffe and Kitty O'Doherty to find and protect the guns that had come into the country in boxes marked as 'cutlery'. Informers at Dublin Castle had given warning that the British had discovered what was really in the boxes and that the house was to be raided by Castle officials; the women successfully transported these two boxes across town, past a couple of policemen, and hid them under the stairs in O'Doherty's house.[73] (See Claude Road, Drumcondra [Dublin 9].)

28 Frederick Street North: Office of Stephen Bollard, editor of *The Hibernian*. HQ of the Ancient Order of Hibernians.[74] (See Great Brunswick Street [Dublin 2]; 31 and 44 Rutland Square.)

Gardiner Row: Home of Linda Kearns, who was born in 1889 in Sligo. A nurse, she opened a first aid station in an empty house in North Great George's Street and treated both Volunteers and British casualties during the Rising.[75] Although she avoided arrest after the Rising, she was imprisoned in 1920 when she was caught smuggling a large consignment of arms in Sligo.

Gardiner Row: Fleming's Hotel; owned by Seán O'Mahoney, who lived here. Tom Clarke stayed with him on Holy Saturday night, thinking that he might be captured otherwise. Next day, Clarke, Tom O'Connor and Seán McGarry[76] returned to the Clarkes' home on Richmond Avenue, where they stayed the night.[77]

14 Gardiner Street Lower: Home of John (Seán, Jack) O'Reilly (30), killed in action at City Hall on 24 April. He is buried in the family plot, St Paul's, Glasnevin Cemetery.

Gloucester Street (now Seán MacDermott Street): Tara Hall Printers' Union; HQ of C Company, 2nd Battalion, Dublin Brigade.

15 Gloucester Street (now Seán MacDermott Street): Painter's Hall. HQ of C Company, 3rd Battalion, Dublin Brigade.

3 Upper Gloucester Street: Home of James Jessop (12), who was killed during the Rising.[78] His brother Christopher died of gastritis a week later, and they are buried in the same grave in Glasnevin Cemetery.

Great Britain Street (now Parnell Street): The Rotunda Hospital. Built in 1757 by Bartholmew Mosse, its official name is the Dublin Lying-in Hospital. Richard Cassell designed the hospital building, John Ensor designed the Round Room concert hall, and James Gandon (architect of the Custom House) designed the entrance block. The hospital was totally dependent on charity and for this reason the buildings and environs were created with an eye to fund-raising. The 'social' rooms of the Rotunda existed to provide entertainment. The 'Round Room' became the 'Rotunda Picture House' and is now the **Ambassador Cinema**; the former 'Supper Rooms' became the **Gate Theatre**, and the 'Pillar Room' is used for concerts. The Roller Rink was in the basement.

On 25 November 1913 Eoin MacNeill and Laurence Kettle (son of A.J. Kettle, aide to Charles Stewart Parnell) held the first meeting to enrol the Irish Volunteers here.[79] They had intended the meeting to be held at the Mansion House but the then lord mayor, Lorcan Sherlock, refused to rent the Dawson Street premises to them. Sherlock later went on the Executive as one of John Redmond's 'forced' nominees. (See 206 Great Brunswick Street [Dublin 2].) The band that started off the night was the St James's Brass and Reed Band. The doors were opened shortly after 8 p.m. and Seán T. O'Kelly chaired the meeting.[80] Eventually 4,000 managed to squeeze into the Rink, while another 3,000 crammed the Concert Room and the adjacent gardens. Over 4,000 people signed up that night. Padraic Pearse was one of the principal speakers. Others were Seán MacDermott, James McMahon, Michael Judge and Councillor Richard O'Carroll. Batt O'Connor and Bulmer Hobson addressed the crowd outside. The IRB pressed all nationalists to join the Volunteers, but the organisation had not backed the ITGWU in the 1913 Lockout. Laurence Kettle was a well-known opponent of the union. 'Cheers for Larkin' was shouted throughout Kettle's speech.[81] When he spoke, fights broke out with union protestors, but the song *God Save Ireland* soon drowned out the disturbances.[82] This marked the continuance of the disagreements between union members and those who became Volunteers and led to Connolly's reluctance to join with the Volunteers. (See Seán O'Casey, the *Workers' Republic*, 70 Eccles Street [Dublin 2], for public disagreements between the ICA and the Volunteers. See Kildare Street [Dublin 2] for the First Provisional Committee of the Irish Volunteers.)

MacNeill stated in his opening speech that the Volunteers meant no ill will towards the Ulster Volunteer Force:

> We do not contemplate any hostility to the Volunteer movement that has already been initiated in parts of Ulster. The strength of that movement consists in men whose kinfolk were amongst the foremost and most resolute in winning freedom for the United States of America . . . The more genuine and successful the local Volunteer movement in Ulster becomes, the more completely does it establish the principle that Irishmen have the right to decide and govern their own national affairs. We have nothing to fear from the existing Volunteers in Ulster nor they from us.[83]

On the Saturday night after the Rising, the defeated Volunteers from the GPO were marched here. In the early hours of Sunday morning Capt. Lea Wilson took charge. Of Seán MacDermott, who because of polio walked with a limp and only with the aid of a cane, he said, 'So you've got cripples in your Army!' Wilson stripped Thomas Clarke and made him stand naked on the Rotunda steps in view of the nurses: 'That old bastard is Commander in Chief. He keeps a tobacco shop across the street. Nice general for your fucking Army.'[84] Michael Collins had Wilson killed in Gorey, Co. Wexford, on 15 June 1920.

65 Great Britain Street (now Parnell Street): Home of Mr and Mrs Maurice Collins. *Who's Who* claims that Bulmer Hobson was held here prior to the Rising.[85] Most commentators agree, however, that he was held at Martin Conlon's home at Cabra Park and that Maurice was one of those guarding him on Holy Saturday.[86] (See Cabra Park [Dublin 7].) Maurice opened a tobacconist and confectioner's shop here after he was released from Frongoch prison.[87]

70 Great Britain Street (now Parnell Street) and Moore Lane (it became Patrick Conway's pub). Padraic Pearse surrendered to Brig. Gen. W.H.M. Lowe, CB, here at 3.30 p.m. on Saturday 29 April 1916. Elizabeth O'Farrell accompanied Pearse. Lowe's son, John, who was also an officer in the British army, accompanied the general. Later John Lowe changed his name to 'John Loder' and became a successful author and film producer in Hollywood.

70, 71 Great Britain Street (now Parnell Street): Elizabeth O'Farrell met Col. Portal and Brig. Gen. W.H.M. Lowe here before being taken to Tom Clarke's shop at 75A Great Britain Street.[88]

75A Great Britain Street (now Parnell Street) (corner of Sackville Street): Tom Clarke's tobacconist's shop, opened in 1909. Clarke was arrested in London on 4 April 1883, and was imprisoned in Millbank, Portland and Chatham prisons as Henry Hammond Wilson. He was finally released on 21 September 1898. He was prisoner number J464. (See 10 Richmond Avenue, Dublin 3.)

Elizabeth O'Farrell was held here as a prisoner while waiting for Gen. Lowe. She then returned to the Rising's leaders in Moore Street with Lowe's note:

From Commander of Dublin Forces

To P. H. Pearse

29 April/16
1.40 P.M.

A woman has come in and tells me you wish to negotiate with me.
I am prepared to receive you in BRITAIN ST at the North End of MOORE ST provided that you surrender unconditionally —
You will proceed up MOORE ST accompanied only by the woman who brings you this note under a white flag —
W.H.M. Lowe
B. Gen.

165 Great Britain Street (now Parnell Street) (and Cavendish Row): National Bank; Elizabeth O'Farrell was subjected to a search here.[89]

204–206 Great Britain Street (now Parnell Street): Williams and Woods, Soap and Sweet Manufacturers, the 'jam factory'; formerly Simpson's Hospital. The factory was full of food and too close to their own lines for the British to shell it. The Ó Rahilly was on his way here when killed, and the Volunteers were also headed in this direction when they escaped from the GPO into Henry Street and then into Moore Street.

North Great George's Street: Linda Kearns set up a Red Cross hospital here during the Rising. She nursed Volunteers and British army casualties alike, for which she was awarded the Red Cross Florence Nightingale Medal for Exceptional Services in 1951.[90]

2 North Great George's Street: The family town house of John Dillon. He spoke out in parliament, condemning the 1916 executions—'Larne begat Dublin'.

On 7 May the Capuchin Fr Aloysius met Dillon, a leading member of the Irish Parliamentary Party, who agreed to do all in his power to persuade the British government to stop the executions. The Rising had taken the Irish Party by surprise, and it was unprepared in its immediate reaction. It was largely due to Fr Aloysius's efforts that Dillon, during a debate on the Rising in the House of Commons five days later, launched a blistering attack on the British government's handling of the situation in Ireland. Dillon intervened with Prime Minister H.H. Asquith to halt the 90 sentences of execution pronounced by 'field court martial' (in camera without defence or jury) under martial law by Gen. Maxwell after the latter declared the rebellion 'treason in time of war'. Dillon insisted that if they went ahead they would 'fill the whole country' with the same type of radicals, while imprisonment, on the other hand, would leave the radicals with as many supporters as could 'fit in a single gaol cell'. He declared that the rebels were 'wrong' but had fought 'a clean fight'. His intervention resulted in a halt to the executions after the fifteenth, though it was apparent how unbridgeable the chasm in Anglo-Irish relations had become following the Rising. The secret manner of the trials and executions had changed public opinion into sympathy for the rebels.[91]

Eamon de Valera defeated Dillon for the East Mayo parliamentary constituency seat in December 1918.

30 North Great George's Street: Home of Christopher Whelan (15), who was an only child and was killed in the Rising. He is buried in Glasnevin Cemetery. He was one of 28 people living in the house.[92]

3 Halston Street: O'Keefe's printers. The *Irish War News* bulletins from the GPO were printed here in 1916. (See Sackville Street Lower for the full texts.) The proprietor was Mr O'Keefe, and his shop was chosen by Joseph Stanley[93] to print the bulletins. Assisting Stanley were M.S. MacSiubhlaigh (Walker), James O'Sullivan, Thomas Ryan and Charles Walker (son of M.S.).[94]

Hardwicke Street: Fianna HQ; Seán Heuston was in charge of training and organisation. (See 34 Camden Street; 12 D'Olier Street [Dublin 2].)

27 Hardwicke Street: Home of Mrs Kissane. Seán MacDermott lived here until he moved to the Munster Hotel the week before the Rising; then on Holy Saturday he moved to the Fleming Hotel on Gardiner Street to stay with Tom Clarke at Seán O'Mahoney's home.

Henry Place: Volunteers escaping from the GPO rushed through here to get from Moore Street to Moore Lane, and thence to Moore Street.[95] (See Moore Street.)

1 Henry Place: Dundon Brothers, tenement house and workrooms.

2 Henry Place: Tenement house.

3 Henry Place: Home of Elizabeth Brady.

4–8 Henry Place: Michael O'Brien and Co., mineral water company. Many of the wounded fleeing the GPO were placed here on the Friday night, as it was better for their rest and quieter than in the crowded houses of Henry Place and Moore Street.[96]

9–10 Henry Place: Tenement houses.

10a–13 Henry Place: Michael O'Brien and Co. stables and lofts.

10 Henry Place, at the corner of Moore Street (behind Cogan's greengrocer's shop): Thomas McKane's family home. The family had remained indoors for the previous two days, having seen a looter being shot and unceremoniously thrown upon a barricade by British troops. Mr McKane, on hearing an attempt to enter the cottage, made for the rear door. At that moment, a Volunteer broke the glass panel with his rifle, which accidentally discharged. A bullet passed through Mr McKane, killing his teenage daughter behind him. Bridget McKane (16) was the first civilian casualty of the retreat from the GPO.[97] She received the last rites from Fr McInerny. Her mother signed her death certificate with an 'x'. The Volunteers were greatly traumatised by her death.[98]

Henry Street: An area with many retail outlets in 1916 and today; 53 buildings were burned on the street during the Rising. The Volunteers fleeing the burning GPO fled out the side door across Henry Street, through Henry Place and Moore Lane, into Moore Street. A post office van was dragged across Henry Street to screen them from the British, who had set up a machine-gun position further to the west on Henry Street.

9–15 Henry Street: Arnott's Department Store. During the Rising, the Volunteers under the command of Frank Henderson bored through the walls of Henry Street buildings from the GPO to here.[99]

21 Henry Street: Home of Jennie Wyse-Power and her husband, John, and son, Charles. John had been a member of the IRB and the Volunteers but was told that he

would be more valuable as a lawyer, free from these associations, and so did not take part in the Rising.[100]

The *Proclamation* was agreed upon here and six signed it: Thomas Clarke, Padraic Pearse, James Connolly, Thomas MacDonagh, Seán MacDermott and Éamonn Ceannt, probably on Tuesday 18 April. Joseph Plunkett signed on Easter Sunday morning. (There has always been confusion over whether the 'signatories' actually affixed their signatures to the paper, but Kathleen Clarke indicated that Tom told her that it was 'signed that night'.[101] Michael Molloy, one of the men who printed the *Proclamation*, said that he carried with him the piece of paper signed by the signatories to the *Proclamation* until he found himself in Richmond Barracks after the surrender, when he chewed it up and spat it out to prevent its discovery.[102])

Jennie (née O'Toole) grew up in Dublin in a nationalist family. She joined the Ladies' Land League in 1881, took an active part in its activities and became a member of its executive.[103] She married John Wyse-Power, a journalist on the *Freeman's Journal* and one of the founders of the Gaelic Athletic Association.

Jennie was an activist all her life. She was involved with the Dublin Women's Suffrage Association and the Gaelic League, and was a founder member and vice-president of Inghínidhe na hÉireann. She was a founder member of Sinn Féin, served on its executive from the beginning and was elected vice-president in 1911. She was elected first president of Cumann na mBan, was elected Poor Law guardian in 1903 and was one of five women elected to Dublin Corporation in 1920. Jennie was a successful businesswoman and her restaurant in Henry Street was a well-known meeting place for nationalists.[104]

During the Rising the Wyse-Powers supplied food to the insurgents and, with their daughter Nancy, later helped to organise relief for prisoners' dependants. Their home was completely destroyed in the fires.[105] Although not the original building, a plaque was placed on the wall of the current building in 2013, noting its importance.

Jennie supported the Treaty and was appointed to the first Seanad of the Irish Free State, where she had an outstanding record as a champion of women's rights from 1922 to 1936.

Her daughter, Nancy Wyse-Power, who had joined Cumann na mBan in 1915, undertook her first mission to Cork on Ash Wednesday of 1916. She had a brush with the authorities as she was delivering the message. Upon her arrival, she discovered that a priest had taken the bag, mistaking it for his own. This led to much trouble on her part, as she and the MacSwiney family, to whom she was delivering the message, spent all the next day trying to retrieve it. Her only consolation was that a priest was less likely to go to the police; in fact, he returned the bag without even mentioning its contents.[106] In a later mission during Easter Week, Nancy sewed a message she was given into the hem of her skirt.

47 Henry Street: Williams's Stores, looted during the Rising.

16 Irvine Crescent (North Dock): Home of Walter Scott (8), who was probably the last child to die of wounds suffered during the Rising. He died in Mercer's Hospital on 5 July from a gunshot wound to the head[107] and is buried in Glasnevin Cemetery.

14–20 Jervis Street: Jervis Street Hospital (now the Jervis Centre). Forty-five fatalities and 550 casualties were treated here during the Rising. The hospital became part of Beaumont Hospital, which was completed in 1987. The site of the hospital is now the Jervis Shopping Centre.

Liffey Street: O'Neill's pub. James Connolly was slightly wounded in his arm on returning from observing positions here on the Thursday morning of the Rising.

30 Liffey Street Upper: The *Gaelic Press* was printed here, as well as all kinds of 'republican' publications and posters during the period. The proprietor was Joseph Stanley, who was in the GPO during the Rising and was the printer in charge of the *Irish War News* bulletins issued from there.[108] (See 3 Halston Street and Sackville Street Lower.)

Marlborough Street (at corner of Cathedral Street): Pro-Cathedral (St Mary's). Dublin's Catholic Cathedral, begun in 1815 and opened in 1825. Fr O'Doherty, a priest here, was shot dead when he went to talk to the rebels, fully vested and with a cross in his hand.

8 Mary Street: Thomas Fallon and Co.; sold Volunteer uniforms, head-dress, badges, etc. Haversacks cost 10d or 1s. 6d; great coats were 25s.; green Cronje hats (named after the Boer leader Gen. Peter A. 'Piet' Cronje) were 1s. 8d; infantry swords in brown leather scabbards were five guineas.

4 Mary's Abbey: Home of Mary Redmond (16), who was killed in the Rising (some lists name her as Mary Raymone or Mary Raymond) and was the daughter of a widow.[109] The family lived with Mary's grandfather in a four-roomed house containing 43 people from seven families.[110]

101 Mecklenburgh Street (now Waterford Street): Home of Paddy Heaney, Peadar Kearney's childhood pal, who collaborated with him in writing the music to *A Soldier's Song*. (See 68 Dorset Street.)

6–8 Moore Lane: The Flag pub. The British killed Robert Dillon, aged 65, the owner, and his wife and child, who were fleeing the fire while running under a flag of truce. Upon seeing this, Padraic Pearse determined to surrender rather than have more civilian casualties. Dillon had carried on the business of The Flag for 35 years.

8 Moore Place: William Mullen (9) was killed here on 28 April.[111] He was shot by Volunteers retreating from the GPO. He died immediately and received no medical attention. He is buried in Glasnevin Cemetery.

Moore Street: An area with many food-sellers in 1916 and today; eleven buildings were burned here during the Rising.[112] Escapees from the GPO left there at 8 p.m. on Friday 28 April, went across Henry Street, through Henry Place and Moore Lane, into Moore Street.[113] As the escapees bored through the walls of houses on Moore Street on Friday night, they stopped and sheltered in many homes and shops, and they spent Friday night in buildings and yards throughout the terrace. There were seventeen wounded, including Connolly, who went into the buildings in Moore Street.

5 Moore Street: Dunne's butchers. After their escape from the GPO on Friday night, 25 April, the Volunteers entered this building and began tunnelling northward between buildings on Moore Street.

10 Moore Street: T.F. Cogan's, greengrocer (the property extended towards Moore Lane from Moore Street and was bounded by Henry Place). Looters took its entire stock, including 'tins of biscuits, Skipper sardines, John West salmon, fruit, OXO cubes, packets of butter, pickles and jam'.[114]

The rebel forces fled the GPO and spread themselves throughout the terrace.[115] Most of the leaders spent Friday night in the Cogan's house at No. 10. Many Volunteers from the GPO passed through this shop to get to the Plunkett shop and home at 16 Moore Street, which was their last Rising HQ. The 'Provisional Government' spent Friday night here and were served breakfast on Saturday morning by Mrs Cogan.[116] During the night the Volunteers, by now exhausted and despondent, were lying low, some sleeping and some saying the rosary in different rooms along the terrace. Some continued to work through the night, boring between buildings towards the north, and by dawn on Saturday the Volunteers had made considerable headway along the terrace, tunnelling their way at different levels from house to house.

11 Moore Street: James Plunkett, china and glass dealer, house, yard and shop.

12 Moore Street: T.F. Cogan, confectionary. P. McManus, a civilian aged 61, was killed here during the Rising.

13 Moore Street: Mrs R.A. Hogan, lodging house.

14 Moore Street: Mrs Norton, china glass warehouse.

15 Moore Street: Home of the Gormans, behind their clothes dealer's and tobacconist shop. At the start of the Rising the shop was looted, and Mrs Gorman put in a claim for '2000 Woodbine cigarettes, 500 Players, 300 Gold Flake and 700 Park Drive'.[117]

Elizabeth O'Farrell went out their door at about 12.45 p.m. on Saturday in order to find the British commander, Brig. Gen. W.H.M. Lowe, CB. She first met Col. H.S. Hodgkin, DSO, who told her to go back, and then said, 'I suppose this will have to be reported'. He reported to Col. Portal, who said, 'Take that Red Cross off her, she is a spy'. Gen. Lowe treated her in a more gentlemanly fashion.[118]

16 Moore Street: Patrick Plunkett's home and poultry shop. (No relation to Joseph Plunkett, or the other Plunketts fighting in the Rising.) J. Doyle, a civilian aged 36, was killed here during the Rising.

On Saturday morning it was decided, in the interests of safety, that the leadership should move up from No. 10 to a halfway point in the terrace of houses, away from a possible attack. They stopped at Plunkett's poultry shop, No. 16, and settled in a back room on the first floor. This was to be the final headquarters of the GPO garrison and the last meeting place of five of the signatories to the *Proclamation*. After breakfast in No. 10, Padraic and Willie Pearse, Tom Clarke, Joseph Plunkett and Seán MacDermott gathered at James Connolly's bedside in No. 16 to determine the course of negotiation to undertake.[119] (Connolly, with some other wounded, had been taken to this house earlier in the morning.[120])

Discussions were then held as to a plan of action. Seán McLoughlin, who had been shuttling between the GPO and the Four Courts all week and was familiar with British posts, was asked to outline the position as he saw it. He made a case for escape towards Henry Street, with a view to meeting up with the 1st Btn Volunteers under the command of Cmdt Ned Daly at the Four Courts. This would require a diversion by way of an attack on the enemy barricade at the junction of Moore Street and Parnell Street by twenty Volunteers. It was planned that, while the barricade was being attacked, all other Volunteers would emerge from the terrace of houses into the lanes opposite and make their way to the Four Courts.[121]

The leaders agreed to this plan, whereupon McLoughlin called for twenty Volunteers for the barricade attack. This group then made their way through the remaining houses towards the Parnell Street end of the terrace. Some time later, they emerged into the rear yard of the last house, Kelly's at No. 25, halting to await further orders. McLoughlin opened the rear gate and stepped into Sackville Lane (now Ó Rahilly Parade) at the side of the house. He was shocked to see the body of The Ó

Rahilly lying in the roadway in a pool of blood, with Volunteer Paddy Shortis lying dead beside him.[122] At this very moment Seán Mac Diarmada arrived and on seeing The Ó Rahilly became deeply upset. They placed covers on both bodies and then, on receiving an order delivered by a messenger, returned to No. 16 to be informed that all preparations for an attack were to be cancelled for one hour.

On arriving back at No. 16, McLoughlin was questioned at length by Pearse as to the likely loss of civilian life in the planned retreat to the Four Courts, as this would involve passing through populous districts no matter what route was taken. McLoughlin agreed that this was the case. This is believed to have greatly influenced Pearse in his decision to end hostilities. He had earlier witnessed the gunning down of the Dillon family on Moore Street as they emerged into the street under a white flag. (See 6–8 Moore Street.) Pearse then ordered McLoughlin to give a ceasefire order to all Volunteers to last one hour. McLoughlin made a tour of the terrace, giving the order, and upon his return was informed by a despondent Tom Clarke that the leaders had decided to ask for terms of surrender.[123] From here, Elizabeth O'Farrell and ultimately Pearse eventually approached British forces to declare the surrender.[124]

Later on Saturday afternoon Séamus Devoy, nephew of the Fenian John Devoy, came to No. 16 to inform those in the house that he had made the necessary arrangements to have the Parnell Street barricade opened to receive Connolly, and the rest of the men began to gather in the street. Lining up and forming ranks with sloped arms, the first group marched off, picking up any stragglers on the way. Next, Willie Pearse headed the main body, waving his white flag. Close behind him walked Tom Clarke, and towards the rear walked Seán Mac Diarmada and Joseph Plunkett,[125] supported by Julia Grenan and Winifred Carney.[126]

In November 1916, Mary Plunkett lodged a claim for damage to her premises: for an 'outside electric lamp, a child's cot, a drawing-room table and four linen sheets'. Her claim was denied, however, because she had filed it after the 18 August deadline.[127]

A recent report recommending its preservation notes that the interior of No. 16 is 'largely complete' in its eighteenth-century form, though in recent decades the buildings along the street have largely fallen into disrepair. In January 2007 Nos 14, 15, 16 and 17 Moore Street became the subjects of a Preservation Order under the National Monuments Act.[128]

17 Moore Street: R.J. Gore, chemist and druggist.

18–19 Moore Street: Unoccupied at the time of the Rising.

20–21 Moore Street: M. and P. Hanlon's fish shop and ice merchants. Hanlon's house was behind. Some GPO escapees stopped here on Friday night, 28 April.[129]

22–23 Moore Street: Price's hardware store.

24–25 Moore Street: Patrick Kelly, fish merchant. The Ó Rahilly crawled into the rear doorway of their shop after he was shot, and then he crawled into Sackville Lane (now Ó Rahilly Parade), where he died. (See Sackville Lane.)

Kelly's delivery van was taken by the British and became part of their barricade at the north end of Moore Street. Mrs Kelly submitted a claim for the van and was compensated after the Rising.[130]

24–25 Moore Street: Miss Matassa, ice cream merchant.

26 Moore Street: McCormack and Fogarty, grocers, tea, wine and spirit merchants.

27 Moore Street: Tenement house.

27a Moore Street: M. Rhuimann, pork butcher.

28 Moore Street: Thomas Byrne, delft and china merchant.

29 Moore Street: Thomas Melling, fruit merchant.

30 Moore Street: P. O'Connor, poulterer.

30½–31–32 Moore Street: Christopher O'Flanagan, poulterer.

Between 41 and 42 Moore Street: Arched entrance to Moore's Market. Seán MacEntee and his men took refuge in the arch during their escape from the GPO.

47B Moore Street: Christy O'Leary's butcher shop. A British soldier was dragged to safety here during the Rising.

57 Moore Street: W. Heavey, a civilian aged 32, was killed here during the Rising.

19 Mountjoy Square East: A Dublin University VAD hospital set up by women graduates and students of Trinity College during the Rising. It treated mostly civilians wounded in the area.[131]

27–28 Mountjoy Square: Joseph Plunkett left Miss Quinn's Private Nursing Home here on Holy Saturday, having had surgery on his neck three weeks prior to the Rising.

Mountjoy Street: Home of Seán McGarry.[132] He had been in charge of the security party on the pier at Howth. He was editor of the *Literary Souvenir* for the O'Donovan Rossa Funeral. (See Finglas Road/Glasnevin Cemetery [Dublin 11].) McGarry accidentally shot Clarke in the elbow on 30 January 1916; the wound never completely healed.

44 Mountjoy Street: Munster Private Hotel, also known as Aras na nGael or Grianan na nGaedheal, owned by Myra T. McCarthy, a staunch republican from Kerry. Seán MacDermott stayed here before the Rising. The week before the Rising MacDermott briefed here the Volunteers who were to go and commandeer a wireless system and transmitter at the Wireless College at Cahersiveen on the Ring of Kerry, in order to broadcast news of the Rising to the world.[133] Present were Denis Daly (leader of the team),[134] Charlie Monaghan, Donal Sheehan and Colm Ó Lochlainn,[135] as well as two men from Cahersiveen: Denis Healy and Con Keating (a skilled wireless operator). They went by train to Limerick, where they met Tommy McInerney, who owned one of the two cars that were to be used in the venture. Keating, Sheehan and Monahan travelled on with McInerney. When Daly and Ó Lochlainn got to Cahirsiveen, the other car never showed up and they decided to return to Dublin. On the train back they heard that McInerney had driven off the Ballykissane Pier in County Kerry and that Sheehan,[136] Monaghan[137] and Keating[138] had drowned.[139]

Parnell Street: See Great Britain Street.

Parnell Square: See Rutland Square.

Poplar Row (and North Strand Road): Wicklow Chemical Manure Company. A force of ICA, originally under the command of Thomas Craven,[140] held this early in the Rising. Vincent Poole was second in command. Frank Henderson ultimately took charge of this force and led it to the GPO.[141] Harry Boland and Harry Colley were in this group of Volunteers.

Prince's Street North: Fifteen buildings were burned here during the Rising.

4–8 Prince's Street North: In 1916 this was an entrance to the offices of the *Freeman's Journal*. Prior to the Rising, the *Journal* was John Redmond's paper and a fierce opponent of the Irish Volunteers. (See 84 Abbey Street Middle.)

3 Richmond Parade: Home of Peadar Kearney at the time of the Rising. He was a member of the garrison at Jacob's Factory. (See 68 Dorset Street Lower.)

Rutland Square (now Parnell Square): The first of Dublin's Georgian squares, its four sides were originally known as Charlemont Row, Cavendish Row, Palace Row and Great Britain Street. The central park was named after the 4th duke of Rutland, who was lord lieutenant of Ireland from 1784 to 1787. It is now named for Home Rule leader Charles Stewart Parnell.

Rutland Square (now Parnell Square): Garden of Remembrance. The GPO prisoners were held in the open overnight here on 29 April 1916. The current garden opened in 1966 on the 50th anniversary of the Rising; designed by architect Daithi Hanly, it features a sunken pool with mosaics depicting discarded weapons. The sculpture is by Oisin Kelly and represents the Children of Lir, an ancient Irish legend about children turned into swans and condemned to live for 900 years—a spell finally broken by St Patrick, who restored them to humanity and baptised them before they died.

Rutland Square (now Parnell Square), 8 Cavendish Row: Grocery shop of Robert MacKenzie. A survivor of the sinking of the *Lusitania*, he was killed on 27 April as he was sitting in his shop.

3 Rutland Square (now Parnell Square): Home of Edward Fannin, a doctor with the Royal Medical Corps.[142] His diary and letters give a clear view of the Rising from the viewpoint of an upper-class family.

4 Rutland Square (now Parnell Square): One-time HQ of the Irish Volunteers.

25 Rutland Square (now Parnell Square): Gaelic League Headquarters (Conradh na Gaeilge). Grocers' Hall/Gaelic League Building. The League was founded here on 31 July 1893. This was the usual parade hall of C Company, 2nd Battalion, prior to the Rising. It was also the Central Branch of Cumann na mBan (the original branch).[143] There were 43 affiliated branches before the Rising. The officers of the Central Branch in 1916 were Kathleen Clarke, president, and Sorcha MacMahon, secretary; branch members included Áine Ceannt,[144] Louise Gavan-Duffy,[145] Niamh Plunkett and Jennie Wyse-Power.

On Easter Sunday night the 2nd Battalion officers and men met here under the command of Thomas MacDonagh. Arms that were hidden here were taken by The Ó Rahilly to the GPO on Monday in his blue De Dion Bouton motorcar, which was later used as a part of a barricade and burned.

25 Rutland Square (now Parnell Square): Offices in the Gaelic League Building of Seán T. O'Kelly, who was president of the Free State from 1945 and became the first president of the Republic of Ireland in 1949.[146]

On 9 September 1914 there was a meeting here of the Supreme Council of the IRB (albeit not exclusively of the IRB: non–IRB members were also present).[147] It was decided that 'England's difficulty is Ireland's opportunity' (Theobald Wolfe Tone) and that there would be a Rising before the end of the war, or if the British tried to enforce conscription. Among those present were Éamonn Ceannt, Thomas Clarke, James Connolly, Arthur Griffith, John MacBride, Seán MacDermott, Seán McGarry, William O'Brien,[148] Seán T. O'Kelly, Padraic Pearse, Joseph Plunkett and James Tobin.[149] The Volunteer 'Advisory Committee' was formed; original members were Pearse and Plunkett and 'a considerable number of Volunteer Officers'. Pearse proposed two resolutions:

(1) Volunteer action during the war should be confined to the defence of Ireland.
(2) Volunteers should announce their intention to occupy the ports, in the event of shortages, to prevent food from being exported.

By December 1914, given its attendant risks of leakage, the 'Volunteer Advisory Committee' was discontinued.

Early in the summer of 1915 the Executive of the IRB approved Ceannt, Pearse and Plunkett as a Military *Committee*. Diarmuid Lynch asserts repeatedly that the 'Military Council' was instituted not by the Supreme Council but by the IRB Executive Council.[150] P.S. O'Hegarty wrote that the Supreme Council, at its last meeting in January 1916, was not convinced that an offensive insurrection was warranted.[151] Desmond Ryan contended that the resolution that 'we fight at the earliest date possible' was apparently adopted with some reservations on the part of some members of the Supreme Council.[152] Yet Denis McCullough has said: 'The decision by the Supreme Council to call a Rising at the earliest possible date, after prolonged discussion under my chairmanship, was unanimous. I know my worth. I was there all the time, working and building up the IRB. But the actual Rising was the work mainly of four men—Pearse, MacDermott, Connolly and Clarke.'[153]

Some months later, when Seán MacDermott was released from prison, he and Thomas Clarke acted as ex-officio members of the Military *Committee*. After the last meeting of the Supreme Council on 16 January 1916, all additions to the renamed Military *Council* were at the discretion of the Executive. After James Connolly's 'disappearance and reappearance' in January 1916, he was co-opted onto the Council. In the second week of April Thomas MacDonagh was co-opted onto the Council, and it thereafter consisted of the seven signatories to the *Proclamation*.

29–30 Rutland Square (now Parnell Square): Vaughan's Hotel, owned by Mrs Vaughan of Clare, who sold it to Tom McGuire, formerly of Limerick. Often used by Volunteers from the country.

Rutland Square (now Parnell Square): Geraghty's Hotel; Neary's Hotel; Meath Hotel; all were located a few doors from Vaughan's Hotel. Volunteers from the country used them all while visiting Dublin for Rising orders.

41 Rutland Square (now Parnell Square): Irish National Foresters' Hall. The GAA often met here. The Wolfe Tone Clubs of Dublin were headquartered here. On Easter Sunday night, 23 April 1916, Volunteers met here for a *céilidhe* after the Rising was 'cancelled'. The 3rd Battalion officers and men met here under the command of Éamon de Valera. On Easter Monday, the 1st Battalion mustered here.

44 Rutland Square (now Parnell Square): Ancient Order of Hibernians Meeting Rooms and Hall (now Kevin Barry Memorial Hall). The AOH was much closer philosophically to the ICA than were the Volunteers. No Protestants were allowed to join.[154] Joseph Scollan, from Derry, was the national director after 1911; he bought 30 rifles from the ICA for £30 in 1915. The commander of the Hibernian Rifles in Dublin in 1916 was John J. Scollan.[155] (See 28 Frederick Street North; 44 Rutland Square; 180 Great Brunswick Street [Dublin 2].)

It became the HQ of the Irish National Volunteers and was used as a drill hall. Dublin Castle had it under surveillance before the Rising because it was thought that the Volunteers stored arms there. It is currently the **Dublin Sinn Féin HQ.**

27 Rutland Street Upper (now Parnell Street): Home of Seán T. O'Kelly in 1916. Padraic and Willie Pearse stayed here for the two nights preceding the Rising. O'Kelly became closely associated with Arthur Griffith in the foundation of Sinn Féin, of which he became secretary from 1908 to 1910. In 1913 he was one of the founding members of the Irish Volunteers, and was appointed staff captain to Pearse in the GPO during the Rising. He became the first accredited diplomat of the Irish Republic, and was sent by Dáil Éireann as envoy to the Paris peace talks at the end of World War I. He became the second president of Ireland, occupying that office when Ireland was declared a republic in 1949.

29 Rutland Street Upper (now Parnell Street): Home of Oscar Traynor[156] at the time of the Rising.

Sackville Lane (now Ó Rahilly Parade): The Ó Rahilly crawled up this laneway after being wounded, and died here.[157] He died slowly: at least four hours after he was shot he was heard calling for water.[158] It is noted that at the moment of surrender, nineteen hours later, a British ambulance came across him, barely alive, but that is probably incorrect. The ambulance driver, Albert Mitchell, made a statement that The Ó Rahilly was alive the next day and that a British officer was then said to remark:

'The more of them that die naturally, the fewer we'll have to shoot', but that seems quite unrealistic.[159]

On Saturday morning Seán McLoughlin, stepping into Sackville Lane from the rear yard of No. 25 Moore Street, was shocked to see the body of The Ó Rahilly lying in the roadway in a pool of blood, with Paddy Shortis lying dead beside him (see 16 Moore Street). He and Seán Mac Diarmada placed covers on both bodies.[160]

Elizabeth O'Farrell saw The Ó Rahilly's body when she returned from her first meeting with Brig. Gen. W.H.M. Lowe in Tom Clarke's shop. Her recollection, and that of McLoughlin, is more likely than that of Mr Mitchell. Miss O'Farrell related that it was 2.30 p.m. on Saturday when she reached Moore Street, and as she passed Sackville Lane again 'she saw Ó Rahilly's corpse lying a few yards up the laneway, his feet against a stone stairway in front of a house, his head towards the street'.[161]

The Ó Rahilly wrote this note to his wife:

Written after I was shot, Darling Nancy I was shot leading a rush up Moore Street, took refuge in a doorway. While I was there I heard the men pointing out where I was + I made a bolt for the lane I am in now. I got more [than] one bullet I think. Tons + tons of love dearie to you + to the boys + to Nell + Anna. It was a good fight anyhow. Please deliver this to Nannie Ó Rahilly, 40 Herbert Park, Dublin. Good bye darling.

A plaque replicating the note was carved by Shane Cullen and placed in Ó Rahilly Parade in 2005.

Sackville Place: Six buildings were burned here during the Rising.

Sackville Street Lower: This ran from Henry Street on the west and Earl Street on the east to O'Connell Bridge. All buildings from No. 1 to No. 47 were burned during the Rising, some as a result of British artillery fire and some from fires started by looters, who set alight both fireworks and lamp oil.

The *Irish Times* reported:

The Hotel Metropole and all that block of buildings for a long distance into Middle Abbey Street were burned down, including the *Freeman's Journal* and *Evening Telegraph* offices, Messrs. Easons, Messrs. Mansfields, and Messrs. Thorn's printing establishment. Then the General Post Office was given to the flames and was destroyed—only the bare walls of this fine building remain. This particular fire extended down Henry Street as far as the large warehouse of Messrs. Arnott and Co., which remained intact but was flooded with water. The Coliseum Theatre was also destroyed.[162]

On the east side of Sackville Street all the shops were burned down from Hopkins's Corner, at O'Connell Bridge, right up to the Tramway Company's office at Cathedral Street. The fire extended backwards and enveloped and destroyed almost all the buildings between Eden Quay and Lower Abbey Street, back to Marlborough Street.

Sackville Street Lower: the General Post Office (GPO). Opened in 1818, it was 200ft long and 150ft wide, with a height of 50ft in three storeys. Its architect was Francis Johnston. (The site had been suggested for the new Catholic cathedral later opened on Marlborough Street, but the authorities of the time did not think it appropriate for a Catholic cathedral to be built in that prime location.) A major edifice of Dublin's eighteenth- and nineteenth-century classical architecture, it was built from mountain granite with a portico of Portland stone. The 50ft-long Ionic portico of six fluted columns has a pediment surmounted with statues by John Smyth of Hibernia, Fidelity and Mercury, and a tympanum decorated with the royal coat of arms.

Pearse read the *Proclamation of the Irish Republic* in front of the GPO at 12.45 p.m. on Monday 24 April 1916 (some reports erroneously cite 12.04 p.m.). Florrie O'Donoghue wrote:

> It was considered essential that the Proclamation should be in such terms and issued in such circumstances that, no matter how the Rising ended, the event would take an authentic place in historic succession to earlier efforts to achieve freedom, and that it redefine in modern terms the unchanging aspiration of the Irish people for sovereign control over their own destinies. That aspiration had to be set on the highest moral plane and expressed publicly in a definite form.[163]

After the Rising, the *Irish Times* reported that 'his audience became progressively bored . . . On a rumour that [Clery's was going to be breached for looting] his audience moved over to the shop windows, and left the speaker finishing his peroration with no one to listen to him but his guard. Like the revolution itself, the proclamation was a fiasco.'[164]

The GPO was taken as the headquarters of the Rising, and outposts were established at the corner of Sackville Street and Bachelor's Walk ('Kelly's Fort'), at O'Connell Bridge, at the corner of Abbey Street Lower and in the Imperial Hotel across from the GPO. Barricades were constructed in Lower Abbey Street and North Earl Street. The understanding was that once the *Proclamation* had been read and the Irish Republic established, the Irish Volunteers and the Irish Citizen Army would merge as the Army of the Irish Republic. There were no forces stationed to the east of the Sackville Street garrisons, and while it could be inferred that that was because there were no British barracks there, it must be noted that the pressure which ultimately crushed the GPO and brought the Rising to a halt came from exactly that quarter.

The detachment that charged the GPO consisted of about 150 men, both Volunteers and Irish Citizen Army. The 'Kimmage Garrison', comprised mostly of men who had come to Ireland from England, was the first unit to occupy the GPO.[165] The detachment that took the GPO was not, however, a single organised military unit and had the disadvantages of a 'piecemeal organisation hurriedly put together'.[166] The first attackers were dangerously overloaded with a motley assortment of weapons: some of the men had Howth rifles, some carried the Italian Martinis they had purchased themselves, others carried shotguns, and some were 'armed' with sledgehammers, picks and a few revolvers. Most were not in uniform, and only a few wore any military dress at all. They ordered the staff and public to leave the building; a few British soldiers were taken prisoner, and they would remain prisoners for the week. The Irish occupied every part of the building, including the roof, and immediately began to knock out windows, loopholing them with ledgers and anything else to hand.

On Tuesday Pearse issued the first of three 'Irish War Bulletins' in a sheet entitled *Irish War News*:

The Irish Republic

(Irish) War News is published today because a momentous thing has happened. The Irish Republic has been declared in Dublin, and a Provisional Government has been appointed to administer its affairs. The following have been named as the Provisional Government:—

    Thomas J. Clarke.

    Seán Mac Diarmada.

    P.H. Pearse.

    James Connolly.

    Thomas Mac Donagh.

    Éamonn Ceannt.

    Joseph Plunkett.

    The Irish Republic was proclaimed by a poster which was prominently displayed in Dublin.

    At 9.30 this morning the following statement was made by Commandant-General, P.H. Pearse:—

    The Irish Republic was proclaimed in Dublin on Easter Monday, 24th April, at 12 noon. Simultaneously with the issue of the Proclamation of the Provisional Government the Dublin Division of the Army of the Republic, including the Irish Volunteers, Citizen Army, Hibernian Rifles, and other bodies, occupied dominating points in the city. The G.P.O. was seized at 12 noon, the Castle was attacked at the same moment, and shortly afterward the Four Courts were occupied. The Irish troops hold the City Hall and dominate the Castle. Attacks were immediately commenced by the British forces and were everywhere repulsed. At the moment of writing this report (9.30 a.m., Tuesday) the Republican forces hold all their positions and the British have nowhere broken through. There has been heavy and continuous fighting for nearly 24 hours, the casualties of the enemy being much more numerous than those on the Republican side. The Republican forces everywhere are fighting with splendid gallantry. The populace of Dublin are plainly with the Republic, and the officers and men are everywhere cheered as they march through the streets. The whole centre of the city is in the hands of the Republic, whose flag flies from the G.P.O.

Commandant General P.H. Pearse is commanding in chief of the Army of the Republic, and is President of the Provisional Government. Commandant General James Connolly is commanding the Dublin districts. Communication with the country is largely out, but reports to hand show the country is rising, and bodies of men from Kildare and Fingall have already reported in Dublin.

Late on Tuesday night a decision was made by Connolly and Pearse to abandon the idea of a second *Irish War News* and they issued another manifesto in a handbill–style proclamation.[167] Pearse read it to a small crowd assembled in front of Nelson's Column that evening:

The Provisional Government
To the
Citizens of Dublin
The Provisional Government of the Irish Republic salutes the Citizens of Dublin on the momentous occasion of the proclamation of a
Sovereign Independent Irish State
Now in the course of being established by Irishmen in Arms.

The Republican forces hold the lines taken up at twelve noon on Easter Monday, and nowhere despite fierce and almost continuous attacks of the British troops, have the lines been broken through. The country is rising in answer to Dublin's call and the final achievement of Ireland's freedom is now, with God's help, only a matter of days. The valour, self-sacrifice, and discipline of Irish men and women are now about to win for our country a glorious place among the nations.

Ireland's honour has already been redeemed; it remains to vindicate her wisdom and her self-control.

All Citizens of Dublin who believe in the rights of their country to be free will give their allegiance and their loyal help to the Irish Republic. There is work for everyone: for the men in the fighting line, and for the women in the provision of food and first aid. Every Irishman and Irishwoman worthy of the name will come forward to help their common country in this her supreme hour.

Able bodied Citizens can help by building barricades in the streets to oppose the advance of British troops. The British troops have been firing on our women and on our Red Cross. On the other hand, Irish Regiments in the British Army have refused to act against their fellow Countrymen.

The Provisional Government hopes that its supporters—which means the vast bulk of the people of Dublin—will preserve order and self-restraint. Such looting as has already occurred has been done by hangers-on of the British Army. Ireland must keep her honour unbesmirched.

We have lived to see an Irish Republic proclaimed. May we live to establish it firmly, and may our children and our children's children enjoy the happiness and prosperity which freedom will bring.

Signed on behalf of the Provisional Government

P.H. Pearse

Commanding in Chief the forces of The Irish Republic and

President of the Provisional Government

Late on Wednesday night, or early on Thursday morning, Pearse wrote more copy for the final *Irish War Bulletin*. The date on this bulletin appears as '88 April 1916', but some of the later sheets have the date as '28 April', so it seems that the printers noticed their mistake and partially rectified it. Thursday, however, was in fact the 27th of April.[168]

Irish Republic

War Bulletin

Thursday Morning, 88 April, 1916

The main positions taken up by the Republican Forces in Dublin at 12 noon on Easter Monday, 24th instant are all still held by us. Our lines are everywhere intact and our positions of great strength.

The Republican Forces have at every point resisted with great gallantry.

Commandant-General Pearse, Commander-in-Chief, and Commandant-General Connolly, commanding in Dublin, thank their brave soldiers.

Despite furious and almost continuous attacks by the British forces, our casualties are few. The British casualties are heavy.

The British troops have continually fired on our Red Cross and even on parties of Red Cross women nurses bearing stretchers. Commandant-General Pearse, commanding in chief for the Republic, has notified Major-General Friend, commanding in chief for the British, that the British prisoners held by the Republican forces will be treated as hostages for the observance on the part of the British of the laws of warfare and humanity, especially as regards the Red Cross.

Commandant-General Pearse, as president of the Provisional Government, has issued a proclamation to the citizens of Dublin, in which he salutes them on the momentous occasion of the proclamation of the Irish Republic, and claims for the Republic the allegiance of every man and woman in Dublin who believes in Ireland's right to be free. Citizens can help the Republican Forces by building barricades in the streets to impede the advance of the British Forces.

Up with the Barricades!

The Republican Forces are in no position to supply bread to the civil population within the lines occupied by them.

A committee of citizens known as the Public Service Committee has been formed to assist in the maintenance of order and in the supply of food to the civil population.

The Provisional Government strongly condemns looting and the wanton destruction of property. The looting that has taken place has been done by the hangers-on of the British forces.

Reports to hand from the country show that Dublin's call is being responded to, and that large areas of the West, South and South-East are now in arms for the Irish Republic.

P.H. Pearse

Commandant-General

From Wednesday on, buildings in Sackville Street came under high-explosive and incendiary fire, mostly from artillery in Westmoreland Street. The Imperial Hotel, located over Clery's department store, across the street from the GPO, was one of the first buildings to be set on fire; soon most buildings between that and the Liffey were in flames. Connolly naively claimed that the British would not use artillery in city areas because as capitalists they would be reluctant to destroy property.

On Friday morning, Pearse issued his last Manifesto from the GPO:

Headquarters, Army of the Irish Republic.

General Post Office, Dublin

28th April 1916, 9.30 a.m.

The Forces of the Irish Republic, which was proclaimed in Dublin, on Easter Monday, 24th April, have been in possession of the central part of the Capital, since 12 noon on that day. Up to yesterday headquarters was in touch with all the main outlying positions, and, despite furious, and almost continuous assaults by British Forces all those positions were then still being held, and the commandants in charge were confident of their ability to hold them for a long time.

During the course of yesterday afternoon, and evening, the enemy succeeded in cutting our communications with our other positions in the City, and Headquarters is today isolated.

The enemy has burnt down whole blocks of houses, apparently with the object of giving themselves a clear field for the play of Artillery and Field guns against us.

We have been bombarded during the evening and night by Shrapnel and Machine Gun fire, but without material damage to our position, which is of great strength.

We are busy completing arrangements for the final defence of Headquarters, and are determined to hold it while buildings last. I desire now, lest I may not have an opportunity later, to pay homage to the gallantry of the soldiers of Irish freedom who have during the past four days been writing with fire and steel the most glorious chapter in the later history of Ireland. Justice can never be done to their heroism, to their discipline, to their gay and unconquerable spirit in the midst of peril and death.

Let me, who have led them into this, speak in my own, and in my fellow commanders' names, and in the name of Ireland present and to come, their praise, and ask those who come after them to remember them.

For four days they have fought and toiled, almost without cessation, almost without sleep, and in the intervals of fighting they have sung songs of the freedom of Ireland. No man has complained, no man has asked 'why?' Each individual has spent himself, happy to pour out his strength for Ireland and for Freedom. If they do not win this fight, they will at least have deserved to win it. But win it they will although they win in death.

Already they have won a great thing. They have redeemed Dublin from many shames, and made her name splendid among cities.

If I were to mention names, my list would be long. I will name only that of Commandant General James Connolly, Commanding the Dublin Division. He lies wounded, but is still the guiding brain of our resistance.

If we accomplish no more than we have accomplished, I am satisfied. I am satisfied that we have saved Ireland's honour. I am satisfied that we should have accomplished more, that we should have accomplished the task of enthroning as well as proclaiming the Irish Republic as a Sovereign State, had our arrangements for a simultaneous Rising of the whole country, with a combined plan as sound as the Dublin plan has proved to be, been allowed to go through on Easter Sunday.

Of the fatal countermanding order which prevented those plans being carried out, I shall not speak further. Both Eoin MacNeill and we have acted in the best interests of Ireland.

For my part, as to anything I have done in this, I am not afraid to face the judgment of God, or the judgment of posterity.

Padraic H. Pearse
Commandant General
Commanding-in-Chief of the Army of the Irish
Republic and President of the Provisional Government[169]

After days of shelling, the garrison at the GPO were forced to abandon their headquarters on Friday night when fire caused by the shells and the oil stores throughout Sackville Street spread to the GPO. The garrison escaped from the side door on Henry Street and crossed over into Henry Place.[170] Fire from the British came from five areas: from a barricade at the junction of Moore Lane and Great Britain Street [Parnell Street]; from the roof of the Rotunda Hospital; from the spire of Findlater's Church; from a tower at the Amiens Street Railway Station [Connolly

Station]; and from a barricade further west on Henry Street.[171] (See Henry Street; Moore Street.) On Saturday Pearse signed a surrender order, and later Connolly and MacDonagh concurred.

PEARSE SURRENDER ORDER, 29 APRIL 1916

In order to prevent the further slaughter of Dublin citizens, and in the hope of saving the lives of our followers, now surrounded and hopelessly outnumbered, the members of the Provisional Government at present at Headquarters have agreed to an unconditional surrender, and the Commandants of the various districts in the City and County will order their commands to lay down arms.

Padraic H. Pearse
29 April 1916
3.45 pm

CONNOLLY SURRENDER ORDER, 29 APRIL 1916

I agree to these conditions for the men only under my command in the Moore Street District and for the men in the Stephen's Green Command.

James Connolly
April 29/16

MACDONAGH SURRENDER ORDER, 30 APRIL 1916

On consultation with Commandant Ceannt and other officers I have decided to agree to unconditional surrender also.

Thomas MacDonagh
30.IV.16
3.15 p.m.

After the Rising, and before the GPO was reconstructed, a temporary 'GPO' was located at 14 Sackville Street. The GPO was reopened in 1929 after renovation.

In 1966 a plaque was placed in the building's alcove near where Pearse read the *Proclamation*. It displays the following message in both English and Irish: 'Here on Easter Monday 1916, Padraic Pearse read the Proclamation of the Irish Republic. From this building he commanded the forces that asserted in arms Ireland's right to freedom. *Is iad a d'aighean an tine beo.*' ('It is they who fanned the living flame'. The last sentence was *not* translated into English.) In the lobby there is a statue of Cúchulainn, sculpted by Oliver Sheppard, dedicated to the 1916 Rising.

1 Sackville Street Lower (and Eden Quay): Hopkins and Hopkins, jewellers and silversmiths. During the Rising it was held by Séamus Robinson,[172] Séamus Lundy and Cormac Turner alone until James Connolly sent ICA member Andy Conroy, a crack shot, as a sniper.

6–7 Sackville Street Lower: Dublin Bread Company. James Stephens described its glass roof as a 'Chinese-like pagoda'. A detail under the command of Fergus O'Kelly[173] held it during the Rising. Set afire on Wednesday, it was described as follows: 'The flames kissing the ball on the dome's summit are singularly impressive. A scene of greater splendour I have never witnessed . . . It was only outdone by the avalanche of flame and smoke that crashed to the ground when the dome collapsed at 5 o'clock.'[174]

10–11 Sackville Street Lower (corner of Abbey Street Lower): Reis and Co. building. The Irish School of Wireless Telegraphy was situated here; it was closed in 1914 and all its apparatus was dismantled then. In the Rising Fergus O'Kelly[175] led six men to take and restore the wireless equipment to get the 'story out to the world'. The first 'broadcast' was at 5.30 p.m. on Tuesday, but the receiver could not be repaired. Johnny 'Blimey' O'Connor was the telegrapher.[176] The building was burned out on Wednesday.

17 Sackville Street Lower: Hoyte and Son, druggists and oilworks, 'The City of Dublin Drug Hall'. The premises housed a mixture of chemicals, methylated spirits, turpentine and oils. It burst into flames during the Rising and many oil drums exploded, giving extra fuel to the flames: 'When Hoyte's first caught fire it was a terrific spectacle, as it burst into one huge flame the moment it was hit. It was a roaring inferno in less than a minute. Stored as it was with chemicals of all sorts and with oils and colours it spouted rockets and stars of every hue and was the most wonderful fireworks show I ever saw.'[177]

20 Sackville Street Lower: Clery's Department Store (first floor of the Imperial Hotel). The history of Clery's dates back to May 1853, when McSwiney, Delany and Co. opened the 'Palatial Mart' or 'New Mart'. Housed in a purpose-built building, the department store was designed to eclipse European outlets of the time. The shop was renamed 30 years later when it was taken over by Michael J. Clery of Limerick. From 1883 to the present day, 'Clery and Co.' has hung over the doors.

Clery's was completely destroyed during the Rising. 'I had the extraordinary experience of seeing the plate-glass windows of Clery's run molten into the channel from the terrific heat', Oscar Traynor wrote.[178]

21–27 Sackville Street Lower: Imperial Hotel, owned by William Martin Murphy. (**Clery's Department Store** now occupies the entire building.) Cmdt W.J. Brennan-Whitmore was the O/C of the Volunteers who took the hotel and the North King Street area; Michael W. O'Brien was second in command of the unit that occupied the hotel. During the Rising, the Plough and the Stars flag of the ICA was raised over it.

Mrs Thomas Dillon (née Geraldine Plunkett) watched the storming of the GPO from here on Easter Monday. She had been married on Sunday in what was supposed to be a double wedding with Grace Gifford and Joseph Plunkett.[179]

33 Sackville Street Lower, at the corner of North Earl Street: The Pillar Café, restaurant and tearooms. Miss McFarland was the manager.

During the Rising Cmdt W.J. Brennan-Whitmore was the O/C of the North King Street area, commanding both ICA and Volunteers. Brennan-Whitmore was one of the few to argue for a guerrilla-type campaign and held that 'the one really big flaw in our effort was the decision to stand and fight in Dublin'. He regarded the defensive plan adopted by the Military Council as a wasted opportunity. The Volunteers might have 'put up a prolonged resistance that would appeal to the fighting instincts of our race and rouse our people out of the apathy they had sunk into', but the defensive strategy consigned them to 'another chapter of failure'. He argued so often and so forcefully that the Military Council told him to put his ideas into a book and submit it to them, but his advice was ignored.[180]

Brennan-Whitmore was charged with taking this building and building barricades. He tried fruitlessly to stop the looting, until he shot into the air. It was his command that set up the 'string and can' communication system from the Imperial Hotel across Sackville Street to the GPO. When Brennan-Whitmore was captured he met the Australian sniper, stationed in Trinity, who hit one of his cans and tried to hit the string.[181] The sniper, 'snap-shooting' from a corner of Trinity College, hit the can several times but was disappointed to have missed the string—from over half a mile away.[182]

The building was completely burned during the Rising.

34 Sackville Street Lower: Noblett's Ltd, wholesale confectioners. It was at the junction of North Earl Street and was occupied by Volunteers under the command of Cmdt W.J. Brennan-Whitmore.

35–39 Sackville Street Lower (corner of Prince's Street): **Hotel Metropole,** demolished during the Rising. Michael Collins came here to escort Joseph Plunkett to the GPO. (Plunkett was moved here from a nursing home on Saturday, and then moved back to the home when the Sunday attack was called off. He was taken to the

Metropole to pick up his weapons on Monday morning.) Harry Boland came here from the GPO, under the command of Oscar Traynor, and then returned to the GPO prior to the surrender.[183]

The building now houses **Eason's Books** and **Penny's**.

40 Sackville Street Lower: Eason's bookshop. British army training manuals were on sale here; Volunteers bought and studied them from before the Rising until the Truce.

Sackville Street Lower: Lord Nelson's Pillar. Standing between Henry Street and North Earl Street, it distinguished Sackville Street Lower from Sackville Street Upper. The original stone was laid on 15 February 1808 and the monument was completed in 1809; it was the first such monument to Admiral Lord Nelson and cost £6,858, raised by public subscription. William Watkins of Norwich designed the pillar, but Nelson's 13ft-tall statue was the work of an Irish sculptor, Thomas Kirk. The pillar stood 134ft high, carved out of white Portland stone, with 168 winding steps to the lookout balcony.

Sackville Street Upper: Eight buildings were burned here during the Rising. Two of the 1916 garrisons were mustered here after their surrender: the Four Courts garrison and the GPO/Moore Street garrison.

5, 6, 7 Sackville Street Upper (corner of Cathedral Street): William Lawrence's Bazaar, a photo, toy and stationery shop; it was looted and burned during the Rising. The shop contained fireworks that were set off, starting fires elsewhere in the street. This was the main photo studio of William Lawrence. Lawrence and his assistant, Robert French, were Ireland's most noted photographers of the time, and the foremost sellers of picture postcards. The fires destroyed hundreds of thousands of glass plate negatives, which were mostly family portraits. The majority of Lawrence's plates of views of Dublin and the countryside were safe in a warehouse in Rathmines.

9 Sackville Street Upper: Dublin United Tramways Offices, destroyed during the Rising.

10 Sackville Street Upper: Hibernian Bible Society, destroyed during the Rising.

21–22 Sackville Street Upper: Gresham Hotel. Opened by Thomas Gresham in the nineteenth century, it was the most luxurious Dublin hotel north of the Liffey. British snipers on its roof poured bullets onto the roof of the GPO from Tuesday onward. It was the surrender point for the 1st Btn Volunteers under Cmdt Ned Daly's command.[184]

Store Street: Dublin City Morgue. Following the Rising, the bodies of two unidentified children were buried from here on the order of Dr M.J. Russell.[185]

Summerhill: Home of John Doyle (15), who died on 26 April in the Mater Misericordiae Hospital of a bullet wound to the lung.[186]

Summerhill, 4 Murphy's Cottages, Gloucester Diamond: Home of Charles Darcy (15), who was killed in the City Hall garrison on 25 April. When he left home to fight, his father told him that he had to choose 'between Liberty Hall and his family'. His family of eight lived here.[187]

57 Lower Wellington Quay: Home of Mary Anne Brunswick (15), who was killed on 28 April. (Her death certificate said that she was killed at 'Wellington Street'.) She suffered a fractured skull and 'laceration of the brain shock' and was with her father when she was killed. Six families lived in the four-roomed house, a total of 27 people.[188]

William's Lane: rear of Independent House (the *Independent* newspaper, owned by William Martin Murphy, was very anti-Volunteers, anti-ITGWU and anti-ICA prior to the Rising, and became more strongly opposed to the Volunteers afterwards). Also on the premises was the *Freeman's Journal*. James Connolly was seriously wounded in his ankle upon returning from here to the GPO late on Thursday afternoon.

North William Street: National School; attended by Seán Connolly, who was killed in the City Hall.

39 North William Street: Home of Sgt, then Lt, Frank Robbins[189] of the ICA. He was in the St Stephen's Green/College of Surgeons garrison.

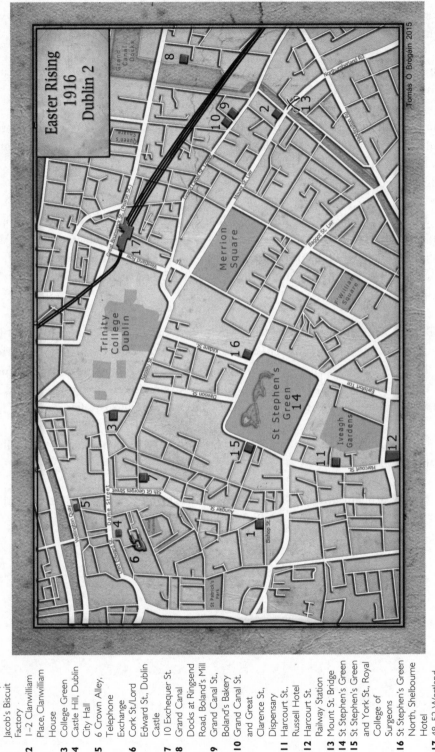

Easter Rising 1916 Dublin 2

Tomás Ó Brógáin 2015

1 26–50 Bishop St., Jacob's Biscuit Factory
2 1–2 Clanwilliam Place, Clanwilliam House
3 College Green
4 Castle Hill, Dublin City Hall
5 6 Crown Alley, Telephone Exchange
6 Cork St/Lord Edward St., Dublin Castle
7 10 Exchequer St.
8 Grand Canal Docks at Ringsend Road, Boland's Mill
9 Grand Canal St., Boland's Bakery
10 Grand Canal St. and Great Clarence St., Dispensary
11 Harcourt St., Russell Hotel
12 Harcourt St. Railway Station
13 Mount St. Bridge
14 St Stephen's Green
15 St Stephen's Green and York St., Royal College of Surgeons
16 St Stephen's Green North, Shelbourne Hotel
17 48–52 Westland Row

Dublin 2

Key locations

Aungier Street
Clanwilliam Place (Clanwilliam House)
College Green
Cork Hill (Dublin City Hall)
Dame Street
Dawson Street
Dublin Castle
Fitzwilliam Square
Fleet Street
Great Brunswick Street (now Pearse Street)
Harcourt Street
Harcourt Street Railway Station
Jacob's Biscuit Factory (now Dublin Institute of
    Technology and the National Archives)
Kildare Street

Leeson Street Upper and Lower
Lord Edward Street
Merrion Square
Mount Street Upper and Lower
Mount Street Bridge (bridge crosses between
    Dublin 2 and Dublin 4)
Nassau Street
Royal College of Surgeons in Ireland
St Stephen's Green
Temple Bar
Trinity College Dublin (TCD)
Westland Row Railway Station (now Pearse
    Station)
York Street

The Irish Volunteers always had their headquarters in Dublin 2, first at 41 Kildare Street, then in 1914 at 206 Great Brunswick Street for a short time, before moving to 2 Dawson Street, which was the HQ of the Dublin Brigade at the time of the Rising. The 3rd Battalion's HQ was at 206 Great Brunswick Street. (Dublin 2 is one of two postal codes to span the Liffey.)

> *'. . . IT WAS GOOD TO BE IN THE ACTION; MORE THAN ONCE I SAW A MAN I AIMED AT FALL'*
> Margaret Skinnider

The Volunteers who mainly lived south of the Liffey composed the 3rd Battalion, under the command of Commandant Éamon de Valera. His command was involved in fighting in Dublin 2 as well as the 'Battle of Mount Street Bridge', which was fought from positions in both Dublin 2 and Dublin 4. (See Dublin 4 for a description of the walking route there.) De Valera's HQ was at Boland's Bakery, which is on the far eastern extreme of Dublin 2 on Grand Canal Street. The Citizen Army, under the command of Major Michael Mallin and Countess Markievicz, took St Stephen's Green and then retreated to the Royal College of Surgeons. Both of those sites and their surrounding areas are easily accessible to walkers.

Trinity College Dublin (TCD) fronts onto College Green and is the most imposing group of buildings in Dublin 2. It was such a perfect grouping of buildings that the British chose it for their headquarters from Tuesday onward. Its very size meant that the Volunteers did not attempt to take it at the start of the Rising because they felt that they could not hold it, but had they known that it was so lightly defended they might have proceeded otherwise. Taking Trinity's OTC arsenal would have provided them with much-needed weapons and ammunition.

Directly across from the front gates of TCD is the Bank of Ireland building, and at that very corner of College Green and Dame Street was where the Volunteers set up their reviewing stand for their parade on St Patrick's Day, 17 March 1916, barely a month before the Rising. At that parade, over 2,000 Volunteers marched past the reviewing stand, with the Commander of the Volunteers, Eoin MacNeill, taking the salute. As one looks upon the area, one should note that the DMP, and especially its G Division intelligence officers, closely watched the parade of armed Volunteers. The Castle authorities made no move to stop the parades, however, or to curtail the other route marches of the Volunteers and Citizen Army, fearing that to do so would actually incite some sort of rebellion.

As one stands in College Green, one is at the crossroads where Irish Citizen Army men and women took their posts on Monday morning. Some mustered at Liberty Hall under the command of Capt. Seán Connolly, then marched across O'Connell Bridge and turned right at the Green, down Dame Street to the City Hall. Another group, under the command of Major Michael Mallin, marched to St Stephen's Green from Liberty Hall, crossing Butt Bridge and making their way down College Street, then into College Green and down Grafton Street to St Stephen's Green.

The intent of the first group has never been entirely clear. Did they intend to take Dublin Castle with such a small force of fewer than 60 men and women? Most commentators feel that they did not intend to take the Castle, and though they shot a guard on the Castle gate and took the upper guardroom, they soon retreated to City Hall. A short walk down Dame Street from College Green will take one down the same route Connolly led his troops. And it was at City Hall that Connolly became the first of the Citizen Army or Volunteers to die in the Rising.

From College Green one can also walk to St Stephen's Green, another battle site in Dublin 2. Here one can visualise that the planning was not carried out nearly as well as at some of the other sites in Dublin. Mallin and his second in command, Countess Markievicz, posted some ICA men in houses overlooking the Green, while others dug trenches to cover the entrances. Mallin then dispatched men to take over nearby Harcourt Street Station and J. and T. Davy's pub in Portobello to the south-west of the Green. But the Green was a vulnerable position, particularly as the large building housing the Shelbourne Hotel overlooked it. The Shelbourne was on the corner of Kildare Street, just as it is today, but the trees in the Green were not nearly as tall in 1916, giving the British riflemen in the hotel an even better view of the Irish positions. Realising this, Mallin had his few men take some houses surrounding the Green and knock out their windows, then blocked the entire perimeter with barricades. Nevertheless, with so many large buildings overlooking the Green and not enough men and women to occupy a useful number of them, the rebels' position rapidly became untenable. As one stands in the Green and looks up at the Shelbourne, which the British occupied on Monday night, one can see just how exposed the Citizen Army position was, and the folly of taking the Green and not the surrounding buildings.

As one walks through the Green, one should take a look at the duck-keeper's house standing right beside one of the lakes, just as it did in 1916. At that time Jack Kearney was the duck-keeper, and both sides stopped firing twice a day so that he could feed the ducks!

Leaving the Green to the west, one should look, too, to the bullet-scarred façade of the Royal College of Surgeons building across the street, to where the St Stephen's Green garrison retreated on Tuesday. Look across the trees of the Green toward the Shelbourne Hotel and one can see just how exposed the front of the building is to fire from the Shelbourne. The College was under constant machine-gun fire all week, and the men and women of the garrison remained there until they surrendered on Sunday.

Dublin 2 provides a fine example of the difficulties of fighting in a city, for both attackers and defenders.

14–18 Aston Quay: McBirney's General Retailers; it had a reputation for the best linens. During the Rising British snipers fired from this location directly across the Liffey on Hopkins and Hopkins, jewellers, on Eden Quay.

26–50 Bishop Street, corner of Peter Row, touching Wexford Street: W. and R. Jacob's Biscuit Factory. A principal garrison during the Rising, under the command of Thomas MacDonagh. (See 2, 7a, 10–15 Peter Street, corner of Bishop Street at intersection of Aungier/Wexford Streets.)

The 2nd Battalion occupied Jacob's Biscuit Factory, almost a mile to the south of the GPO. Thomas McDonagh was O/C[190] and Major John MacBride[191] was second in command, with Michael O'Hanrahan next in line.

The building was a massive triangular structure filling most of the area between Peter Street and Bishop Street. It was difficult for the British to assault because it was surrounded by a labyrinth of streets, as well as myriad small houses that hindered the use of artillery.[192] It had two tall towers, which provided a view over much of the city. MacDonagh posted men in buildings in Camden Street, Wexford Street, Aungier Street and other streets in the area, making Jacob's an even more difficult target for the British military. As 150 men and women invaded the building, they informed the caretaker, Thomas Orr, and the watchman on duty, Henry Fitzgerald, what they were doing, and Orr called George Jacob and the manager, Mr Dawson. Both Jacob and Dawson came to the building where the Volunteers had assembled all the workers and placed them under guard. After a short time all the workers were released, but Orr remained in his apartment in the building for the duration of the Rising, and Fitzgerald stayed with him.[193]

Within hours of the garrison taking over, Volunteers on Wexford Street and Camden Street put a company of British soldiers travelling from Portobello Barracks to Dublin Castle to flight. Barmack's Malthouse in New Row/Fumbally Lane was taken, and four DMP policemen were detained there. Thereafter, the main action for the Jacob's garrison was sniping at Portobello Barracks and other military positions that were overlooked by the two towers.

McDonagh surrendered the garrison on Sunday about 2.30 p.m. after reading the unconditional surrender to the men. Because they had seen so little action during the week, and were kept in the dark as to the progress of the Rising, the surrender came as a surprise to many of the men and women of the garrison.

Currently the buildings house the Dublin Institute of Technology, with its main entrance on Peter Row at the corner of Aungier/Wexford Streets, and the National Archives, entered from Bishop Street. (The Dublin Institute of Technology entrance on Aungier Street at Peter Row is in Dublin 2, while the entrance to the National Archives on Bishop Street is in Dublin 8.)

Bride Street and Ross Road: Éamonn Ceannt and Thomas MacDonagh surrendered their garrisons to Major de Courcy Wheeler at this location.

34 Camden Street Lower: The first meeting of Fianna na hÉireann in Dublin took place here on 16 August 1909: Bulmer Hobson (president), Countess Markievicz (vice-president), Padraic Ó Riain (secretary)[194] and Liam Mellows (appointed National Organiser). Most members wore kilts with double-breasted dark green tunics, but senior officers wore breeches and leggings. Their headdress was the Baden-Powell Scout hat. They shared a motto with St Enda's: 'Strength in our arms, Truth on our lips, Purity in our hearts'.[195]

The following Fianna were killed or executed in the Rising:

Con Colbert (executed 8 May),[196] William Frank [Goban] Burke (South Dublin Union),[197] Brendan Donellan (South Dublin Union),[198] James Fox (St Stephen's Green),[199] Seán Healy (carrying dispatches from Jacob's),[200] Seán Heuston (executed 8 May),[201] Seán Howard (Four Courts),[202] James Kelly (died in the Mater Hospital; it is not known where he was shot),[203] Gerard Keogh (carrying dispatches, he was shot outside Trinity)[204] and Frederick Ryan (attacking the Russell Hotel from the College of Surgeons).[205]

The Volunteers used these premises as a drill hall. It was the fourth meeting place of K Company (3rd Battalion) after the Rising.[206]

42 Camden Street: Delahunt's pub. On Monday night the pub was seized by a party of Volunteers led by Lt James Shiels. When the British troops attacked the position, Richard O'Carroll was fatally wounded on Wednesday.[207] He was travelling along Camden Street when he was pulled from his motor-cycle combination by a British officer, Captain J.C. Bowen-Colthurst, and shot; he died nine days later in Portobello Hospital.[208] He was a member of Dublin Corporation, where he represented the Labour Party for several years, and was the general secretary of the Incorporated Brick and Stone Layers' Union. He left a widow and seven children, whose ages ranged from thirteen years to a few weeks. (See Rathmines Road/Portobello Barracks [Dublin 6].)

67 Camden Street Lower: Home of Councillor Richard O'Carroll, who was shot by Capt. J.C. Bowen-Colthurst. (See Rathmines Road, Portobello Barracks [Dublin 6].)

Castle Street (8 Bristol Buildings): Home of Florence Williams. She received the Military Medal from the British for her heroic medical treatment of men inside and outside Dublin Castle during the Rising.

16 Castle Street: Dublin Municipal Buildings, where Éamonn Ceannt worked in the city Treasurer's Department.

28 Charlemont Street: Home of Christopher Cathcart (10), who was killed on Easter Monday.[209] He died in Portobello Barracks from a gunshot wound, which he received while he was walking on the street. His family of eleven shared a six-roomed house with three other families, a total of 27 people.[210]

1–2 Clanwilliam Place, corner of Mount Street Lower: Clanwilliam House. The home of Miss Wilson, it was occupied during the Rising by elements of Éamon de Valera's Boland Mills garrison. (See Mount Street Bridge; 25 Northumberland Road [Dublin 4].) This became known as the battle of Mount Street Bridge, as the British troops were halted trying to cross the bridge into the city.[211] Clanwilliam House was on the city (east) side of the intersection and canal; St Stephen's Parochial Hall[212] was on the opposite (south) side of the Grand Canal, on the west side of the street, and was the most exposed of the three positions. Across from the Parochial Hall was the schoolhouse (the Volunteers were forced from this position early in the battle); 25 Northumberland Road was on the same side of the canal as the Parochial Hall but further to the south-east, about 300 yards towards Kingstown (Dún Laoghaire).

There were thirteen men in the three main outposts after the school was evacuated. Patrick J. Doyle was the O/C in the Parochial Hall; he and Joe Clarke, William Christian and James (P.B.?) McGrath held off the Sherwood Foresters from their position for as long as they could, and then fled to Percy Place, where they were captured. George Reynolds was O/C in Clanwilliam House; he was killed, as were Richard Murphy[213] and Patrick Doyle (company musketry instructor).[214] Willie Ronan, James Doyle,[215] Thomas Walsh and James Walsh survived.[216]

Reynolds was born in Dublin and educated in the Synge Street Christian Brothers' School. James Doyle (17) had his rifle shot out of his hands. Richard Murphy was killed as he fired from the middle windows, partially reclining on a chair. He was to be married a week later. The Walsh brothers were using Howth Mausers. At one point Patrick Doyle suddenly stopped firing and spoke no more; he was an inveterate talker, and when one of the Walshes shook him he fell over dead. A soda siphon was used to dowse a fire and it was shot out of Jim Walsh's hand. The survivors abandoned the burning house only when they ran out of ammunition.

> Time after time the enemy's attempts to cross the bridge were foiled by the magnificent heroism and gallantry of the small garrison of men in Clanwilliam House, supported by the three men in the Parochial Hall . . . The bridge presented a terrible spectacle, as did also the greater portion of Northumberland Road as it was actually a wriggling mass of khaki. The men whom I despatched to Roberts yard frustrated an attempted enemy advance on the canal bank made through a place known as Pembroke Cottages, and had they been able to get on the canal bank, they would have been able to direct an oblique and very effective fire on Clanwilliam House. Luckily, however, this was averted . . . on several occasions.[217]

In this engagement the Sherwood Foresters' casualties included three officers killed and fourteen wounded, and 216 other ranks killed or wounded. (See Mount Street Bridge for complete description of the battle and list of British killed.) Three-quarters of the Sherwood Foresters who fought at Mount Street Bridge had no more than three months' service and no training in street fighting.[218] 'A lot of their [British] losses were their own fault. They made sitting ducks for amateur riflemen.'[219] The inexperience of the British troops was most notably demonstrated when one of the first soldiers to fire a volley fell to the ground crying out 'I've been shot'. His company commander, Capt. Frank Pragnell, examined the boy and exclaimed angrily, 'Good God, man! You're not hit—it's only the recoil'.[220]

The Clanwilliam House of the Rising was destroyed, but the site is now occupied by a modern office building named Clanwilliam House.

College Green: Bank of Ireland; former Irish Parliament House of Lords. The Bank took possession on 24 August 1803 following the Act of Union. The Upper Chamber remains as it was when the building housed the Irish parliament. The reviewing stand for the Volunteers' Parade on St Patrick's Day 1916 was here. Over

2,000 Volunteers filed past MacNeill on the reviewing stand. They assembled at St Michael's and St John's Church for a 9.00 a.m. Mass, and then paraded at noon.[221]

College Green: Trinity College Dublin (TCD). Founded in 1592 by Queen Elizabeth I, it was built on land confiscated from the Priory of All Hallows. Its full name is the College of the Holy and Undivided Trinity.

Major Tate, the O/C of the Officer Training Corps (OTC) here, was away, but on Easter Monday Capt. Alton, Lt A.A. Luce of the Royal Irish Rifles (a Trinity professor who was at the time on leave from France owing to the measles) and Lt G. Waterhouse were in the college and took charge of the OTC.[222] Waterhouse, professor of German, took command. They ordered the gates to be shut, and with 50 men of the OTC prepared to defend the college until troops from the Curragh arrived. The expected attack never came.

The Volunteers and the Citizen Army made no attempt to capture it. It was the most central and commanding position in the city, and also had many military stores in the OTC depot, containing hundreds of rifles and thousands of rounds of ammunition. Ultimately some 4,000 British troops were billeted on the college grounds. Brig. Gen. W.H.M. Lowe made it his HQ during the Rising.

The provost at that time was J.P. Mahaffy.[223]

1 College Green (College Street): office of John R. Reynolds. This was also the first office used by Kathleen Clarke for the Irish Volunteers' Dependants' Fund prior to its amalgamation with the Irish National Aid Association, when it moved to 10 Exchequer Street. Clarke originally submitted the name 'Irish Republican Prisoners' Dependants' Fund', but that was not accepted by the censors and so no funds could be solicited in periodicals until the name was changed. Joseph McGrath was the first secretary of the combined Fund. Reynolds was ordered by the English military officials to deport himself to Coventry, England, and remained there until 1917. (See 10 Exchequer Street.)

7 College Green: The O'Connell Press printed *The Eye Opener*, a strongly nationalist paper. Thomas Dickson was the editor, and he was shot in the same tragic incident during the Rising as Francis Sheehy-Skeffington and Patrick MacIntyre. C.S. Andrews called *The Eye Opener* 'a scandal sheet which was non-political but directed at exposing the sex life of British officers'.[224] Others noted that *The Eye Opener* was 'rabidly loyalist'. (See Rathmines Road/Portobello Barracks [Dublin 6].)

12–14 College Green: Star Assurance Building. Headquarters for the Dublin Fire and Property Losses Association, which paid out compensation for property destroyed in the Rising.[225] The Association was established under the leadership of William Martin

Murphy. The British government agreed to indemnify approved claims. Compensation claims were made for looted stores and damages to both commercial and residential premises, vans and delivery vehicles. About 60 claims were submitted and approved, with over half coming from Moore Street traders. The rest were from premises in the immediate area. The deadline for submitting claims was 18 August 1916.

16 College Green: Office of Walter Hume, assessor of property destroyed in the Rising.[226]

Cork Hill (at Dame Street): Dublin City Hall. The Church of St Mary del Dam was originally built here; it was demolished to make way for the Royal Exchange building, completed in 1779. The building was taken over by Dublin Corporation as its City Hall in 1852. The city's motto is *Obedienta Civium Urbis Felicitas*, roughly translated as 'Happy the city whose citizens obey'. The Dublin City Council of the Dublin Corporation met here.

City Hall was held on Easter Monday 1916 by a garrison primarily from the Irish Citizen Army. Seán Connolly was the O/C of the Volunteer/ICA force.[227] He led a detachment of 40 ICA men and women from Liberty Hall through College Green and down Dame Street to the gate of Dublin Castle. They threw a home-made bomb (which failed to explode) at the policeman on duty at the gate of the Castle, then seized the Castle guardroom. When they charged the Castle gate, DMP Constable James O'Brien raised his arm and told them to halt. Connolly shot O'Brien in the head. Constable O'Brien was 48, had been a constable for 21 years and was the first casualty of the Rising. As they could not hold the Castle, they withdrew to the City Hall, which abutted the Castle Yard and its executive offices. Connolly also posted ICA men and women at the *Evening Mail* and *Daily Express* building at the corner of Parliament Street and Cork Hill, as well as throughout buildings in the Parliament Street and High Street area.

Later Connolly was killed on the roof, becoming the first rebel casualty of the Rising.

Cork Hill (and 1–3 Parliament Street): Henry and James, outfitters; outpost of City Hall garrison during the Rising.

Cork Hill (and 30–40 Parliament Street): *Mail and Express* office (sometimes called *Daily Express*); outpost of City Hall garrison during the Rising.

6 Crown Alley: Telephone Exchange. One of the early moves planned by the Volunteers was to disrupt communications by cutting telephone and telegraph links, thereby delaying the British ability to request assistance in Dublin and for

reinforcements to be summoned from England.[228] The telegraph connection to Dublin was broken at 12.20 p.m. on Monday, but the telephone system was kept working. Crucially, the five female operators kept the system operating after the Rising started, sleeping in the cellar and dodging bullets that came in the windows. The British did not arrive at the Exchange until 5 p.m. on Monday, but when they took over the system civilians could only receive calls, not initiate them.[229]

It was planned to take control of Dublin's telegraph and telephone systems, and to control British communication with England. Capt. Dermot Lynch was given the task of obtaining information about the telephone and telegraph systems in Dublin, and to determine how to disable them so that the British could not use them to call for reinforcements in Ireland or from England. Richard Mulcahy, an employee in the Post Office Department, was assigned to assist Lynch. Upon the outbreak of hostilities the following operations were planned.

- Mulcahy would cut and destroy the cable and telephone lines from Dublin to Belfast and England at Raheny. This was accomplished.
- George and Sam King were to destroy the signal junction points in Lombard Street and Palace Street, so as to destroy the lines from Dublin Castle to London. This, too, was accomplished.
- Martin King was to destroy the junction point outside the Crown Alley Telephone Exchange that would disable the Dublin telephone system.

Martin King was in command of the ICA contingent that was supposed to capture the exchange. It could have been occupied by the ICA early in the Rising, but they were deterred by a 'shawlie' who yelled, 'Go back, boys, the place is crammed with military'. Because they did not wait, King, who was detailed to cut the wires here, could not find them, so he reported to his post at St Stephen's Green.[230] The exchange remained in operation all Monday afternoon with no guards and the Volunteers could easily have taken it. Finally, it was taken over by the British about five hours later.

Dawson Street: The Mansion House, the official residence of the lord mayor of Dublin since 1713. Lord Mayor James M. Gallagher called Dublin 'Louvain by the Liffey' after the destruction of the Rising.

2 Dawson Street: Irish Volunteer HQ from late 1914, and HQ of the Dublin Brigade at the time of the Rising. (See 144 and 206 Great Brunswick Street, 41 Kildare Street.) The Fianna also had an office here. Michael O'Hanrahan worked here as a clerk before the Rising.

The *Irish Volunteer*, edited by Eoin MacNeill, was printed here. In an early issue Padraic Pearse wrote: 'We want recruits because we are absolutely determined to take action, the moment action becomes a duty . . .'.[231] The paper was suppressed and was subsequently printed by a pro–Unionist printer in Belfast. The last issue was dated 22 April 1916. (It was said that the Orangemen of Belfast were 'not loyal to the Crown so much as to the half-crown' and they would always print whatever was sent to them with payment.)

On 19 April 1916, MacNeill drafted an order in response to the 'Castle Document' that included the following instructions:

> Your object will be to preserve the arms and organisation of the Irish Volunteers, and the measures taken by you will be directed to that purpose.
>
> In general you will arrange that your men defend themselves and each other in small groups so placed that they may be best able to hold out.
>
> Each group must be provided with sufficient supplies of food, or be certain of access to such supplies.[232]

(See Larkfield, Kimmage, The Castle Document [Dublin 6W].)

On 22 April 1916, the last issue of the *Irish Volunteer* printed a notice that signalled to Dublin Castle an imminent manoeuvre by the Volunteers:

> Arrangements are now near completion in all the more important Brigade areas for the holding of a very interesting series of manoeuvres at Easter. In some instances the arrangements contemplate a one or two-day bivouac. As for Easter, the Dublin programme may well stand as a model for others.[233]

Dublin Castle: Construction began in 1204 under the orders of King John. The entrance used to be on Castle Street; now the main route is on Lord Edward Street. The statue of 'Justice' is above the old Castle Gate; small holes are drilled in her scales to drain water so that they don't become 'unbalanced' in the rain:

> The Statue of Justice
> Mark well her station
> Her face to the Castle
> And her arse to the Nation.

When the Rising began the Castle was nearly empty of British troops; it was a bank holiday and many had gone to the Fairyhouse Races. (The Irish Grand National was run there on Easter Monday and was won by All Sorts.) As the Rising continued, the Castle filled up with troops and was not attacked by the rebels.

There has never been consensus on the Volunteers' intent in attacking Dublin Castle.[234] Many have contended that it was never the intention of the Volunteers and

ICA to seize the Castle, as they did not believe that it would be easy to capture, and it would be very difficult (if not impossible) to hold.[235] *Irish War News* reported that 'the Castle was attacked'.[236] Others felt that the Castle could be taken but not held, and it couldn't be destroyed, as there was a Red Cross Hospital there.[237] Some hold that attempts to take the Castle were a designed part of the Rising but were unsuccessful.[238] Finally, still others conclude that the reduced strength as a result of the countermanding order precluded its capture.[239]

On the first day of the Rising, Baron Wimborne, the lord lieutenant, issued the following proclamation:

> Whereas, an attempt, instigated and designed by the foreign enemies of our King and Country to incite rebellion in Ireland and thus endanger the safety of the United Kingdom, has been made by a reckless, though small, body of men, who have been guilty of insurrectionary acts in the City of Dublin:
>
> Now, we, Ivor Churchill, Baron Wimborne, Lord Lieutenant-General and Governor-General of Ireland, do hereby warn all His Majesty's subjects that the sternest measures are being, and will be, taken for the prompt suppression of the existing disturbances, and the restoration of order:
>
> And we do hereby enjoin all loyal and law-abiding citizens to abstain from any acts of conduct which might interfere with the action of the Executive Government, and, in particular, we warn all citizens of the danger of unnecessarily frequenting the streets or public places, and of assembling in crowds.
>
> Given under our seal, this 24th day of April, 1916.

A sniper in the Bermingham Tower was responsible for 53 rebel casualties before he was killed on Saturday.

The Church of the Most Holy Trinity in the Castle has been a Catholic church since 1943. It was the viceroy's chapel at the time of the Rising.

Earlsfort Terrace: During the Rising, 3rd Battalion A Company mustered here under Capt. Joseph O'Connor, who led his men to Grand Canal Street, Upper Lotts Road and elsewhere.[240] Thirty-four men of 3rd Battalion C Company mustered here under Capt. Simon Donnelly.[241] Donnelly marched his men to Upper Mount Street, where they met Michael Malone and George Reynolds and proceeded on to Boland's Bakery.

Earlsfort Terrace (at corner of Hatch Street): University College Dublin (UCD). Founded in 1851 as the Catholic University of Ireland on St Stephen's Green. Padraic Pearse attended Catholic University and took a BA in 1901. He was soon called to the Bar, but practised little as a barrister. (Later he described the lawyer's craft as 'the most ignoble . . . the most wicked of all professions'.[242])

3 Lower Erne Place: Home of John Kirwan (15), who was killed in the Rising.[243]

6 Essex Street West: Home of a civilian, Henry B. Knowles, killed at his home during the Rising while watching the fighting in the streets.

Exchange Street Lower: Church of Saints Michael and John. On 17 March 1916 over 2,000 Volunteers assembled here and then marched to College Green, where they filed past Eoin MacNeill on the reviewing stand. They assembled here for a 9.00 a.m. Mass, and then paraded at noon.[244] The sound of the Angelus bell ringing from this church over the River Liffey was heard by the ICA as they marched up Dame Street to seize City Hall.

10 Exchequer Street: Irish National Aid Association. Initially under the direction of George Gavan-Duffy and Alderman Patrick Corrigan, it combined with Kathleen Clarke's Irish Volunteers' Dependants' Fund to form the Irish National Aid and Volunteers' Dependants' Fund.[245] (See 1 College Green.)

> On 17th June [1916] Mrs. Clarke suggested that a fund should be opened to help the dependants of Volunteers and that the fund should be known as the Volunteers' Dependants Fund. It was opened by a subscription from Mrs. Clarke of either £20 or £25, and from my own family and my own relatives and friends in Dublin who helped me I obtained about £15.
>
> Paddy Holohan obtained something like £30 from the area that he had visited . . .
>
> As there were two funds being collected for the Volunteers' dependants, one formed by Mrs. Clarke known as the Volunteers' Dependants Fund, and the other known as the National Aid Fund, there was a conference called by the committees of both Funds and it was decided to amalgamate the two Funds, but no definite decision was then arrived at.
>
> At that conference I met Greg Murphy who was then Leinster Treasurer of the I.R.B., and in the course of conversation he told me that he would try and get some others of the officials of the I.R.B. to have it re-organised, but I do not remember anything further about the organization until some months afterwards.[246]

Clarke originally submitted the name 'Irish Republican Prisoners' Dependants' Fund', but that was not accepted by the censors and therefore no funds could be solicited in periodicals. The name was then changed to the 'Irish Volunteers' Dependants' Fund', which was deemed acceptable by the censors. Joseph McGrath was the first secretary of the combined fund.

Clarke did not initially consider this proposed merger a sensible one. She had come to see the IVDF as a sacred torch passed to her by her dead husband.[247] She saw it as republican property and would not allow it to merge with a fund that was partly administered by non-republican parliamentarians. She insisted, therefore, that a number of personnel whom she considered parliamentarian be removed from the INAA before she would merge her organisation with it. The National Aid fund may have been running a little low, however, as Nancy Wyse-Power later alleged that it was when 'the Volunteer Aid funds ran out' that the merger of the two organisations occurred.[248] Thus, when the Irish-American group Clan na nGael sent two delegates to Ireland with a substantial sum of money and a merger proposal, the financial position of the National Aid fund might have been what forced them into negotiations with Clarke's Volunteers' Dependants' Fund. After the negotiations, in September the Inspector General of the RIC reported the merger of the two groups as follows:

> The Irish National Aid Association and the Irish Volunteer Dependants' Fund were amalgamated during the month at the instigation of two American delegates—A. Murphy and J. Gill—who brought over a contribution of £5,000 collected under the patronage of Cardinal Farley of New York. The amalgamated fund now amounts to £28,000 . . . Therefore it may be assumed that it is under Sinn Féin control.[249]

Whatever the financial situation of the National Aid fund, it is quite clear by her account and that of the Inspector General that the merger occurred on Clarke's terms.[250] The new organisation was called the Irish National Aid and Volunteers' Dependants' Fund (INAVDF).

This was the first 'real' office: Kathleen Clarke, president; Áine Ceannt, vice-president;[251] Máire Nic Shiubhlaigh, treasurer; E. MacRaghnaill, secretary; Margaret Pearse, Muriel MacDonagh, Eily O'Hanrahan,[252] Madge Daly[253] and Lila Colbert, directors.

20 Fitzwilliam Square: Home of Dr R. Travers Smith, visiting physician to Richmond Hospital, where he treated casualties of the Rising.

32 Fitzwilliam Square: Home of Miss Meade; converted to a field hospital during the Rising.

35 Fitzwilliam Square: Home of Miss Fletcher; converted to a field hospital during the Rising.

69 Fitzwilliam Square: Home of A.A. McConnell, Ireland's first neurosurgeon and a

surgeon at Richmond Hospital, where he treated casualties of the Rising.

13 Fleet Street: Wood Printing Works. The office of *New Ireland*, edited by David Gwynn and then by Patrick J. (Paddy) Little. Prior to the Rising, *New Ireland* was the 'official' organ of the Redmondite National Volunteers under Little. Staff included Austin Clarke, Mario Esposito, Frank Gallagher,[254] Kathleen Goodfellow, Fred Higgins, Peadar Kearney, Stephen MacKenna, Séamus McManus, Andrew Malone, Jack Morrow, Liam Ó Briain,[255] Padraic Ó Conaire, Rory O'Connor, Michael Scott, Liam Slattery and Jack B.Yeats.

New Ireland was the first to publish the 'Castle Document' just before the Rising. According to Little's account, Rory O'Connor produced the document at a meeting at Dr Séamus O'Kelly's house at 53 Rathgar Road.[256] Alderman Thomas Kelly read it at a Dublin Corporation meeting on 19 April, and he indicated that he had received it from Little.[257] (See 53 Rathgar Road [Dublin 6]; Kimmage, Larkfield, 'The Castle Document' [Dublin 6W].)

2 Fownes Street: Lawlor's. This was a money exchange that also sold guns and ammunition. Prior to the Rising, Volunteers 'thronged' Lawlor's, buying bandoliers, canteens, belts, haversacks, swords, bayonets and all sorts of 'military' material.

21 Fownes Street: Home of Patrick MacIntyre; he was 38 when he was killed along with Francis Sheehy-Skeffington in Portobello Barracks during the Rising, and he is buried in Mount Jerome Cemetery. He was editor of *The Searchlight*, which was noted as a 'nationalist newspaper that was rabidly anti-German'. During the Lockout of 1913 he edited the anti-striker paper, *The Toiler*. (See Rathmines Road/Portobello Barracks [Dublin 6].)

Fumbally Lane (off Clanbrassil Street at New Row): Barmack's Malthouse. An outpost of the Jacob's 2nd Battalion Volunteers. Peadar Kearney (Peadar Ó Cearnaigh) was one of a group that seized Barmack's. Upon being informed of the surrender, he was one of those who argued for a mass breakout to the hills.

7 Fumbally Lane: Home of Eleanor Warbrook (15), who was shot in the jaw during the Rising and died in the Meath Hospital.[258] One of seven children, she is buried in Mount Jerome Cemetery.

Grafton Street (at Trinity College Dublin): Ponsonby and Gibbs, booksellers. Irish Volunteer companies bought the *English Infantry Manual, 1911* here, for the price of one shilling. Other large sellers were the *King's Regulations* and *Small Wars: Their Principle and Practice*.

1 Grafton Street: Home of the provost of Trinity College. During the Rising Trinity's provost was Dr J.P. Mahaffy, who memorably wrote on one occasion: 'In Ireland the inevitable never happens, the unexpected always'.[259]

14 Grafton Street: Office of Trinity College Officers' Training Corps Commemorative Fund, whose secretary was Lewis Beatty.

22a Grafton Street: D.A. Stoker, jewellers. Stoker was in the GPO buying stamps when it was overrun in the Rising. On 3 May, the evening before she married Joseph Plunkett in Kilmainham Gaol, Grace Gifford bought her wedding ring here.

Grand Canal Street: Sir Patrick Dun's Hospital. Sir Arthur Ball was a surgeon here in 1916. The official records indicate that 79 military and 69 rebels and civilians were treated here during the Rising; ten of the military and eleven of the civilians were either dead on arrival or died thereafter. Almost all of the casualties were a result of the fighting around Mount Street Bridge.

Grand Canal Docks at Ringsend Road: Boland's Flour Mills. De Valera's 3rd Battalion occupied the Mills, but it was the Bakery that was the area's centre of operations.[260]

Grand Canal Street: Boland's Bakery. This was an important strategic stronghold because it covered the railway line out of the Westland Row terminus. Éamon de Valera's HQ was actually in a small dispensary next door, at the corner of Grand Canal Street and Great Clarence Street (now Macken Street).[261] De Valera knew every inch of the territory and did not reduce his area of responsibility, though Eoin MacNeill's order greatly reduced the men who mustered. De Valera has been depicted as one who scorned danger almost to the point of recklessness. He had the great confidence of all his men that he was a leader who was capable of the unexpected stroke that would extricate them from danger. 'De Valera certainly knew every inch of the area under his command ... It was characteristic of de Valera to attempt the impossible and he made no reduction in the scale of his operations notwithstanding the fact that less than one-fifth of the men allotted to his command had responded to the mobilization order. He might have sat down in Boland's and waited to be dug out of it, but that was not his way.'[262] In contrast, others held that de Valera's leadership at Boland's Mills was questionable.[263]

On Thursday afternoon, shelling from a one-pounder gun taken from HMY *Helga* began from the corner of Percy Lane.[264] De Valera ordered Capt. Michael Cullen to lead a party to raise a flag on top of a tall, disused water tower of the abandoned Ringsend Distillery just north of the railroad line, and this attracted the shelling. (The first shell from the gun on Percy Lane missed the tower and landed in the water near the *Helga*. Thinking she was under fire, the *Helga* fired back. That was soon sorted out.) The tower was hit, rupturing the water tank and almost drowning the defenders, but the British had been fooled and this saved Boland's.[265]

De Valera had not slept during the early days of the Rising and for two days prior to it. By Thursday/Friday he was exhausted: 'I can't trust the men—they'll leave their posts if I fall asleep, if I don't watch them'. When Lt James FitzGerald assured his O/C that he'd sit by him, de Valera relented and fell asleep immediately. Soon he awoke screaming, 'Set fire to the railway!'[266] De Valera insisted that papers be dipped in whiskey and used to set fire to the waiting rooms and rolling stock, but another officer, Capt. John McMahon, O/C of B Company, 'eventually persuaded de Valera to reason and the fires were put out. De Valera quickly regained his composure'.[267] Late on Friday de Valera ordered the bakery to be evacuated, but there was nowhere for the Volunteers to go, so they reoccupied it and remained in their positions until their surrender on Sunday.[268]

Following the garrison's surrender, de Valera was taken into captivity and held in the Weights and Measures Department of Ballsbridge Town Hall on Merrion Road. This was on the opposite side of the city to the main body of arrested Volunteers detained in Kilmainham Gaol or Richmond Barracks. He remained in Ballsbridge during the first of the executions and was transferred to Richmond Barracks only on 8 May. (See Richmond Barracks [Dublin 8].)

Grattan Street: Éamon de Valera surrendered the Boland's Volunteers here. He surrendered to Capt. E.J. Hitzen, O/C of the 5th Lincolnshire Regiment.[269]

1–8 Great Brunswick Street (now Pearse Street) (corner of Townsend Street): Dublin Metropolitan Police (G-Division) HQ.

27 Great Brunswick Street (now Pearse Street): Pearse family home. The father, James, was a monument sculptor and sculpted many of the figures crowning Dublin buildings. He was a great believer in personal freedom, as well as national freedom from England, and wrote a pamphlet on it in 1886.[270] Emily Susanna Fox, his first wife, whom he married in 1864, bore James three children: a daughter, Mary Emily, and later two others, of whom only James Vincent survived infancy. Margaret Brady was his second wife; he married her in October 1877. Margaret was a nineteen-year-old girl who worked in a local stationer's shop that he frequented. Her family originally hailed from an Irish-speaking district of County Meath and had been forced by the disastrous effects of the Famine to migrate to Dublin in search of work. There they had become moderately successful, eventually coming to hold several pieces of property in a working-class area of the city, where Margaret was born. Despite her family's initial reluctance to see her marry someone so recently widowed, with two children and somewhat older than her, the wedding eventually went ahead. She bore him four children, two boys and two girls: Margaret, Patrick (Padraic),[271] William (Willie)[272] and Mary Bridget (Brigid). At the time of the births of Padraic and William, baptismal records show the family name still spelled 'Pierce'. Padraic was born here on 10 November 1879, and was christened Patrick Henry Pierce after the American patriot. He had a cast in his left eye, and was quite aware of it; he always had his profile photos taken from his right side.[273] William was born here in 1881. It is now home to the Ireland Institute.

144 Great Brunswick Street (now Pearse Street): St Andrew's Club. The 3rd Battalion of Volunteers had been instructed to assemble here prior to the Rising. De Valera was also using this as his HQ. The building is now part of Dublin City Library and Archive (138–144 Pearse Street). The head of Lord Nelson's statue, shot at during the Rising, is now on display in the Library. Lord Nelson's Pillar was blown up in 1966. (See Sackville Street Lower [Dublin 1].)

180 Great Brunswick Street (now Pearse Street): 'Red Hand' division of the Ancient Order of Hibernians. (See 28 Frederick Street North, 44 Rutland Square [Dublin 1].)

206 Great Brunswick Street (now Pearse Street): HQ of the Dublin Brigade for a short time in 1914, and of the 3rd Battalion of the Irish Volunteers at the time of the Rising. (See 2 Dawson Street, 41 Kildare Street.)

Great Clarence Street South (now Macken Street): Peadar Macken (37) was elected an alderman in the North Dock Ward in 1913. An officer during the Rising, he reprimanded a Volunteer who kept ignoring the order for silence.[274] The truculent Volunteer shot him through the heart.[275] His body was taken to the dispensary in Grand Canal Street where de Valera had his headquarters and was buried in the dispensary yard,[276] then reinterred in Glasnevin Cemetery. At the time, the street on which he fought was named Great Clarence Street, but it was renamed Macken Street in his honour.

10 Hackett's Court: Home of Philip Walsh (11), who was shot in the abdomen during the Rising and died in Mercer's Hospital.[277] He is buried in Glasnevin Cemetery.

Harcourt Street (and corner of Cuffe Street): Little's pub, one of the key defence points for St Stephen's Green during the Rising.

6 Harcourt Street: Home of John, Cardinal Newman (1801–90). In 1910 Arthur Griffith acquired permanent rooms here and thereafter it was the headquarters of Sinn Féin and the Inghínidhe na hÉireann branch of Cumann na mBan. Griffith disapproved of the Rising, and after he heard of MacNeill's countermanding order he hoped that that would prevent it. There is some evidence, however, that when it was clear that the Rising would go on he sought to join the rebels, but was told his most important work lay ahead.[278]

The Volunteers used the building as a drill hall before and after the Rising.

Harcourt Street (and 103–104 St Stephen's Green): Russell Hotel; occupied by the British during the Rising. Margaret Skinnider, a mathematics teacher originally from Glasgow, was wounded on Wednesday of Easter Week when she was in a party sent to set fire to the hotel. Wounded three times (in the right arm, right side and back), she was carried back to the College of Surgeons on St Stephen's Green by William (Bill) Partridge. At Christmas 1915 she had brought detonators to Ireland on the boat from Glasgow. She wrote *Doing My Bit for Ireland.* Writing about her role as a sniper on the roof of the College of Surgeons, she said: 'It was dark there, full of smoke, a din of firing, but it was good to be in the action; more than once I saw a man I aimed at fall'.[279]

Harcourt Street Station: This was a terminus of the Dublin and South-Eastern Railway (along with Westland Row Station), in use from its construction in 1859 until 1959. It served as the terminus of the railway from Dublin to Bray in County Wicklow.

This major railway station was of strategic importance. It was the rebels' plan to occupy it and prevent British reinforcements being brought from the south to Dublin. Taken early in the Rising by a detachment of the ICA under Capt. Richard McCormack, it was evacuated almost immediately because it was indefensible.[280]

12 Harrington Street: Home of Thomas Dickson, editor of *The Eye Opener*; killed along with Francis Sheehy-Skeffington, he is buried in Glasnevin Cemetery. (See College Green; Rathmines Road/Portobello Barracks [Dublin 6].)

Hatch Street: A detachment of the ICA under Sgt Frank Robbins was to defend this area and build barricades all around St Stephen's Green.[281]

20 Hatch Street: Home of Dr Ella Webb, the Lady District Superintendent of the St John's Ambulance Brigade of Ireland since 1914. She helped to set up an emergency hospital at the Brigade's headquarters at 14 Merrion Square during the Rising and cycled daily through the firing line to visit the hospital.[282] Dr Webb was later awarded an MBE for her work for the St John's Ambulance Brigade.[283]

4 High Street: Home of Freddie Ryan (17). A member of the St Stephen's Green garrison, he was killed while trying to set fire to the Russell Hotel, in the same raid in which Margaret Skinnider was wounded.[284]

Holles Street: National Maternity Hospital, which opened to all during the Rising. Known usually as Holles Street Hospital, it opened in 1884. Elizabeth O'Farrell later worked here as a midwife.

41 Kildare Street: first HQ of the Irish Volunteers, 1913–14, before a move to 206 Great Brunswick Street in 1914, and then to 2 Dawson Street, which was the HQ of the Dublin Brigade at the time of the Rising.

The first Provisional Committee of the Irish Volunteers operated from here. The formal executive of 30 was established after the Volunteer Convention of 1914. The affiliations noted are those at the time of the inception of the Volunteers (November 1913), not as they became later:[285] Piaras Béaslaí (IRB); Roger Casement; Éamonn Ceannt (IRB); Con Colbert (IRB); James Deakin; Seán Fitzgibbon; Liam Gogan;[286] John Gore (United Irish League, Irish Parliamentary Party); Bulmer Hobson (IRB); Michael J. Judge (Ancient Order of Hibernians); Laurence J. Kettle (Ancient Order of Hibernians, United Irish League, Irish Parliamentary Party); Tom Kettle (United Irish League, Irish Parliamentary Party); James Lenehan (Ancient Order of Hibernians); Michael Lonergan (IRB);[287] Thomas MacDonagh; Eoin MacNeill; Seán MacDermott (IRB); Peadar Macken (IRB); Éamon Martin (IRB);[288] Liam Mellows (IRB); Col. Maurice Moore (United Irish League, Irish Parliamentary Party); Seámus O'Connor (IRB); Colm Ó Lochlainn (IRB);[289] The Ó Rahilly; Peter O'Reilly (Ancient Order of Hibernians); Padraic Ó Riain (IRB);[290] Robert Page (IRB); Padraic Pearse;[291] Joseph Plunkett; John P. Walsh (Ancient Order of Hibernians); and Peadar White.

King Street South: Gaiety Theatre. The manager in 1916 was Charles Hyland, whose son, C. Hanchette Hyland (29), was killed while looking out the back door of his home at 3 Percy Place (near Northumberland Road [Dublin 4]). The Carl Rosa Opera Company often played here. The D'Oyly Carte Opera Company opened on 24 April 1916.

Leeson Park: Litton Hall; auxiliary hospital during the Rising.[292]

89–90 Leeson Street Lower: Catholic University School, run by the Marist Community. Fr Watters was the president. He was killed at the Clanwilliam House fighting at Mount Street Bridge.

Lombard Street East: Peter Lanigan's timber yard. On St Patrick's Day 1858, James

Stephens established the Irish *Revolutionary* Brotherhood here, but the name was soon changed to the Irish *Republican* Brotherhood.

29 Longwood Avenue: Home of James Grace, who fought at 25 Northumberland Road in the Rising and survived.[293]

Mercer Street: Mercer's Hospital. The street and hospital were named after Mary Mercer, who founded the hospital for the poor in 1734. It was built on the site of the ancient St Stephen's Church and the even older leper hospital. Sixteen dead civilians and 278 injured non-combatants as well as four dead and five wounded British soldiers were treated here during the Rising.

14 Merrion Square: HQ of the St John's Ambulance Brigade of Dublin.[294]
The training and volunteer work of the St John's Ambulance Brigade stems from the Venerable Order of St John, which had its beginnings in an eleventh-century Jerusalem hospital built to care for pilgrims. In 1903 Dr (later Sir) John Lumsden formed the first division in Ireland at the Guinness Brewery, and it became known as the St James Gate division. In 1905 the City of Dublin Division was formed, the first unit open to the public for membership; in 1909 women were allowed to join the ranks, with the formation of the first nursing division.

The Brigade was involved in many major events in Irish history, including treating casualties from the clashes during the Lockout of 1913. From 1914 many members served in World War I, providing medical aid for those injured in combat. The Brigade became most prominent in Dublin during the Rising, however, when it treated casualties on both sides and fed and cared for evacuees.

17–18 Molesworth Street: Masonic Lodge, also known as the Freemason's Hall. During the Rising it was occupied by the Volunteers and surrounded by the British. The British withdrew and the Volunteers abandoned the hall. There was Masonic influence on both sides.

25–26 Molesworth Street: Buswell's Hotel. Roger Casement, Erskine Childers and Bulmer Hobson met here at the end of June 1914 to plan the landing of guns at Howth.

Mount Street Bridge (over Grand Canal): This was in Éamon de Valera's 3rd Battalion area.[295] Some of the heaviest fighting during the Rising took place here on Wednesday 26 April 1916.[296] (See 1, 2 Clanwilliam Place, Grand Canal Street; 25 Northumberland Road [Dublin 4], Pembroke Road [Dublin 4].) (The Bridge crosses between Dublin 2 and Dublin 4.)

Among the first British troops called to Ireland were the Sherwood Foresters.[297] Known officially as the Nottinghamshire and Derbyshire Regiment, it was created in 1881 in England by combining the 45th (Nottinghamshire) and 95th (Derbyshire) Regiments of Foot.[298] On 25 April 'two infantry brigades were sent, the 176th and the 178th . . . Each brigade was made up of two battalions of the Sherwood Foresters, and as [Captain Arthur] Lee noted, "most of our 'men' were merely boys, Derby Recruits, who had been in uniform about 6 or 8 weeks".'[299] The Foresters left their training barracks at Watford, Hertfordshire, and travelled on troop trains to Liverpool. Upon arrival, they and their sparse gear were loaded onto two cargo ships: the 2/5th and 2/6th battalions aboard the HMS *Munster*, and the 2/7th and 2/8th on the SS *Patriotic*. The 2/8th Battalion had been assigned four Lewis guns (light machine-guns used during World War I), two of which had been loaded on the trains with them as they travelled to Liverpool. When they arrived, however, three companies were to be sent immediately to Ireland, while D Company and the guns were left behind for the next transport. Lt Col. W.C. Oates noted this fatal mistake:

> The value of the presence of even two of these guns in Dublin next day would have been incalculable, and the British Army seems fated to have its work blocked or rendered as difficult as possible by officials dressed with a little brief authority, whose orders may not be questioned and who rarely have to answer for after results.[300]

Tired, seasick and disoriented after their overnight voyage from Liverpool, the Foresters disembarked on Wednesday morning in Kingstown (now Dún Laoghaire), where their officers issued live ammunition for the first time but ensured that the men pointed their rifles safely out to sea as they charged their weapons—just in case of accidents amongst such unskilled soldiers.[301] The officers, all volunteers from English public schools, breakfasted at St George's harbourside yacht club, while the men opened tins of bully beef and biscuits. Some of the men thought that they had landed in France. They were excited, keen, anxious and apprehensive. They were raw troops,[302] many of whom had never fired a live cartridge, had had training only in trench fighting, had left their machine-guns in Liverpool, had no grenades at first, and were completely overwhelmed by urban/street fighting.[303] One column headed to the Royal Hospital, Kilmainham, by way of the Stillorgan–Donnybrook–South Circular Road route and reached it without incident.[304] The other column was ordered to head to Trinity College and marched into a massacre.[305]

The Sherwoods marched from Kingstown up to Sandymount by Merrion Road, then through Pembroke Road (see Pembroke Road, Carrisbrook House [Dublin 4]), then finally into Northumberland Road. The march to Dublin was not easy, as each of the men carried full packs, weapons and 130 rounds of ammunition. The locals were not afraid of the British, though. Indeed, they seemed welcoming towards the Foresters, bringing them water to refresh them on their hot trek.[306] Along their march through the suburbs, the Foresters learned valuable pieces of information about the rebels' positions and strength. One cyclist with the 178th Brigade, Corporal B.C. Webster, said:

> We heard startling accounts of the rising of the rebels, half Dublin was on fire we were told ... Our orders were to take no prisoners, 'Shoot them all' was the order ... Some said there were 15,000 Sinn Féiners in Dublin, while others were lower estimates.[307]

They were told to be on the lookout for the green uniforms of the rebels, particularly along Northumberland Road, which was to be the site of the Foresters' biggest losses.

The column continued to advance, with C Company (Capt. Pragnell) in the lead, accompanied by the O/C, Lt Colonel Fane, followed by A Company (Capt. Wright) and B Company (Capt. Hanson), with the reserve, D Company (Capt. Cooper), bringing up the rear. C Company advanced in a box formation, with the front platoon in line and the following platoons advancing along the pavement in column, the intention being that they could cover any side streets and clear houses, if required.

At about 12.25 p.m. the leading platoon came under fire from the defenders of 25 Northumberland Road, Lt Michael Malone and James Grace. About 200 yards further down the road, other Volunteers waited in the schoolhouse and Parochial Hall, and about 100 yards further along on the other side of the canal still more Volunteers were in Clanwilliam House, which commanded Mount Street Bridge. All these buildings had been prepared for resistance, with barricades on the lower floors and loopholed windows, and were manned by thirteen Volunteers of the 3rd Battalion who were excellent marksmen with plenty of ammunition.[308] From a military viewpoint, Clanwilliam House could hardly have been better sited, with a commanding view up Northumberland Road and across Mount Street Bridge.

Among the first British officers to fall was Capt. F.C. Dietrichsen, most likely by the fire of Malone and Grace. Soon other officers were falling, as the Volunteers picked them off from the upper floors. The loss of the officers caused great confusion amongst the raw Robin Hoods, some of whom had only been in uniform for three months and almost none of whom had ever previously been under fire.

The confusion mounted as the inexperienced troops and officers struggled to pinpoint the enemy positions, and a number of houses were stormed at bayonet point without success. The soldiers fell back to the opposite side of the road, not yet knowing whence the shots had come. They deployed along Northumberland Road, returning fire when they could. But street-fighting with rifles is an ineffective response to a well-positioned urban enemy behind good and organised cover. Pte James Woods of the 2/7th Battalion recalled:

We arrived in Dublin about 1 o'clock, as near as I can remember, and immediately came into action. Really, we are lucky to be able to tell the tale, as no sooner had we halted and got down ready we were fired on from all quarters. We retired for a few yards amidst a veritable hail of bullets. The worst part of the job was, we did not know who our enemy were, with the result that we had to be careful when we fired.[309]

Soon after 5 p.m. another attempt to storm the house at No. 25 was undertaken, with the use of grenades brought up from the nearby Elm Park bombing school. Malone and Grace were in the process of retreating from the house when the door was blown in. Grace dived into the cellar and took cover, escaping the grenades thrown in after him. Malone was shot dead as he descended the stairs. Malone and Grace had held the battalion at bay for some five hours and inflicted heavy casualties on the troops.

With No. 25 taken, the battalion was now faced with fire coming from the direction of the school buildings further down Northumberland Road and from Clanwilliam House across the bridge. Col. Oates of the 2/8th Battalion hastily outlined a plan to rush across the bridge and storm Clanwilliam House, having received orders that a flanking move was not permitted. The plan seemed to be rather basic and similar to those that had ended with such heavy casualties for the 2/7th throughout the day. A combined force of attackers stormed across Mount Street Bridge, throwing grenades into the windows of Clanwilliam House. The fight for the house was even more severe than for 25 Northumberland Road, as more and more British tried to advance across the bridge and were cut down. The British infantry had been trained to advance towards enemy lines on the sound of a whistle; it was the only tactic they knew. Now, every twenty minutes, on the sound of a British Army whistle, the Robin Hoods again charged their enemy. Later, some described the British advance as looking like an oncoming 'khaki serpent'.[310] Finally, a shower of grenades had the unintended consequence of igniting the gas supply to the houses, and soon both Clanwilliam House and the adjoining house were ablaze.

The British side suffered their greatest casualties of the Rising here: three officers were killed and fourteen others wounded, while fourteen other ranks were killed and another 216 wounded. The British gave full credit to the defensive positions and the courage of the Volunteers, saying after the Rising that if every position had been defended with such skill and determination the insurrection would have lasted three times as long.[311]

The British dead were:[312]

Capt. and Adjutant Frederick Christian Dietrichsen
Lt Percy C. Perry
2Lt William Victor Hawken

Pte John Blissitt
Pte Joseph H. Bradford
Pte Charles T. Dixon
Pte Alfred G. Elliott
Pte Ernest Farnsworth
Pte Joseph Goss
Pte Arthur Holbrook
Cpl Charles Hoyle
Pte Percy Jeffs
Pte William Lang
Pte Thomas Miller
Pte A. Sibley
Pte Walter A. Tunnicliffe
Pte George Wylde

Besides the above, twelve men were so seriously wounded that they were discharged from the Army. As Dublin was considered 'Home service', the men killed or discharged earned no medals, as only overseas service counted in this regard. The twelve men discharged as a result of their wounds did qualify for a Silver War Badge, which was intended to show that they had 'done their bit' for King and Country.

As a 'reward' for their gallantry, troops from the Sherwood Foresters were chosen to form the firing squads for the leaders of the Rising who were executed in Kilmainham Gaol. Brigadier J. Young was in charge at the Gaol and laid down the procedures for the executions; the first prisoner to be executed was paraded at 3.30 a.m. to face a firing squad of twelve men. The commander of the firing squad was Major Charles Harold Heathcote, second in command of the regiment. Major Heathcote was sent to Richmond Barracks to take charge of the prisoners and their effects and escort them to Kilmainham. He took with him B Company and Capt. Orr and Lt Maine (acting as Adjutant). They were under the command of Provost Marshall Col. Fraser. As is customary in firing squads, eleven of the soldiers had live rounds in their weapons and one round was a blank. The officers loaded the weapons for the soldiers, so no soldier knew whether his weapon contained the blank round or a live one. If necessary, the officer commanding shot the prisoner in the head with a handgun as a *coup de grâce*. While Major Heathcote was identified as the commander, the regiment also followed the custom of not identifying the men who were in the firing squad, and the regimental records have no listing of the squad members. (See Inchicore Road, Kilmainham Gaol [Dublin 8].)

101 Mount Street Lower: Home of the Walker family. One sister, Annie, was an Abbey actress and became famous as Eileen O'Doherty. Another sister, Mary, also

became an Abbey actress, known as Máire nic Shiubhlaigh. The entire family was heavily involved in revolutionary activities, following the lead of the father, Matthew, who was a printer by trade and carried on his business here under the name of the Tower Press. Annie married Joe Stanley, another printer, who with Matthew Walker printed the *Irish War News* for Padraic Pearse during the Rising.[313] (See 3 Hatch Street, GPO, Sackville Street Lower [Dublin 1].)

Mount Street, 8 Stephen's Place (Grattan Court, off Mount Street): Home of Christopher Andrews (14), a schoolboy who was killed by a gunshot in the Rising.[314] (He is sometimes identified as 'J. Andrews'.) In this five-roomed tenement there were nine separate families, totalling 37 people.[315]

28 Mountpleasant Avenue Upper: Home of J.J. Coade; shot by Capt. J.C. Bowen-Colthurst in Portobello Barracks, he is buried in Glasnevin Cemetery.[316] (See Rathmines Road/Portobello Barracks [Dublin 6].)

1–3 Parliament Street: Henry and James' Outfitters; an outpost of the Irish Citizen Army garrison at City Hall during the Rising.[317]

5–7 Parliament Street: Royal Exchange Hotel; Cmdt W.J. Brennan-Whitmore stayed here prior to the Rising.

38–40 Parliament Street: Office of the *Dublin Evening Mail*, an outpost of the Irish Citizen Army garrison at City Hall during the Rising.

Patrick Street: St Patrick's Park, next to St Patrick's Cathedral. Thomas MacDonagh came here with Brig. Gen. W.H.M. Lowe to discuss surrender.

2, 7a, 10–15 Peter Street (corner of Bishop Street): W. and R. Jacob's Biscuit Factory. A principal garrison during the 1916 Rising under the command of Thomas MacDonagh. (See 26–50 Bishop Street, corner of Peter Row, touching Aungier/Wexford Streets.)

15 Peter Street: Elizabeth O'Farrell met Thomas MacDonagh here bringing Padraic Pearse's order to surrender.[318]

22–28 Peter Street: Adelaide Hospital. A boy named O'Toole (14) was brought here during the Rising and died in the hospital.[319]

33 Richmond Street South (and Charlemont Mall): Overlooking Portobello

Bridge, J. and T. Davy's pub. The name was subsequently changed to Shearson's and it is now called the Portobello Pub. Joe Doyle (a Sgt in the ICA) and James Joyce (an ICA member) were barmen here prior to the Rising. Doyle led sixteen men in the occupation of Davy's. Michael Kelly led another section of sixteen to a position on the railway bridge crossing of the Grand Canal in support of the Davy's men, and this section was to cover the Davy's retreat. Both sections removed themselves to join the St Stephen's Green garrison on Tuesday.

Ross Road and Bride Street: Éamonn Ceannt and Thomas MacDonagh surrendered their garrisons to Major de Courcy Wheeler here at 3.15 p.m. on Sunday 30 April, ending the Rising.

2 St Andrew's Street: Office of A. Corrigan, solicitor for some of the Volunteers. He was asked to write many wills in the week before the Rising.

St Stephen's Green: Covering about 60 acres and with eight gates, the Green is named after St Stephen's Church and Leper Hospital, sited from 1224 to 1639 in the vicinity of Mercer Street. In 1877 Sir Arthur Guinness paid for it to be refurbished; it was placed under the management of the Board of Works, and was reopened in 1880. There are monuments here to Countess Markievicz, the Fianna, Robert Emmet, James Clarence Mangan, Tom Kettle, James Joyce, Jeremiah O'Donovan Rossa, Theobald Wolfe Tone, Oscar Wilde and W.B. Yeats; there is also a Famine memorial. The Fusilier's Arch is at the Grafton Street entrance (a Boer War monument to the Dublin Fusiliers); older Dubliners often called that entrance the 'Traitor's Gate'.

Members of the Irish Citizen Army under the command of Major Michael Mallin occupied the Green.[320] A party numbering about 40 marched to the Green from Liberty Hall, via Butt Bridge, College Street, College Green and Grafton Street, but as the week wore on the strength of the garrison rose to approximately 140 men and women. The Green was one of the first areas occupied. When it was taken, DMP Constable Michael Lahiff of College Street Station was on duty and was shot for 'refusing to leave his post'.[321]

(It is often said that Constable Lahiff was shot by Countess Markievicz.[322] When the Green was taken, Markievicz was delivering arms and supplies to the City Hall with Dr Kathleen Lynn. Markievicz was to have acted as liaison between the Green and the GPO, but when she reported to the Green Mallin co-opted her as his second in command. Upon arriving, she was detailed to inspect the defences and came to the Harcourt Street corner, where a group of Volunteers were arguing with a DMP member who refused to leave his post. It is said that she raised her Mauser handgun and other Volunteers also raised their guns. Three shots rang out and Constable Michael Lahiff was killed.[323] She was supposed to have shouted 'I shot him! I shot him!', but no witness statement definitively places her at the Harcourt Street corner at that time. In contrast, an eyewitness account recalls her in the Green, with a cigarette in her mouth and a pistol in her hand: '. . . a lady in a green uniform . . . breeches, slouch hat with green feathers, the feathers were the only feminine appearance, holding a revolver in one hand and a cigarette in the other, was standing on the footpath giving orders to the men . . .'. Geraldine Fitzgerald was a nurse at St Patrick's Jubilee Nurses' Home, 101 St Stephen's Green South. She wrote that the nurses had just begun lunch when they saw the woman and 'recognised her as the Countess de Markievicz—such a specimen of womanhood . . . We had only been looking a few minutes when we saw a policeman walking down the path . . . he had only gone a short way when we heard a shot and he fell on his face. The Countess ran triumphantly into the Green shouting 'I got him' . . . We rushed for bandages . . . but we could not stop his life blood ebbing away.'[324] Markievicz did take part in the firing later that day, when a party of Royal Irish Rifles came along Camden Street, and also took part in the sniping from the roof of the College of Surgeons. At the surrender, she removed her 'Peter the Painter' Mauser and kissed it before handing it over.[325])

Mallin posted some ICA men in houses overlooking the Green, while others dug trenches to cover the entrances and blocked the entire perimeter with barricades.[326] Mallin then dispatched men to take over Harcourt Street Station and J. and T. Davy's pub in Portobello. Mallin had served twelve years in the Royal Fusiliers in the British Army and had some experience in military planning as a non-commissioned officer. But the Green was a vulnerable position, as it was overlooked by the Shelbourne Hotel; when the British forces occupied the hotel during Monday night holding the Green became untenable. With so many large buildings overlooking the Green and not enough men and women to occupy a useful number of them, the rebels' position rapidly became impossible.[327]

The Green, Harcourt Street Station, Hatch Street, and the railway bridge in Harcourt Road commanding the South Circular Road were deemed vital positions by Connolly, and no fewer than eleven streets led into the Green itself. This was both a boon and a bane for the garrison, as it provided a most important position for the ICA but also gave the British several access routes. As with the other garrisons, this one was greatly hampered by MacNeill's countermanding order. Only skeleton garrisons held the outlying positions, and all outlying posts were abandoned early in the week, withdrawing to the College of Surgeons on St Stephen's Green West.

It was deemed impossible to occupy the Shelbourne owing to lack of numbers. Davy's pub was taken but abandoned. The Harcourt Street Station post could hold out only until 3 p.m. on Monday.[328] The Green was abandoned completely on Tuesday when it came under machine-gun fire from British forces, particularly from the Shelbourne, and the rebels were forced to withdraw across the street to the stout Royal College of Surgeons building. (See 123 St Stephen's Green [west].) But as Gen. Lowe concentrated on the GPO and the Four Courts, the College of Surgeons garrison was isolated and involved in little further action besides reconnaissance forays until the Sunday surrender order.

17 St Stephen's Green (north): Dublin University Club (now the Kildare Street and University Club). The pageboy Walter McKay, aged seventeen, testified that he saw Countess Markievicz aim and fire through the windows at the members of the club. This testimony was used by the court martial to convict her on the two charges that she 'took part in an armed rebellion against His Majesty the King and did attempt to cause disaffection among the civilian population of His Majesty'. She always denied that she shot at the club.

27–32 St Stephen's Green (north, corner of Kildare Street): Shelbourne Hotel. Opened in 1824 by Martin Burke, originally from County Tipperary. The general manager from 1904 to 1930 was G.R.F. Olden.[329]

James Connolly led the Citizen Army on a mock manoeuvre around St Stephen's Green a few weeks before the Rising and commented that the Shelbourne would be a suitable barracks, with a plentiful supply of food and beds. It was also the highest building of those surrounding the Green, and should have been taken in lieu of taking the Green itself. The hotel was left undefended by the Volunteers, not because they did not recognise its importance but primarily because 50 Volunteers and ICA men who were to have taken it simply had not shown up.[330] Certainly the Green became indefensible once the British occupied the Shelbourne.

During the Rising, there were over 100 British soldiers in the hotel, under the command of Capt. Carl Elliotson and Capt. Andrews. Paddy Kelly, a Shelbourne porter, made stealthy forays to the roof at frequent intervals to signal with flags to the rebels in St Stephen's Green, as did Eileen Costello. Doreen Carphim (8) was killed on Monday while walking past the hotel.[331]

In May 1916 the Commission to Inquire into the Rising met here under the chairmanship of Lord Hardinge of Penshurst. The other members of the Commission were Mr Justice Montague Shearman and Sir Mackenzie Chalmers. Hardinge had been viceroy of India for six years. Chalmers was a KCB and undersecretary of state, and had been on many royal commissions. Shearman seemed to have no qualifications at all and the papers of the time could only describe him as 'a jolly good sport who played rugby for Oxford'.[332]

51 St Stephen's Green (east): Office of James V. Healy, Atlas Insurance Co.; insured many buildings destroyed in the Rising and the Civil War.

86–87 St Stephen's Green (south): University Church is not visible from the street, lying behind the door of the house at No. 87. James Grace[333] (25 Northumberland Road [Dublin 4]) reported here at 11.00 a.m. on Easter Monday; the company O/C was Simon Donnelly,[334] but only about 34 members of the company's roster of over a hundred showed up.

90 St Stephen's Green (south): Home of Irish historian Alice Stopford Green, widow of the British historian John Richard Green, between 1918 and 1929.[335] When she lived in London she was responsible for raising most of the funds for the purchase of the Howth rifles, which cost £1,500. The largest single contributor was Capt. George Fitz Hardinge Berkeley, with Mrs Green the next largest subscriber; Roger Casement, Erskine Childers and his wife, Mary Spring-Rice, Conor and Hugh O'Brien, Lord Ashbourne, Lady Young and Minnie Ryan subscribed the rest of the money.[336] All were Protestants of Anglo-Irish stock. The idea was that the money should be used to purchase arms, to bring them to Ireland, to sell them to the Irish Volunteers and to reimburse the subscribers.[337] They did, in fact, get their money back.

Childers stayed here following his service in the British army during World War I. IRA/Volunteers often stayed here during the War of Independence, and the house was repeatedly raided. Máire Comerford worked here as a secretary.[338]

113 St Stephen's Green (west): Home of Michael Donnelly. He approved the occupation of his home during the Rising.

123 St Stephen's Green (west) at York Street: Royal College of Surgeons in Ireland. There are three statues atop the royal coat of arms: Athena, goddess of wisdom and war; Asklepios, god of medicine; and Hygeia, goddess of health. The college was opened to women in 1885.

Countess Markievicz and Major Michael Mallin surrendered the St Stephen's Green/College of Surgeons garrison to Major de Courcy Wheeler on nearby York Street. Members of the Anglo-Irish community had always been disturbed by one of their own participating in all the events of the period, from the Lockout on, but they were particularly shocked to see a woman of their own class taking part in the Rising. That attitude is expressly indicated in the diaries of Elsie Mahaffy, who was explicit in her condemnation of Markievicz.[339]

The college suffered little structural damage, though the pockmarked columns are evidence of the bullets that hit them. Some portraits were cut out of their frames and made into leggings, and the life-size portrait of Queen Victoria was cut into fragments.

Sir John Rogerson's Quay: Birthplace of Elizabeth More O'Farrell in 1884. (See Great Britain Street, Moore Street, and Sackville Lane [Dublin 1].) In 2007 a monument to Elizabeth O'Farrell was unveiled here.[340]

Sir John Rogerson's Quay: Home of Julia Grenan. With Elizabeth More O'Farrell, she conveyed the instructions for the surrender of the Volunteers who fled the GPO and were in buildings in Moore Street. Most commentators agree that the woman's name was Julia Grenan, although Brian O'Higgins has it spelled 'Grennan'.[341] *Last words* by Piaras MacLochlainn, published by the Kilmainham Gaol Restoration Society in 1971, names her as Julia Grenan.[342] *Who's who* names her as 'Sheila Grennan'.[343] She also wrote articles under the name 'Julia Grenan' shortly after the Rising.[344] She is buried in Glasnevin Cemetery in the same grave as her great friend Elizabeth O'Farrell, and it should be noted that the gravestone reads 'And her faithful comrade and lifelong friend—Sheila Grenan'.

Tara Street (corner of Great Brunswick Street, now Pearse Street): Central Fire Station opened in 1900. British machine-guns were taken out of Trinity College, winched to the top of the tower, and fired across the Liffey at Liberty Hall.

9 Temple Bar: Printer Robert Latchford was prosecuted and fined £5 under DORA in June 1916 for printing a statement purportedly made by Thomas MacDonagh from the dock. (See 41 Amiens Street and 45A Capel Street [Dublin 1].)

Gentlemen of the Court Martial

I choose to think that you have done your duty, according to your lights, in sentencing me to death. I thank you for your courtesy. It would not be seemly for me to go to my doom without trying to express, however inadequately, my sense of the high honour I enjoy in being of those predestined in this generation to die for Irish Freedom. You will, perhaps, understand this sentiment, for it is one to which an Imperial poet of a bygone age bore immortal testimony: ''Tis sweet and glorious to die for one's country'. You would all be proud to die for Britain, your Imperial patron, and I am proud and happy to die for Ireland, my glorious Fatherland.

There is not much left to say. The Proclamation of the Irish Republic has been adduced in evidence against me as one of the signatories; you think it is already a dead and buried letter, but it lives, it lives. From minds alight with Ireland's vivid intellect it sprang; in hearts aflame with Ireland's mighty love it was conceived. Such documents do not die.

The British occupation of Ireland has never for more than one hundred years been compelled to confront in the field a Rising so formidable as that which overwhelming forces have for the moment succeeded in quelling. This Rising did not result from accidental circumstances. It came in due recurrent season as the necessary outcome of forces that are ever at work. The fierce pulsation of resurgent pride that disclaims servitude may one day cease to throb in the heart of Ireland—but the heart of Ireland will that day be dead. While Ireland lives, the brain and brawn of her manhood will strive to destroy the last vestige of British rule in her territory.

In this ceaseless struggle, there will be, as there has been, and must be an eternal ebb and flow. But, let England make no mistake. The generous high-bred youth of Ireland will never fail to answer the call of war to win their country's freedom. Other and tamer methods they will leave to other and tamer men; but they must do it or die.

It will be said that our movement was foredoomed to failure. It had proved so. Yet it might have been otherwise. There is always a chance for brave men who challenge fortune. That we had such a chance none knows so well as your statesmen and military experts. The mass of the people of Ireland will doubtless salve their consciences to sleep for another generation by the now exploded fable that Ireland cannot successfully fight England. We do not profess to represent the mass of the people of Ireland. We stand for the intellect and the soul of Ireland. To Ireland's intellect and soul the inert mass, drugged and degenerate by ages of servitude, must, in the distant day of resurrection, render homage and free service—receiving in return the vivifying impress of a free people.

Gentlemen, you have sentenced me to death and I accept your sentence with joy and pride, since it is for Ireland I am to die. I go to join the goodly company of men who died for Ireland, the least of whom was worthier than I can claim to be; and that noble band are, themselves, but a small section of that great unnumbered army of martyrs, whose Captain is the Christ Who died on Calvary. Of every white-robed knight in all that goodly company, we are the spiritual kin. The forms of heroes flit before my vision; and there is one, the star of whose destiny sways my own; there is one, the key-note of whose nature chimes harmoniously with the swan-song of my soul. It is the great Florentine, Savonarola, whose weapon was not the sword but prayer and teaching. The seed he sowed fructifies to this day in God's Church.

Take me away, and let my blood bedew the sacred soil of Ireland. I die in the certainty that once more the seed will fructify.

Thomas MacDonagh
Address to his Court Martial—2 May 1916

The speech's authenticity was questioned but it was wholly accepted as true by MacDonagh's family.[345]

12 Temple Lane: Printer Paul Curtis was similarly prosecuted and fined under DORA for printing the same statement.

Townsend Street (corner of Great Brunswick Street): DMP Barracks. This was the HQ of the detective division ('G' Division) of the DMP.

128 Townsend Street: Home of Mary Kelly (12), who died on 30 April from a gunshot wound suffered during the Rising.[346] She was the daughter of a man serving in the British Army in France, and is buried in Deansgrange cemetery.

Westland Row: St Andrew's Church. Built with the assistance of Daniel O'Connell between 1832 and 1837, it was the first church built on a main road after Catholic Emancipation. Willie Pearse sculpted the Mater Dolorosa statue that is on display here.[347]

20 Westland Row: Office of Daniel Maher, solicitor. Pearse left letters with Maher 'to be opened in case of my death', including his will and other documents/instructions of a financial character.

45–46 Westland Row: Christian Brothers' School; Brother Maunsell, from County Kerry, and Brother Craven were noted teachers here. Attended by Padraic and Willie Pearse (starting in 1891)[348] and by Desmond Ryan in 1907.

48–52 Westland Row: Westland Row Railway Station, now Pearse Station. It was the first railway station in Ireland, built in 1834, and was the terminus for the Dublin–Kingstown Railway, also known as the Dublin and South-Eastern Railway. (Harcourt Street Station was another terminus for the line.) At first it just ran commuter trains south to Kingstown (Dún Laoghaire), but in 1881 it was connected to Amiens Street Station (Connolly Station) by means of the Loopline Bridge, since it was deemed impractical to build a tunnel under the Liffey.

This was the main railway station for the Dublin and South-Eastern Railway and was of great strategic importance. It was the Volunteers' plan to occupy it and prevent British reinforcements being brought to Dublin through the station. Third Battalion Volunteers of B company under the command of Capt. John McMahon quickly seized it, cut telephone wires and seized signal boxes, and the rails toward the Kingstown line were sabotaged as far south as Merrion Gates. Volunteers under Capt. Joseph O'Connor and Capt. McMahon were charged to snipe and fight running battles

Following the Rising, British troops and Dublin policemen place barbed wire around City Hall to keep all curiosity-seekers out. The interior of the hall did not suffer much damage because it was retaken so quickly by the British.

Clanwilliam House on Clanwilliam Place, at the east corner of Lower Mount Street. Sited right at Mount Street Bridge and held by seven Volunteers, it was a prime position from which the Volunteers could fire on British troops trying to cross the bridge.

The Royal College of Surgeons was located on St Stephen's Green West. It was occupied by Volunteers and Irish Citizen Army men and women who retreated from their positions in the Green after coming under fire from the Shelbourne Hotel.

Born Constance Gore-Booth in County Sligo, she married a Polish count and was thereafter known as Countess Markievicz. Despite her aristocratic background, she devoted her life to Irish republicanism and helping the poor, and she was second in command at St Stephen's Green.

The Citizen Army, under the command of Major Michael Mallin Countess Markievicz, took St Stephen's Green and then retreat to the Royal College of Surgeons. Mallin and Markievicz surrendered the garrison to Major de Courcy Wheeler on near York Street. She removed her 'Peter the Painter' Mauser and ki it before handing it over.

Seán Connolly led a detachment of 40 ICA men and women from Liberty Hall down Dame Street to the gate of Dublin Castle. They threw a home-made bomb (which failed to explode) at the policeman on duty at the gate of the Castle and then seized the Castle guardroom, but soon retreated to the City Hall.

Harcourt Street Railway Station was the main railway station for the Dublin and South-Eastern Railway and was of strategic importance. It was the rebels' plan to occupy it and prevent British reinforcements being brought from the south to Dublin. Taken early in the Rising by men of the Citizen Army, it was abandoned almost immediately because it was indefensible.

Mount Street Bridge, site of the bloodiest single battle of the Rising, crosses over the Grand Canal between Dublin 2 and Dublin 4. Here the burned-out remains of Clanwilliam House can be seen on the left of the photograph.

British troops took the Shelbourne Hotel on Monday night. They placed many machine-guns in its windows and maintained a constant fire on the St Stephen's Green garrison, necessitating the latter's retreat to the Royal College of Surgeons.

Located at the corner of Tara Street and Great Brunswick Street (now Pearse Street), the Tara Street Central Fire Station opened in 1900. British machine-guns were taken out of Trinity College, winched to the top of the tower and fired across the Liffey at Liberty Hall.

On Easter Monday John MacBride was on his way to have lunch with his brother (who was to be married) when he unexpectedly met a Volunteer column led by Thomas MacDonagh and was told that the Rising was under way. He was 'invited' to participate. It was a complete accident, for which he was executed as a Rising leader on 5 May.

St Andrew's Church on Westland Row was built with the assistance of Daniel O'Connell between 1832 and 1837. It was the first Catholic church built on a main road after Catholic Emancipation. Willie Pearse sculpted the Mater Dolorosa statue that is on display here.

Westland Row Railway Station (now Pearse Station) was the first railway station in Ireland and was the terminus for the Dublin and South-Eastern Railway. At first it just ran commuter trains south to Kingstown, but in 1881 it was connected to Amiens Street Station (Connolly Station) by means of the Loopline Bridge, since it was deemed impractical to build a tunnel under the Liffey.

Thousands of prisoners arrested after the Rising were taken to prisons in England and Wales. Most were released just before Christmas 1916 and they received a tumultuous welcome upon their return to Ireland. Most of them came through Westland Row Railway Station.

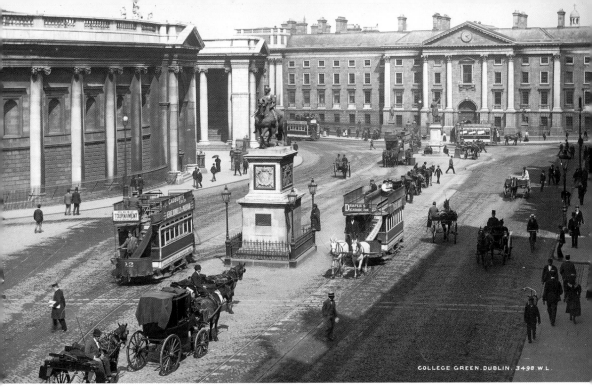

College Green, showing the Bank of Ireland (L) and Trinity College Dublin (R). Note the lack of trees. Unlike today, there were few or no trees on many central Dublin streets, giving long-range lines of fire for both sides. The same was true for the area around Mount Street Bridge, enabling the Volunteers to engage the British from well-hidden positions.

British Lancers often paraded in Dublin, and they were also used as scouts when trouble arose. These Lancers passing Trinity College are like the Lancers who were ambushed in front of the GPO, and another group who were waylaid in front of the Four Courts, at the start of the Rising.

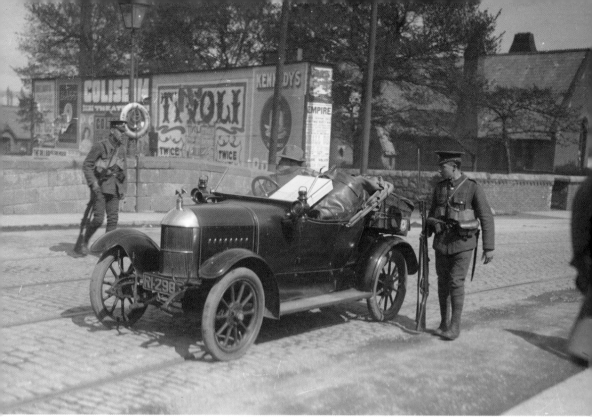

British troops inspecting a motorcar on Mount Street Bridge, the scene of some of the bloodiest fighting. The bridge connected Northumberland Road to Lower Mount Street across the Grand Canal, and after the Rising British troops stopped and searched cars entering the city centre.

British troops marching in from Kingstown took Northumberland Road through Dublin 4. Lt Michael Malone and James Grace occupied the house at No. 25 and inflicted severe casualties on the British, holding them at bay for almost five hours. Grace survived but Malone was killed.

around the railway to maintain control of it, so that troops coming from Kingstown would have to march to Dublin. (See Mount Street Bridge.[349]) It remained under Volunteer control until the surrender on 3 May.

Westland Row at Densil Street: Oriel House. De Valera hoped to occupy many of the tall buildings in the area, in particular Oriel House, which would have dominated British movements in Merrion Street and Lincoln Place. He even selected Volunteers to attack it, but repeatedly felt the attack was too risky and withdrew men from the area.

Westmoreland Street: The British placed eighteen-pound artillery pieces here to shell Lower Sackville Street during the Rising, and destroyed many buildings.

Westmoreland Street: Carlisle House; *Irish Independent* offices.

31 Westmoreland Street: Main office of the *Irish Times*. (See Abbey Street Lower [Dublin 1].)

4 Wicklow Street: Wicklow Hotel, next to Weir's Jewellers, one building away from Grafton Street. On Easter Monday John MacBride was on his way to have lunch here with his brother (who was to be married) when he unexpectedly met a Volunteer column led by Thomas MacDonagh at St Stephen's Green and was told that the Rising was under way. He was 'invited' to participate and that is how he ended up at Jacob's. It was a complete accident, for which he was executed.

MacBride was a native of Westport, Co. Mayo, and was a draper's assistant there in his early life. He emigrated to South Africa, and during the Boer War took a leading part as one of the leaders of the Irish Brigade fighting the British. The government of South Africa conferred the rank of Major on him. Upon his return, he married Maud Gonne and they had one son, Seán. In the years leading up to the Rising he was a water bailiff for Dublin Corporation.

South William Street: Home of Richard Murphy, who was killed in the Rising in Clanwilliam House.

41 York Street: Dublin Conservative Workingmen's Club. Many Protestant workers belonged to this club. It was one of the first centres for Volunteer recruitment after their establishment on 25 November 1913.[350] The 3rd Battalion of the Dublin Brigade met here before the Rising.

45 York Street: Home of John H. McNamara (12), who was shot and died in Mercer's Hospital on 28 April.[351] He is buried in Mount Jerome Cemetery.

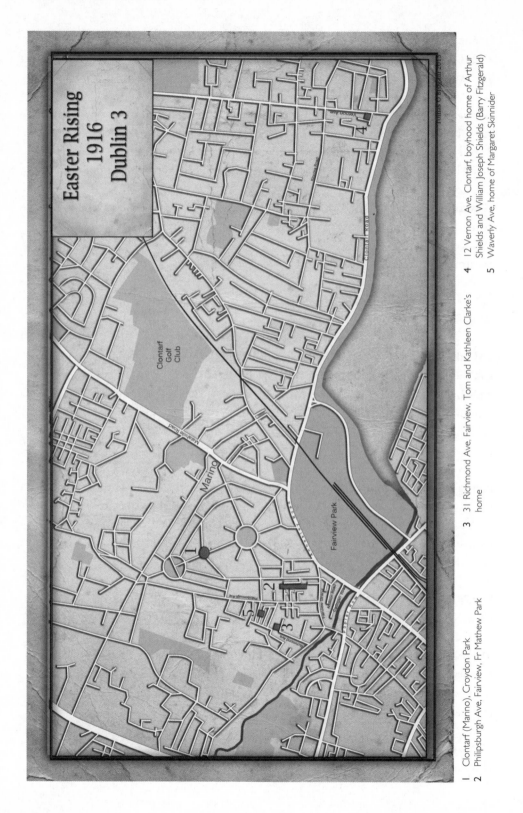

Easter Rising
1916
Dublin 3

1 Clontarf (Marino), Croydon Park
2 Philipsburgh Ave, Fairview, Fr Mathew Park
3 31 Richmond Ave, Fairview, Tom and Kathleen Clarke's home
4 12 Vernon Ave, Clontarf, boyhood home of Arthur Shields and William Joseph Shields (Barry Fitzgerald)
5 Waverly Ave, home of Margaret Skinnider

Dublin 3

Key locations

Ballybough	Fairview
Clontarf	Fr Mathew Park
Croke Park	Marino
Croydon Park	Richmond Avenue

C lontarf lies on the north side of the estuary of one of Dublin's three main rivers, the Tolka, which reaches the sea at the Raheny end of the district. Noted for the Battle of Clontarf in 1014 at which Brian Boru defeated the Danes, Clontarf lacks a single 'village centre' but has a range of commercial centres in several locations, mainly focused around Vernon Avenue. Clontarf adjoins Fairview, Marino and Raheny and is in the Dublin 3 postal zone. By the early nineteenth century Clontarf had become a popular holiday resort for the citizens of Dublin, who came out from the city to enjoy bathing in the sea or in the hot and cold seawater baths. A key arrival at Clontarf was Sir Benjamin Lee Guinness, son of Arthur Guinness II, who purchased various lands in Clontarf and Raheny, combining them to form St Anne's Estate, the remnants of which form St Anne's Park in Raheny (Dublin 5). With its open areas, Dublin 3 was perfect for drilling, and the Volunteers and Citizen Army took advantage of Croydon Park and Fr Mathew Park.

> *'I WAS THEN WHAT I HAD BEEN, AND WHAT I STILL AM, AN IRISH NATIONALIST'*
>
> Tom Clarke

Clonliffe Road, 6 Holycross Cottages: Home of William Fox (13),[352] who was killed while walking past St Mary's Pro-Cathedral on Marlborough Street.

Clontarf Town Hall: The Volunteer Military Council frequently met here prior to the Rising. Michael McGinn, its curator, was a friend of Padraic Pearse and was an old IRB man himself. Michael and his brother, Tom, both fought in the GPO.

Clontarf (Marino): Croydon Park. The Park had been taken over by the ITGWU several years before the Rising, and was used by Capt. Jack White for drilling the Irish Citizen Army.[353] In October 1913 about 500 workers travelled here to enlist in the army that was being discussed. Their names were taken, but they heard no more until Capt. White took up James Connolly's announcement of the ICA the next month. After the 1913 Lockout, White offered Countess Markievicz £50 to buy shoes for the workers so that they could drill and form a real army, and Croydon Park was the primary training area for the ICA. There were three acres of park and a house on the grounds. After James Larkin left for America in October 1914 the ITGWU sold the estate.

Fairview Strand: Gilbey's Wine Branch Depot, on the north-west side of the Tolka Bridge. Harry Boland fought here during the Rising with the Volunteers commanded by Frank Henderson, before going with them to the GPO.[354]

Fairview Strand: Lambe's pub, on the north-east side of Tolka Bridge. There was a small garrison here under the command of Seán Russell, before they went to the GPO with the rest of Henderson's men.

Jones Road: Croke Park. The grounds were originally acquired by the GAA in 1913 and were named after Archbishop Thomas Croke of Cashel, patron of the Association.

30 O'Connell Villas, Fairview: Home of Michael W. O'Reilly.[355] Quartermaster of the Volunteers prior to the Rising, he became O/C at Frongoch prison camp.[356]

Philipsburgh Avenue, Fairview: Fr Mathew Park. On Sunday 26 July 1914, four Battalions of the Dublin Volunteers assembled in Fr Mathew Park. About 1,000 men formed up under their company commanders and an officer in uniform on horseback. Various companies marched from the park: first the cyclist corps, then the signalling corps, then the various companies, including a small detachment of Fianna with an ambulance cart. Almost all of the marchers were unaware of their destination or the purpose of the march. As they marched, they were joined by several more Volunteer companies, including those from Lusk, Skerries and Donabate.

The march progressed through Sutton and Baldoyle before reaching its destination in Howth at about 1 p.m. The head of the march came to a halt at the tram terminus at the entrance to the East Pier. The Volunteers had marched to Howth to accept the rifles and ammunition brought in by Erskine Childers in his yacht, *Asgard*. (See 90 St Stephen's Green South [Dublin 2] and Howth [Dublin 13].)

The 2nd Battalion companies paraded here during Easter Week 1916. Fr Walter McDonnell, a Fairview curate, came into the park on Monday, heard confessions and blessed the Volunteers.

31 Richmond Avenue, Fairview: Tom and Kathleen Clarke's home at the time of the Rising; she lived here after the Rising with their sons. Though Clarke stayed at Fleming's Hotel on Holy Saturday night, he, Seán McGarry[357] and Tom O'Connor returned to stay here on Easter Sunday night.

Kathleen was one of the most well-known women of the period and one of very few privy to the plans of the Rising. She served as a TD for the Dublin Mid constituency and was the first female lord mayor of Dublin. Born Kathleen Daly in Limerick, she preferred to be known as Caitlín Bean Uí Chléirigh and has this inscription on her headstone. Tom Clarke met her uncle, John Daly, while in prison, and married Kathleen, 21 years his junior, on his release in 1898. Kathleen was specifically given the responsibility to 'carry on' the IRB following the Rising, as Tom knew that many of its leaders would be killed or imprisoned. For her role, it was said that she was one of only two women (Una Brennan being the other) to be sworn into the IRB. 'On Holy Thursday, [she] was sent to Limerick with dispatches. I took my three children with me to leave them with my mother, so that I could be free to take on the duty assigned to me in the Rising.'[358] After the Rising and her imprisonment, Kathleen was unwell and moved her sons to her uncle's home in Limerick until 1917. This house was let furnished to P.S. O'Hegarty during this time, and when she returned to Dublin she took a furnished house in Dundrum for a while. After her release, she headed the Irish National Aid and Volunteers' Dependants' Fund. (See 10 Exchequer Street [Dublin 2].) She was elected unopposed as a Sinn Féin TD to the Second Dáil Éireann in May 1921. Always adamantly against the Treaty, she failed to be re-elected in 1922; she was elected to the short-lived Fifth Dáil in June 1927, but again lost her seat in September 1927 and failed to regain it. She was elected to the Seanad in 1928 and retained her seat in two subsequent elections until the seat was abolished in 1936. She was lord mayor of Dublin from 1939 to 1941. She unsuccessfully contested the 1948 Dáil Éireann election on behalf of Clann na Poblachta. Following her death, aged 94, in 1972 she received the rare honour of a state funeral.

16 Russell Street, North Circular Road: Home of Seán MacDermott; in 1916 Dublin Castle recorded his address as 500 North Circular Road. Born in Kiltyclogher, Co. Leitrim, he spent his early years in Scotland and the United States. On his return to Ireland he became a nationalist, joining every nationalist organisation. Trained in republicanism by Bulmer Hobson in Belfast, he became the full-time organiser for the Irish Volunteers and cycled all over Ireland despite being crippled by polio. The protégé of Tom Clarke, he was executed after the Rising on 12 May 1916.

3 Seafield Road, Clontarf: Home of Arthur Shields at the time of the Rising. (See Vernon Avenue; Walworth Road [Dublin 8].)

10 Summer Street, North Circular Road: Home of Capt. Jack White at the time of the Rising.

12 Vernon Avenue, Clontarf: Childhood home of Arthur Shields and William Joseph Shields (Barry FitzGerald), noted Abbey Theatre actors at this time and during the twenties. Arthur was in the GPO. He never changed his name and was in John Ford's film *The Quiet Man* with his brother, who by then was known as Barry FitzGerald. (See 1 Walworth Road [Dublin 8].)

Waverly Avenue: Home of Margaret Skinnider, a mathematics teacher from Glasgow, who operated as an ICA member when in Ireland.[359] After she joined Cumann na mBan, she was involved in smuggling weapons and explosives to Ireland.[360] She would carry the detonators in her hat and wrapped the wires around her body. At Christmas 1915 she brought detonators to Ireland on the boat from Glasgow. She was sent away from her post at the College of Surgeons many times carrying dispatches, and when she left her post she changed into civilian clothes, rode on her bicycle and changed back into her uniform on her return. She was wounded on Wednesday when she was in a party sent to set fire to the Russell Hotel and was carried back to the college by Bill Partridge. She wrote about her role as a sniper on the roof of the College of Surgeons: 'It was dark there, full of smoke, a din of firing, but it was good to be in the action; more than once I saw a man I aimed at fall'.[361] She applied for a pension for her service, but was rejected at first because she was a woman. After repeated submissions, her application was finally approved in 1938. (See Harcourt Street, Russell Hotel [Dublin 2].)

5 Windsor Villas, Clontarf: Childhood home of the Henderson family. Some of the Howth rifles were hidden under the floorboards here. Frank[362] wrote *Narratives: Frank Henderson's Easter Rising*.[363] He was in the GPO and was later a captive at Frongoch. Leo was also in the GPO[364] and became a leading IRA/Republican figure. He led the raid on Ferguson's garage which was the prelude to the attack on the Four Courts in 1922, and spent the rest of the Civil War in Mountjoy Prison.

Dublin 4

Key locations

Ailesbury Road
Baggot Street, Upper and Lower
Ballsbridge
Beggar's Bush Barracks
Donnybrook
Haddington Road
Herbert Road
Irishtown

Merrion Road/Square
Mount Street Bridge (bridge crosses between
    Dublin 2 and Dublin 4)
Northumberland Road
Pembroke Road
Ringsend
Sandymount
Shelbourne Road

> '*WE KNOW WHAT WE ARE*
> *DYING FOR, THANK GOD THE*
> *DAY HAS COME*'
> *Lt Michael Malone*

Dublin 4 is now one of the more upmarket districts in Dublin, but in 1916 it was the scene of the single bloodiest battle of the Rising. The district includes Ballsbridge and Beggar's Bush Barracks, then Sandymount on the way to what was then Kingstown and is now Dún Laoghaire, the harbour town eight miles to the south-east of Dublin.

Beggar's Bush Barracks is located on Haddington Road, bordered by Shelbourne Road on the east, and dates from 1827. It was a recruit-training depot in 1916, and at the time of the Rising had a very small garrison in residence. Like other buildings and complexes in Dublin, it could have been taken by a minimal number of Irish troops, but the Rising's planners didn't know this, and it probably couldn't have been held anyway. Today the Barracks holds many offices for governmental buildings, as well as housing for pensioners. One can walk through the public areas, and one really should—it gives an idea of just how substantial the British military positions in the heart of Dublin were in 1916.

Dublin 4 was the area towards which British reinforcements disembarking at Kingstown marched to get to the centre of town. While one may not want to walk the entire way from Dún Laoghaire, imagine the condition of the British troops who walked that distance to fight on these streets. The week of the Rising was quite hot in Dublin for that time of year—many older Dubliners called any warm day 'Rising weather' for many years thereafter. So, as you stand in the street, imagine the condition of the British soldiers marching all that way in the thick serge uniforms of the time! The 'Battle of Mount Street Bridge' began on Wednesday morning and continued until early Thursday. It demonstrated the difficulty for the British in street-fighting.

To set the scene, note that Clanwilliam House was on the city side of the bridge, on the east side of the intersection of Northumberland Road and the Grand Canal

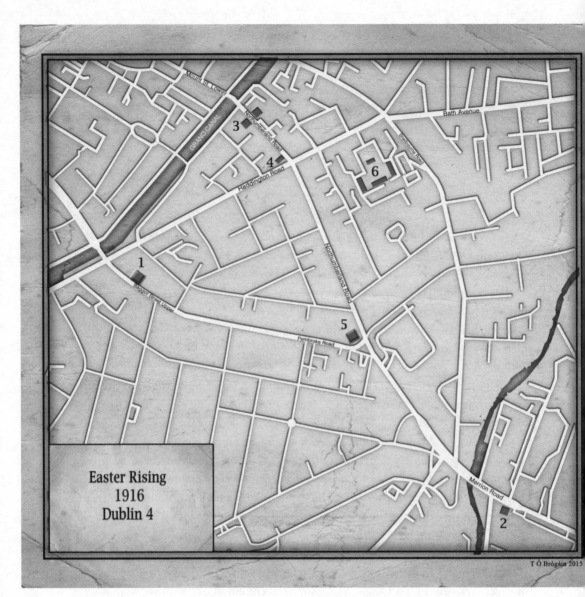

T Ó Brógáin 2015

1 16–18 Baggot St. Upper, Royal City of Dublin
   Hospital

2 Merrion Road, Ballsbridge, Pembroke/Ballsbridge
   Town Hall

3 1–5 Northumberland Road, St Stephen's Schoolhouse
   and Parochial Hall

4 25 Northumberland Road, at corner of Haddington
   Road, single family home

5 122–124 Pembroke Road, at Northumberland Road,
   Carrisbrook House

6 Shelbourne Road, Beggar's Bush Barracks

(actually in Dublin 2); St Stephen's Parochial Hall was on the opposite side (the south side) of the Grand Canal on the west side of the street; 25 Northumberland Road was on the same side of the canal as the Parochial Hall but further to the south-east, towards Kingstown (Dún Laoghaire). Volunteers of the 3rd Battalion, under the overall command of Cmdt Éamon de Valera, had prepared all these buildings for resistance with barricades on the lower floors. From a military standpoint, Clanwilliam House could hardly have been better sited, with a commanding view up Northumberland Road and across Mount Street Bridge. Stand on the bridge and look north at the house and then south down Northumberland Road and you'll get a perfect feeling for what the British soldiers were marching into. The thirteen Volunteers at 25 Northumberland Road, Clanwilliam House and the Parochial Hall were perfectly deployed, and excellent marksmen with plenty of ammunition manned all positions.

Among the first British troops called to Ireland were the Sherwood Foresters. They arrived in Kingstown on Wednesday morning, tired, seasick and disoriented. One column headed to the Royal Hospital, Kilmainham, and reached it without incident. The other column was ordered to head to Trinity College and Beggar's Bush Barracks and marched into an ambush.

At about 12.25 p.m. on Wednesday the leading platoon of Sherwoods came under fire from the defenders of 25 Northumberland Road, Lt Michael Malone and James Grace. More Volunteers waited in the schoolhouse and parochial hall, some 200 yards further down the road, and in Clanwilliam House, which commanded Mount Street Bridge.

The confusion of the British troops mounted as the inexperienced troops and officers struggled to pinpoint the enemy positions, and a number of houses were stormed at bayonet point without success. Several of the British officers were among the first to fall, and this caused great confusion amongst the raw Robin Hoods, some of whom had only been in uniform for three months and most of whom had never been under fire before. Poignantly, among the first to fall was Captain F.C. Dietrichsen, who was with his troops when he saw his wife, Beatrice, and his two children on the street watching the troops arrive. Without his knowledge, his wife (née Mitchell, of the Dublin wine merchant family) had brought them to Ireland for safekeeping from Zeppelin raids in England. He greeted and hugged them—just before he was killed in front of 25 Northumberland Road. He was buried in Deansgrange Cemetery.

When No. 25 was taken late in the afternoon, the British were then faced with fire coming from the direction of the school buildings further down Northumberland Road and from Clanwilliam House across the bridge. The fight for Clanwilliam House was even more severe than for 25 Northumberland Road, as more and more British tried to advance across the bridge and were cut down. Later some described the British advance as looking like an oncoming 'khaki serpent'. Finally, a shower of grenades had the unintended consequence of igniting the gas supply to the houses and soon both

Clanwilliam House and the adjoining house were ablaze.

The British suffered their greatest casualties of the Rising here: three officers were killed and fourteen others wounded, and 216 other ranks were either killed or wounded. The British gave full credit to the defensive positions and the courage of the Volunteers, saying after the Rising that if every position had been defended with such skill and determination the insurrection would have lasted three times as long.

As one walks between the positions one can see just how daunting it was for the British—and one gains a better appreciation for the planning of the Irish, which has often been dismissed.

16–18 Baggot Street Upper: Royal City of Dublin Hospital; commonly called Baggot Street Hospital. Dr Alfred Parsons, Alfred Fannin's brother-in-law, worked here.[365] He was a leading Dublin doctor, included J.M. Synge among his patients, and was singled out for his great service during the Rising. He was taken to Dublin Castle to examine James Connolly and was asked whether Connolly was 'fit to be shot'. Parsons answered, 'A man is never fit to be shot'. He also gave evidence that Capt. J.C. Bowen-Colthurst, the officer who unlawfully shot Francis Sheehy-Skeffington during the Rising, 'was far from normal and he was unbalanced'. Parsons suggested that this had been brought on by the strain of fighting at the front in the war.[366] (See Rathmines Road/Portobello Barracks [Dublin 6].)

Belmont Avenue, Donnybrook: Home of Mrs Áine (Annie) Heron, a judge of the Dáil Éireann/Republican Courts. She was in the Four Courts, and she was pregnant with her third child when she went out to fight in the Rising.[367]

Elgin Road: Home of Count and Countess Plunkett after 1916. George and Jack Plunkett also lived here upon their return from internment camps after the Rising.[368]

Haddington Road: St Mary's Church. British snipers climbed to the belfry here, overlooking the whole of 25 Northumberland Road and the Clanwilliam House area. The curate here was Revd James Doyle.[369]

103 Haddington Road: Home of Margaret (Mary?) Veale (13), who died on 4 May of wounds sustained during the Rising.[370] She was killed when 'she used binoculars to look out of the window of her house'.[371]

17 Herbert Park, Ballsbridge: Home of F.H. Browning, who led one column of the Georgius Rex on Northumberland Road and was killed there. (See Northumberland Road.)

18 Herbert Park, Ballsbridge: Home of Mr and Mrs Arthur Mitchell; he was the director of Jameson's Distillery, while she left a diary of the times that is very revealing of the attitude of the upper classes during the Rising.[372] Of the fires she wrote: 'Dublin is in flames in many places like Sodom and Gomorra; and it makes one feel quite sick'.

19 Herbert Park, Ballsbridge: Home of Eoin and Agnes MacNeill in 1914. He was professor of early and medieval history at UCD and chief of staff of the Irish Volunteers, and she was on the Provisional Committee of Cumann na mBan.[373] By April 1916 they were living in Rathfarnham; their home there was known as Woodtown Park. (James MacNeill, Eoin's brother, acquired the house in 1915. See Rathfarnham, Woodtown Park [Dublin 14].) (See 53 Rathgar Road [Dublin 6].)

32 Herbert Park, Ballsbridge: Home of Alfred and Violet Fannin, owner of Fannin's medical and surgical supply on Grafton Street; it remained in the family until their son Eustace died in 1985 and it is now an ambassadorial residence.[374] Alfred's letters provide a valuable insight into the life of upper-class citizens in Dublin during the Rising.

40 Herbert Park, Ballsbridge: Home of The Ó Rahilly, Michael Joseph O'Rahilly. His wife was Nancy Marie Browne O'Rahilly (usually known as 'Nannie'), originally from Philadelphia; she was on the Provisional Committee of Cumann na mBan.[375] He was Eoin MacNeill's publisher. (See Sackville Lane [Dublin 1].)

Herbert Road at corner of Newbridge Avenue: Fairfield House. Home of James Stephens, founder of the IRB.

Merrion Road, Ballsbridge: Pembroke/Ballsbridge Town Hall, Ballsbridge. The township included Ballsbridge, Ringsend, Irishtown, Donnybrook and Sandymount. C.P. O'Neill was the chairman of the Urban Council during the Rising; J.C. Manly was town clerk. The 177th Infantry Brigade (the Lincolnshire Regiment) of the 59th (North Midland) Division commandeered the Town Hall after the Rising.

Following his garrison's surrender, de Valera was taken into captivity and held in the Weights and Measures Department of Ballsbridge Town Hall on Merrion Road.[376] This was on the opposite side of the city to the main body of arrested Volunteers, who were detained in Kilmainham Gaol or Richmond Barracks. He remained in Ballsbridge during the first of the executions and was transferred to Richmond Barracks only on 8 May. (See Richmond Barracks [Dublin 8].)

9 Merrion Road, Sandymount: Home of Maire Comerford. Born in County Wicklow in 1892, she was in Dublin during the Rising. She volunteered to aid

Countess Markievicz in St Stephen's Green but was turned away and carried dispatches for the GPO garrison. Later she worked for the countess. She joined Cumann na mBan in 1918 and was extremely valuable to Michael Collins as a courier and source.[377]

Mount Street Bridge: Bridge crosses between Dublin 2 and Dublin 4. See Dublin 2 for full description of the battle surrounding the bridge. (See 25 Northumberland Road.)

1–5 Northumberland Road: St Stephen's Schoolhouse and Parochial Hall. The hall was on the same side of the road as 25 Northumberland Road, near the Grand Canal. Patrick Doyle (leader), Joe Clarke, William Christian and James (P.B.?) McGrath held off the Sherwood Foresters from here as long as they could, then fled to Percy Place, where they were captured. St Stephen's Parish School was across the road.[378] Denis O'Donoghue, Robert Cooper, James H. Doyle and James (Séamus) Kavanaugh occupied the school building until their position became untenable. They were withdrawn early in the week and occupied Robert's Builders' Yard, providing covering fire for those in Clanwilliam House. (See No. 25 below; Mount Street Bridge [Dublin 2].)

25 Northumberland Road (corner of Haddington Road) (see 1–2 Clanwilliam Place [Dublin 2], Mount Street Bridge [Dublin 2]): Clanwilliam House was on the city (east) side of the intersection and canal; St Stephen's Parochial Hall[379] was on the opposite (south) side of the Grand Canal on the west side of the street (and was the most exposed of the three positions); across from the parochial hall was the schoolhouse (the Volunteers were forced from this position early in the battle); 25 Northumberland Road was on the same side of the canal as the parochial hall but some 300 yards further to the south-east. There were thirteen men in the three main outposts after the school was evacuated. Situated as it is at the corner of Haddington Road, the house gave a clear line of fire to the main gate of Beggar's Bush Barracks.

Lt Michael Malone was killed at the top of the house (he had been Éamon de Valera's ADC).[380] James Grace (in the basement) survived but was captured.[381] (He had a revolver and four bullets left when he hid in the garden.) Malone sent Paddy Byrne and Michael Rowe home (without their weapons and ammunition) because he didn't think that anyone would survive: 'They're only children—too young to die'.[382]

The Volunteers first opened fire on the 1st Dublin Battalion Associated Volunteer Corps, the Georgius Rex ('the George Royals'), who were returning from manoeuvres at Tickmonock in the Dublin hills. They were a part-time volunteer veteran corps, a 'home defence force' composed of old rugby club members, ex-British Army soldiers, and business and professional men. They were based at Beggar's Bush

Barracks and Kingstown. They had originally marched in civilian clothes with armbands bearing the 'G.R.' insignia, but after formal recognition they wore khaki uniforms with 'Georgius Rex' on their belts. The majority being elderly, the force was also known derisively as 'God's Rejected', the 'Gorgeous Wrecks' or 'Methusiliers'. The GRs had been out on a field day in the Dublin mountains south of the city when they heard the news of the Rising. According to one account, the information that they received led them to conclude that the fighting was in the centre of the city and away from the direction of their barracks. They were carrying rifles but no ammunition. The battalion had been divided into two sections for the field manoeuvres and they took separate routes back to the barracks. The larger section, under Major G.A. Harris of Trinity College OTC, though coming under some fire, managed to reach the security of the barracks with only one casualty.

Sub-Cmdt F.H. Browning, who was killed, led the other section of the GRs. He was a graduate of TCD, an outstanding cricketer and president of the Irish Rugby Union; he played for his university as well as for the Wanderers, and founded the Irish Rugby Volunteer Corps. Known as 'Chicken' Browning, he was one of the best cricketers Ireland ever produced. This smaller group of about 40 men under Browning's command had taken the route back that brought them onto Northumberland Road, where they were fired on at close range. Seven were wounded and five were killed outright—Browning, Reginald Clery, John Gibbs, Thomas Harborne and James Nolan. G. Hosford was shot by a sniper while in Beggar's Bush Barracks and died later.

Once it was realised that the GRs were unable to return fire and were, in effect, unarmed, the insurgents immediately ceased firing, and the incident was regretted when the full facts were understood. Moreover, when it became known in the city that a group of elderly and defenceless men had been shot down, public reaction against the Volunteers was very hostile. That evening Pearse was forced to give an order prohibiting firing on anyone not carrying weapons, whether or not they were in uniform.[383] The GRs, however, knew that the Rising had begun before they started their march back to Beggar's Bush Barracks. Lord Molony, the head of the Corps, ordered them back to the barracks, and he also telephoned Secretary Nathan to offer the GRs' services; he admitted later that it 'was not anticipated they would be attacked on their return march, but it is clear they came back with the intention of assisting the military authorities and that the latter were aware of their purpose'.[384]

The first regular British troops to come under fire were the Sherwood Foresters, the 7th and 8th Battalions, part of the 178th Infantry Brigade, who had arrived in Kingstown from Liverpool that morning. Sherwood officers Lt Col. W.C. Oates and Col. E.W.S.K. Maconchy, CB, CIE, DSO, were ordered to go straight to Beggar's Bush Barracks and through the Mount Street Bridge area, even though they had been warned of the casualties to the Georgius Rex reserves. Their troops were raw and inexperienced;[385] many of them had never fired a live cartridge, had had training only in trench fighting, had no grenades at first, and were completely overwhelmed by urban/street fighting.[386]

The Sherwoods marched from Kingstown up to Sandymount by Merrion Road, through Pembroke Road (see Pembroke Road, Carrisbrook House) and then into Northumberland Road. C Company (under Capt. Pragnell) took the lead, accompanied by the O/C, Lt Col. Fane, followed by A Company (Capt. Wright) and B Company (Capt. Hanson), with the reserve, D Company (Capt. Cooper), bringing up the rear. C Company advanced in a box formation, with the front platoon in line and the following platoons advancing along the pavement in column, the intention being that they could cover any side streets and clear houses if required.

At about 12.25 p.m. the leading platoon came under fire from 25 Northumberland Road, then manned only by Lt Michael Malone and James Grace. Further down the road, more Volunteers waited patiently in the parochial hall and in Clanwilliam House, which commanded Mount Street Bridge. All these buildings had been prepared for resistance, with barricades on the lower floors. The firing by Malone and Grace was to be the signal to the other defenders to engage the advancing British troops, and they began to lay down harassing fire on the British troops taking shelter behind the little cover available.

Among the first to fall was Capt. F.C. Dietrichsen, most likely by the fire of Malone and Grace, shortly after greeting his wife and children on the street. Soon other officers were falling, as the Volunteers picked them off from the upper floors. The loss of the officers caused great confusion amongst the raw Robin Hoods, some of whom had only been in uniform for three months and most of whom had never been under fire before.

The confusion mounted as the inexperienced troops and officers struggled to pinpoint the enemy positions, and a number of houses were stormed at bayonet point without success. Soon after 5 p.m. another attempt to storm the house at No. 25 was undertaken, with the use of grenades brought up from the nearby Elm Park bombing school. Malone and Grace were in the process of retreating from the house when the door was blown in. Grace dived into the cellar and took cover, but Malone was shot dead as he descended the stairs. Malone and Grace had held the battalion at bay for some five hours and had inflicted heavy casualties on them. With No. 25 taken, the British were now faced with fire coming from the direction of the school buildings further down Northumberland Road and from Clanwilliam House across the bridge.

The British suffered their greatest casualties of the Rising here: three officers were killed and fourteen others wounded, and 216 other ranks were either killed or wounded. (See Mount Street Bridge [Dublin 2] for list of the British killed.) Holden Stoddart, superintendent of the St John's Ambulance Brigade, was killed as he accompanied a stretcher party to aid a wounded soldier here.[387]

Three bodies were buried in the grounds of the parochial hall, and Malone's body was buried at 25 Northumberland Road. These bodies were not removed until 12 May 1916.

29, 31, 33 Northumberland Road: Used as field hospitals by the Sherwood Foresters during the fighting at the bridge.

54 Northumberland Road: Home of Mary Ellen (Nell) Humphreys, a sister of The Ó Rahilly, at the time of the Rising. She and her husband David, an eye surgeon from Limerick, moved here in 1909, and she was involved in nationalist activities from her arrival in Dublin. She continued those activities after the Rising and was very opposed to the Treaty. Always interested in design, she was largely responsible for the family home at 36 Ailesbury Road, to which the family moved from here. She was in the GPO several times during the Rising, but she was captured in the vicinity of her home here and was imprisoned.

122–124 Pembroke Road (and Northumberland Road): **Carrisbrook House**, an outpost of de Valera's garrison at Boland's Bakery. The house was taken over early in the Rising but it was abandoned, as no safe escape route was available.

3 Percy Place: Home of C. Hanchette Hyland (29), a dentist. When the fighting started, he donned a white coat and went out to help the wounded, and survived unscathed. The next morning, he was merely looking out his back door when he was shot dead.

Shelbourne Road: Beggar's Bush Barracks. Part of the task of de Valera's 3rd Battalion was to 'dominate' the barracks, but they made no attempt to do so. The British had few troops there and it could have been taken. 'There was nothing in Beggar's Bush Barracks, if only they had rushed it.'[388] On Tuesday, a sentry here came to Capt. Gerrard and reported that he had just shot two young girls. When asked why, the sentry replied: 'I thought they were rebels. I was told they were dressed in all classes of attire.'

The barracks was not a regular military establishment and there were only two regular British officers present on Monday. Their sole defence consisted of sixteen service rifles (which the men did not know how to use) and little ammunition. They held the barracks until the Sherwood Foresters arrived.[389]

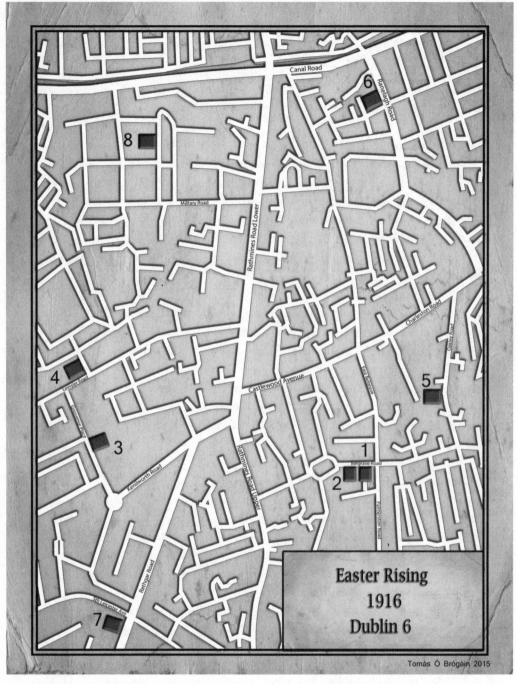

Easter Rising
1916
Dublin 6

Tomás Ó Brógáin 2015

1 7 Belgrave Road, Rathmines, home of Alderman
   Thomas Kelly
2 9 Belgrave Road, Rathmines, home of Dr Kathleen
   Lynn and Madeleine ffrench-Mullen
3 11 Grosvenor Place, Rathmines (now No. 21), home
   of Hanna and Francis Sheehy-Skeffington

4 49B Leinster Road, Rathmines, home of Countess
   Constance Markievicz
5 21 Oakley Road, Ranelagh, Cullenswood House
6 19 Ranelagh Road, Ryan family home
7 53 Rathgar Road, home of Dr Séamus Kelly
8 Rathmines Road, Portobello Barracks

Dublin 6

Key locations

Belgrave Road
Cullenswood House—St Enda's—
   St Ita's
Portobello Barracks (Rathmines Road)
   (now Cathal Brugha Barracks)

Ranelagh
Rathgar
Rathmines

D ublin 6 is a primarily residential area in the south of County Dublin. Rathmines has a long history, stretching back to the fourteenth century. At that time Rathmines and its surrounding hinterland were part of the ecclesiastical lands called *Cuallu* or *Cuallan*, later the vast parish of Cullenswood, which gave its name to a nearby area and to Cullenswood Road, on which Padraic Pearse first founded his school, St Enda's, in Cullenswood House. Rathmines was a popular southern suburb of Dublin, attracting the wealthy and powerful seeking refuge from the poor living conditions of the city from the middle of the nineteenth century.

'[FRANCIS SHEEHY-SKEFFINGTON] WAS BESIDES, I THINK, THE HONESTEST MAN IN IRELAND'
Robert Lynd

Early in the twentieth century Rathmines, and particularly Belgrave Road, became known for all the republicans living there. Count and Countess Plunkett, Alderman Thomas Kelly, Robert and Una Brennan, Nora Connolly O'Brien, Count and Countess Markievicz, Agnes O'Farrelly and Kathleen Lynn were among those living in the area.

Dr Kathleen Lynn was one of the most noted women of the period, and also served as a member of the Citizen Army in the Rising. As the medical officer in the City Hall (Dublin 2), she was the one who surrendered the garrison after its ICA leaders were killed. Appalled by the fact that 16% of Dublin infants were dying from preventable diseases, in 1919 Dr Lynn and her partner Madeleine ffrench-Mullen founded St Ultan's Children's Hospital as a hospital 'for the medical treatment of infants under one year of age'. With due reference to her treatment by her medical masters while training at the Adelaide Hospital, Dr Lynn was 'adamant that the staff of St Ultan's would be confined to women medical staff only'. (Though she was the first woman to be elected a resident doctor at the Adelaide Hospital, prejudice prevented her from going into residence there.) St Ultan's became the front line in the battle against infant mortality, and provided the opportunity for Dr Dorothy Price to continue her research on childhood tuberculosis, leading to the establishing of the research unit at the hospital. They introduced a Montessori ward in the hospital and made a significant contribution to the eradication of tuberculosis in Ireland.

Francis and Hanna Sheehy-Skeffington, both known for their suffrage activism and pacifism, also lived in Dublin 6, on Belgrave Road. Francis was one of Dublin's most revered pacifists and eccentrics. He was individualistic in disposition and unconventional in temperament; he refused to shave and wore knickerbockers and long socks. As an ardent proponent of rights for women, he prominently wore a badge that read *Votes for Women*. Shortly after he married, he organised a petition to lobby for women to be admitted to UCD on the same basis as men. Both Sheehy-Skeffingtons supported Home Rule but were not supporters of the Volunteers. Strangely, in spite of his pacifist views Francis was on the first committee of the Irish Citizen Army. He and Hanna took opposing positions towards the Rising. He advocated his pacifist principles and preferred civil disobedience, while Hanna brought food to the rebels in the General Post Office and the Royal College of Surgeons. Francis attempted to raise a citizen's force to quell the looting but attracted no followers. On his way home from one of his forays into the city centre he was arrested.

Dublin 6 is also home to Portobello Barracks (now Cathal Brugha Barracks, named after the hero of the South Dublin Union [Dublin 8]). Infamously, during the Rising it was the scene of one of the most notorious British atrocities, when Capt. J.C. Bowen-Colthurst murdered Francis Sheehy-Skeffington and J.J. Coade (a young man aged about nineteen returning from a sodality meeting and unaware of the curfew), as well as two magazine editors, Patrick MacIntyre and Thomas Dickson, who had nothing to do with the Rising. Although no action was taken against Bowen-Colthurst at first, he was finally tried after Major Sir Francis Vane put his career on the line in order to bring him to justice. A court martial on 6 June 1916 found Bowen-Colthurst guilty but insane; he was confined in the Broadmoor Criminal Lunatic Asylum but was later released.

At various times James Joyce, Éamon de Valera, Taoiseach Jack Lynch and Bram Stoker also lived in Rathgar.

7 Belgrave Road, Rathmines: Home of Thomas Kelly, Dublin alderman. He read the 'Castle Document' (allegedly 'forged' by Joseph Plunkett) at the Dublin Corporation meeting on 19 April 1916. (See 53 Rathgar Road; Kimmage, Larkfield [Dublin 6W].)

7 Belgrave Road, Rathmines: Home of Hanna Sheehy-Skeffington. Hanna lived here after Francis's murder and after being evicted from 11 (now 21) Grosvenor Place, Rathmines, where she lived with Francis and their son Owen. She was a judge of the Dáil Éireann/Republican Courts and was a member of the first Fianna Fáil executive in 1926. Rosamund Jacob sometimes lodged here. (See Grosvenor Place.)

9 Belgrave Road, Rathmines: Home of Dr Kathleen Lynn and Madeleine ffrench-Mullen.

Born in Cong, Co. Mayo, and educated in Dublin, England and Germany, Dr Lynn qualified as a doctor in 1899. She saw a great deal of poverty as a child and recalled: 'The local doctor was a fount of help and hope so I decided to become a doctor'. Awarded degrees in surgery and medicine from the Royal University in 1899, having interned at Holles Street Hospital (1897–9), the Rotunda Hospital (1899), the Royal Victoria Eye and Ear Hospital (1899) and the Richmond Lunatic Asylum, she became a Fellow of the Royal College of Surgeons in Ireland in 1909.[390] She fought in the Rising, was imprisoned and deported, but was released in 1918 to fight the influenza epidemic of that year.[391] She died in September 1955 and was given a military funeral, as she was a commanding officer during the Rising.[392]

Madeleine ffrench-Mullen was a member of the Irish Women's Franchise League and a staunch supporter of James Connolly as a member of the Irish Citizen Army, serving in the Liberty Hall soup kitchens during the 1913 Lockout. A frequent contributor to *Bean na hÉireann*, she had a lifelong commitment to the causes of labour and women's rights and the emancipation of the working class. She invested a significant portion of her life in building the Irish Women's Workers' Union, and was elected a vice-president in 1917 (as was Dr Lynn). During the Rising she commanded the medical detachment at St Stephen's Green and was imprisoned in Richmond Barracks and Kilmainham Gaol.

In 1919 Dr Lynn and Miss ffrench-Mullen founded St Ultan's Children's Hospital and it became a locus for the eradication of tuberculosis in Dublin's children.

Helena Molony often lodged here.[393]

11 Bushy Park Road, Rathgar: Home of Mrs Jackson; converted to an auxiliary hospital during the Rising.[394]

11 Grosvenor Place, Rathmines (now No. 21): Home of Francis and Hanna Sheehy-Skeffington and their son Owen;[395] situated just on the other side of Portobello Bridge over the Grand Canal from Portobello Barracks.

Francis was the first lay registrar of University College Dublin; he resigned after a dispute in which he favoured allowing academic status to women. He was 37 when he was murdered during the Rising and is buried in Glasnevin Cemetery.[396] Just after his death Hanna and Owen were evicted and moved to 43 Moyne Road, Rathmines.

Born on 27 May 1877 in Kanturk, Co. Cork, Hanna was raised in County Tipperary. Her father was an MP and she had an early memory of visiting her uncle, Fr Eugene Sheehy, in Kilmainham Gaol for Land League activities. She attended the Dominican Convent School in Eccles Street, Dublin, being among the first generation of women to benefit from the new educational reforms.[397] She attended the Royal

University, receiving a BA in 1899 and an MA in 1902.[398] When she and fellow student Francis Skeffington were married on 27 June 1903 they combined their surnames, and she gave her husband the credit for awakening her commitment to women's issues. They had one son, Owen.[399]

Hanna and Frank were friendly with James Connolly; they supported the labour movement during the 1913 Lockout but took no active part in the 1916 Rising. As pacifists they had been critical in the *Irish Citizen* of recruitment for the British Army, and as feminists they denounced the subordination of Cumann na mBan to the Irish Volunteers. (Curiously for a pacifist, Frank was on the first Council of the Irish Citizen Army and served as co-vice-chairman.)

(See 7 Belgrave Road, Moyne Road; Rathmines Road/Portobello Barracks.)

49B Leinster Road, Rathmines: Surrey House; home of Countess Constance Gore-Booth Markievicz.[400] She moved into the house in 1912. James Connolly and his family lived here between 1913 and 1916. Prior to the Rising it was a great meeting and gathering place for nationalists.[401] *The Spark* and the *Workers' Republic* were printed here. (See 70 Eccles Street [Dublin 2].) The January 1916 article/editorial 'What is Our Programme?' clearly stated their position:

> Mark well then our programme. While the war lasts and Ireland still is a subject nation we shall continue to urge her to fight for her freedom.
>
> We shall continue, in season and out of season, to teach that the 'farflung battle line' of England is weakest at the point nearest its heart, that Ireland is in that position of tactical advantage, that a defeat of England in India, Egypt, the Balkans or Flanders would not be so dangerous to the British Empire as any conflict of armed forces in Ireland, that the time for Ireland's battle is NOW, the place for Ireland's battle is HERE.
>
> That a strong man may deal lusty blows with his fists against a host of surrounding foes and conquer, but will succumb if a child sticks a pin in his heart.
>
> But the moment peace is once admitted by the British Government as being a subject ripe for discussion, *that moment OUR policy will be for peace* and in direct opposition to all talk or preparation for armed revolution.
>
> We will be no party to leading out Irish patriots to meet the might of an England at peace. The moment peace is in the air we shall strictly confine ourselves, and lend all our influence to the work of turning the thought of Labour in Ireland to the work of peaceful reconstruction.
>
> That is our programme. You can now compare it with the programme of those who bid you hold your hand now, and thus put it in the power of the enemy to patch up a temporary peace, turn round and smash you at his leisure, and then go to war again with the Irish question settled—in the graves of Irish patriots.

We fear that is what is going to happen. It is to our mind inconceivable that the British public should allow conscription to be applied to England and not to Ireland. Nor do the British Government desire it. But that Government will use the cry of the necessities of war to force conscription upon the people of England, and will then make a temporary peace, and turn round to force Ireland to accept the same terms as have been forced upon England.

The English public will gladly see this done—misfortune likes company. The situation will then shape itself thus: the Irish Volunteers who are pledged to fight conscription will either need to swallow their pledge, and see the young men of Ireland conscripted, or will need to resent conscription, and engage the military force of England at a time when England is at peace.

This is what the diplomacy of England is working for, what the stupidity of some of our leaders who imagine they are Wolfe Tones is making possible. It is our duty, it is the duty of all who wish to save Ireland from such shame or such slaughter to strengthen the hand of the leaders who are for action as against those who are playing the hands of the enemy.

We are neither rash nor cowardly—we know our opportunity when we see it and we know when it has gone. We know that at the end of this England will have at least an army of one million men, or *more than ten soldiers for every adult male in Ireland*. And these soldiers are veterans of the greatest war in history.

We shall not want to fight those men. We shall devote our attention to organising their comrades who return to civil life, to organising them trade unions and Labour parties to secure them their rights in civil life.

Unless we emigrate to some country where there are men.[402]

This was published the day after Connolly's return from his 'kidnapping' but was undoubtedly written before it. (See Dolphin's Barn [Dublin 8].)

The house became a de facto headquarters for the Fianna. The older members gathered here and a small firing range was set up in the basement. These members became known as the 'Surrey House clique'. There was also a wireless set and the Fianna were trained in its use, leading to a raid by the DMP. After the raid the Fianna moved their headquarters to proper rooms at 12 D'Olier Street (Dublin 2).

43 Moyne Road, Rathmines: Home of Hanna Sheehy-Skeffington and her son Owen after they were evicted from Grosvenor Place following Francis's murder. They then moved to Belgrave Road. (See Belgrave Road, Grosvenor Place, Rathmines Road/Portobello Barracks.)

21 Oakley Road, Ranelagh: Cullenswood House. Padraic Pearse's *Scoil Éanna*, St Enda's School. (See Grange Road, Rathfarnham [Dublin 14].) Later St Ita's School.

This was the first site of St Enda's, founded by Padraic Pearse and Thomas MacDonagh and opened on 8 September 1908. It was originally conceived as St Lorcan's School but took the name St Enda's from the patron saint of Pearse's beloved Aran Islands. When St Enda's moved to a site on Grange Road in Rathfarnham (the Hermitage) in 1910, this site became St Ita's. Mrs Pearse reopened St Enda's here after the Rising while the Hermitage was occupied by British troops, and then moved back to the Grange Road site.

Cullenswood House currently houses Gaelscoil Lios na nÓg, an Irish-language primary school founded in 1996.

29 Oakley Road, Ranelagh: The Grace House; Thomas MacDonagh's home. He moved here in 1910 in order to be closer to St Enda's. Muriel Gifford (sister of Grace Gifford Plunkett) married Thomas MacDonagh on 3 January 1912. Grace Gifford stayed here at the time of the Rising.

Oakley Road, Ranelagh: 'The Mill House'; Bulmer Hobson's home.[403] Hobson was the only Quaker among the Volunteer leaders.[404] In collaboration with Tom Clarke, Hobson was part of the group that reorganised the IRB, and along with Eoin MacNeill was a leader of the Irish Volunteers. (See Wynn's Hotel, Abbey Street Lower and Rotunda Hospital, Great Britain Street [Dublin 1]; 206 Great Brunswick Street [Dublin 2]; Cabra Park, Martin Conlon's home [Dublin 7].)

Palmerston Road, Rathmines, 8 Temple Villas: Home of Grace Gifford Plunkett. This was the address she listed on her wedding engagement announcement.[405] She and Joseph Plunkett became engaged on 2 December 1915 and announced their engagement on 11 February 1916.

Both Grace and her sister Muriel, Thomas MacDonagh's wife, were fervent nationalists and converts to Catholicism. It was said that 'whenever those vivacious girls entered a gloomy Sinn Féin room, they turned it into a flower garden'. Grace was an artist with a special talent for caricatures, and she left a lovely painting of the Madonna in her cell at Kilmainham Gaol, where she was imprisoned during the Civil War.[406]

3 Pembroke Cottages: Home of Bridget Stewart (11), who was shot and died on 28 April in Royal City Hospital.[407] Another casualty, Margaret McGuinness (54), was killed in the Rising and was listed as having this address.

19 Ranelagh Road: The Ryan family home. Jim and his sisters lived here before the Rising.[408] Mary Kate (Kit) married Seán T. O'Kelly, but the couple had no children; Ellen (Nell) never married; Mary Josephine (Min) became Mrs Richard Mulcahy and they had six children; Phyllis became Seán T. O'Kelly's second wife two years after her

sister's death, but they, too, were childless.[409]

Although Kit and Nell had taken no part in the Rising, they were both imprisoned. Phyllis and Min brought food and messages to the GPO. Min escaped arrest and was sent to the US to coordinate with John Devoy and Clan na Gael.

Min and Phyllis visited Seán MacDermott in Kilmainham[410] (Min was his fiancée) and they were the last two to see him:

> He preferred to talk of casual matters, asking about different people we knew, enjoying little jokes almost as though we were in Bewley's. He had worked and planned for Irish Independence since boyhood. His last words, save for his prayers, were 'God Save Ireland'. At four o'clock, when the shooting was done, a gentle rain began to fall—the tears of Dark Rosaleen.[411]

53 Rathgar Road: Home of Dr Séamus O'Kelly (Ó Ceallaigh). Arthur Griffith,[412] Thomas MacDonagh, Eoin MacNeill, The Ó Rahilly, Seán Fitzgibbon,[413] Liam Ó Briain,[414] Joseph Plunkett and Seán MacDermott met here at various times on Holy Saturday night (22 April). MacNeill determined that the 'Castle Document' was a fake, and that the *Aud* had been captured/sunk and no German arms were forthcoming.[415] (See 7 Belgrave Road, Rathmines; Kimmage, Larkfield [Dublin 6W].)

At first, MacNeill had been convinced that this document relayed the true intentions of Dublin Castle. In response, he issued the following order to the Volunteers:

> Your object will be to preserve the arms and organisation of the Irish Volunteers . . . In general, you will arrange that your men defend themselves and each other in small groups . . .

When MacNeill found that he had been deceived about the Rising, that the 'Castle Document' may have been forged, that Roger Casement had been captured in Tralee and that the German arms ship *Aud* had been lost, he cancelled the manoeuvres scheduled for Easter. He dispatched messengers throughout the country with countermanding orders for the Sunday Rising: 'Volunteers completely deceived. All orders for special action are hereby cancelled, and on no account will action be taken.'[416] He issued an order on Saturday night, published in the next day's *Sunday Independent*:

> Owing to the very critical position, all orders given to Irish Volunteers for tomorrow, Easter Sunday, are hereby rescinded, and no parades, marches, or other movements of Irish Volunteers will take place. Each individual Volunteer will obey this order strictly in every particular.[417]

The members of the IRB's Military Council (Pearse, Clarke, Connolly, Ceannt, MacDonagh, Plunkett and MacDermott) angrily decided to call a meeting in Liberty Hall on Easter Sunday morning.

> I saw Eoin MacNeill's countermanding order in the paper and heard the discussion in Liberty Hall. Connolly was there. They were all heartbroken and when they were not crying they were cursing. I kept thinking 'does this mean that we are not going to go out?' There were thousands like us. It was foolish of MacNeill and those to think they could call it off. They could not. Many of us thought we would go out single-handed, if necessary.[418]

In that meeting, the Rising's leaders determined that to delay further would be fatal for their plans: the Rising was rescheduled for Monday at noon. The Military Council made two equally important decisions: (1) to send dispatches immediately to the various commands *confirming* MacNeill's cancellation of that day's manoeuvres; and (2) that the Rising would commence the next day at noon, and that dispatches to that effect would be sent out on Sunday night. The first decision was intended to remove the possibility that units outside Dublin might start their operations before the Dublin battalions could revise their plans and occupy their allotted positions on Easter Monday. Moreover, Pearse intended that this would obviate any further action by MacNeill. Alternatively, it was thought that if the British became aware of this follow-up to MacNeill's order their suspicions would be allayed.

On Friday morning, toward the end of the Rising, Pearse issued a War Bulletin from the GPO that included the following:

> If we accomplish no more than we have accomplished, I am satisfied. I am satisfied that we have saved Ireland's honour. I am satisfied that we should have accomplished more, that we should have accomplished the task of enthroning as well as proclaiming the Irish Republic as a Sovereign State, had our arrangements for a simultaneous Rising of the whole country, with a combined plan as sound as the Dublin plan has proved to be, been allowed to go through on Easter Sunday. Of the fatal countermanding order which prevented those plans being carried out, I shall not speak further. Both Eoin MacNeill and we have acted in the best interests of Ireland.[419]

But the views of the members of the Military Council were well known and were not so kindly ambiguous. Plunkett was reported to have spoken to Pearse of 'how much bigger an event it would have been had the original plans gone forward unchecked'.[420] Piaras Béaslaí recorded that Tom Clarke told him: 'Our plans were so perfect, and now everything is spoiled. I feel as if I'd like to go away in a corner and cry.'[421] In Kilmainham Gaol Clarke told his wife, Kathleen, of MacNeill: 'I want you to see to it that our people know of his [MacNeill's] treachery to us. He must never be allowed back into the national life of the country, for sure as he is, so sure he will act treacherously in a crisis. He is a weak man, but I know every effort will be made to whitewash him.'[422] Seán MacDermott said 'We have been betrayed again'.[423] Éamonn Ceannt told his wife, Áine, 'MacNeill has ruined us, he has stopped the Rising'.[424] While Ceannt planned to sleep away from home on Saturday, he later remarked to her: 'I may thank MacNeill that I can sleep in my own home—the cancelling of manoeuvres will lead the British to think everything is all right'.[425]

MacNeill later addressed his decision:

. . . all that was actually counted upon was shipments of sufficient arms and ammunition.

This obviously was a vital need. Without equipment we could do nothing. But when at last word came that the shipments were on their way, Easter Sunday was fixed as the date for the beginning of hostilities, always conditional on the safe arrival of the arms and ammunition. At least this was my understanding. And that was where I was in error! I did not know that a little coterie among our leaders was inspired with an idea of the intrinsic value of martyrdom for martyrdom's sake! But I will come to that presently.

Of course, without those German arms and ammunition they must have failed in any event had I not issued the countermanding orders but in the resultant confusion, with our forces in all parts of the country, notably in Cork, remaining passive, it seemed that this mad act of desperation by a mere handful of men poorly equipped and with no support to depend upon would constitute the most lamentable, futile gesture in the annals of Ireland's struggling centuries. Undoubtedly this would have been the case had it not been for England's stupidity!

The truth, as I afterwards learned it, was that Clarke and Pearse and MacDonagh and the others had deliberately planned to go down to certain defeat and death. If ever seven men were animated by pure martyrdom it was these patriots. They were willing to give their lives to move their countrymen to work together in the cause they would thus ennoble. And yet how easily instead they might have found themselves a laughing stock!

If England had only used the Dublin police force instead of high explosive shells and all the paraphernalia of war, arrested the leaders on a charge of disturbing the peace or, perhaps, trespass and regarded the feint in its true light, the prank of irresponsible idealists not to be taken seriously, she could have led a world to join in ironic laughter! In that fashion the cause of Irish freedom could have been set back a generation. Every Irishman must thank God that England made the mistake of treating it seriously, thereby giving it a dignity with which nothing else could have invested it.

The seven martyrs went to martyrs' deaths. Their fondest dreams were exceeded. Ireland's freedom was at last in sight!

This explanation, I trust, will establish once and for all my motive in issuing those orders.[426]

(See Kimmage, Larkfield, 'The Castle Document' [Dublin 6W].)

Rathmines Road: Portobello Barracks (now Cathal Brugha Barracks). Opened in 1815, it was generally a cavalry barracks, but in 1888 the cavalry left for Marlborough Barracks in Cabra. In 1916 the 3rd Reserve Battalion of the Royal Irish Rifles was stationed here under the command of Lt Col. McCammond, who was on sick leave, and command devolved on Major J. Rosborough.

Capt. J.C. Bowen-Colthurst murdered Francis Sheehy-Skeffington here, along with J.J. Coade (a young man aged about nineteen returning from a sodality meeting and unaware of the curfew) and two magazine editors, Patrick MacIntyre and Thomas Dickson.[427]

Sheehy-Skeffington was one of Dublin's most noted pacifists and eccentrics. He often took up a station in front of the Custom House and began expounding on any topic of the day that displeased him. Both Connolly and Pearse thought him a man of high principle, though he argued with their wishes for a physical-force rebellion. After seeing some of the looting on Sackville Street on the first day of the Rising, he wished to establish a committee to halt such action. Sheehy-Skeffington's intent was to establish a 'citizen's police force' to prevent looting. His 'manifesto' read:

When there are no regular police on the streets, it becomes the duty of the citizens to police the streets themselves—to prevent such spasmodic looting as has taken place in a few streets. Citizens (men and women) who are willing to this end are asked to attend at Westmoreland Church at five o'clock this Tuesday afternoon.

There were no volunteers for his force.[428]

On Tuesday evening Sheehy-Skeffington decided to return to his home near the Portobello Bridge. As he neared Portobello Barracks, the pickets stopped him, arrested him and detained him inside the barracks.[429] When Bowen-Colthurst returned at midnight, he took charge of Sheehy-Skeffington, intending to use him as a hostage. Bowen-Colthurst then headed up the Rathmines Road, several times firing his pistol into the air. At Rathmines Church he found two boys who had just left a sodality meeting and ordered them to stop. To avoid trouble, J.J. Coade (19) turned away. Bowen-Colthurst ordered a soldier to bash his head with a rifle, and as Coade fell to the ground Bowen-Colthurst shot him dead.[430]

After killing Coade, Bowen-Colthurst led his small patrol to a pub owned by Alderman James Kelly and they wrecked it. Possibly Bowen-Colthurst confused Alderman *James* Kelly with Sinn Féin Alderman *Tom* Kelly. In the pub, Bowen-Colthurst arrested two newspaper editors who were there and had nothing to do with the Rising: Thomas Dickson and Patrick MacIntyre Then the men returned to Portobello Barracks, where Bowen-Colthurst told Sheehy-Skeffington to say his prayers. When Sheehy-Skeffington refused, Bowen-Colthurst told his men to remove their hats and he prayed for them all.

At his trial, Bowen-Colthurst testified that he spent the night looking over documents he had seized from the men and came to the conclusion that they were all 'very suspicious and dangerous characters'. He told the officer in charge of the guardroom that he was 'taking the prisoners out into the yard and shooting them as it is the right thing to do'.[431] Later he described all three as 'leaders of the rebels' and desperate men who would 'try to escape'.[432]

Bowen-Colthurst was a sixteen-year veteran of the Royal Irish Rifles in India, was seriously wounded in France and often said this prayer there: 'O Lord God, if it shall please Thee to take away the life of this man, forgive him for Christ's sake. Amen'.[433] Bowen-Colthurst found the biblical quotation he was looking for that evening in the Gospel of Luke: 'But those mine enemies, which would not that I should reign over them, bring hither and slay them before me'.[434]

All the deceased were Catholic. Fr F. O'Loughlin, an Army chaplain, administered the last rites; they were buried in Portobello Barracks and then were reinterred after the Rising. Fr O'Loughlin presided at their exhumation and read the service at their reinterment.

Hanna Sheehy-Skeffington's two sisters, Mrs Mary Kettle and Mrs Margaret Culhane, went to Portobello Barracks and were arrested on a charge of 'talking to Sinn Féiners'—meaning Hanna and Francis.[435]

Bowen-Colthurst attempted a cover-up and ordered the ransacking of Sheehy-Skeffington's home, looking for evidence to implicate him. Major Sir Francis Fletcher Vane was in overall charge of defence at Portobello Barracks but was not present when these executions took place. He arrived shortly afterwards and was horrified at what had unfolded. He recognised the killings as murder, and called upon Hanna Sheehy-Skeffington.[436]

Vane reported to the deputy commander of the garrison, Major Rosborough, that Bowen-Colthurst was mentally deranged. Rosborough telephoned Dublin Castle and was told to bury the bodies. Vane subsequently travelled to London, where he met Lord Kitchener on 3 May 1916. A telegram was sent to Gen. John Maxwell, commander-in-chief of British forces in Ireland, ordering the arrest of Bowen-Colthurst, but Maxwell refused to arrest him. Vane put his career on the line and Bowen-Colthurst was eventually arrested on 6 June, charged with murder and court-martialled.

Vane was subsequently relieved of all duties and left the army.

Is the hon. Gentleman aware that Colonel Maconochie [sic], on the 8th May, reported as follows on Sir Francis Vane: 'That he rendered valuable assistance, that his dispositions were excellent, and that he recommended him to be mentioned in dispatches, and to be permitted to return to the front'; and whether it is a fact that Sir J. Maxwell has now discontinued his services solely because he reported, and insisted upon reporting, the murder of Skeffington and others in Portobello Barracks?[437]

A court martial on 6 June 1916 found that Bowen-Colthurst was guilty but insane; he was confined in the Broadmoor Criminal Lunatic Asylum, but was later released. A British inquiry found that there was 'no incriminating evidence' on any of the men shot.[438]

Seán O'Casey wrote:

In this new wine a lowly life like a pearl has been dissolved; a life untarnished by worldly ambition or selfish perception; a life of mourning struggle and valorous effort sacrificed humbly and fearlessly for the general good; sacrificed under circumstances that stripped the offering of all the draperies of martyrdom. Unwept, except by a few, unhonoured and unsung—for no national society of Sheehy-Skeffington, like the tiny mustard seed today, will possibly grow into a tree that will afford shade and rest to many souls overheated with the stress and toil of barren politics.

He was the living antithesis of the Easter insurrection: a spirit of peace enveloped in the flame and rage and hatred of the contending elements, absolutely free from all its terrifying madness; and yet he was the purified soul of revolt against not only one nation's injustice to another, but he was also the soul of revolt against man's inhumanity to man. And in this blazing pyre of national differences his beautiful nature, as far as this world is concerned, was consumed, leaving behind a hallowed and inspiring memory of the perfect love that casteth out fear, against which there can be no law.

In Sheehy-Skeffington, and not in Connolly, fell the first martyr to Irish Socialism, for he linked Ireland not only with the little nations struggling for self-expression but with the world's humanity struggling for a higher life. He indeed was the ripest ear of corn that fell in Easter week, and as it is true that when an ear of corn falls into the ground and dies it bringeth forth much fruit, so will the sown body of Sheehy-Skeffington bring forth, ultimately, in the hearts of his beloved people, the rich crop of goodly thoughts which shall strengthen us all in our onward march towards the fuller development of our national and social life.[439]

In his book of essays, Robert Lynd characterised Sheehy-Skeffington's death as one that Ireland could ill afford:

Sheehy-Skeffington's death at the hands of soldiers in the Dublin rising stirs the imagination all the more profoundly because not merely was he innocent of any crime, but he seemed to be almost the only person left in Ireland who was an irreconcilable believer in peace . . .

Skeffington was constantly in a minority of one even in the house of his friends . . .

Orthodox members of all leagues have a way of passing resolutions and then going asleep for the rest of the year. Skeffington's resolutions all had the object of waking people up.

He did not believe in tact or compromise. He believed in fighting for principles. And he was always doing it . . . As a result, Skeffington was constantly at odds with the majority. He became a sort of legend as an interrupter of the somnolent. One thought of his red beard as a storm-signal, and of his long knicker-bockers as an assertion of principle at all times and in all places. Every orthodoxy in Dublin regarded him as an eccentric . . .

But however much one differed from him, one could still watch his fighting and heretical progress with immense admiration for his devotion and courage. He was a 'bonnie fighter'.

He was besides, I think, the honestest man in Ireland.

How generous was the spirit in which, in those days of insurrection, the police having been withdrawn from the streets of Dublin, he set out for the danger-zone to remind the poor and the starved of their duties of citizenship! That lonely mission to put down looting in the streets was a worthy last act in a life devoted to noble causes.

'You will find out your mistake afterwards', he said to the soldiers who were about to shoot him and having said so he died smiling.

Ireland, and the world, could ill afford to lose so good a citizen, so daring, so energetic, so challenging, so individual. Probably he would never have been the leader of a large party in Irish politics however long he had lived. But as a guerrilla critic in advance of his age, he would have been of infinite service in a self-governing Ireland.

He was less a dreamer than a propagandist. But every humanitarian cause in Ireland, while gaining an example, has lost a heroic champion through his death.[440]

Portobello Barracks is now known as **Cathal Brugha Barracks** and houses the Irish Military Archives, including the **Bureau of Military History**.

5 Sandford Terrace, Ranelagh: Home of Mrs Augustine (Elsie) Henry. A wealthy lady, she kept a diary of all she observed during the Rising and how it affected the citizenry of Dublin.[441] Her diaries are an invaluable source for how Dubliners assessed the situation, but they also demonstrate how many rumours were in circulation: for example, she indicated that the Volunteers had a 'machine gun mounted on the top of the Post Office and they were firing with it'. It is known, however, that the Volunteers had no machine-guns.

12 Villiers Road, Rathmines: Home of H.J. Tipping; he was the controller of the GPO and was in charge of opening accounts and funding after the Rising.

Dublin 6W

Key locations

Harold's Cross
Kimmage

L arkfield, in Kimmage, Co. Dublin, has the
Dublin 6W postal code. Located in south-
west Dublin, it can be reached by taking
Harold's Cross Road to Kimmage Road. The
estate was on the boundary of Rathmines and
Kimmage and is between what were then the
rural villages of Crumlin, Kimmage and Terenure.

> '*First, the following
> persons are to be placed
> under arrest—All
> members of the Sinn Féin
> National Council . . . '*
> *from the 'Castle Document'*

Commandant Éamonn Ceannt's 4th Battalion trained and billeted here before
the Rising. Nearly all the men in the 'Kimmage Garrison' were born in or came from
England, or were Irishmen 'on the run'. The men were not, however, commonly
known by that name until about mid-century, when the Bureau of Military History
started taking Witness Statements. Men from the Kimmage Garrison, along with men
from the ICA, formed the core of the Irish troops that stormed the GPO on Monday.
Almost all were members of the Gaelic League and/or the GAA, and the IRB has
been accused of 'hijacking' those organisations for recruiting purposes.

In 1913 Countess Josephine Plunkett took a lease on Larkfield House and mill.
Countess Plunkett was the wife of George Noble Plunkett (a papal count) and they
had seven children. One of their sons, Joseph, was a signatory to the *Proclamation* and
was executed after the Rising. Two other sons, Jack and George, also fought, and their
daughter, Geraldine, was in the Imperial Hotel directly across from the GPO when it
was attacked on Monday. The countess was a wealthy woman in her own right. On
her marriage she retained total control of her inheritance and went on to speculate by
acquiring other properties. When she took the lease on the Larkfield property her sole
intention was to generate rental income by subletting the property.

Countess Plunkett set about making some changes. According to Geraldine
Plunkett Dillon, her mother dismantled the internal structure of the mill's boiler-
house and created two four-roomed cottages. Within the mill there were now two
businesses in operation. Brothers James and George Quinn, who were poplin-weavers,
worked with their loom making silk poplin. Another brother, Thomas, who was a
baker, operated a small bakery.

Sometime early in 1914 Larkfield became the operational base for the 4th
Battalion. This came about through the activities of Joseph and his brothers George

and Jack, as well as under the leadership of Cmdt Éamonn Ceannt. The first meeting of the 4th Battalion took place at the Larkfield mill in January 1914; the mill was established as the battalion's headquarters, and the Volunteers had use of the shooting range at Larkfield. The 4th Battalion advertised their activities in the *Irish Volunteer* in April 1914: 'The battalion HQ is at Larkfield Kimmage Road. There are full facilities for indoor and outdoor drill and on fine moonlit nights, the men drill in the open. All the companies of this battalion drill at Larkfield.'

In 1914 Geraldine Dillon moved to Larkfield. She had become the main carer for her brother Joseph, who was suffering from advanced glandular tuberculosis. Joseph continued with his writings and planning for the Rising and he was able to make use of the printing press that had been set up here. By autumn of 1915 Geraldine had moved the Plunkett family into the house: her brothers Joseph, George and Jack and their father, Count Plunkett, joined her. Her mother was in the USA at this time. By then Joseph was a member of the IRB Military Council and a planner of military operations for the Irish Volunteers. He spent much of 1915 travelling to and from Germany, receiving medical treatment while meeting with Roger Casement and seeking German support for the IRB's plans for a rising. When he was in Dublin he stayed at Larkfield and it became his headquarters. Consequently, the executive of the Irish Volunteers held several meetings at Larkfield. By early 1916 the activity at the Larkfield mill became more intense, as it was transformed into an armed camp, with about 90 men living on the premises.

Later, it is said, Joseph utilised a small hand-press here on which the 'Castle Document' was printed on 13 April 1916. This document alleged that the Castle authorities proposed to arrest many important and well-known public figures, and to raid the business premises and residences of them and several other persons, including the residence of the archbishop of Dublin, William Walsh. It became known as the 'Castle Document' and was read to the Dublin Corporation by Alderman Thomas Kelly. Kelly was very well respected and so the document was believed, but most now think that Plunkett had it 'forged' on the press here.

On Easter Monday the members of this Kimmage Garrison took a tram into Dublin to join the Rising, and George paid the tuppenny fare for all the men.

Kimmage, Larkfield: Home of Count and Countess Plunkett. The 4th Battalion of the Dublin Brigade trained and billeted here before the Rising.[442] Nearly all the men in the 'Kimmage Garrison' were born in or came from England, or were Irishmen who were 'on the run'. Men from the garrison, along with men from the ICA, formed the core of the GPO garrison.[443]

The first meeting of the 4th Battalion took place here on 21 January 1914, shortly after the Volunteers were founded. The battalion comprised six companies; each

Grace Gifford and Joseph Plunkett became engaged on 2 December 1915. Grace and her sister Muriel, wife of Thomas MacDonagh, were fervent nationalists and converts to Catholicism. It was said that 'whenever those vivacious girls entered a gloomy Sinn Féin room, they turned it into a flower garden'. Grace was an artist with a special talent for caricatures.

Kathleen Clarke was married to Thomas Clarke in the United States in 1901. She was one of the most well-known women of the period and one of very few privy to the plans of the Rising. She served as a TD for Dublin and was the first female lord mayor of Dublin.

Fairview Park is an urban park to the north of central Dublin in Dublin 3. Volunteers met here before the Rising to practise drilling, as well as some tactical training.

Portobello Barracks (now Cathal Brugha Barracks) was opened in 1815. British Capt. J.C. Bowen-Colthurst murdered Francis Sheehy-Skeffington here, along with J.J. Coade (a young man aged about nineteen returning from a sodality meeting and unaware of the curfew) and two magazine editors, Patrick MacIntyre and Thomas Dickson.

Broadstone Railway Station. The Volunteers only held it for a short while, as the British retook it on Tuesday. While they held it, they blew up the permanent way, seized a steam engine and placed it on the up-line to block all incoming trains. They destroyed the signal system and cut telegraph lines.

The bodies of the fourteen men executed in Dublin were buried in the yard of Arbour Hill Detention Centre in a pit of quicklime. All were taken there directly after their execution, and some DMP and British soldiers reported that they were buried in the order in which they were executed.

Edward (Ned) Daly was O/C of the 1st Battalion in the area around the Four Courts and Dublin 7. As regards his preparations, strategy and the actual tactics used during the week, the British noted that his Volunteers had situated themselves to inflict maximum casualties on the English troops with minimum loss to themselves and they gave Daly much credit.

Fr Mathew was a Franciscan priest and a very successful preacher and teetotalist reformer in the mid-eighteenth century. Fr Mathew Hall on Church Street was used as a hospital during the Rising. His statue on O'Connell Street was sculpted by Mary Redmond.

The 1st Battalion, led by Cmdt Edward (Ned) Daly, occupied the Four Courts and the adjacent streets on the north bank of the River Liffey. Daly established his defences around buildings that allowed his limited forces as much movement between positions as possible.

Volunteers of the 1st Battalion attacked the British Linenhall Barracks, demanding the surrender of the troops within. When they refused, the Volunteers set bombs at the gate, and finally the British did surrender. The Volunteers set it alight and, though they subsequently tried to control the fire, it burned until Friday.

TO MY MOTHER

My gift to you hath been the gift of sorrow,
My one return for your rich gifts to me,
Your gift of life, your gift of love and pity,
Your gift of sanity, your gift of faith
(For who hath had such faith as yours
Since the old time, and what were my poor faith
Without your strong belief to found upon?)
For all these precious things my gift to you
Is sorrow. I have seen
Your dear face line, your face soft to my touch,
Familiar to my hands and to my lips
Since I was little:
I have seen
How you have battled with your tears for me,
And with a proud glad look, although your heart
Was breaking. O Mother (for you know me)
You must have known, when I was silent,
That some strange thing within me kept me dumb,
Some strange deep thing, when I should shout my love?
I have sobbed in secret
For that reserve which yet I could not master.
I would have brought royal gifts, and I have brought you
Sorrow and tears: and yet, it may be
That I have brought you something else besides —
The memory of my deed and of my name
A splendid thing which shall not pass away.
When men speak of me, in praise or in dispraise,
You will not heed, but treasure your own memory
Of your first son.

Dublin's Arbour Hill Detention Barracks housed the prisoners prior to their executions. Padraic Pearse, Thomas MacDonagh and Joseph Plunkett were well-known poets, and the Rising became known as the 'Poets' Rebellion'. 'To My Mother' was a poem that Pearse wrote specifically at the request of his mother, Margaret.

The British established Marlborough Barracks in 1888, and the cavalry that was quartered at Portobello Barracks was moved to here. At the time of the Rising, squadrons of the 5th and 12th Lancers of the 6th Cavalry were billeted at Marlborough Barracks (approximate strength 885).

The Royal Barracks (now Collins Barracks, a part of the National Museum of Ireland) was built in 1702 and further extended in the late eighteenth and nineteenth centuries. The complex's main buildings are neoclassical in style. Prior to the Rising, the Barracks housed the 10th Royal Dublin Fusiliers (approximate strength 470—37 officers, 430 other ranks).

From 3 May until 12 May, the leaders of the Rising were executed by firing squad in Kilmainham Gaol. Eleven of the soldiers had live rounds in their weapons, and one round was a blank. Officers loaded the weapons so that no soldier knew whether his weapon contained the blank round or a live one. (Thomas Kent was executed by firing squad on 9 May at Cork Detention Barracks.)

Paddy Holohan led about twenty Volunteers to the Magazine Fort in Phoenix Park. Their mission was to explode the munitions there — and the noise of that explosion was to be the signal to the other rebels throughout Dublin that the Rising was under way. They were only able to detonate a small quantity of the munitions, so the signal didn't work.

Cornelius (Con) Colbert led a Volunteer garrison in Watkin's Brewery, and then they moved to the South Dublin Union. He commanded the Volunteers in the entire Marrowbone Lane Post. He was 28 when he was executed on 8 May.

Fourteen men were executed in Kilmainham Gaol for their participation in the Rising. All the Dublin executions took place in the Stonebreaker's Yard of the Gaol.

Seán Heuston was ordered to hold the Mendicity Institute for Monday afternoon. He asked for and received a small number of reinforcements from the GPO, bringing his garrison to about 35 men, and they held for three days. At 25, Heuston was the youngest executed.

The courts martial following the Rising were held at Richmond Barracks, directed by Brig. Gen. Charles Blackader. The Brigadier said of Padraic Pearse: 'I have just done one of the hardest tasks I have ever had to do. I have had to condemn one of the finest characters I have ever come across. There must be something very wrong in the state of things, that makes a man like that a rebel.'

met here on a different night of the week, and then on Sunday they met for full drilling and manoeuvres.[444] Almost all the men were members of the Gaelic League and the GAA, and many believed that those organisations were 'hijacked' by the IRB for recruiting purposes.[445] Arthur Agnew,[446] Joseph Gleeson,[447] Joe Good,[448] John (Blimey) O'Connor[449] and Séamus Robinson[450] were among those who came from England and who lived and worked here prior to the Rising. Peadar Bracken,[451] Séamus Brennan, Denis Daly[452] and Francis and Michael Flanagan were among those Irishmen who were 'on the run'. Michael Collins, aide-de-camp to Joseph Plunkett in the Rising, worked for the Plunketts here and was at the location almost daily, but he had lodgings in Mountjoy Street. Collins was employed by the Plunketts to try to sort out the family's financial records.

There was a mill on the property where Volunteers manufactured most of the pikes, buckshot and bayonets used in the Rising. There was also a small hand-press here, on which it is said that the 'Castle Document' was printed on 13 April 1916. This document alleged that the Castle authorities proposed to arrest many important and well-known public figures, and to raid the homes and residences of them and several other persons, including the residence of the archbishop of Dublin, William Walsh:

The following precautionary measures have been sanctioned by the Irish Office on the recommendation of the General Officer Commanding the Forces in Ireland. All preparations will be made to put these measures in force immediately on receipt of an order issued from the Chief Secretary's Office, Dublin Castle, and signed by the undersecretary and the General Officer Commanding the Forces in Ireland.

First, the following persons are to be placed under arrest—All members of the Sinn Féin National Council; the Central Executive Irish Sinn Féin Volunteers; General Council Irish Sinn Féin Volunteers; County Board Irish Sinn Féin Volunteers; Executive Committee National Volunteers; Coisde Gnotha Committee Gaelic League. See list (a) three and four and Supplemenatary List (a) two . . .

. . . Dublin Metropolitan Police and Royal Irish Constabulary Forces in Dublin City will be confined to barracks under the direction of Competent Military Authority.

An order will be issued to inhabitants of the city to remain in their houses until such time as Competent Military Authority may direct or otherwise permit; pickets chosen from units of Territorial Forces will be placed at all points marked on maps three and four. Accompanying mounted patrols will continuously visit all points and report every hour.

The following premises will be occupied by adequate forces and all necessary

Secret Orders issued to Military Officers.

The cipher from which this document is copied does not indicate punctuation or capitals.

" The following precautionary measures have been sanctioned by the Irish Office on the recommendation of the General Officer Commanding the Forces in Ireland. All preparations will be made to put these measures in force immediately on receipt of an Order issued from the Chief Secretary's Office, Dublin Castle, and signed by the Under Secretary and the General Officer Commanding the Forces in Ireland. First, the following persons to be placed under arrest :— All members of the Sinn Fein National Council, the Central Executive Irish Sinn Fein Volunteers, General Council Irish Sinn Fein Volunteers, County Board Irish Sinn Fein Volunteers, Executive Committee National Volunteers, Coisde Gnota Committee Gaelic League. See list A 3 and 4 and supplementary list A 2. . . . . . Dublin Metropolitan Police and Royal Irish Constabulary Forces in Dublin City will be confined to barracks under the direction of the Competent Military Authority. An order will be issued to inhabitants of city to remain in their houses until such time as the Competent Military Authority may otherwise direct or permit. Pickets chosen from units of Territorial Force will be placed at all points marked on Maps 3 and 4. Accompanying mounted patrols will continuously visit all points and report every hour. The following premises will be occupied by adequate forces, and all necessary measures used without need of reference to Headquarters. First, premises known as Liberty Hall, Beresford Place ; No. 6 Harcourt Street, Sinn Fein building; No. 2 Dawson Street, Headquarters Volunteers ; No. 12 D'Olier Street, 'Nationality' Office ; No. 25 Rutland Square, Gaelic League Office ; No. 41 Rutland Square, Foresters' Hall ; Sinn Fein Volunteer premises in city ; all National Volunteer premises in city ; Trades Council premises, Capel Street ; Surrey House, Leinster Road, Rathmines. THE FOLLOWING PREMISES WILL BE ISOLATED, AND ALL COMMUNICATION TO OR FROM PREVENTED :— PREMISES KNOWN AS ARCHBISHOP'S HOUSE, DRUMCONDRA ; MANSION HOUSE, DAWSON STREET ; No. 40 Herbert Park ; Larkfield, Kimmage Road ; Woodtown Park, Ballyboden ; Saint Enda's College, Hermitage, Rathfarnham ; and in addition premises in list 5 D, see Maps 3 and 4."

The 'Castle Document' printed on 13 April 1916. This document alleged that the Castle authorities proposed to arrest many important and well-known public figures. Today it is commonly held that 'it was not (as has usually been said) a forgery, but it was "sexed up" by Joseph Plunkett.

measures used without reference to headquarters—First, premises known as Liberty Hall, Beresford Place; number six Harcourt Street, Sinn Féin Building; number two Dawson Street, Headquarters Volunteers; number twelve D'Olier Street, Nationality Office; number twenty-five Rutland Square, Gaelic League Office; number forty-one Rutland Square, Foresters' Hall; Sinn Féin Volunteer premises in city; all National Volunteer premises in city; Trade Council premises, Capel Street; Surrey House, Leinster Road, Rathmines.

The following premises will be isolated and all communication to or from prevented—Premises known as Archbishop's House, Drumcondra; Mansion House, Dawson St; number forty Herbert Park; Larkfield, Kimmage Road; Woodtown Park, Ballyboden; Saint Enda's College, Hermitage, Rathfarnham; and in addition premises in List five (d). See Maps three and four.[453]

The general consensus today is that Joseph Plunkett created the document in Miss Quinn's Private Nursing Home in Mountjoy Square (where he was being treated for tuberculosis) and then sent it with Rory O'Connor to Kimmage. O'Connor took it to George Plunkett and Colm Ó Lochlainn to print it.[454] Its provenance has never been proven, however.

The document contained several 'errors' that Joseph Plunkett was unlikely to have made. For example, in the 'original' of the document, the Archbishop's palace was incorrectly designated as *Ara Coeli*, when that was the name of Cardinal Logue's home in Armagh. 'Jack Plunkett was immediately sent on his motor bike to the nursing home and returned with the message from his brother: "Make it Archbishop's House".'[455]

This document was branded as bogus by the British authorities, then and now, but Grace Gifford Plunkett stated that she was present while Plunkett decoded part of it.[456] In addition, Eugene Smith, a telegrapher at the time in Dublin Castle, gave Patrick J. Little a signed and witnessed statement that he recognised the document as genuine and abstracted from the Castle files.[457] Thomas MacDonagh's son, Donagh, claimed that there really was a secret order from a file in Dublin Castle directing that 'immediately on receipt of an Order from the Chief Secretary's Office, Dublin Castle, and signed by the undersecretary and the General Officer Commanding the Forces in Ireland', all the leaders of the different separatist organisations should be arrested.[458] Desmond Ryan wrote: 'Forgery is a strong word, but that *in its final form* the document was a forgery no doubt can exist whatever . . .' (emphasis added).[459] In Kilmainham, on the night before he was executed, Seán MacDermott swore to Msgr Patrick Browne that the document was genuine.[460] Éamonn Ceannt told his wife, Áine, that the document was genuine and he never doubted it.[461]

Alderman Thomas (Tom) Kelly read the document at the Dublin Corporation meeting on 19 April. He was highly regarded by all parties, and thus the document was taken very seriously. (See 7 Belgrave Road, Rathmines [Dublin 6]; 53 Rathgar Road [Dublin 6].) It seems that the scepticism regarding the document may have been overdone, and there was a basis for believing that there was an underlying document from which the final was 'forged'.[462] Today it is commonly held that 'it [the Document] was not (as has usually been said) a forgery, but it was "sexed up" (by Joseph Plunkett) to make the plans appear imminent, to try to get MacNeill to support immediate action'.[463]

Phoenix Park

'OH, SIR, SIR, DON'T SHOOT
ME. I'M AN IRISHMAN AND
THE FATHER OF SEVEN
CHILDREN . . .'
sentry at the Magazine Fort

Fianna members attacked the **Magazine Fort** here after their football game on Monday morning. The explosion coming from the attack on the fort was supposed to provide the signal to start the Rising.

Paddy Daly was the leader of the Fianna who assaulted the Magazine Fort; some months before the Rising he got a job with a building firm making repairs at the fort and he knew its layout. Fianna members who attacked the fort included Paddy Daly, Patrick (Paddy) Boland, Frank Gaskin,[464] Bob Gilligan, Garry Holohan,[465] Patrick H. (Paddy) Holohan (brother of Garry), Louis Marie, Christopher Martin, Éamon Martin,[466] Herbert (Barney) Mellows, John (Jack, Seán) Murphy,[467] John O'Brien, Bernard Parker and Timothy (Tom) Roche. Tom Roche commandeered a horse-drawn jaunting car as an 'escape vehicle'.

The fort was under the command of a temporary officer, who was at the Fairyhouse races with the keys to the ordnance sections in his pocket. The fort's O/C was Col. George Playfair, who was serving with an Irish regiment in France. His family still lived in the fort. At first, Mrs Isabel Playfair, her two sons and a daughter were detained in their residence. When they were released and told to leave the area, her son George ran first to a DMP constable and then headed toward Islandbridge Barracks. Garry Holohan chased after him on a bicycle and, when Playfair would not stop, Holohan had to shoot him to prevent him from sounding the alarm.

When [I] reached Rutland cottages the house was packed with men and they were still arriving on foot and on bicycles. We distributed automatic pistols to the men who had no small arms and made everyone leave his rifle in the house and remove his equipment. Then we sent them to the Phoenix Park in Batches, some on bicycles and some on the Ballybough tram. Paddy Daly and I went on bicycles and called at Whelan's on Ormond Quay Upper, where we bought a football. After a few minutes chat together, as if we were a football team with followers, we moved around to the front of the Fort in a casual way, some of the lads kicking the ball from one to the other. When we got near the gate they rushed the sentry who was standing outside, and then another party rushed in and took the guardroom completely by surprise. I was detailed off with Barney Mellows to take the sentry on the parapet. I rushed straight through the Fort, which is a rather large place, and I had some difficulty in locating him. I eventually saw him looking at me over a roof. I rushed towards him, calling on him to surrender. He came towards me with his bayonet pointed towards me. I fired a shot and he fell, and at that moment Barney came along the parapet. The poor sentry was crying, 'Oh, sir, sir, don't shoot me. I'm an Irishman and the father of seven children.' . . . When I met Paddy Daly he told me he could not find the key of the high-explosives store and he had set the charges in the small-arms ammunition store. Éamon and I lit the charges and my brother Pat gave us a hand. While we were placing the charges, most of the attacking party were clearing away. We informed the prisoners that one of their men was injured and told them to give him attention. We also ordered them not to go down the Park in the direction of the city. We took the guards' rifles and went to the waiting hackney car . . . I followed behind the car on my bicycle. As the car turned towards the gate leading to the Chapelizod Road we noticed a youth of about 17 years of age running towards the gate. He stopped and spoke to the policeman who was in the middle of the road directing the traffic, and then ran away in the middle of the road towards Islandbridge. I left the hack and followed him, and when he got to the corner of Islandbridge Road he ran towards one of the big houses, evidently with the intention of giving the alarm. I jumped off my bicycle, and just as the door opened I shot him from the gate. At that moment the car arrived at the junction of the road and two large explosions took place in the Fort. The lads on the car started to cheer, and then they thought it wiser to put the rifles that were in their hands into the well of the car.[468]

Dublin 7

Key locations

Arbour Hill

Blacquire Bridge, North Circular Road (Irish Volunteer Monument)

Broadstone Railway Station

Cabra

Church Street

Four Courts

Irish Volunteer Monument

King's Inns

Linenhall Street

Marlborough Barracks (now McKee Barracks), Cabra

North Dublin Union

North King Street

Ormond Quay

Phibsborough ('Phibsboro')

Stoneybatter

Commandant Edward (Ned) Daly's Volunteer 1st Battalion was primarily drawn from men who lived north of the Liffey and west of Sackville (O'Connell) Street. As a result, Daly and his men knew their area intimately, and this enabled them to pick positions for urban ambushes that completely confused and stifled the British. One must never forget the contribution of women to the Rising, and in Daly's case they were a vital part of his garrison. Over 40 women fought alongside the men; some acted as couriers on the most dangerous missions, some performed medical duties and some were engaged in the shooting itself.

'THE IRISH REPUBLIC HAD BEEN PROCLAIMED AT 12 NOON BY COMDT GEN. PATRICK PEARSE'
Cmdt Ned Daly

Daly's men and women fought throughout Dublin 7, and its key positions were in Church Street, in the Four Courts complex and North King Street. Some of Dublin's fiercest fighting took place here, and as one walks in the King Street area one realises the nature of urban fighting—the kind of battle that led to the British atrocities there.

Daly set up his headquarters first in North Brunswick Street and later in Church Street, and established his defences for the 1st Battalion in the Four Courts area around buildings that allowed his limited forces as much movement as possible between positions. He reconnoitred his command area exhaustively and established his posts in positions allowing crossing fields of fire, cover and concealment. The British barracks in Dublin were primarily to the west and south, and Daly placed his forces in areas that allowed them to intercept forces coming from Marlborough Barracks (now McKee Barracks in Phoenix Park) and Royal Barracks (now Collins Barracks on the quays and a part of the National Museum of Ireland) towards the GPO.

Most of the Volunteers mustered in Blackhall Place and at the area around 138–142 Church Street, the Capuchin Franciscan Friary, and 131–137 Church Street,

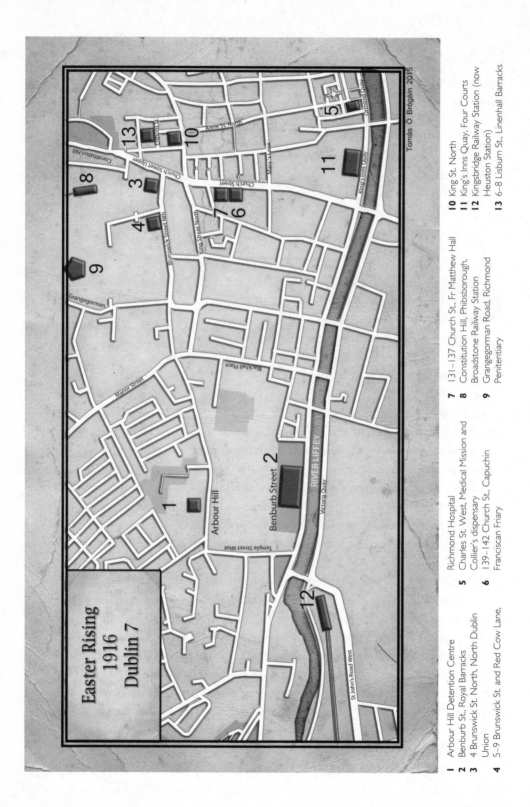

Easter Rising
1916
Dublin 7

Tomás Ó Brógáin 2015

1 Arbour Hill Detention Centre
2 Benburb St., Royal Barracks
3 4 Brunswick St. North, North Dublin
   Union
4 5–9 Brunswick St. and Red Cow Lane,

5 Richmond Hospital
   Charles St. West, Medical Mission and
   Collier's dispensary
6 139–142 Church St., Capuchin
   Franciscan Friary

7 131–137 Church St., Fr Matthew Hall
8 Constitution Hill, Phibsborough,
   Broadstone Railway Station
9 Grangegorman Road, Richmond
   Penitentiary

10 King St. North
11 King's Inns Quay, Four Courts
12 Kingsbridge Railway Station (now
    Heuston Station)
13 6–8 Lisburn St., Linenhall Barracks

Fr Mathew Hall, also known as Capuchin Hall. A plaque on the wall of the hall commemorates its importance during the Rising, as it was a headquarters under Daly's 1st Battalion before the battalion moved to the Four Courts on Friday. All week the hall was used as a hospital. If one were to walk south on Church Street to the quays, one would be taking the route most of the Volunteers took when they stormed the Four Courts complex. As the Four Courts is right on the Liffey quays, no troops could get past the Volunteers, and as one stands at the front of the Courts one sees that the British had to attack them from across the Liffey.

The position that Daly's men took was so well sited that on Monday they opened fire on a troop of Royal Lancers who were escorting a load of ammunition from the North Wall to Phoenix Park. Two of the Lancers were killed, the ammunition was abandoned on the quays, and the surviving Lancers had to take cover in a medical mission in nearby Charles Street.

Walking west along the Liffey from the Four Courts, it is only a short distance to Royal (Collins) Barracks, where British Lancers and infantry were stationed in 1916. There is an exhibition on the Rising on permanent display in Collins Barracks and one would be well advised to stop there.

Directly north of Collins Barracks is Arbour Hill Detention Centre. Built in 1835 and redesigned in 1845, it was the smallest of Dublin's Victorian prisons. Upon his arrival on Friday to take command, Major Gen. Sir John Grenfell Maxwell first issued a proclamation indicating that he would take all measures necessary to quell the Rising. His second command was to have a limepit dug in the yard of Arbour Hill Prison (large enough for 50 bodies, it was claimed), and that is where the executed 1916 leaders were buried: in a communal grave and covered with quicklime. Some DMP and British soldiers reported that they were buried in the order in which they were executed. Behind the pit where they are entombed is a wall with the *Proclamation of the Irish Republic* inscribed in Irish and English.

If one were to walk back to the Four Courts and then north on Church Street, one would shortly come to King Street North, which was the scene of the British atrocities by the South Staffordshire Regiment (South Staffs) on Saturday 29 April. Five South Staffs officers were wounded and 42 men killed, mostly in this street, but thereafter the British took fourteen unarmed men who had nothing to do with the Rising to the basements of houses and shot and bayoneted them. Perhaps the actions of the British troops can be traced to Brig. Gen. W.H.M. Lowe's orders, which included the following: 'No hesitation should be shown in dealing with these rebels. By their action they had placed themselves outside the law. They must not be made prisoners.' An inquest held the British responsible for murder but no individuals were ever tried. Gen. Maxwell explained it all away: 'Possibly unfortunate incidents, which we should regret now, may have occurred . . . it is even possible that under the horrors of this particular attack some of them "saw red". That is the inevitable consequence of a rebellion of this kind. It was allowed to come into being among these people, and could not be suppressed by velvet-glove methods where our troops were so desperately opposed and attacked.'

Walking further north on Church Street one comes to Constitution Hill in Phibsborough, which was the site of Broadstone Railway Station at the time. Broadstone Station, the terminus of the Midland and Great Western Railway, was the most monumental of the five railway termini of Dublin. The Volunteers who were sent to take it were too undermanned, but they did blow up the right-of-way tracks. Then they went to the nearby Linenhall Barracks and set it on fire.

All this was done by Volunteers of the 1st Battalion under the command of Commandant Ned Daly, and all in a very small area of Dublin 7.

Arbour Hill: Arbour Hill Detention Centre; built in 1835 and redesigned in 1845, it was the smallest of Dublin's Victorian prisons.[469] The bodies of the fourteen men executed in Dublin are buried here in a pit of quicklime; some DMP and British soldiers reported that they were buried in the order in which they were executed.[470]

Upon his arrival to take command on Friday 28 April 1916, Major Gen. Sir John Grenfell Maxwell first issued a proclamation indicating that he would take all measures necessary to quell the Rising. His second command was to have a large limepit dug in the yard of Arbour Hill Prison, and that is where those executed were to be buried.[471] He had already decided on executing the leaders.

The executions of the fourteen leaders in Dublin were carried out in Kilmainham Gaol from 3 May to 12 May. Maxwell ordered the men to be certified as dead by a medical officer and to have a label bearing their name pinned to their breast. The bodies would then be removed immediately to an ambulance, which, when full, was to drive to Arbour Hill Barracks, where the bodies were to be put in a grave alongside one another, covered in quicklime and the grave filled in. One of the officers with the party was to keep a note of the identity of each body that was placed in the grave, and a priest was to be available to attend the 'funeral service'. (See Inchicore Road, Kilmainham Gaol [Dublin 8].)

The stipulation about the burial of the remains in quicklime came from the very top, because Maxwell was determined from the outset that the bodies of the executed men would not be released to their families, for fear that the men's graves might become a place of pilgrimage or, worse, a rallying point for further insurrection:

Irish sentimentality will turn these graves into martyrs' shrines to which annual processions etc. will be made which will cause constant irritation in this country.[472]

The graves are located under a low mound on a terrace of Wicklow granite in what was once the old prison yard. Behind the pit where they are entombed is a wall bearing the *Proclamation of the Irish Republic* inscribed in Irish and English. On the prison wall opposite the grave site is a plaque bearing the names of others who gave their lives in 1916. The current memorial was started in 1955, and the grave is surrounded by limestone kerbing into which the names of those interred are incised in Irish at the head and English at the bottom. Michael Biggs, a Dublin letter-cutter and sculptor, carved the 4,800 four-inch letters of the *Proclamation*, beginning in 1959.

27 Arran Quay: Home of Bridget Allen (16), who was killed on 27 April.[473] She was a 'packer' who was 'killed by a bullet wound, and she received no medical attention'. She is buried in Glasnevin Cemetery. The family moved from 128 Thomas Street, where nineteen people lived in the house.[474]

9 Bridge Street Lower: Limerick Clothing Factory; 300 Irish Volunteer uniforms were ordered from here in 1914, to be made from material supplied by Morrogh Brothers at Douglas Woollen Mills in Cork.

4 Brunswick Street North: North Dublin Union. A poorhouse north of the Four Courts, it was occupied by Ned Daly's men of the 1st Battalion. Next door was the Convent of St John of the Sisters of St Vincent de Paul. The nuns supported the Volunteers, prayed with them, and pleaded with God for their safe return. Daly's men knew the sisters by name: Sisters Brigid, Agnes, Patrick, Monica and Louise.[475]

Though occupied, there was little fighting around the Union. Volunteer snipers operated briefly from its rooftops, but left after protests that they were endangering the inmates' lives. Residents of the area, particularly from North King Street, progressively evacuated their homes and fled for safety to the Union, which held about 400 refugees by the week's end.[476] (See Church Street and King's Inn Quay for 1st Battalion.)

Now St Lawrence's Hospital.

5–9 Brunswick Street and Red Cow Lane: Richmond Hospital. Fifteen dead and 200 wounded were received here during the Rising. It was a teaching hospital for surgery; Sir Thomas Myles, former president of the Royal College of Surgeons in Ireland, and A.A. McConnell, Ireland's first neurosurgeon, both practised here, as did Sir William Stoker, Sir William Thomson and Sir Conway Dwyer. Oliver St John Gogarty studied here and was a clinical clerk for Sir Thomas Myles. Myles was the skipper of the *Chotah*, the vessel that landed arms at Kilkoole, Co. Wicklow, on 1 August 1914.[477] (See Kilcoole, Co. Wicklow.) All of them treated casualties at the hospital during and after the Rising.

About a week after the Rising, members of the DMP came looking for Volunteers Patrick (Paddy) Daly and Liam Archer,[478] but the house surgeon, Michael

Bourke, informed the policemen that they had been discharged. When the policemen then asked about Éamon Martin, Bourke told them that Martin was dying.[479]

All the Volunteers treated in the Richmond Hospital evaded arrest and this was partly due to assistance from hospital staff.

Cabra Park: Home of Martin Conlon. Bulmer Hobson was held here from just before the Rising.[480] He was arrested on the orders of the Leinster Executive of the IRB, acting on the orders of the Military Council.[481] Éamonn Ceannt remembered walking with Thomas MacDonagh, who remarked: 'Bulmer Hobson is the evil genius of the Volunteers and if we could separate MacNeill from his influence all would be well'.[482] Seán T. O'Kelly was sent from the GPO on the night of Easter Monday to have him released. He was held by Conlon, Michael Lynch, Con O'Donovan,[483] Maurice Collins[484] and Seán Tobin. (See 65 Great Britain Street [Dublin 2].)

24 Cabra Road, Phibsborough: Home of Louise Gavan-Duffy, member of the initial Provisional Committee of Cumann na mBan and its Hon. Secretary.

The sister of George Gavan-Duffy, later minister for foreign affairs in the first Dáil Éireann, Louise Gavan-Duffy founded Scoil Bhríde, Ireland's first Gaelscoil for girls. She travelled through Dublin on Easter Monday, arriving finally at the GPO, where she asked to see Pearse: 'I said to him that I wanted to be in the field but that I felt that the Rebellion was a frightful mistake, that it could not possibly succeed, and that it was, therefore, wrong'. Pearse suggested that she help out in the kitchens, and she agreed to this, since it was not active service. She stayed there until the GPO was evacuated on Friday, and next morning went to Jacob's biscuit factory 'to see what they were going to do there'.[485] (See St Ita's, 21 Oakley Road, Ranelagh: Cullenswood House [Dublin 6].)

Charles Street West: Medical Mission and Collier's Dispensary. On Monday, Volunteers in the Four Courts fired upon Royal Lancers escorting a shipment of ammunition from the North Wall to Marlborough Barracks in Phoenix Park. Two Lancers were killed, including their O/C, Lt Sheppard. (These were *not* the Lancers under the command of Col. Hammond, sent from Marlborough Barracks to investigate the fighting, who trotted down Lower Sackville Street and were attacked in front of the GPO.)

The surviving Royal Lancers, under the command of 2Lt Hunter, took this building on Monday afternoon. They also took Collier's Dispensary across the street. The Volunteers took a lance from one of the dead Lancers, attached a tricolour to it and placed it in the middle of North King Street, where it remained for the duration.

Daly's men from the Four Courts made a determined effort to burn out the Lancers on Wednesday. A party firing from the Chancery Lane gate peppered the Mission, while two Volunteers flung a bundle of rags and paper soaked in oil through a window. This 'bomb' was ineffective, and Paddy Daly was wounded in the attempt.[486] Later in the week the Lancers' sniping on the Four Courts inspired the Volunteers there to try to set it on fire again by shooting a flaming arrow into the Mission, but that, too, failed. The Lancers remained in the outposts, under heavy fire, until Friday, when the British sent armoured cars into Charles Street to rescue the trapped Lancers and retrieve the body of Lt Sheppard.

Church Street: St Michan the Martyr's Church, named after an eleventh-century Viking martyr-bishop. There was a Volunteer garrison in the nearby Four Courts in the Rising, and British firing on that garrison, and return fire by the Volunteers, greatly damaged the church.

5 Church Street: Home of Volunteer Michael Lennon.[487] Peadar Clancy led a group of Volunteers from the Four Courts and converted the house into a canteen and first-aid post. Brigid Lyons (Thornton) hid here after the Rising.[488]

79–80 Church Street: Monks' Bakery; during the Rising, Cmdt Daly oversaw the distribution of bread from here to the local residents, who depended on the bakery for their food.

93 Church Street: Home of William O'Neill (16), who was a 'labourer' and was killed here during the Rising.[489] (In some lists he is named as William Neill.) He is buried in Glasnevin Cemetery.

138–142 Church Street: Capuchin Franciscan friary; and 131–137 Church Street: Fr Mathew Hall, also known as Capuchin Hall. Named after Fr Theobald Mathew (1790–1861), who preached against alcohol abuse throughout Ireland and the US. He was *very* successful in getting the Irish to take the teetotal 'pledge'. The building was used as a hospital in 1916, and there is a plaque on the wall commemorating its importance during the Rising.

Cmdt Ned Daly chose this area for the headquarters of his 1st Battalion. Daly's troops engaged the British in a haphazard and widespread battle, and the area they were to hold presented many tactical problems to them as defenders, as well as to the attacking British.[490] Daly set up his headquarters first in North Brunswick Street and later in Church Street, and established his defences for the 1st Battalion in the Four Courts area around buildings that allowed his limited forces as much movement as possible between positions.[491] (See Brunswick Street North [North Dublin Union], and King's Inns Quay.)

From the re-establishment of the Irish Province of the Capuchin Order in 1885 there had been strong links between its members and the emerging national movement. It was clear that the cultural resurgence associated with the 'Irish Ireland' movement deeply influenced the men who were drawn to Capuchin religious life.

Even before the Province was reconstituted in the 1800s Fr Albert Mitchell, an ardent nationalist, made a particular point of always wearing Irish-made garments and vigorously championed homemade products. Later, Fr Aloysius Travers preached a 'Buy Irish Campaign'. Fr Edwin Fitzgibbon played a leading role in promoting Gaelic games. Many of the friars were fluent Irish-speakers, and Fr Augustine Hayden and Fr Albert Bibby were to the forefront in fostering interest in the native language through the Gaelic League (Conradh na Gaelige).

The friars who attended those executed in Kilmainham Gaol lived here, and they were instrumental in bringing the British and the battalion O/Cs together at the end of the Rising (Fathers Albert Bibby, Aloysius Travers,[492] Augustine Hayden,[493] Columbus Murphy and Sebastian O'Brien).

William Patrick Travers was born into a prominent, devoutly Catholic Cork family on 20 March 1870. He entered the Capuchin Order in 1887, took the religious name of Aloysius and was ordained a priest in 1894. Fr Aloysius was involved in ministering to the Rising leaders during their imprisonment and was present at the execution of James Connolly in Kilmainham Gaol on 12 May 1916. He wrote a Witness Statement which clearly indicates that he felt most at home among the working classes of Dublin, and noted his experiences throughout Easter Week.

During Easter Week the Father Mathew Feis was scheduled, and a small boy was shot on Monday afternoon. The children were quickly rounded up and placed under the stage for safety, and from that time on Fr Aloysius helped in the Fr Mathew Hall, which was quickly turned into a hospital by the Volunteers and Cumann na mBan. On Sunday Fr Aloysius was one of the priests who were asked to carry the notice of surrender to the various Volunteer/Citizen Army garrisons. Fr Aloysius and Fr Augustine went to Richmond Barracks to speak to Padraic Pearse, and then to Dublin Castle to confer with Connolly. Both men indicated that the surrender was their wish and the two friars were deputed to take the orders to Thomas MacDonagh's command in Jacob's factory and then to relay the orders to Éamonn Ceannt and his men in the South Dublin Union. After both commanders were brought to parley with British Gen. Lowe, the commands were surrendered.

Fr Aloysius and Fr Augustine were called to Kilmainham Gaol to minister to Pearse, Clarke and MacDonagh on the morning of their executions. On that night of 2–3 May, Fr Aloysius, walking in the corridor, saw a light shining through the spyhole in Pearse's cell: 'Pearse was there kneeling and the light showing on his face as he clasped the crucifix'. Fr Aloysius had brought this crucifix with him to the Gaol and had left it with Pearse earlier. Pearse scratched his initials, 'P.M.P.' (for the Irish form of his name, Pádraic MacPiarais), on the back of the crucifix as a memento for Fr Aloysius. The crucifix was preserved in the Church Street Friary and is of wood with brass figures of Our Lord, Our Lady and the skull and crossbones. On 3 May Fathers Aloysius and Augustine were not permitted to stay with the condemned men, Pearse, Clarke and MacDonagh, until their execution but had to leave Kilmainham Gaol between 2 and 3 a.m. Fr Aloysius protested so strongly that priests were thereafter allowed to stay with the men until their executions.

Fr Aloysius was permitted to accompany Connolly from Dublin Castle when he was executed on 12 May, and to be present at Kilmainham with Connolly to the end. Connolly requested to see Fr Aloysius but before going Fr Aloysius had to promise that he would act only as a priest. When Connolly was informed by Fr Aloysius that it was only as a priest that he could see him, Connolly said: 'It is as a priest I want to see you. I have seen and heard of the brave conduct of priests and nuns during the week and I believe that they are the best friends of the workers.' On the morning of 12 May word was sent to Church Street asking Fr Aloysius to go to Dublin Castle to see Connolly. Fr Aloysius heard his confession, gave him Holy Communion and went with him in the ambulance to Kilmainham, and was there when Connolly was executed. After Connolly's execution a British captain said: 'Fr Aloysius, they are the bravest and cleanest lot of men I have ever met'. Aloysius agreed that all the men were brave. 'They were clean in the eyes of the British captain and they were clean too in the eyes of God.' Aloysius always commented on the faithfulness of those executed: 'I think we owe it to the young people of this country to put the spiritual aspect of the lives of these men before them as an ideal to follow'.

Thomas Bibby was born on 24 October 1877 in Bagnalstown, Co. Carlow. He entered the Capuchin novitiate at Rochestown on 7 July 1894 and took the religious name Albert. He was solemnly professed on 8 May 1900 and was ordained a priest at Church Street on 23 February 1902.

In the aftermath of the Rising Fr Albert ministered to a number of rebel prisoners in Kilmainham Gaol and in other locations. He and Fr Augustine were called to Kilmainham Gaol on the night of 7–8 May in order to minister to the four men who were to be executed in the morning: Seán Heuston, Michael Mallin, Con Colbert and Éamonn Ceannt. Upon arriving at the Gaol, Fr Augustine went to Ceannt's cell, while Fr Albert attended to Michael Mallin and Con Colbert. Fr Albert did not remain in their cells long, and then went to see Seán Heuston.[494]

In the *Capuchin Annual* of 1942 Fr Albert gave a remarkable account of his time with Heuston. According to that account, Heuston was

kneeling beside a small table with his Rosary beads in his hand and on the table was a little piece of candle and some letters which he had just written to some relatives and friends. He wore his overcoat as the morning was extremely cold and none of these men received those little comforts that are provided for even the greatest criminals while awaiting sentence of death.

Fr Albert said that Heuston had been to Confession and Mass that morning and was not afraid to die. According to Albert's account, Heuston 'awaited the end not only with the calmness and fortitude which peace of mind brings to noble souls, but during the last quarter of an hour he spoke of soon meeting again Padraic MacPhiarais and the other leaders who had already gone before him'. Heuston's brother Michael, who was studying to be a Dominican priest, saw him, as did Fr Patrick Browne. In addition, his mother, sister, aunt and a first cousin saw him. Heuston wrote to his sister, a Dominican nun:

> Let there be no talk of 'foolish enterprises'. I have no vain regrets. If you really love me, teach the children the history of their own land and teach them that the cause of Caitlin ni h-Uallachain never dies. Ireland shall be free from the centre to the sea as soon as the people of Ireland believe in the necessity for Ireland's freedom and are prepared to make the necessary sacrifices to obtain it.[495]

Fr Albert walked to the Stonebreaker's Yard with Heuston, and they saw Fr Augustine and Michael Mallin as they passed in the hallway. When they reached the yard, the blindfolded Heuston bent and kissed a cross that Fr Albert held in his hand. In the yard, Fr Albert wrote,

> . . . there was a box (seemingly a soap box) and Seán was told to sit down on it. He was perfectly calm and said with me for the last time 'My Jesus, mercy'. I scarcely had moved away a few yards when a volley went off, and this noble soldier of Irish freedom fell dead. I rushed over to anoint him. His whole face seemed transformed, and lit up with a grandeur and brightness that I had never before noticed.

Fr Albert said that Heuston's last message to him was: 'Remember me to the boys of the Fianna. Remember me to Miceal Staines and to his brothers and to all the boys at Blackhall Street.'[496]

Of Heuston's death, Fr Albert wrote:

> Later on his remains and those of the others were conveyed to Arbour Hill military detention barracks, where they were buried in the outer yard, in a trench which holds the mortal remains of Ireland's noblest and bravest sons. Never before did I realise that man could fight so bravely, and die so beautifully and so fearlessly as did the heroes of Easter Week. On the morning of Seán Heuston's death, I would have given the world to have been in his place, he died in such a noble and sacred cause and went forth to meet . . .

John Hayden was born in November 1870 to William and Mary Hayden (née Morrisey). He took the religious name of Augustine on entering the Capuchin Order in November 1885. He cultivated a strong interest in the Gaelic Revival and in particular in preserving the Irish language. During Easter Week, Fr Augustine helped the Cumann na mBan women in the hospital in Fr Mathew Hall, and then on Thursday he went to the Volunteer position in the Four Courts. Fr Augustine wrote a Witness Statement and detailed his activities under fire in the Four Courts area on Thursday and Friday, dismissing his bravery by saying, 'Well, I felt that I might be badly wounded but I would not be killed outright'.[497]

On Saturday morning, Fr Augustine went to the British lines to explain that Fr Mathew Hall was being used as a Red Cross Hospital:

In this I explained that I was a Capuchian [sic] priest, that the Hall was being used as a hospital, that I was there in charge of the wounded, and that, under the circumstances, I asked the favour of an interview. Having seen the Colonel at the barricade, after some considerable delay, he brought back to me the oral answer he had received and delivered it to me in words that I shall never forget. 'He said, Father, that we were all rebels and outlaws and that we would get none of the amenities of war'.

Fr Augustine was instrumental in conveying the surrender orders through the Dublin garrisons, and he particularly facilitated the meetings between British officers and Cmdt Thomas MacDonagh at Jacob's Factory and Cmdt Éamonn Ceannt at the South Dublin Union.

After the Rising courts martial, Fr Augustine attended the Volunteers and leaders in their cells in Richmond Barracks and Kilmainham, many in the hours before they were executed. He saw Padraic Pearse, Éamonn Ceannt, Seán McDermott, Con Colbert and John MacBride in Kilmainham.

Daniel V. Murphy was born on 17 June 1881 in Cork. His parents were James and Sarah Murphy (née Flynn). He studied at the Capuchin College, Rochestown, and took the religious name Columbus. In 1916 Fr Columbus was assigned to the Capuchin Friary on Church Street, and during the Rising he played an important role in bringing about a cessation of hostilities. Like the other Capuchin friars who ministered to the Volunteers during the Rising, and to the leaders prior to their executions, Fr Columbus wrote a diary recording his experiences and it was later published.[498]

The day after the surrender of the Four Courts garrison on 29 April there was still confusion in North King Street and in other locations as to whether this was a truce or a complete surrender. To clarify the situation for those Volunteers still fighting and who had not received proper notice of the Irish surrender, Fr Columbus went to the Four Courts in an effort to retrieve Pearse's note which had led to the surrender of Cmdt Ned Daly. Failing in this effort, Fr Columbus crossed the river to Dublin Castle to see whether someone there had the note. He met a British officer and explained to him that he needed the document to convince the Volunteers in the North King Street area that the Rising was over. The officer suggested that he should go in person to Pearse at Arbour Hill Detention Barracks and ask him to rewrite the surrender note. Gen. Maxwell received him courteously. Fr Columbus asked to be allowed to see Pearse and the others held there, and his request was granted. Fr Columbus wrote that Maxwell expressed his horror at the loss of life and destruction of property, but said: 'Oh, but we will make those beggars pay for it'. Fr Columbus replied, 'The blood of martyrs is the seed of martyrs'. 'Are you backing them up, then?' asked Maxwell. Concluding that prudence was the better part of valour, Columbus said nothing further.

Fr Columbus was taken to Arbour Hill Barracks to see Pearse. Pearse was seated in his cell with his head bowed and sunk deep into his arms, resting on a little table. He looked a sad, forlorn, exhausted figure. Disturbed by the opening of the cell door, he slowly raised his head. He had the vacant, dazed look of someone waking from sleep. Then, recognising the Capuchin habit, he got up quickly, stretched out his hand and said: 'Oh, Father, the loss of life, the destruction! But, please God, it won't be in vain.' Fr Columbus explained briefly why he had come, and asked Pearse to rewrite the surrender order. Pearse agreed, saying that his one wish was to prevent further loss of life and property.

In the governor's office, Pearse wrote:

> In order to prevent the further slaughter of Dublin citizens, and in the hope of saving the lives of our followers, now surrounded and hopelessly outnumbered, the members of the Provisional Government at present at Headquarters have agreed to an unconditional surrender, and the Commandants of the various districts in the City and County will order their commands to lay down arms.

Shaking hands with Fr Columbus, Pearse said: 'Hurry, Father, as time is precious and perhaps there are lives depending on it'. The next time Fr Columbus saw Pearse was shortly before his execution.

Between 30 April and 4 May Fr Columbus was called on to minister to the prisoners in Kilmainham Gaol prior to their executions. On Tuesday 2 May, a car drove up to the friary in Church Street, carrying two soldiers who told Fr Columbus that Fr Aloysius was required at Kilmainham Gaol. Within minutes the car drove off with Fr Aloysius. Later Fr Columbus answered the door again. Two policemen handed him a written message that had just been phoned through to the Bridewell. The note read: 'Please tell the Franciscan Fathers at Church Street that the two men they wish to see at Kilmainham Detention Prison should be seen by them tonight'. Fr Columbus consulted his superior, who agreed that Columbus should go. On his way, he met the car carrying Fr Aloysius and they travelled together to Kilmainham Gaol. When they arrived, they were shown into a little room. There Fr Columbus was informed that three men were to be shot at daybreak. Fr Aloysius went to see Thomas MacDonagh.

Fr Columbus went into Thomas Clarke's cell, where he remained for about an hour. Clarke told him that the three men had been court-martialled early that morning, but that sentence had not been passed on them until after 5 p.m. He also said that he had received no food since breakfast and that he would like something to eat. At Fr Columbus's request, one of the soldiers went to get a couple of biscuits and a tin of water. Fr Columbus wrote that Clarke, grateful for the biscuits, gave his Volunteer badge to the priest as a souvenir. Clarke, however, later told his wife, Kathleen, that Fr Columbus told him that he had to 'admit that he had done a great wrong' in order to get absolution. Kathleen wrote that Clarke said that he threw Fr Columbus out: 'I'm not a bit sorry for what I did. I glory in it. And if that means I'm not entitled to absolution, then I'll have to go to the next world without it. To say I'm sorry would be a lie and I am not going to face my God with a lie on my tongue.'[499]

The governor told Fr Columbus that Tom Clarke's wife and Willie Pearse were on their way, but that the visit of MacDonagh's sister, a nun, was out of the question because of practical difficulties. When MacDonagh was told this he was so disappointed and upset that Fr Columbus promised that he himself would bring her to the prison if at all possible.

Later he was given a car to fetch MacDonagh's sister, and he was able to return to the prison with both Sister Francesca and the Mistress of Novices. Fr Columbus conducted Sister Francesca to her brother's cell with only the flickering of a candle to light the way, then left to fetch the holy oils for anointing the men. When he returned to the prison, he found that the governor was anxious to get the nuns to leave, as time was almost up. Sister Francesca was numbed and dazed with grief. To gain more time she asked for a lock of her brother's hair as a keepsake. But there were no scissors. The governor then produced a penknife with a small scissors attached. It was given to Sister Francesca but she could not use it, as her shaking fingers refused to work. A soldier took it from her, cut off a lock of her brother's hair and handed it to her. Finally, after she had hung her rosary beads around her brother's neck, Fr Columbus led her away and supported her down the stairs to the military car outside. Sister Francesca received the rosary back the next day from Fr Aloysius, though six beads had been shot off.[500]

When Fr Columbus re-entered the prison, the governor informed him that both priests would have to leave immediately as it was now 3.20 a.m. 'We have not finished giving the rites of the church to the men,' said Fr Columbus, and he explained that the anointings could only be given after the shootings. 'Well, in that case,' said the governor, 'it cannot be done at all, as it is written in the regulations that all except officials have to leave the prison.' The priests were surprised and indignant but were unable to change the governor's mind. Having administered the sacraments of Confession and Holy Communion, the priests accepted the ruling but lodged a formal complaint. Then they said a last farewell to the three prisoners, without telling them that they would not be present at the shootings.

The following night, Fr Columbus was awakened shortly before 3 a.m. and told that he was wanted again at Kilmainham. As he came downstairs he saw Fathers Augustine, Albert and Sebastian waiting for him. At Kilmainham an excited governor told them that four men were to be shot at 3.25 a.m., and that there was only a short time left for the priests to exercise their ministry. He asked that one priest go to each man, but their protest from the night before had had its effect, as he added: 'Of course this time you will remain for the executions and do all that is necessary for them'.

As Fr Columbus knew Edward Daly, he went to his cell. Fr Albert attended to Michael O'Hanrahan, Fr Augustine to Willie Pearse and Fr Sebastian to Joseph Plunkett. When he entered Daly's cell, Fr Columbus saw a look of relief and gladness appear on Daly's face. When it was realised that Holy Communion had not been brought to Plunkett, who was in a different wing, Fr Columbus went there and literally gave him the Sacrament as he was being led from his cell. Anxious to see Daly for the last time, Fr Columbus rushed back, only to discover that Daly had already been led out for execution. As Fr Columbus proceeded to follow him, the shots rang out.

Fr Columbus went back to where the other prisoners stood chatting with each other, with the priests and with the soldiers. Fr Columbus wrote that the whole process was callously informal:

> The governor said a name and gave a signal. The prisoner shook hands all round. His hands were then tied behind his back, and a bandage placed over his eyes. Two soldiers took up their places, one on either side to guide the prisoner, and the priest went in front.

Fr Columbus wrote of the actual executions:

> When the prisoner reached the outer door another soldier pinned a piece of white paper over his heart. The procession went along one yard, then through a gate leading to the next. Here the firing squad of 12 soldiers was waiting, rifles loaded. An officer stood to the left, a little in advance; on the right were the governor and the doctor. The prisoner was led in front of the firing squad and was turned to face it. The two soldiers guiding him withdrew quickly to one side. There was a silent signal from the officer; then a deafening volley. The prisoner fell on a heap on the ground—dead.

(See Inchicore Road, Kilmainham Gaol [Dublin 8].)

North Circular Road: Home of Conor (Con) Collins. He was sent to Tralee to take charge of the wireless arrangements at the Wireless College at Cahersiveen on the Ring of Kerry, but the plan went awry when the car bringing others drove off the Ballykissane Pier on the way to Cahersiveen.[501] (See 44 Mountjoy Street [Dublin 1].)

Collins and Austin Stack heard that Sir Roger Casement had landed from a submarine and had been captured; they went in search of him but were taken into a police barracks at Causeway, where Stack pulled his revolver. Collins and Stack escaped from the barracks but were later re-arrested and imprisoned after the Rising.

Collins was TD for Limerick West from 1919 to 1923. From 1922 he abstained from attendance as an opponent of the Treaty.

67 Connaught Street, Phibsborough: Home of Michael O'Hanrahan; he lived here with his mother, his brother, Henry (Harry), and his sisters, Áine (Ciss), Máire and Eily.[502] The O'Hanrahan family was from County Carlow and they lived there until Michael was a young man. Michael was second in command of the 2nd Battalion Volunteers in Jacob's Biscuit Factory. Eily was also in Jacob's during the Rising and Thomas MacDonagh sent her back to the house for a time, as there were arms hidden here and he directed her to give them out to the men he sent with her.[503] (See Jacob's Biscuit Factory, Bishop Street [Dublin 2].)

Constitution Hill, Phibsborough: Broadstone Railway Station, the terminus of the Midland and Great Western Railway, with lines from Galway and Athlone. The station was opened in 1847 and ran trains until 1937. Sited on a hill, its most dramatic feature was a railway shed with a huge colonnade. Designed by Richard Turner, the shed proved too ambitious for the span and was replaced after it collapsed in the early 1850s. Closed as a railway station in 1937, it is now a bus station.

This was the most monumental of the five railway termini of Dublin and the Volunteers only held it for a short while, as the British retook it on Tuesday 25 April. On Monday night Sam O'Reilly was put in charge of a detail assigned to blow up the Midland Railway lines near the Broadstone Station. They blew up the permanent way, seized a steam engine and placed it on the up-line to block all incoming trains. They destroyed the signal system and cut telegraph lines. The official report described their work:

> During Monday night troops had been ordered over the line and the rebels, having become aware of the fact, took steps with the object of wrecking expected troop trains. An abortive effort to destroy a culvert near the Liffey junction was made, and during the early hours of the morning, the cattle special, proceeding in advance of the troop train, was derailed and wrecked. On the same morning an engine in steam at the Broadstone was seized by the rebels and placed on the

up-line, and started, those in charge jumping off as soon as the engine began to gather speed. This act would have resulted in disaster if the runaway locomotive had met a troop train coming from the opposite direction but fortunately it was thrown off the line at the Liffey junction points. In consequence of this derailment, the troop trains could not come into the city. All telegraph wires were cut and service from Dublin was completely suspended.[504]

27 Corporation Buildings: Home of Christina Caffrey (2, who was killed on 27 April. She was shot at home while being held in her mother's arms—the bullet went through her mother's hand before entering Christina's back.[505] She died in the North Dublin Union Hospital and is buried in Glasnevin Cemetery.[506] Her mother applied for and received £40 compensation for being unable to work owing to a hand injury, but no compensation for the death of Christina.

32–38 Eccles Street (and Berkeley Road): Mater Misericordiae Hospital. Originally established by Catherine McAuley's Sisters of Mercy as the House of Mercy for Women on Baggot Street in the 1820s. Prior to and during the Rising, Dublin Castle believed that many of the nuns at the hospital were Volunteers or sympathisers.[507]

70 Eccles Street: Home of Helena Molony, nominal 'owner' of *The Worker* and the *Workers' Republic* on behalf of James Connolly and Countess Markievicz.[508] An actress by profession, Helena Molony was also an active Irishwoman before, during and after the Rising. She was involved in the early years of Cumann na mBan and edited the women's newspaper, *Bean na hÉireann*. She later served as an officer in the Irish Citizen Army and was part of the group that stormed the City Hall. She was imprisoned after the Rising, and attempted to escape using a spoon to dig a tunnel.[509] She failed, but as a result the female prisoners were no longer allowed to eat with utensils. She remained a great friend of Constance Markievicz until the countess's early death. Following the Rising, Molony went back to work at the Abbey, but continued with the Irish Women's Workers' Union and became more involved politically. After the establishment of Dáil Éireann in 1919 she became an adviser to the Provisional Government, though she never ran for the Dáil. After 1922 she had to decide whether to continue as a professional actress or as a full-time trade union official; she chose the latter and left the stage.[510]

The *Workers' Republic* was the successor to *The Worker*, which had been suppressed after six issues and which was itself the successor to the *Irish Worker*, which had been suppressed in December 1914 and finally stopped in February 1915. In September 1914 Connolly wrote: 'A resurrection! Aye, out of the grave of the first Irishman murdered for protesting against Ireland's participation in this thrice-accursed war there will arise a new Spirit of Irish Revolution. We defy you! Do your worst!' (See 49B Leinster Road, Rathmines: Surrey House [Dublin 6].)

Henrietta Lane: Messrs McMaster Hodgeson. A wholesale drug firm and purveyor of oils, it was burned during the Rising and its burning oils contributed greatly to the fires.

16 Henrietta Place: Home of John Gibney (5), who died during the Rising as a result of 'cannonading', according to the records of Glasnevin Cemetery, where he is buried.[511]

Inns Quay: See King's Inns Quay.

Irish Volunteer Monument, Phibsborough (Blacquiere Bridge, North Circular Road): The Royal Canal passed there and that part of the North Circular Road was a bridge over it. The monument commemorates those who fought in the Rising and in the War of Independence. It was cast by Leo Broe and unveiled on 19 February 1939.

King Street North (and Church Street): Reilly's Pub (became known as 'Reilly's Fort'). Jack Shouldice commanded a unit here during the Rising.[512] The 1st Battallion Volunteers held this building for eighteen hours; they were almost on their own, cut off from the Four Courts and the other outposts, but they held their position.[513] Patrick O'Flanagan was killed here.[514]
    Now the Tap Bar.

4 King Street North: Home of Charles Kavanagh (15), who was shot during the Rising and died in St Joseph's Hospital.[515] He is buried in Glasnevin Cemetery.

King Street North (see King Street North Nos 27, 168, 170, 172, 174, 177, following, and 27 Little Britain Street, below): Atrocities were committed here by the South Staffordshire Regiment (South Staffs), under the command of Lt Col. Henry Taylor, on Saturday 29 April 1916.[516] Taylor refused to attend the inquest that followed the Rising. Five South Staffs officers were wounded and 42 men killed, mostly in this street. Perhaps the actions of the British troops can be traced to Brig. Gen. W.H.M. Lowe's orders, which included the following: 'No hesitation should be shown in dealing with these rebels. By their action they had placed themselves outside the law. They must not be made prisoners.'[517]
    In his written statement to the inquest, Lt Col. Taylor wrote:

The operations in the portion of King St between Linenhall St and Church St were conducted under circumstances of the greatest difficulty and danger for the troops engaged, who were subject to severe fire, not only from behind several rebel barricades . . . but from practically every house in that portion of King St and other buildings overlooking it.

Strong evidence of these difficulties and dangers is afforded by the fact that from 10 am on the 28th of April until 2 pm on the 29th to force their way along King St from Linenhall St to Church St, a distance of some 150 yards only; and that the casualties sustained by the regiment (the great majority of which occurred at this spot) included five officers (including two Captains) wounded, eleven NCOs and men killed and twenty eight wounded.

I am satisfied that during these operations the troops under my command showed great moderation and restraint under exceptionally difficult and trying circumstances.

The court refused to accept Taylor's statement.[518]

Sir Edward Troup, the investigating law officer of the Home Office, told Prime Minister Herbert Asquith with regard to one of these incidents:

The source of the mischief was the military order to take no prisoners. This in itself may have been justifiable, but it should have been made clear that it did not mean that an unarmed rebel might be shot after he had been taken prisoner . . . I have no doubt that if the evidence were published, he [Sgt Robert Flood, see No. 177 below] should be tried for murder.

In his advice to Asquith, Troup admitted that if the events had occurred in England 'the right course would be to refer the cases to the DPP [Director of Public Prosecutions]'.[519]

The verdict of the coroner, Dr Louis A. Byrne, was that

We find the said Patrick Bealen [see No. 177 below] died from shock and haemorrhage, resulting from bullet wounds inflicted by a soldier, or soldiers, in whose custody he was, an unarmed and inoffensive prisoner. We consider that the explanation given by the military authorities is very unsatisfactory, and we believe that if the military authorities had any inclination they could produce the officer in charge.[520]

On 18 May, Gen. Sir John Maxwell issued the following statement:

Possibly unfortunate incidents, which we should regret now, may have occurred

... it is even possible that under the horrors of this particular attack some of them 'saw red'. That is the inevitable consequence of a rebellion of this kind. It was allowed to come into being among these people, and could not be suppressed by velvet-glove methods where our troops were so desperately opposed and attacked.[521]

He repeated his statement in a letter to the *Daily Mail*: 'A revolt of this kind could not be suppressed with velvet-glove methods'.[522]

In contrast, in all matters of discipline and morale Cmdt Ned Daly had high standards for those under his command in this area. After the Rising, British Capt. Brereton, who was held prisoner in the Four Courts, said: 'The Sinn Féiners observed all the rules of civilised warfare and fought clean. They proved they were men of education, incapable of acts of brutality.'[523]

27 King Street North: One of the first rebel barricades was thrown across the street here.

27 King Street North: Louth Dairy, kept by Mrs Lawless. It was here that Peadar Lawless (21), James McCartney (36, an American citizen), James Finnegan Jr (40) and Patrick Hoey (25) were murdered by the South Staffs.

168 King Street North: Home of Thomas and Christopher Hickey (16).[524] This was a butcher's shop, and the sons worked there with their father. Mrs Hickey was in her shop when the men were taken from here to 170 North King Street and murdered on Saturday 29 April. Mrs Hickey testified at the inquest:

> When I rushed into the room, there I saw my darling son. He was lying on the ground, his face darkened, and his two hands raised above his head as if in silent supplication. I kissed him and put his little cap under his head, and settled his hands for death. Then I turned, and in another place I saw poor Tom [her husband] lying on the ground. 'Oh Jesus', I cried. 'My poor husband too'. And not far off lay the corpse of poor Connolly. I reeled round and remembered no more, as the soldier hustled me down the stairs and into the street.[525]

Both men are buried in an unmarked grave in Deansgrange Cemetery.

Kate Kelly, who did housework for the Hickeys, was a most colourful and damning witness at the inquest, as she witnessed the deaths of Christopher Hickey and Peter Connolly.

170 King Street North: Peter Connolly (39, lived at 164 North King Street; he was

a member of Redmond's Volunteers but did not participate in the Rising), Thomas Hickey (38) and Christopher Hickey (16) were murdered here by South Staffs. They were removed from Hickey's victualler's shop at 168 North King Street.

172 King Street North: Michael Hughes (36) (Mick and Sally Hughes owned this house) and John Walsh (56) were murdered here by South Staffs.

174 King Street North: Michael Noonan (34), who owned a newsagency and tobacconist shop here, and George Ennis (51) were murdered here by South Staffs. Anne Fennel was a resident here and a witness:

> As well as I can recollect it was between 5 and 6 am on Easter Saturday morning when the military burst into the shop. There were one or more officers in command and about thirty soldiers. They burst in like wild beasts and shouted harshly at us. The officer shouted 'Hands up' and ordered the two men, Ennis and Noonan, upstairs. As poor Mrs Ennis saw her husband being led upstairs she clung to him and refused to be parted from him and said 'I want to go with him'. One of the soldiers pulled her off and put a bayonet to her ear and uttered the foulest language. Then they took the men upstairs and locked us women in the shop parlour, and told us not to move in peril of our lives. After a long time, it must have been a couple of hours, we heard a noise at the parlour door, and to our horror poor Mr Ennis crawled in. He was bleeding to death, and when the military left the house he crept down the stairs to see his wife for the last time. He said 'O Kate, they have killed me. They killed poor Noonan, too, I stayed with him as long as I could'.[526]

177 King Street North: A 'licensed public house' owned by Mrs Mary O'Rourke. Patrick Bealen (30)[527] and James Healy (44, a labourer at Jameson's Distillery) were murdered here by South Staffs Sgt Flood and Cpl Bullock, who were spirited away to England prior to the 'line-up' of the South Staffs for ID purposes.

On 20 May 1916, the *Irish Catholic* reported and opined:

> A Dublin Coroner's jury on Tuesday found that Patrick Bealen and James Healy, whose bodies were found buried in a cellar in North King Street, died from the result of bullet wounds inflicted by the military, in whose custody they were unarmed and unoffending prisoners.
>
> The jury 'found that the said Patrick Bealen died from shock and hemorrhage, resulting from bullet wounds inflicted by a soldier, or soldiers, in whose custody he was, an unarmed and unoffending prisoner'.
>
> They considered the explanation given by the military authorities as very

unsatisfactory and expressed the opinion that the latter could produce the officer in charge ... Little as we approve the rebellion, we are not going to remain silent when unoffending fellow citizens are killed in cold blood and the responsible local military chiefs take no adequate steps to secure investigation.[528]

King's Inns Quay (between Richmond and Whitworth bridges): The Four Courts. These were: Exchequer (presided over by the chief baron of the exchequer); Chancellory (presided over by the lord chancellor); King's Bench (presided over by a chief justice); and Common Pleas (presided over by a chief justice). Previously, the site was the priory of the Friars Preachers, a monastery confiscated after Henry VIII proclaimed himself king of Ireland and head of the Church.

The King's Inns is the governing body of Irish barristers. The full title is the Benchers of the Honourable Society of the King's Inns.

The 1st Battalion, led by Cmdt Edward (Ned) Daly, occupied the Four Courts and the adjacent streets on the north bank of the River Liffey, almost a mile to the west of the GPO.[529] Daly set up his headquarters first in North Brunswick Street and later in Church Street; he established his defences in the Four Courts area around buildings that allowed his limited forces as much movement between positions as possible.[530] Because of Eoin MacNeill's cancellation order Daly's command was greatly reduced in size.[531] His troops engaged the British in a haphazard and widespread battle, and the area they were to hold presented many tactical problems to them as defenders, as well as to the attacking British.[532] He reconnoitred his command area exhaustively and established his posts in positions allowing crossing fields of fire, cover and concealment.[533] The 1st Battalion was to occupy and hold the Four Courts area, and to form a line from there to Cabra, where it was to link up with the 5th Battalion. Daly's command area extended from the Cabra and North Circular roads to the north, east towards the Bolton Street approach to North King Street, and west to North Brunswick Street as far as Red Cow Lane.[534] This area controlled the main approach routes from the west of Dublin to the centre of the city. As regards his preparations, strategy and the actual tactics used during the week, the British noted that 'in this North King Street they had situated themselves as to be able to inflict maximum casualties on the English troops with minimum loss to themselves' and they gave Daly much credit.[535] Daly placed his forces in areas that allowed them to intercept British troops coming from Marlborough Barracks and Royal Barracks toward the GPO.

The first skirmish in the area occurred on Monday afternoon, when Volunteers in the Four Courts ambushed a party of Lancers escorting lorries loaded with munitions. (See Charles Street.) On Wednesday the Volunteers captured two enemy positions in the area: the Bridewell, which was held by police, and Linenhall Barracks, which was occupied by unarmed army clerks. By Thursday the South Staffordshire[536] and Sherwood Foresters regiments effectively cordoned off the area. The fighting continued until Saturday evening, when the news of Pearse's surrender filtered through.

Joseph McGuinness led the garrison that occupied the Four Courts. They entered through the Chancellory gate. The garrison was largely composed of the 'football teams' that had tried to blow up the Magazine Fort in Phoenix Park. (See Phoenix Park.)

In all matters of discipline and morale Daly had high standards for those under his command. After the Rising, British Capt. Brereton, who was held prisoner in the Four Courts, said: 'The Sinn Féiners observed all the rules of civilised warfare and fought clean. They proved they were men of education, incapable of acts of brutality.'[537]

32 King's Inn Street: Home of Mrs O'Toole, probably a friend of a soldier to whom Tom Clarke gave a letter for Kathleen while he was in Kilmainham Gaol.[538]

Linenhall Street: Trueform Shoe Shop; during the Rising looters started fires here and the building was burned down.

Linenhall Street: Linen Hall; erected in 1728. Once the distribution centre for Irish linen, before that trade moved to Belfast.

6–8 Lisburn Street: Linenhall Barracks. A high protective wall surrounded the building when it eventually became a British military barracks, opened in 1873.

Held by 40 members of the British Army Pay Corps, during the Rising it was attacked by Volunteers of the 1st Battalion under the command of Capt. Denis O'Callaghan and Garry Holohan.[539] Capt. O'Callaghan was sent to capture Broadstone Station but, acting on his own initiative, he felt that his force was too small and so diverted his men to occupy tenement houses on North King Street. He led the assault on the Linenhall Barracks and demanded that the British troops surrender. When they refused, the Volunteers set bombs at the gate, and finally the British did surrender. The Volunteers set it alight and, though they subsequently tried to control the fire, it burned until Friday.[540] In 1916 and during the War of Independence it was the HQ of the British Army Pay Department.

The building was mostly burned in the Rising and closed in 1928. The site now contains housing.

27 Little Britain Street: On Friday of the Rising, soldiers of the South Staffs killed James Moore at his front door here.[541] The inquiry by Sir Edward Troup found that 'he was probably a perfectly innocent person'.[542] (See King Street North.)

24 Manor Place: Home of (John) Joseph Byrne, who fought under Seán Heuston at the Mendicity Institute during the Rising. He worked as a messenger for the Great Southern and Western Railway, and was sentenced to three years' penal servitude after the Rising.[543]

Marlborough Barracks (now McKee Barracks), Cabra: The British established Marlborough Barracks in 1888, and the cavalry that were quartered at Portobello Barracks (see Dublin 6) were moved to here. At the time of the Rising, squadrons of the 5th and 12th Lancers of the 6th Cavalry were billeted at Marlborough Barracks (approximate strength 885).

It was renamed McKee Barracks in 1926, after Richard (Dick) McKee, O/C of the Dublin Brigade in the War of Independence, who was murdered in Dublin Castle on Bloody Sunday, 21 November 1920. McKee was a member of the 2nd Battalion and fought in Jacob's Biscuit Factory in the Rising.

14 Ormond Quay Lower: Lalor Ltd, ecclesiastical candle-makers. Cathal Brugha was the managing director.

9 Ormond Quay Upper: Office of Arthur Griffith's *Sinn Féin* newspaper from 1906 until 1914. It moved here from Fownes Street. (It was preceded in Fownes Street by his *United Irishman* newspaper.)[544]

17 Ormond Quay Upper: Whelan and Son, music and literary publishers. First published *A Soldier's Song* in 1908. (See 68 Dorset Street Lower [Dublin 1].) Some military equipment was also on sale here before the Rising. Dublin Castle thought it a Sinn Féin HQ before the Rising.

Parkgate Street: British Army Pay Corps HQ. At the end of the Rising, Padraic Pearse was taken here to meet Gen. Maxwell. Ironically, the office where Pearse was held captive after signing the surrender became the office of the Irish minister for defence.

188 Phibsborough Road: Home of John (Seán) Healy (14). A Fianna member, he was apprenticed to his father as a plumber. He never received any mobilisation orders, so on Tuesday he reported to Jacob's Biscuit Factory and was sent home by Thomas MacDonagh for being too young. He was given an urgent dispatch to carry to Phibsborough Bridge, but was killed on the way home.[545] He died in the Mater Misericordiae Hospital two days after being shot.

205 Phibsborough Road: Home of James Kelly (15), who was killed during the Rising.[546]

16 Rathdown Road: The Belton family home. Seán Hurley found Michael Collins a room here on Collins's return from London in January 1916.

Red Cow Lane: Cullen's Builders' Yard. Lt William O'Carroll used his revolver to blow the lock off the gate, and his men hauled out lorries and building material to erect a barricade across Red Cow Lane and North Brunswick Street.[547]

2 Sitric Place: Home of Patrick Ryan (13), who was killed in the Rising and is buried in Glasnevin Cemetery.[548] Two other children predeceased him, and two siblings survived.

13 Stafford Street (now Wolfe Tone Street): City Printing Works; it printed the *Irish Worker* for James Connolly, as well as many ICA posters and handbills.

Stonybatter, 18 Manor Place: Home of John Francis Foster (2), who was shot in his pram near Fr Mathew Hall on Easter Monday.[549] He was 'shot in the head at the level of the ears' and was one of the first killed in the Rising. He is buried in Glasnevin Cemetery. Piaras Béaslaí wrote: 'A second lancer galloped up Church Street and was shot down after he killed a child'.[550]

Temple Street: Temple Street Children's Hospital, where Dr Ada English worked during the Rising. She was later a member of the Second Dáil Éireann, and voted against the Treaty.

Temple Street: D Company of the 1st Battalion, Dublin Brigade, mustered here under Capt. Seán Heuston for the Rising, before heading for the Mendicity Institute.

3 Yarnhall Street: Patrick Mahon, printer, printed *Irish Freedom* here.

Dublin 8

Key locations

Dolphin's Barn
Inchicore Road
Islandbridge
James's Street
Kilmainham Gaol
Kingsbridge Station
Mendicity Institute
Merchant's Quay

Richmond Barracks, Inchicore
Royal Hospital, Kilmainham (now the Irish
    Museum of Modern Art)
South Circular Road
South Dublin Union (now St James's Hospital)
The Coombe
Usher's Island

Commandant Éamonn Ceannt was O/C of the Volunteer 4th Battalion. He and his wife, Áine, lived on Dolphin's Terrace in Dolphin's Barn, Dublin 8. They often had meetings of the Volunteer leadership at their home from 1913 to 1916.

Cmdt Éamonn Ceannt wrote in his diary: IS IONGANTACH AN LÁ É SEO, IS IONGANTACH AN LÁ DOM-SA FREISIN É *(*'TODAY IS A WONDERFUL DAY AND IT'S ALSO A WONDERFUL DAY FOR ME'*). That was the day he joined the IRB.*

One of the more curious happenings in Dolphin's Barn took place in January 1916, when James Connolly met with the Military Council of the Volunteers and they stayed in a brickworks here for three days. An agreement was reached for the Irish Citizen Army and Volunteers to work together towards a rising at Easter. Connolly agreed to abandon his openly declared intention to strike independently with the Irish Citizen Army. Prior to this, the Military Council regarded Connolly as endangering the Volunteers' plans. It is unclear, however, whether Connolly was really prepared to lead out the ICA alone, or whether he was trying to provoke the authorities into attacking him and the ITGWU. Some earlier writers were of the opinion that Connolly was 'kidnapped' and held here, but most now agree that he met with the Council voluntarily. In any case, from February 1916 onward the 'War Parties' in the ICA, IRB and the Volunteers were a united bloc. Then in the first week of February there was a meeting at the Ceannts' home of Ceannt, Tom Clarke, James Connolly, Seán MacDermott and Padraic Pearse (Thomas MacDonagh and Joseph Plunkett were absent). These men formed the Military Council, and they made the final plans for the Rising.

Dublin 8 was also home to many of the Volunteers of the 4th Battalion, and they mustered at Emerald Square in Dolphin's Barn, just off Cork Street. Ceannt told them: 'The Irish Republic has been proclaimed and here are your orders'. If one goes to Emerald Square and walks west onto James's Walk to St James's Hospital, one will be walking the exact route taken by Ceannt and his men on their way to take over the

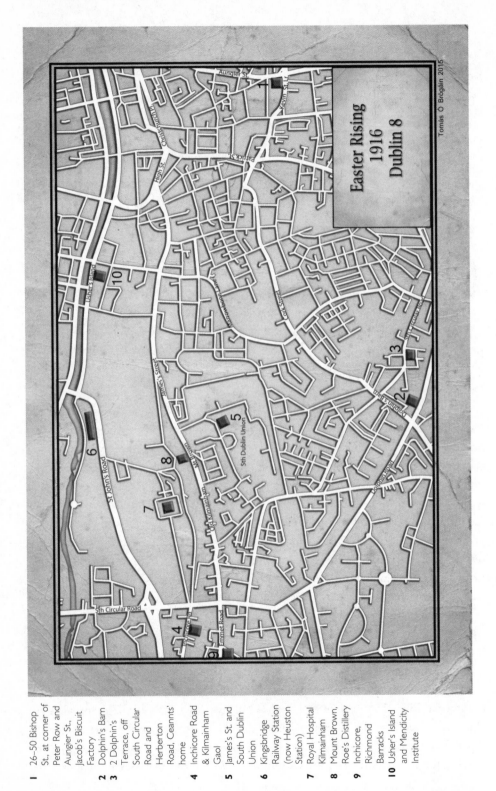

Easter Rising
1916
Dublin 8

Tomás Ó Brógáin 2015

1 26–50 Bishop St., at corner of Peter Row and Aungier St., Jacob's Biscuit Factory
2 Dolphin's Barn
3 2 Dolphin's Terrace, off South Circular Road and Herberton Road, Ceannts' home
4 Inchicore Road & Kilmainham Gaol
5 James's St. and South Dublin Union
6 Kingsbridge Railway Station (now Heuston Station)
7 Royal Hospital Kilmainham
8 Mount Brown, Roe's Distillery
9 Inchicore, Richmond Barracks
10 Usher's Island and Mendicity Institute

South Dublin Union by its Rialto Gate. At the time, the South Dublin Union (now St James's Hospital) was a huge workhouse, and, like all the battalions, Ceannt's was severely limited by the cancellation order. Ceannt could have used 1,000 men to hold the Union, but he had less than 60 to do the job.

Then one should walk to Ardee Street, Marrowbone Lane and Roe's Distillery, Mount Brown, just as Ceannt's Volunteers did on Monday morning.

One of those fighting in the Union was Cathal Brugha, one of the most celebrated fighters of the Rising. He was severely wounded (25 bullet fragments were taken from his body), and at one time he single-handedly held one of the buildings— sitting with his back against a wall, he was singing *God Save Ireland* and daring the British to come closer.

Dublin 8 was also the position of another garrison, that of Cmdt Thomas MacDonagh's 2nd Battalion in Jacob's Biscuit Factory. (This is now mostly the Dublin Institute of Technology, with its entrance at the intersection of Aungier Street/Wexford Street and Bishop Street, while a smaller portion of the original factory is now the National Archives of Ireland, further west on Bishop Street. The Dublin Institute of Technology entrance on Aungier Street at Peter Row is in Dublin 2, and the entrance to the National Archives on Bishop Street is in Dublin 8. [See Dublin 2.]) About 200 Volunteers, including about twelve members of Cumann na mBan, held it during the Rising. They mustered in St Stephen's Green and left just as the ICA contingent arrived to occupy that area. The factory was a virtually unchallenged stronghold during the Rising and didn't have to defend against frontal attack. Forty Volunteers were sent from there to reinforce the Portobello area and twenty more were sent back to St Stephen's Green.

Also in Dublin 8 was the Mendicity Institute, a home for the destitute of Dublin. Directly across the Liffey from Royal Barracks (now Collins Barracks) on Usher's Island, during the Rising it was held by D Company, 1st Battalion, under Capt. Seán Heuston. Heuston's command was a part of Cmdt Ned Daly's battalion, which otherwise was posted north of the Liffey (see Dublin 7). Their task was to delay British deployment of any troops from Inchicore Barracks, located to the west, and to hinder all troops leaving Royal Barracks. Approximately 30 Volunteers, all between the ages of eighteen and 25, were in the garrison—thirteen Volunteers from Swords, under the command of Richard Coleman, and seventeen Fianna held out against approximately 400 Royal Dublin Fusiliers. Heuston was only 25 years old and was instructed to hold this position for two hours—they held for three days. There were 28 survivors and two killed. Seán Heuston was the youngest of those executed, and Dublin's Heuston Railway Station was named after him. The Institute was destroyed but was later rebuilt as a homeless shelter.

Dublin 8 was the scene of some of the most courageous events of the Rising.

8, 10, 11–12 and 22 Ardee Street: Watkin's Brewery; Con Colbert's headquarters, from which the garrison moved to the South Dublin Union during Easter week.[551]

26–50 Bishop Street, corner of Peter Row, touching Wexford Street: W. and R. Jacob's Biscuit Factory. A principal garrison during the 1916 Rising under the command of Thomas MacDonagh. (See 2, 7a, 10–15 Peter Street, corner of Bishop Street at intersection of Aungier Street/Wexford Street [Dublin 2].) Currently the buildings house the Dublin Institute of Technology, with its main entrance on Peter Row at the corner of Aungier Street/Wexford Street, and the National Archives, with its entrance on Bishop Street. (The Dublin Institute of Technology entrance on Aungier Street at Peter Row is in Dublin 2, and the entrance to the National Archives on Bishop Street is in Dublin 8.) (See Dublin 2.)

Dolphin's Barn, Dublin: James Connolly met with the Military Council of the Volunteers on 19 January 1916 and they stayed in a brickworks here until 22 January. An agreement was reached that the ICA and Volunteers would work together towards a rising at Easter. Connolly agreed to abandon his openly declared intention to strike independently with the ICA. Prior to this, the Military Council regarded Connolly as endangering the Volunteers' plans, while he was suspicious of them as 'would-be Wolfe Tones—legally seditious and peacefully revolutionary'. Week by week his writings in the *Workers' Republic* intensified the lack of understanding between the Volunteers and the ICA. Some have speculated that Connolly was not prepared to lead the ICA out alone but was merely trying to goad the English authorities into attacking him or the ICA and the Union. Certainly an attack by the British would have given him that civilian empathy, so it is also unclear whether the Dublin Castle authorities would have taken such a 'bait' if that were Connolly's intention. Others contend that the Military Council simply preferred their own plans and timing for the Rising.

Some earlier writers asserted that Connolly was 'kidnapped' on 19 January 1916 and held here, but most now agree that he met with the Council voluntarily.[552] In September 1914 Connolly had attended a meeting at 25 Rutland Square with senior IRB officials, including Thomas Clarke, Seán MacDermott, Padraic Pearse, Joseph Plunkett, Éamonn Ceannt and Thomas MacDonagh, at which the prospect of a rising was openly discussed. Connolly was enthusiastic at that meeting, convinced that an Irish revolution would have to be a two-stage process in which the struggle to overthrow capitalism would have to be preceded by a rebellion to gain independence from Britain.[553] (See 25 Rutland Square [Dublin 1].)

In May 1915 Seán MacDermott told the Supreme Council of the IRB that 'we'll have to do something about this bloody fellow Connolly. He's going about shouting out his mouth all over the place and we're afraid he'll bring the Rising down on us before we are ready.'[554] Pearse and Eoin MacNeill met with Connolly in early January

1916 in an unsuccessful attempt to restrain him from any premature action. It is believed that after this meeting Pearse reported to the Military Council that Connolly needed to be brought into their confidence about the planned date for a rising.

There has always been this speculation about Connolly's disappearance, and recent authors have concluded that he met agreeably with the Military Council rather than being forcibly kidnapped and detained for the three days[555]—particularly so since even Michael Mallin of the ICA realised that the English were not likely to 'take' Connolly and leave the other ICA and Volunteer leaders in place, and the Volunteers really didn't want to kidnap him.[556] These latest theories seem to agree only that Connolly spent those three days in secret consultation, probably with Pearse, Clarke and Plunkett,[557] and that he did so on his own initiative and/or their invitation, without any question of coercion or military detention.[558] In any case, from February 1916 onward, the 'War Parties' in the ICA, IRB and the Volunteers were a united bloc.

Volunteers Frank Daly and Éamon Dore[559] were the ones sent to escort him to Dolphin's Barn.[560] Upon his return he went to Countess Markievicz's home. The next day, when William O'Brien asked him where he had been, Connolly would not tell him. To Helena Molony he replied 'That would be telling you', though his final word to her was that he 'had walked 40 miles that day, and I have converted my enemies'.[561] To Markievicz he said that he had been 'through hell'.[562]

2 Dolphin's Terrace, Dolphin's Barn/Rialto (off South Circular Road and Herberton Road): Home of Éamonn and Áine Ceannt. Ceannt was quite tall at about 6ft and he was an excellent musician, playing the uilleann pipes before Pope Pius X in Rome in 1908. The family was originally from County Galway, though they moved to Dublin when Éamonn was very young. His father was a member of the RIC. Éamonn was born on 21 September 1881, reputedly in the RIC Barracks in Ballymoe, and christened Edmund Kent. He taught at St Enda's and was an official in the City Treasurer's Office of Dublin Corporation. On 12 December 1912 Ceannt wrote in his diary: *'Is iongantach an la e seo, is iongantach an la dom-sa freisin e'*. ['Today is a wonderful day and it's also a wonderful day for me'.] That was the day he joined the IRB.[563] As commandant of the 4th Battalion, Ceannt was a man of iron resolution, more naturally a physical-force man than any of the other leaders.

A native of Dublin, Áine (née Frances [Franny] O'Brennan) was an avid member of the Gaelic League and met Éamonn at one of their meetings. They married in 1905, in a ceremony entirely in Irish, and thereafter she always signed her name Áine B. E. Ceannt, i.e. Áine Bean Éamoinn Ceannt.[564] They had one son, Ronan. After the Rising Áine moved into a more public role and became an active member of Cumann na mBan, serving as vice-president from 1917 to 1925. She was a member of the Standing Committee of Sinn Féin from 1917 to 1925 and served on the District Council of Rathmines. In 1920–1 she acted as a judge for the Dáil

Éireann/Republican Courts. She was a founder in 1920 of the Irish White Cross, which cared for so many orphans of the wars in Ireland, and later wrote a history of the White Cross after it closed in 1941. Its chairman, James Webb, described her thus: 'It would only be fair to say that SHE WAS the Association'.[565]

From the time of the establishment of the Volunteers in November 1913, meetings were held in the Ceannts' home. Ceannt was director of communications, and representatives from all over the country came to meet him there. From there he monitored a system by which a 'Volunteer Post', known as '*An Post Gaelach*', was set up. Various houses were offered to act as reception depots for letters; the sender would leave the letter and a penny (the postage at the time) at one of these depots, and a postman would collect the letters and penny and deliver all letters within the area surrounding Dublin.

In January 1916 the Military Council started to meet regularly in the Ceannts' home. At the time, the Council consisted of Padraic Pearse, Tom Clarke, Seán MacDermott, Joseph Plunkett and Ceannt. Later James Connolly and Thomas MacDonagh were co-opted onto the Council. Of all the members of the Council, Ceannt was closest to Connolly's social views, though Pearse was not far behind.

In the first week of February 1916 there was a meeting here of Ceannt, Tom Clarke, James Connolly, Seán MacDermott and Padraic Pearse (Thomas MacDonagh and Joseph Plunkett were absent). It had already been determined that the Rising would take place at Easter, and final plans had to be made for the distribution of arms which the Council expected to be delivered on a ship coming from Germany.

In early March there was another group meeting at the Ceannts' in order to finalise plans for a march by all the Dublin battalions to College Green on 17 March. The Volunteers were to assemble at SS Michael and John's Church for a special Mass, and Ceannt's 4th Battalion comprised the Guard of Honour. The Volunteers would then march with rifles and fixed bayonets from O'Connell Street into College Green and form a square in front of the Bank of Ireland building, from where they would be reviewed by their O/C, Eoin MacNeill. After the inspection, Ceannt's battalion marched back to Dolphin's Barn, where Ceannt addressed them and they sang *The Soldier's Song* before being dismissed. That was the last time the Volunteers marched through Dublin before the Rising.

In the week leading up to the Rising, the Ceannt home was a constant meeting place for the members of the Military Council, as well as the members of Ceannt's own battalion. On Holy Saturday Éamonn and Áine Ceannt went to Dalkey to visit a friend and have lunch, but Áine wrote that Éamonn was determined to be back at their home before 4.00 p.m. That night he told her that the Rising was planned for the next day, and they brought to their home the tricolour that Áine and her sister, Lily O'Brennan, had had made. They sprinkled the flag with Easter Water. Later Éamonn left, expecting the Rising to begin on Sunday morning. He returned about

2.30 a.m. after receiving the news of MacNeill's countermanding order, cancelling the Rising planned for Easter Sunday. While Ceannt had planned to sleep away from home on Saturday, he later remarked to Áine: 'I may thank MacNeill that I can sleep in my own home—the cancelling of manoeuvres will lead the British to think everything is all right'. He never slept there again.

The 4th Battalion was assigned to take the South Dublin Union workhouse during the Rising. The workhouse, formerly known as Queen Anne's Mansions, was begun in 1702 and is now St James's Hospital. Located quite near the Ceannt home, the Union was an urban battlefield within the larger Dublin urban battlefield. Ceannt was an inveterate planner; Áine wrote that he had maps of the layout and constantly had members of his battalion to their house to discuss how best to attack and hold positions there. It was composed of almost a dozen large buildings, all of which were built with several wings, and surrounded by twice that number of smaller buildings. The entire Union was a maze: each building and cul-de-sac was part of a labyrinth of open areas, streets and courtyards, as well as active hospitals and infirmaries housing over 3,000 patients and medical personnel at the time of the Rising.

The Union was home to over 3,280 persons and had residences for doctors and nurses, as well as churches, workshops, dormitories and fields. Ceannt decided not to evacuate those living there but moved them to buildings draped with Red Cross flags. Following all his planning, Ceannt masterfully placed his troops in the best positions; as a result, they were never beaten but only surrendered on Pearse's orders on Sunday.[566]

Emerald Square, Dolphin's Barn (off Cork Street): The 4th Battalion of the Volunteers mustered here under Éamonn Ceannt: 'The Irish Republic has been proclaimed and here are your orders'. Ceannt expected 1,000 men but only about 100 showed up.[567] Ceannt sent a detail by James's Street to the South Dublin Union, and a detail by the Rialto Gate. Then he sent details to Ardee Street and Marrowbone Lane, and to Roe's Distillery, Mount Brown.

Inchicore Road: Kilmainham Gaol. There was a prison on this site dating back to the twelfth century; originally it was known as the 'Dismal House of Little Ease'. By the eighteenth century the extant building was in deplorable condition and had to be replaced. The current gaol was opened in 1796 on a site known as Gallows Hill, altered in 1857 and reopened in 1863. Over the main door is a bronze relief of five entangled snakes, known as the 'Demons of Crime', twisted and chained together to represent a warning to all who passed through the gates.

The Gaol ceased to operate as a convict prison in 1911 and had been taken over by the British army for use as a detention barracks for military prisoners. It lacked even basic amenities, and its most significant part was the former Stonebreaker's Yard, where the executions took place. Because the gasworks had been disabled during the Rising, the entire Gaol was lit only by candles for the duration of the executions. Major Lennon was in charge of all the prisoners at Kilmainham.[568]

As a 'reward' for their gallantry, troops from the Sherwood Foresters, the regiment whose ranks were so decimated at Mount Street Bridge, were chosen to form the firing squads for the leaders of the Rising who were executed in Kilmainham Gaol. Brigadier J. Young was in charge at the Gaol and laid down the procedures for the executions after the Rising. The first prisoner to be executed was paraded at 3.30 a.m. to face a firing squad of twelve men. The commander of the firing squad was Major Charles Harold Heathcote, second in command of the regiment. Major Heathcote was sent to Richmond Barracks to take charge of the prisoners and their effects and to escort them to Kilmainham. He took B Company with him, as well as Capt. Orr and Lt Maine (acting as adjutant). They were under the command of Provost Marshal Col. Fraser.

As is customary in firing squads, eleven of the soldiers had live rounds in their weapons while the twelfth had a blank. The officers loaded the weapons for the soldiers, so that no soldier knew whether his weapon contained the blank round or a live one. If necessary, the commanding officer delivered the *coup de grâce* by shooting the prisoner in the head with a handgun. While Major Heathcote was identified as the commander, the regiment also followed the custom of not identifying the men who were in the firing squad, and the regimental records have no listing of the squad members.

Capt. A.A. Dickson remembered the day that he was to send his company to fulfil their orders:

> I was to march my firing-squad of a Sergeant and twelve men to a space cut off from the execution-point by a projecting wall; halt them to ground arms there; march them forward twelve paces to halt with their backs to their rifles each of which I was then to load and replace on the ground. Thus no man knew whether his rifle had been loaded with blank or with ball; each was therefore left not knowing whether he personally had shot the man or not. The men were then marched back to pick up their rifles and hold them, at attention under my eye, until word came that the prisoner was to be led out; they must then be marched round and halted facing the execution wall.[569]

A priest would be present as each prisoner was led out to the execution spot; the Foresters were given the order to fire and were immediately ordered to march back behind the dividing wall, where their rifles would be emptied and the cartridges taken away, again to prevent the soldiers from knowing who fired the fatal bullets, and the weapons were cleaned. This procedure was to be followed for every execution party, and Dickson made sure to follow the instructions to the letter.

The marriage of Grace Gifford and Joseph Plunkett, presided over by Fr Eugene McCarthy, took place at 11.30 p.m. on 3 May in a candlelit ceremony in the chapel. Two soldiers of the Royal Irish Regiment, John Smith and John Lockerby, signed the register as witnesses. In 1949 Grace completed her Witness Statement and recounted her memory of the wedding. She was taken to the Gaol at 6.00 p.m. and kept waiting until around 11.30 p.m.

> When I saw him [Joe], on the day before his execution, I found him in exactly the same state of mind. He was so unselfish he never thought of himself. He was not frightened not at all, not the slightest. I am sure he must have been worn out after the week's experiences, but he did not show any signs of it—not in the least. He was quite calm.
>
> I was never left alone with him, even after the marriage ceremony. I was brought in and was put in front of the altar; and he was brought down the steps; and the cuffs were taken off him; and the chaplain went on with the ceremony; then the cuffs were put on him again.
>
> I was not alone with him—not for a minute. I had no private conversation with him at all. I just came away then.

Immediately after the wedding, Fr McCarthy took Grace back to 53 James's Street, which was the home of Mr Byrne, bell-ringer at St James's Church.[570] She rested there until she was awakened at 2 a.m. The military sent a car for her and she was taken back to the Gaol to see Joe for ten minutes before he was executed:

> There would be a guard there, and you could not talk . . . I was just a few moments there to get married, and then again a few minutes to say good-bye that night; and a man stood there with his watch in his hand, and said: 'Ten minutes'.

After this last visit, Fr McCarthy escorted her to a convent on Thomas Street, where she spent the remainder of the night, and then she went to her sister Katherine's home on Philipsburg Avenue in Fairview.

(See Church Street [Dublin 7] for the stories of the Capuchin friars who attended those executed in Kilmainham Gaol.)

Kilmainham Gaol was closed in 1924. Éamon de Valera was the last prisoner.

James's Street: South Dublin Union Workhouse (now St James's Hospital). Formerly known as Queen Anne's Mansions, the building was begun in 1702. During the Rising it was held by Cmdt Éamonn Ceannt and the 4th Battalion Volunteers.[571] The Union was home to over 3,280 persons and had residences for doctors and nurses, as well as churches, workshops, dormitories and fields. Ceannt decided not to evacuate those living there but moved them to buildings draped with Red Cross flags. The main outposts were Jameson's Distillery in Marrowbone Lane, Watkins's Brewery in Ardee Street and Roe's Distillery in Mount Brown.[572]

Ceannt could have used 2,000 men to man the entire estate, but he had only 43 Volunteers in the Union. Almost immediately, he withdrew his men from the main gate and outer walls to the inner buildings, because the British surrounded them.[573] The Volunteers occupied buildings here from Easter Monday. On Thursday, Major Sir Francis Vane took command of a column of British troops under Lt Col. W.C. Oates. Ceannt and the Volunteers were surrounded, but in comparative peace, after Thursday night until they surrendered on Sunday. (Ceannt had fewer than 60 Volunteers under his command here at any one time; he surrendered 42—Cathal Brugha was missing.)

There were several open fields surrounding the buildings, stretching southwards from the Volunteer HQ to the Grand Canal: the Master's Fields, McCaffrey Estate and the Orchard Fields. Nurse Margaretta Keogh (Kehoe?),[574] who worked in the Union Hospital, was killed here, the first woman to die in the Rising. She was killed at No. 2 Hospital Building when she went to the aid of a fallen Volunteer and was shot by a British soldier who thought she was one of the Volunteers.

Cathal Brugha single-handedly saved the Volunteers' position here by his courage. For two hours he held the British at a courtyard, defending the Nurses' Home unaided. Alone he forced the British to retreat. He was propped against a wall singing *God Save Ireland* when Ceannt and the Volunteers came to get him. He had been wounded 25 times—'5 dangerous bullet wounds, 9 serious and 11 slight'—and survived, though he never fully recovered the use of his legs. A Carmelite nun and a Red Cross worker took him to the Union Hospital on Friday morning, then to the hospital in Dublin Castle. The British ultimately released him: they did not think he could be of any future danger because he was hurt so badly.[575] 'When he walked,' it was said afterwards, 'one could hear the bullets rattlin'.'

James's Street: St James's Church. Fr Eugene McCarthy ministered here. He married Grace Gifford and Joseph Plunkett. On their wedding certificate, Plunkett was listed as a bachelor with an occupation of 'gentleman', while Grace was listed as a spinster with an occupation of artist. The two British soldiers who were 'witnesses' were John Smith and John Lockerby ('Sgt 3rd Battalion, the Royal Iniskillen Regiment'). At the presbytery here, Fr McCarthy and Grace Gifford Plunkett were 'assaulted' by British troops after her wedding, when they searched the premises and 'roughly handled them both'.[576]

Fr McCarthy also saw James Connolly in Dublin Castle. He said that Connolly was first strapped to a chair, but his wounds were so bad that the chair toppled over. The chair was put upright but again fell over. Finally, Fr McCarthy said, 'a stretcher was brought out and Connolly was strapped to it in a slanting position against the wall and the volley rang out'.[577] Along with Fr Aloysius, Fr McCarthy anointed Connolly after the execution.[578]

53 James's Street: Home of Mr Byrne, bell-ringer at St James's. Grace Gifford Plunkett rested here after her wedding and was awakened at 2 a.m. and taken to Kilmainham to see Joseph Plunkett for ten minutes before he was executed. Then Fr McCarthy escorted her to lodgings on Thomas Street, where she spent the remainder of the night.

174 James's Street: Home of W.T. and Philip Cosgrave and their stepbrother Frank (Goban) Burke. It is situated across from the South Dublin Union, where they all fought and where Goban Burke was killed.[579] The section commander of C Company, South Dublin Union, Burke was on sentry duty in the corridor of the Nurses' Home, and they were constantly under fire from machine-guns in the Royal Hospital. As Burke leaned over to light a cigarette from James Fogarty's pipe, a shot hit him in the neck, killing him instantly.[580] Burke's death had a profound effect on W.T. Cosgrave; he blamed himself in later years for involving Burke in the fighting.[581]

Kilmainham: Royal Hospital. The Hospital was established in 1684 to house old soldiers disabled in the wars of the time. This was the HQ of the British military in Ireland at the time of the Rising.

Upon his arrival on Friday to take command, Major Gen. Sir John Grenfell Maxwell, KCB, CMG, CVO, DSO, issued the following proclamation:

> Most vigorous measures will be taken by me to stop the loss of life and damage to property which certain misguided persons are causing by their armed resistance to the law. If necessary, I shall not hesitate to destroy all buildings within any area occupied by rebels, and I warn all persons within the area now surrounded by his Majesty's troops forthwith to leave such areas.[582]

His next command was to have a limepit dug in the yard of Arbour Hill Barracks (large enough for 50 bodies, it was claimed), and that is where the executed were buried.[583] (See Arbour Hill Detention Barracks [Dublin 7].)

It remained a home for soldiers until 1927, was remodelled in 1991 and is now the Irish Museum of Modern Art.

Kingsbridge Station (now Seán Heuston Station). The station was in the area assigned to the 4th Battalion under Cmdt Éamonn Ceannt, but it was never taken. Ceannt's orders were to prevent troops from Richmond and Islandbridge Barracks from moving into the city, and the station would have provided a perfect position from which to operate. It has been suggested that Ceannt considered the task of seizing the station, but when so few Volunteers reported on Monday he reported that to Connolly, and Connolly ordered Cmdt Ned Daly to send Seán Heuston to the Mendicity Institute instead.[584] The first British troops to arrive in Dublin were the 3rd Reserve Cavalry Brigade from the Curragh, and they arrived at Kingsbridge Station at 4.15 p.m. on Monday afternoon.

14–21 Marrowbone Lane: Guinness buildings.[585] Fr Eugene Nevin was the chaplain for the Volunteers stationed here.[586] It was James (Séamus) Murphy's HQ during the Rising; he put hats and jackets on brush handles and put them in windows to 'increase' the size of his 'garrison'.[587]

43–45 Marrowbone Lane: Marrowbone Lane Distillery, usually known as Jameson's Distillery.

Mount Brown: Roe's Distillery. Capt. Thomas (Tommy) McCarthy brought in a load of ammunition to the distillery:[588]

> We occupied Roe's Distillery from Monday morning. We did not anticipate any hindrance in our ingress into the building . . . I then gave orders to my Company to get their trench tools, and we had to bash in the gate. During all this delay we were being exposed to the tower of the old men's Home, and they had a commanding view from which we were directly under fire in our present Position. We had to smash the gate in and also some of our lads scaled the wall, which was covered with glass, and got in and opened the gate. I went up afterwards and demanded every key of the place from Boyd. He was a bit hesitant at first, but I said, 'If you don't deliver the keys I'll have to take them off your corpse'. He delivered up the keys then. During the time we were trying to knock down the gate we were practically attacked by the rabble in Bow Lane, and I will never forget it as long as I live. 'Leave down your —— rifles', they shouted, 'and we'll beat the —— out of you'. They were most menacing to Our Lads.

McCarthy and his garrison mysteriously left Roe's Distillery on Thursday. He didn't tell 4th Battalion Cmdt Éamonn Ceannt—they just left their post, which left the flank of the Union exposed.[589] McCarthy stated:

> After withdrawing it was a case of every man for himself. Some of them succeeded in getting into other posts. After our withdrawal from this post there was no reaction except that I was a much maligned man, but I still say that under

similar circumstances I would adopt the same attitude, and I have never yet apologized for our action.[590]

Their withdrawal weakened the entire South Dublin Union area's defences.

Richmond Barracks, Inchicore. The courts martial following the Rising were held here.[591] (James Connolly's was held in Dublin Castle because of his injuries.) Brig. Gen. Charles Blackader, CB, DSO, Col. E.W.S.K Maconchy and two other military officers directed them. The Brigadier said of Padraic Pearse: 'I have just done one of the hardest tasks I have ever had to do. I have had to condemn one of the finest characters I have ever come across. There must be something very wrong in the state of things, that makes a man like that a rebel.'[592] The prosecutor was William Wylie.[593] Although Wylie fought against the rebels, he was strongly opposed to the speed and secrecy of the trials. He was rebuffed in his proposal to allow the defendants defence counsel, and only after MacDonagh's execution were they allowed to call witnesses. Alderman Laurence O'Neill, lord mayor of Dublin, refused to act as Crown Prosecutor but acted as Counsel for the Defence.

They all faced the same basic charge, which was handed to them only moments before the trial: that they 'did an act, to wit did take part in an armed rebellion and in the waging of war against His Majesty the King, such an act being of such a nature as to be calculated to be prejudicial to the defence of the realm, being done with the intention and purpose of assisting the enemy'. In some cases there was an additional charge that they 'did attempt to cause disaffection among the civil population of His Majesty'.[594] All the defendants except Willie Pearse pleaded not guilty. Daly attempted to plead guilty to just one part of the charge ('did take part in an armed rebellion') but he was told that this was not permitted. Ned Daly was prisoner No. 21, Willie Pearse was prisoner No. 27 and Seán MacDermott was prisoner No. 91; James Connolly was designated prisoner No. 90, though he was never actually a resident prisoner here.

In reporting to Asquith regarding the executions, Maxwell wrote:

In view of the gravity of the Rebellion and its connection with German intrigue and propaganda and in view of the great loss of life and destruction of property resulting therefrom, the General Officer Commanding in Chief Irish Command [Maxwell] has found it imperative to inflict the most severe sentences on the organisers of this detestable Rising and on the Commanders who took an actual part in the actual fighting which occurred. It is hoped that these examples will be sufficient to act as a deterrent to intriguers and to bring home to them that the murder of Her [sic] Majesty's subjects or other acts calculated to imperil the safety of the realm will not be tolerated.[595]

De Valera was tried here on 8 May. There has always been confusion as to whether de Valera evaded execution because of his American citizenship. His own view was that none of the American connection had the 'slightest influence' on his escaping execution.[596] He said:

> What was decisive was that Tom Ashe, who was likely to be executed, and myself were court-martialled on the same day and just about the time when [English Prime Minister Herbert] Asquith made the public statement that no further executions would take place except those who had signed the *Proclamation*.
>
> The fact that I was born in America would not, I believe, I am convinced, have saved me. I know of nothing in international law which could be cited in my defence or made an excuse for American intervention, except, perhaps, to see I got a fair trial.[597]

The prosecutor, Judge Wylie, gave this account of the ending of the executions:

> Maxwell: 'Who is next on the list?'
> Wylie: 'Connolly.'
> Maxwell: 'We can't let him off; who is next?'
> Wylie: 'De Valera.'
> Maxwell: 'Is he someone important?'
> Wylie: 'No. He is a school-master who was taken at Boland's Mill.'
> Maxwell: 'All right, we will go ahead with Connolly and stop with this fellow.'[598]

Countess Markievicz was also tried here and was sentenced to death, although her sentence was commuted to penal servitude for life because of her sex. Some controversy has arisen about her conduct at the court martial. She always claimed that she would have preferred to share the fate of the male leaders,[599] but it has been alleged that at her trial she broke down and begged that her life be spared solely on account of her sex.[600] In her diary of the events of the Rising, Elsie Mahaffy wrote:

> Her court martial was theatrical. The court president, Brigadier-General Blackadder [*sic*], was so nervous of her that he got out his revolver and put it on the table in front of him. In the formal record of the trial she is said to have stated: 'I went out to fight for Ireland and it doesn't matter what happens to me. I did what I thought was right and I stand by it'. That was untrue. All her 'dash' and 'go' left her . . . she utterly broke down, cried and sobbed and tried to incite pity in General Blackadder [*sic*]; it was a terrible scene—the gaunt wreck of a once lovely lady.[601]

In his unpublished memoir, Wylie claimed that the countess broke down, pleading 'I am only a woman, you cannot shoot a woman, you must not shoot a woman':

> I saw the general getting out his revolver and putting it on the table beside him. But he need not have troubled for she curled up completely. 'I am only a woman', she cried, 'and you cannot shoot a woman, you must not shoot a woman'. She never stopped moaning the whole time she was in the courtroom . . . She crumpled up . . . I think we all felt slightly disgusted, [at a person who] had been preaching to a lot of silly boys, death and glory, die for your Country etc., and yet she was literally crawling. I won't say any more; it revolts me still.[602]

6 Riverdale Terrace, Inchicore: Home of the Holland family, including sons Dan, Frank, Robert and Walter. All but Walter were members of the IRB. All were Volunteers and fought in the South Dublin Union in the Rising. Robert and his company set out to equip themselves by buying rifles from British soldiers.[603]

Rutledge Terrace: The McGrath family lived here in 1916, and the two eldest sons, George and Joseph, were active in the Volunteers in the Rising. Afterwards, George, the eldest son, became controller-general of finances in the Free State government. Joe, the second eldest, was elected to Dáil Éireann in 1918 and became substitute minister for labour in 1920–1; after the Treaty he became minister for labour and, after September 1922, minister for industry and commerce, including the former ministry for labour. He left politics in 1924 and went into business, founding the Irish Sweepstakes.

2 St Augustine Street: Home of Joseph Murray (14), who was killed in the Rising.[604]

South Circular Road: Home of George Percy Sainsbury (9), who died at Haroldville Terrace on 27 April of wounds caused by the Rising.[605] He is buried in Mount Jerome Cemetery.

Thomas Street: Fr Eugene McCarthy found lodgings here for Grace Gifford Plunkett on the morning of 4 May, after he presided at her marriage to Joseph Plunkett.

74 Thomas Street: Home of Jimmy Fox (16), a Fianna member who was killed in the St Stephen's Green garrison.[606] He was the youngest of seven children.[607]

Usher's Island: Mendicity Institute, directly across the Liffey from the Royal Barracks (now Collins Barracks). This was formerly Moira House, home of the earl and countess of Moira. He was an opponent of the Union, was a governor-general of India and became marquess of Hastings. He was a friend, supporter and protector of Robert Emmet and Theobald Wolfe Tone, Lord Edward and Lady Pamela FitzGerald, and Michael Dwyer. They and other 'rebels' often dined here. It was given to the citizens of Dublin as an 'Institution for the Suppression of Mendicancy in Dublin' in 1826. In the days of the Rising, as in earlier times, mendicants were not permitted to enter through the front door.[608] The Institute was only open to people who had normally been resident within the ring of the two circular roads for three months. The intention was that the able-bodied could earn enough in the Institute, over and above what they were charged for their food, to pay for their lodgings. In order not to break up families there was a girls' and a boys' school.[609]

In the Rising it was held by D Company, 1st Battalion, under Capt. Seán Heuston. Approximately 35 Volunteers, all between the ages of eighteen and 25, were in the garrison. About twelve Volunteers from Swords, under the command of Richard Coleman, and 25 Fianna held out against approximately 400 Royal Dublin Fusiliers. Some contend that Heuston's men were not supposed to be sent there in the original plan, but that Ceannt and Connolly, realising that they could not occupy the Guinness buildings and Kingsbridge Station because of the restricted turnout on Monday, sent the Fianna there as an alternative.[610]

Capt. Heuston led the Fianna to take and hold the Mendicity Institute, which was west of Daly's other positions and located on Usher's Island on the south side of the Liffey (on the opposite side to the Four Courts). Heuston was originally charged to hold the Institute for the afternoon but asked for and received a small number of reinforcements from the GPO, bringing his garrison to about 35 men. He was ordered to control the route between Royal Barracks and the Four Courts, and to prevent the British from crossing Church Street Bridge. A tall wall with wooden gates surrounded the large building, and Heuston's men immediately barricaded themselves into the rooms of the Institute. Windows were knocked out and loopholed with furniture and sandbags, and the Fianna, expecting the British to use incendiaries, strategically placed buckets of water throughout.

Capt. Richard Balfe wrote a thorough description of the action:

When we reached the Mendicity Institute we broke one small door and entered ... On the stroke of twelve o'clock a small party of sappers came along unarmed. We allowed these to pass knowing what was coming along. In a few minutes the main body of troops in column of route came into view. We had sixteen men altogether including officers. All had Lee-Enfield rifles. Every man had at least 100 rounds of ammunition. Myself and some others had 500 rounds each. Two shots were fired rapidly and the commanding officer dropped. I heard afterwards that he was shot between the eyes and in the heart. The column halted right opposite to us after the two shots and it was a case of fire and one could not miss. The column were four deep. There were from 200 to 250 at least in the column. At the time we had been putting out a tricolour flag and we saw the officer in front drawing his sword and pointing towards it. This was the officer who was immediately shot dead. The firing became continuous and rapid and it eased off. Some of the British soldiers tried to protect themselves against the quay wall and eventually ran up side streets and in through houses. The casualties were numerous and the ambulance was a considerable time removing the wounded. At four o'clock p.m., they came down eight deep. They must not have known where the first attack had come from, as the officer who first saw us was immediately shot dead. We altered our tactics then and we concentrated firing on the rear of the column. As they were nearly at Queen Street Bridge [now Liam Mellows Bridge, connecting Queen Street and Arran Quay] we suddenly concentrated the firing on the head of the column. The column stopped. It was just a matter of firing as rapidly as possible into a solid body.[611]

The Fianna were well-trained marksmen and disciplined troops who were told to remain stealthily at their posts until Heuston gave the signal to fire on any British attempting to advance on the interior positions of the Four Courts garrison. When the 10th Royal Dublin Fusiliers left Royal Barracks, they marched up the north quays with no advance scouts and did not reconnoitre the area. As they came abreast of the Institute, Heuston's men fired in unison on the column, taking it completely by surprise. Here the Volunteers and Fianna were much better prepared than the professional British soldiers. It could always be argued that an 'ambush' will favour an amateur, but in this case the British simply marched down the road without taking any fundamental precautions, and suffered heavy casualties for their arrogance. The British forces began to overwhelm Heuston's men and the Institute was finally surrounded on Wednesday. By then the British were close enough to lob grenades into the building, many of which were thrown back.

Ultimately, Heuston estimated that his small garrison faced an assault by 300–400 British troops, necessitating his surrender. He had held for three days when he had been asked to hold for three hours, infuriating the British that so few youngsters held them off for so long. A British sniper in Roe's Distillery killed Peter Wilson from Swords as the men were being formed up after the surrender.[612] Dick Balfe[613] and Liam Staines were badly wounded.[614] Later, James Brennan wrote:

> We had almost run out of ammunition. Dog-tired, without food, trapped, hopelessly outnumbered, we had reached the limit of our endurance. After consultation with the rest of us, Seán decided that the only hope for the wounded and indeed, for the safety of all of us, was to surrender.[615]

The garrison consisted of:

Capt. Seán Heuston (executed)
Capt. Richard (Dick) C. Balfe
#616 Capt. Richard (Dick) Coleman
James Joseph (Séamus) Brennan
Frederick John Brooks
John Joseph Byrne
John Clarke
Seán (John) Cody
James Crenigan
John Francis (Frank) Cullen
John (Seán) Derrington
William Patrick (Liam) Derrington
Seán Harrington
Patrick Kelly (Padraig Ó Ceallaigh)
Richard (Dick) Kelly
Tom Kelly
George Levins
John (Seán) McLoughlin (MacLoughlin)
James Marks
William Meehan
William (Liam) Murnane
Joseph Norton
Joseph O'Brien (Seosamh Ó Broin)
William O'Dea
Thomas O'Kelly
Thomas Peppard
Edward Joseph (Eddie) Roach (de
    Roiste)
Joseph Roche (Roach)
Liam Roche (de Roiste)
Michael Scully (Mícheál Ó Scollaighe)
William F. (Liam) Staines
Patrick J. (Paddy Joe) Stephenson
James Wilson
Peter Wilson (killed)
William (Beck) Wilson
William (Cody) Wilson

It was the home of Michael (Mick) Colgan, a participant in the landing of the guns at Howth in July 1914, who fought at Jacob's factory in the Rising. A founder of the Irish Bookbinders and Allied Trades Union, he was president of the Dublin Trades Union Council in 1937, and president of the Irish Trade Union Congress in 1941–2. He was elected to the Seanad in 1943, 1948 and 1951.

The 1916 Institution Annual Report indicated:

Owing to the SF rebellion that took place in the city of Dublin during Easter week, the committee regret to say that the premises were taken possession of by members of the SF Society and as a consequence the house was considerably injured. The sum received from the government was £286 15s but the committee had to expend £391 9s in absolutely necessary work.

Today an Office of the Eastern Health Board occupies the site. The front wall, gates and side buildings are all that remain of the Institute.

4 Vincent Street, Goldenbridge: Home of Eugene Lynch (8), who was killed on 28 April. He is buried in Goldenbridge.[617]

1 Walworth Road, Portobello: Birthplace of Arthur and William Joseph Shields. William Joseph, who became known as Barry FitzGerald, was born on 10 March 1888. Educated to enter the banking business, he was bitten by the acting bug and joined Dublin's Abbey Players. He famously starred in the Abbey Theatre production of Seán O'Casey's *Juno and the Paycock* and, many years later, in John Ford's film *The quiet man*. He received an Oscar for his role in *Going my way*. Arthur was born on 15 February 1896 and was in the GPO during the Rising. He was imprisoned at Frongoch.[618] He never changed his name; he also had a long film career in the US and was in *The quiet man* with his brother. (See 12 Vernon Avenue [Dublin 3].)

Weaver Square: The Inghínidhe Branch of Cumann na mBan, attached to the Volunteer 4th Battalion, mustered here at 11.00 a.m. on Easter Monday.[619]

Whitefriar Street, entrance on Aungier Street: Church of Our Lady of Mount Carmel (Carmelite Church). Fr McCabe was the prior in 1916. He went to Jacob's Biscuit Factory on Monday to tell the Volunteers that the Rising was an 'insane enterprise'. He singularly failed to make an impression during a very heated argument—in the middle of which a Volunteer on an upper floor dropped a bag of flour on him. He left the factory, defeated, and white as a sheet from head to toe.[620]

7 Whitefriar Street: Home of Moses Doyle (9), who was killed in his home near Jacob's Biscuit Factory on Easter Monday.[621] He is buried in Glasnevin Cemetery. His family of six shared a two-roomed house with two other families, twelve persons in all.[622]

Dublin 9

Key locations

Belcamp Park
Drumcondra

13 Alphonsus Road, Drumcondra: Home of Lily M. O'Brennan, Áine Ceannt's sister.[623] Áine Ceannt stayed here while Éamonn was in Richmond Barracks and Kilmainham Gaol, because her home in Dolphin's Barn had been trashed by British soldiers searching the residence.

Áine wrote:

'HE IS GONE TO HEAVEN'
a Capuchin friar to
Áine Ceannt

> Thursday morning's paper brought the news of the execution of Pearse, MacDonagh and Clarke, and I believe in that same paper it said that it was stated in the House of Commons that a sentence of three years' penal servitude had been imposed on Éamonn and three others. I do not know who the other three were. When I read this I was delighted, but at the same time I thought it very hard that MacDonagh, who to my mind had not been so deeply involved until the last moment, should have suffered execution . . .
>
> During this period I was labouring under the delusion that my husband had been sentenced to three years, but my sister-in-law, who lived in Drumcondra, traced me to Mrs Brugha's home and told me that I need not believe what I saw in the papers, that four more had been executed, Willie Pearse, Ned Daly, Michael O'Hanrahan and Joe Plunkett. She suggested that I come over with her and call down to the priests in Church Street, where the only reliable information could be obtained. She also told me that the military escort sent for Mrs MacDonagh had failed to reach her, so that Mrs MacDonagh had no final interview with her husband before his execution. Bearing this in mind I decided to stay up all night . . .
>
> That evening I went down with my sister-in-law to Church Street, and for the first time met Father Albert. He warned me to take no counsel with anyone I met, and to be very discreet in all I said. I stayed in Drumcondra that night as it was too late to cross the bridges . . .
>
> I arrived at Kilmainham, was shown in, and found Éamonn in a cell with no seating accommodation and no bedding, not even a bed of straw. The first thing

I noticed was that his Sam Brown belt was gone, and that his uniform was slightly torn. A sergeant stood at the door while we spoke, and we could say very little, but I gathered from Éamonn that he had heard about the supposed three years' sentence and he felt it would worry me. I said to him that the Rising was an awful fiasco, and he replied, 'No, it was the biggest thing since '98. They told me here that the railway lines were up'. Those were Éamonn's words . . .

He gave me Cathal Brugha's watch to give to Mrs Brugha, and some money which he had on him . . .

I left Éamonn after getting a promise that he would send for me no matter what was going to happen . . .

. . . an Army officer arrived with a note to say that my husband would like to see myself and his sister. We went out to the car and there we found that this soldier had already collected Richard Kent and Michael Kent, brothers.

We reached Kilmainham and had about twenty minutes' interview with my husband. He was in a different cell, and had been given a couple of boards, on which I presume he rested. He also had a soap box, a chair, a candle and pen and ink.

No executions had taken place for some days, I think MacBride's execution had taken place on Friday, and the soldiers were coming in and out in a jocose manner, saying such things as, 'It's a long way to Tipperary', and, 'You never know what will happen'. Éamonn said his mind had been disturbed. He said, 'I was quite prepared to walk out of this at a quarter to four in the morning, but all this has upset me'. He told me he had sent for Father Augustine to come to him . . .

As I was still in doubt as to the outcome of the morning, I remained up all night with my sister-in-law, and each hour we knelt down and said the Rosary. From three o'clock I remained praying until about half past five, when I knew that everything would be over if the executions were to take place.

At six o'clock curfew was lifted, and we made our way down to Church Street. It was a glorious summer morning, and when we arrived at the Priory I asked for Father Augustine.

He sent down another Friar who told me that Father Augustine had only come, celebrated Mass and had gone to his room, but that if I wished he would get up and come down to me. I said no, that I only wanted to know the truth, and this priest said, 'He is gone to Heaven'.

At about ten o'clock on 8th May my sister-in-law accompanied me to Church Street, where we met Father Augustine.

He gave me full details of Éamonn's last moments, and I think enough praise could not be given to both Father Augustine, O.F.M. Cap., and to his comrade Father Albert, for all they did for the executed men.

Father Augustine told me that Éamonn had held his, Father Augustine's, crucifix in his hands, and the last words he spoke were, 'My Jesus, Mercy'.

In every case it would appear as if it was necessary for the officer in charge of the firing party to dispatch the victim by a revolver shot. Father Augustine thought that this was a dreadful thing. He gave me two letters which he had brought from the jail; one was my husband's personal letter to me, and the other was a letter which he left more or less for the Irish nation.[624]

Arran Road, Drumcondra: Seán O'Shea's home. Kitty O'Doherty was sent here to move some arms:

We had a last *Céilidhe* coming off on the Saturday night before Palm Sunday in the Banba Hall, which belonged to the Grocers' Curates Association. It was the Cumann na mBan final *Céilidhe*. On the Wednesday or Thursday night before it, I and a number of members of Cumann na mBan were in the Library of 25 Parnell Square holding a final meeting. There were two men outside—Séamus O'Connor and Mícheál O'Hanrahan . . . I said: 'What is it?' Séamus O'Connor said: 'There is a job to be done'. I was very used to hearing that. I said: 'What is that?' He was very excited, and told me, hurriedly, about guns that were in O'Shea's in Arran Road, Drumcondra. He said: 'You must get them. We want you to save them.' . . . I turned round immediately, and went back into the room. I asked the girls to volunteer. I said: 'I want volunteers. There is a job to be done'. Nobody said a word. After a little while I looked round at them. I said to Brighid Foley: 'Brighid Foley, do you refuse to come?' So Brighid came, and Effie Taaffe too . . . I would like to explain the position leading up to my being asked to save the guns. Information about everything practically used to come out from the Castle. We had our own men in there, who were helping the movement, as well as earning their own living, by working there. Any raids that were threatened, any bits of information from the country, or any telegrams—all these things were made known. They were brought to the Castle, and then our friends in the Castle passed them on to us, thus proving that this bit of information came out from there regarding Seán O'Shea and the arms. Arms were being got into the country in any and every possible way . . . He was connected with the Irish Cutlery Company on the Quays. I don't know whether he was actually a member of the Volunteers, or not. He was very sympathetic. He was getting in small arms, under cover of a War Permit, which he had for the purpose of getting in stuff for his firm. This day that these two men called for me, the boxes of stuff came in to the North Wall for Seán O'Shea, and, although they were marked 'War Permit', somebody opened them, and 'phoned to the Castle that Seán O'Shea's stuff contained small arms . . . Actually, the word 'bayonets' was told to me too, but I could not say, not having seen them. When our man in the Castle was told, he immediately sent out word to Séamus O'Connor's office. Séamus was a Solicitor. O'Connor knew that O'Shea's house would be raided, and that the stuff from the previous day had gone on to the house.

The women moved the arms to the O'Doherty house on Claude Road.[625]

Belcamp Park: Countess Markievicz leased this as a training centre for Na Fianna Éireann.

30 Claude Road, Drumcondra: Home of Kitty O'Doherty.

> I had myself a regular arsenal under the floor in my sitting-room. I can give you plenty of proof. It was my husband, of course, who really was responsible, but he was away travelling, and I was in charge. I had dozens of bandoliers. I know nothing about firearms. I never claim to do what I did not do. I had these bandoliers, with bullets stuck in them—.303. They were either bought from British soldiers, coming home while the war was on, or got by some other means. Then I had some of the Howth Rifles, which were not very good, as they were too heavy.[626]

She carried dispatches to County Kerry, and on Thursday of Easter week she carried messages to Kinnegad.

Drumcondra: Archbishop Dr William Walsh's house. His feelings were always nationalist, but he thought the Rising 'madness'. Count Plunkett went to inform him of the Rising, as he had been asked to do by the pope.[627] Walsh was ill and Plunkett was giving the message to Walsh's secretary, Fr Curran, when word came of the fighting at the GPO.

Éamon de Valera stayed in the gate lodge here in 1919 prior to leaving for New York.

82 Lower Drumcondra Road: Home of Piaras Béaslaí, Battalion Adjutant of the 4th Battalion.

71 Richmond Road, Drumcondra: Home of Richard Kent, brother of Éamonn Ceannt.

Dublin 11

Key location
Glasnevin Cemetery, Finglas Road

Officially opened in 1832, Glasnevin Cemetery, Finglas Road is the largest cemetery in Ireland, opened after a series of events prompted Daniel O'Connell to establish a burial place for the Catholic nation of Ireland.[628] Its official name is Prospect Cemetery.

Among others, the following are buried in Glasnevin Cemetery, many in the 'Republican Plot':

'MY SOUL TO HEAVEN, MY HEART TO ROME, MY BODY TO IRELAND'
Daniel O'Connell

William Phillip Allen (Manchester Martyr)
Thomas Ashe
Kevin Barry (reinterred from Mountjoy Prison on 1 November 2000)
Piaras Béaslaí
Brendan Behan
Harry Boland
Cathal Brugha (Charles William St John Burgess)
Thomas Bryan (reinterred from Mountjoy Prison on 1 November 2000)
Lucy Byrne (née Smyth)★
Mary Byrne★
Winifred Byrne (Somerville)★
Marie Carron★
Sir Roger Casement (reinterred 1 March 1965)
John Keegan Casey (the Fenian poet 'Leo')
Erskine Childers (Molly)
Peadar Clancy
J.J. Coade
Michael Collins
Peg Conlon★
Ina Connolly★
Nora Connolly (O'Brien)★

Rauri (Roddy) Connolly
Marcella Cosgrave★
Kitty Kiernan Cronin
James Daley (Connaught Ranger Mutiny)
Charlotte Despard
Éamon de Valera (Sinéad)
Anne Devlin (Robert Emmet's housekeeper)
Anastasia Anne Devlin★
John Devoy
Thomas Dickson
Patrick Doyle (reinterred from Mountjoy Prison on 1 November 2000)
Frank Duff
Emily Elliott (Ledwith)★
Marie English★
Ellen Ennis★ (Costigan)
Frank Flood (reinterred from Mountjoy Prison on 1 November 2000)
Edmund Foley (reinterred from Mountjoy Prison on 1 November 2000)
Charles Gavan-Duffy
Louise Gavan-Duffy★
Sheila (Julia) Grenan★
Arthur Griffith
Timothy Healy
Denis Caulfield Heron
Revd Gerald Manley Hopkins, SJ
Mary Kavanaugh (Duggan)★
Sarah Kealy★
Peadar Kearney
Delia Larkin
James Larkin
Michael Larkin (Manchester Martyr)
James Fintan Lalor
Philomena Lucas (Morkan)★
Maud Gonne MacBride
Seán MacBride
Muriel Gifford MacDonagh
Michael Malone
Mary Mapother★
Countess Constance Gore Booth Markievicz
Josephine McGowan (née O'Keefe)★
Dick McKee

Mary McLoughlin★

Terence Bellew McManus (first Fenian funeral)

Patrick (Paddy) Moran (reinterred from Mountjoy Prison on 1 November 2000)

Kathleen Murphy★

Marie NicShiulaigh (Price)★

Michael O'Brien (Manchester Martyr)

Daniel O'Connell—'My soul to heaven, my heart to Rome, my body to Ireland'

Batt O'Connor (Máire)

Patrick O'Donnell (the Avenger)

Eoin O'Duffy

Elizabeth More O'Farrell★

Revd Michael O'Flanagan

Eily O'Hanrahan★

Brian O'Higgins (Anna)

Kevin O'Higgins

Annie O'Keefe★

John O'Leary

John O'Mahoney

James O'Mara

Gearóid O'Sullivan

Mary O'Sullivan (O'Carroll)★

The Ó Rahilly (Michael Joseph) (Nancy)

Margaret Quinn★

Charles Stewart Parnell

John (Seán) A. Pinkman

Grace Gifford Plunkett

Bridie Richards★

Jeremiah O'Donovan Rossa

Molly O'Reilly (Corcoran)

Patrick (P.J.) Rutledge

Bernard Ryan (reinterred from Mountjoy Prison on 1 November 2000)

Catherine Ryan★

Frank Ryan

Phyllis Ryan★

Francis Sheehy-Skeffington (Hanna)

Margaret Skinnider★

James Stephens—'A day, an hour, of virtuous liberty is worth a whole eternity in
    bondage'

Nora Thornton★

Sadie Tierney★

Oscar Traynor

Thomas Traynor (reinterred from Mountjoy Prison on 1 November 2000)

Margaret Walsh (Jenkinson)★

Archbishop William Walsh

Thomas Whelan (reinterred from Mountjoy Prison on 1 November 2000)

Jennie Wyse-Power★

Nancy Wyse-Power★

Monument to Hunger Strikers 1917, 1981

★(Cumann na mBan member who served in the 1916 Rising)

Jeremiah O'Donovan Rossa was buried here after a great Fenian funeral. Rossa had founded the Phoenix Society in 1856, and died in America in July 1915. Padraic Pearse gave the graveside oration and William Oman of the Irish Citizen Army played the Last Post.[629]

Rossa was imprisoned in 1865, was released in 1871 and went into exile in America. While in jail, Rossa spent 123 days on a bread-and-water punishment diet, 231 days on a penal-class diet in a darkened cell, 28 days in a completely dark cell and 34 days with his hands manacled behind his back. After this he was occasionally punished for singing. At his trial, he had been accused of 'inciting the lower classes to believe they might expect a redistribution of property'.[630] Rossa died in New York City on 29 June 1915, and the funeral was held in Glasnevin Cemetery on 1 August. Kathleen McDonnell wrote that it was 'a chance for the Irish to prove that a dead patriot is at once a challenge to British tyranny and an inspiration to his own people'.[631] Seán McGarry approached James Connolly to write an article for the programme, and was taken aback when Connolly replied: 'When are you fellows going to stop blathering about *dead* Fenians? Why don't you get a few *live* ones for a change? Rossa was prepared to fight England *at peace*. You fellows won't fight her *at war*! Between the Molly Maguires and the Molly Coddles we'll [the ICA] be landed in the soup!'[632] Later Tom Clarke talked to Connolly, and Connolly wrote an article in which he managed to turn a dead Fenian into a live incitement to revolution:

> The Irish Citizen Army in its constitution pledges its members to fight for a Republican Freedom for Ireland. Its members are, therefore, of the number who believe that at the call of duty they may have to lay down their lives for Ireland, and have so trained themselves that at the worst the laying down of their lives shall constitute the starting point of another glorious tradition—a tradition that will keep alive the soul of the nation.
>
> We are, therefore, present to honour O'Donovan Rossa by right of our faith in the separate destiny of our country and our faith in the ability of the Irish Workers to achieve that destiny.[633]

Many women from Cumann na mBan marched in military formation to Glasnevin Cemetery for the funeral.

> Large Contingents of women marched in the O'Donovan Rossa funeral procession, taking an integral part of it and as far as discipline, bearing, and physical endurance went, proved themselves fully equal to the men.
>
> The comments of the crowd on the women (usually friendly) were instructive, for they were almost invariably hailed as 'Suffragettes', the presumption naturally being that all women who take part in public life in any way must be connected with the movement of Votes for Women.[634]

It was at this funeral that Pearse made his most famous speech:

> It has seemed right, before we turn away from this place in which we have laid the mortal remains of O'Donovan Rossa, that one among us should, in the name of all, speak the praise of that valiant man, and endeavour to formulate the thought and the hope that are in us as we stand around his grave. And if there is anything that makes it fitting that I, rather than some other, I rather than one of the grey-haired men who were young with him and shared in his labour and in his suffering, should speak here, it is perhaps that I may be taken as speaking on behalf of a new generation that has been re-baptised in the Fenian faith, and that has accepted the responsibility of carrying out the Fenian programme. I propose to you then that, here by the grave of this unrepentant Fenian, we renew our baptismal vows; that, here by the grave of this unconquered and unconquerable man, we ask of God, each one for himself, such unshakeable purpose, such high and gallant courage, such unbreakable strength of soul as belonged to O'Donovan Rossa.
>
> Deliberately here we avow ourselves, as he avowed himself in the dock, Irishmen of one allegiance only. We of the Irish Volunteers, and you others who are associated with us in to-day's task and duty, are bound together and must stand together henceforth in brotherly union for the achievement of the freedom of Ireland. And we know only one definition of freedom: it is Tone's definition, it is Mitchel's definition, it is Rossa's definition. Let no man blaspheme the cause that the dead generations of Ireland served by giving it any other name and definition than their name and their definition.
>
> We stand at Rossa's grave not in sadness but rather in exaltation of spirit that it has been given to us to come thus into so close a communion with that brave and splendid Gael. Splendid and holy causes are served by men who are themselves splendid and holy. O'Donovan Rossa was splendid in the proud manhood of him, splendid in the heroic grace of him, splendid in the Gaelic

strength and clarity and truth of him. And all that splendour and pride and strength was compatible with a humility and a simplicity of devotion to Ireland, to all that was olden and beautiful and Gaelic in Ireland, the holiness and simplicity of patriotism of a Michael O'Clery or of an Eoghan O'Growney. The clear true eyes of this man almost alone in his day visioned Ireland as we of to-day would surely have her: not free merely, but Gaelic as well; not Gaelic merely, but free as well.

In a closer spiritual communion with him now than ever before or perhaps ever again, in a spiritual communion with those of his day, living and dead, who suffered with him in English prisons, in communion of spirit too with our own dear comrades who suffer in English prisons to-day, and speaking on their behalf as well as our own, we pledge to Ireland our love, and we pledge to English rule in Ireland our hate. This is a place of peace, sacred to the dead, where men should speak with all charity and with all restraint; but I hold it a Christian thing, as O'Donovan Rossa held it, to hate evil, to hate untruth, to hate oppression, and, hating them, to strive to overthrow them. Our foes are strong and wise and wary; but, strong and wise and wary as they are, they cannot undo the miracles of God who ripens in the hearts of young men the seeds sown by the young men of a former generation. And the seeds sown by the young men of '65 and '67 are coming to their miraculous ripening to-day. Rulers and Defenders of Realms had need to be wary if they would guard against such processes. Life springs from death; and from the graves of patriot men and women spring living nations. The Defenders of this Realm have worked well in secret and in the open. They think that they have pacified Ireland. They think that they have purchased half of us and intimidated the other half. They think that they have foreseen everything, think that they have provided against everything; but the fools, the fools, the fools!— they have left us our Fenian dead, and while Ireland holds these graves, Ireland unfree shall never be at peace.[635]

Pearse was the figurehead speaker pushed forward by Tom Clarke, in spite of stiff opposition from many IRB men who disliked Pearse personally and suspected him of political opportunism. Yet Clarke saw in Pearse the qualities necessary for leadership. He was not only a gifted writer and speaker but also an idealist and romantic visionary whose clarity of purpose and air of nobility appealed to Clarke. It was only after this oration that Pearse began to be taken seriously as a real IRB leader.

Dublin 13
Key location
Howth

A rms were landed at Howth on 26 July 1914. The Ó Rahilly and Mary Spring-Rice primarily planned the purchase of the Howth rifles, which cost £1,500.[636] The largest single contributor was Capt. George Fitz Hardinge Berkeley, with Mrs Alice Stopford Green the next largest subscriber; Roger Casement, Erskine Childers and his wife,[637] Mary Spring-Rice, Conor and Hugh O'Brien, Lord Ashbourne, Lady Young and Minnie Ryan subscribed the rest of the money.[638] All were Protestants of Anglo-Irish stock. The idea was that the money should be used to purchase arms, to bring them to Ireland, to sell the arms to the Irish Volunteers, and to reimburse the subscribers.[639] They did, in fact, get their money back.

'CUMANN NA MBAN MEMBERS ARE NOT THE AUXILIARIES OR HANDMAIDENS OR CAMP FOLLOWERS OF THE VOLUNTEERS—WE ARE THEIR ALLIES'
Mary Colum

The Ó Rahilly directed Darrell Figgis and Childers to the firm in Hamburg where they purchased the arms—1,500 rifles and 45,000 rounds of ammunition. The *Asgard* landed 900 rifles and 26,000 rounds of ammunition, and the rest was landed by the *Kelpie* in Kilcoole, Co. Wicklow.[640]

The plot was simple enough. Once bought from the Hamburg-based arms dealer Moritz Magnus der Jungere (who also supplied the anti-Home Rule UVF), the guns and ammunition were taken to Hamburg from their warehouse in Liège. From there they were transferred by the tugboat *Gladiator* south-west through the North Sea to the Ruytingen Lightship, moored in the English Channel on a sandbank close to the mouth of the River Scheldt and the French port of Dunkirk. At that point the *Gladiator*, with Figgis on board, was met by the *Asgard*, captained by Childers, and the *Kelpie*, captained by O'Brien, and the cargo was split between the two yachts: 900 guns and 25,000 bullets were offloaded onto the *Asgard*, and the remaining 600 guns and 20,000 bullets onto the *Kelpie*. The rifles were Mausers, Gewehr 71s, .31 calibre with a single-shot magazine.

On board the *Asgard* were Childers, his wife Molly, Mary Spring-Rice,[641] an English army officer named Gordon Shephard,[642] and two Donegal fishermen, Patrick McGinley and Charles Duggan. The yacht was a wedding present to the Childers and was designed and built in Norway in 1905.

About 1,000 Volunteers mustered and marched out to Howth that day. Various companies marched from Fr Mathew Park in Fairview (see Dublin 3): first the cyclist corps, then the signalling corps, and then the various companies, including a small detachment of Fianna Scouts with an ambulance cart. Almost all of the marchers were unaware of their destination or the purpose of the march. As the march proceeded towards its destination, it was joined by several more Volunteer companies, including those from Lusk, Skerries and Donabate. The Lusk corps, numbering about 150, were accompanied by the Very Reverend Thomas Byrne, parish priest of Lusk.

The march progressed through Sutton and Baldoyle before reaching Howth about 1 p.m. A small group distracted onlookers with a drill display, while the *Asgard* entered the harbour and docked alongside a group of Volunteers. There were several descriptions of how the guns were unloaded but all agreed that it was done with great speed. Father Byrne addressed a few words of congratulations as the Volunteers departed. Seán Heuston was in charge of the transport, meaning the Fianna ambulance cart. In spite of all the British efforts, the cart brought its entire cargo back to Dublin.[643]

In a cold wind and rain the Volunteers started their march back. On their way to Dublin they met with two or three detachments of police. Several companies of Volunteers branched off the main road to return to their various homes; the remaining Volunteers continued peacefully until they reached the Howth Road, where several soldiers of the King's Own Scottish Borderers were seen getting off a tram. A company of policemen formed up on the pavement, while the Borderers formed up across the road with fixed bayonets, blocking the progress of the march.

William Vesey Harrel, assistant commissioner of the Dublin Metropolitan Police, approached the head of the column of Volunteers and asked who was in charge. Darrell Figgis came forward and Commissioner Harrel requested that they surrender their arms. This request was refused; Figgis pointed out that, as the Ulster Volunteers had been parading fully armed for three weeks, this march was not breaking any law. Figgis offered to surrender to police if the march was allowed to disperse. Mr Harrel replied, 'I mean to have those guns'. Figgis and Harrel went to a private garden to discuss the situation. Unbeknownst to Harrel, Figgis had given the order that the Volunteers should form a line across the road. While the front line stood firm, those in the rear were instructed to slip away quietly with their rifles. Figgis managed to hold Harrel in conversation long enough for the vast majority of the Volunteers to disappear with their rifles. The military succeeded in capturing only nineteen. (See Bachelor's Walk [Dublin 1]; 90 St Stephen's Green south [Dublin 2]; Fr Mathew Park [Dublin 3]; and Kilcoole, Co. Wicklow.)[644]

Howth: Wentworth Cottage, home of Mary M. Colum, member of the Provisional Committee of Cumann na mBan and its Hon. Secretary. She was a teacher at St Ita's school for girls, the sister school to Pearse's St Enda's school for boys. In *Irish Freedom* she explained the role of Cumann na mBan: 'Cumann na mBan members are not the auxiliaries or handmaidens or camp followers of the Volunteers—we are their allies'.[645]

Dublin 14

Key locations
Rathfarnham
St Enda's (Grange Road)

D ublin 14 is the site of St Enda's School, or *Scoil Éanna*, the secondary school for boys set up by Padraic Pearse. Pearse originally opened his school in 1908 in Cullenswood House on Oakley Road in Ranelagh (see Dublin 6). It was named after St Enda of Aran, who abandoned the heroic life of a warrior to teach a devoted band of scholars in the remote seclusion of the Aran Islands. St Enda's offered an education, through the Irish language, that sought to inspire and nurture its pupils. It particularly stressed the arts and dramatics, and everything was given an Irish approach. In 1910 Pearse moved his innovative and experimental school to its present site on Grange Road in Rathfarnham, and it was situated here until the British army occupied it after the Rising. Formerly known as 'the Hermitage', it was an eighteenth-century house, set in 50 acres of woods and parklands, enhanced by a lake and river near its boundary. It boasts a wide variety of flora and fauna, currently interpreted in a specially dedicated nature study centre. In the centre of the park is the Pearse Museum, housed in Pearse's home and the school.

'IF I DIE IT SHALL BE FROM THE EXCESS OF LOVE I BEAR THE GAEL'

Padraic Pearse

The current exhibitions give visitors a sense of the spirit of the house during Pearse's time. His study and the family sitting-room are preserved, allowing very personal glimpses into the private life of Pearse and his family. Side by side with these rooms are the more public spaces in which Pearse's pupils lived and worked, rooms such as the school dormitory, study hall and chapel.

Pearse was not a practical businessman, but he was never one to let lack of finances get in the way of his plans. He elicited promises from prominent nationalists, as proponents of Irish heritage, that they would give him whatever limited financial support they could, and, when applicable, would enrol their children in his school. The school proved a successful experiment, but was never fully to escape the shadow of looming financial woes. In fact, it would not have survived the crucial first few years without the devoted aid of his good friend and assistant headmaster Thomas MacDonagh and the solid dedication of his brother Willie. Both were executed with Pearse after the Rising. After its first two years the school was doing quite well, all things considered. At this point, when most people would work on more fully establishing the school and perhaps working on an endowment, Pearse instead became more ambitious and moved his school to Rathfarnham.

Pearse fell in love with the Hermitage because, in addition to having a majestic pastoral setting, it had a connection with one of his personal heroes, Robert Emmet. It was here that Emmet had courted his love, Sarah Curran, who lived nearby. Sarah's father, John Philpott Curran, Ireland's foremost legal scholar of the late 1700s and early 1800s, owned 'The Priory', just across the road from St Enda's. He did not look kindly on Sarah's beloved Robert, forcing them to the grounds of the Hermitage for their trysts. It was Sarah whom Emmet returned to Dublin to see, which led to his capture. Curran treated Sarah abominably in regard to the affair, probably because it might have imperilled his promotion to the Bench. Though Curran defended all the other United Irishmen, he rejected Emmet's appeal for assistance. The 'Emmet Walk' can still be found at St Enda's.

The Hermitage, while perfect for Pearse's idyllic image of what he had hoped to achieve, predictably proved to be a financial disaster. The extra distance from Dublin centre made it less practical for the day schoolboys, forcing many of them to drop out, with not enough making the switch to boarders. In addition to this school, Pearse had the added expenses of Cullenswood House, where he established a similar school for girls, St Ita's, when St Enda's moved here. The costs of operating the two schools led Pearse into major financial difficulties. With bankruptcy looming, he was forced to look to the US for further funding. He barely raised enough money on a February 1914 lecture tour to keep the schools solvent, but the tour gave him some useful contacts among the exiled Fenians who would prove to play a large part in Ireland's near political future.

After 1913, when Pearse became so involved with the Volunteers, he left St Enda's with a less devoted master than it had previously. He had opened his school with the promises of many to send their sons there. But his radical politics made some moderate supporters question what their children might be exposed to, and some, notably Eoin MacNeill, the nominal leader of the Volunteers, removed their children from Pearse's influence.

Following the Rising and the execution of the Pearse brothers, their mother reopened St Enda's back at Cullenwood House, but the school returned to the Hermitage in 1919. Pearse's martyrdom and the international fame that the Rising had given him made raising funds easier than before, and the following year Mrs Pearse raised enough to buy the property that Pearse could never afford in his lifetime. The school eventually closed its doors for good in 1935. Mrs Pearse left the property to her daughter, Senator Margaret Pearse, and upon her death the property was turned over to the State. Today the Hermitage stands as the Pearse Museum, dedicated to the memory of the school's founder.

A committee of nationalist and separatist men and women was established to plan the O'Donovan Rossa funeral. It included four men who were executed after the Rising: Thomas MacDonagh, Edward (Ned) Daly, Tom Clarke and John MacBride. It also included two men who were leaders after the Rising: Arthur Griffith and Éamon de Valera.

On 1 August 1915 Jeremiah O'Donovan Rossa was buried in Glasnevin Cemetery. Rossa founded the Phoenix Society in 1856. He was imprisoned in 1865, was released in 1871 and went into exile in America, where he died in July 1915. At his trial, he had been accused of 'inciting the lower classes to believe they might expect a redistribution of property'.

On 26 July 1914 Erskine Childers piloted his boat, *Asgard*, into Howth Harbour. The vessel landed about 900 rifles and 26,000 rounds of ammunition, which were to form the basis of the arms the Volunteers used in the Rising.

The yacht *Asgard* had been sailed from the North Sea to Howth Harbour, loaded with guns for the Volunteers. It was crewed by Erskine Childers, his wife Molly (left), Mary Spring-Rice (right), an English army officer named Gordon Shephard and two Donegal fishermen, Patrick McGinley and Charles Duggan.

About 1,000 Volunteers mustered and marched out to Howth on 26 July 1914 to meet the *Asgard*. When they reached the pier, a small group distracted any onlookers with a drill display, while the *Asgard* entered the harbour and docked alongside a group of Volunteers. There were several descriptions of how the guns were unloaded from the yacht but all agreed that it was done with considerable speed.

In 1908 Padraic Pearse founded his first Irish school, St Enda's, in Cullenswood House on Oakley Road in Ranelagh. When St Enda's moved to a site (The Hermitage) on Grange Road in Rathfarnham in 1910, this site became St Ita's.

In founding St Enda's, Padraic Pearse was intent on providing a child-centred education for its pupils. Pearse believed that language was intrinsic to the identity of a nation. He felt that the Irish school system raised Ireland's youth to be *good* Englishmen or *obedient* Irishmen but *not good Irishmen*, so an alternative was needed.

requested by parents. Elocution, vocal and instrumental music and physical drill are also taught.

Domestic Arrangements.

The College also maintains a private and homelike character. The pupils live rather under the conditions which prevail in a large family than under the somewhat harsh discipline of ordinary boarding schools. An important point is that their domestic welfare is in charge of ladies, a fact which, in conjunction with its private character, renders the College specially suited for the education of sensitive or delicate boys.

The College re-opens on 15th September, 1916.

A competent staff of teachers has been appointed.

TERMS:

Day Pupils—Inclusive Fee for ordinary Course:
Boys under 10, 6 guineas per annum.
,, ,, 13, 8 ,, ,,
,, over 13, 10 ,, ,,

Boarders—Boys under 13, 35 gns. per annum.
,, over 13, 38 ,, ,,

For further particulars apply to **Mrs. Pearse.**

H 26446l

Sзoιl Éαnnα

St. Enda's College

❧

(Day and Boarding School for Boys)
Cullenswood House, Oakley Rd.,
Ranelagh, Dublin.

❧

PROSPECTUS - 1916-17

Padraic Pearse's St Enda's School (*Scoil Éanna*) was seen as a huge educational experiment at the time, with Pearse intent on providing a child-centred education. For Pearse, saving the Irish language from extinction was a cultural priority of the utmost importance, and he felt that the key to saving the language would be a sympathetic education system. To show that this would work, he opened St Enda's.

In 1916 Eoin MacNeill, O/C of the Volunteers, lived at Woodtown Park in Rathfarnham, in the foothills of the Dublin Mountains. (James MacNeill, Eoin's brother, acquired the house in 1915.) It was here, in the early hours of Good Friday, 21 April, that MacNeill was informed that the Rising was planned for Easter Sunday.

Thomas Ashe was O/C of the 5th Battalion. In 1917 he was imprisoned for sedition after making an incendiary speech, and he led a hunger strike in Mountjoy Prison. His lung was pierced during force-feeding and he was taken to the Mater Hospital, where he died on 25 September 1917.

The Fianna na hÉireann were established in Dublin on 16 August 1909. Most members wore kilts with double-breasted dark green tunics, but senior officers wore breeches and leggings. Their headdress was the Baden-Powell Scout hat. They shared a motto with St Enda's: 'Strength in our arms, Truth on our lips, Purity in our hearts'.

Members of Fianna na hÉireann marching to Bodenstown in 1912. (*An Phoblacht*)

Robert Ballagh's iconic poster of the leaders of the Rising. Note James Connolly in the forefront.

Execution at Kilmainham, May 1916—contemporary painting, artist unknown. (National Museum of Ireland)

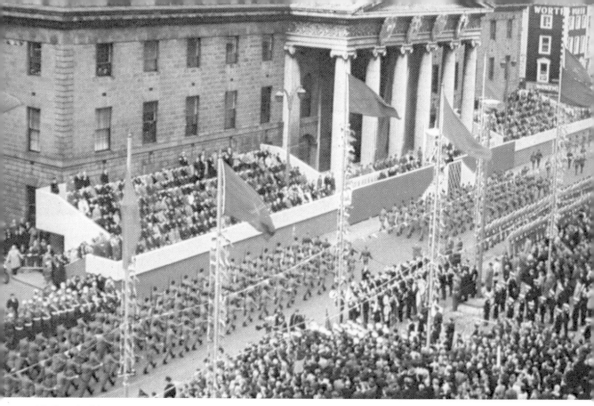

Marking the 50th anniversary of the Rising, the military parade passes the GPO on Easter Sunday, 10 April 1966.
(Cuimhneachán 1916–1966)

Survivors of the Rising met from time to time, and these men are shown at Croke Park wearing medals awarded them for their service.
The man seated on the far right is Jimmy Slattery, who served in Jacob's Biscuit Factory, and who lost his arm in the attack on the Custom House on 25 May 1921.

Anyone travelling close to Rathfarnham should seek out the Pearse Museum, and allow time to walk its grounds.[646]

Grange Road, Rathfarnham: 'The Hermitage'. St Enda's (*Scoil Éanna*) was situated here from 1910 until the British army occupied it after the Rising.[647] (See 21 Oakley Road, Ranelagh: Cullenswood House [Dublin 6].)

The school was known for liberal teaching methods and unyielding nationalism. Its motto was 'Truth on our lips, strength in our hands, and purity in our hearts'. Irish was the school language at St Enda's; only the sciences, in which an Irish vocabulary was lacking, were taught in English. Pearse always insisted on the importance of the Gaelic Revival over all other kinds of 'nationalistic work'.

> When Ireland's language is established, her own distinctive culture is assured . . .
> All phases of a nation's life will most assuredly adjust themselves on national lines
> as best suited to the national character is safeguarded by its strongest bulwark.[648]

Scoil Éanna was seen as a huge educational experiment at the time, with Pearse intent on providing a child-centred education for its pupils. Pearse believed that language was intrinsic to the identity of a nation. He felt that the Irish school system raised Ireland's youth to be *good* Englishmen or *obedient* Irishmen but not *good Irishmen*, so an alternative was needed. For Pearse, saving the Irish language from extinction was a cultural priority of the utmost importance, and he felt that the key would be a sympathetic education system. To show that this would work, he opened St Enda's.

> Our children are the 'raw material'; we desiderate for their education 'modern
> methods' which must be 'efficient' but 'cheap'; we send them to Clongowes to be
> 'Finished'; when 'finished' they are 'turned out'; specialists 'grind' them for the
> English Civil Service and the so-called liberal professions; in each of our great
> colleges there is a department known as the 'scrapheap,' though officially called
> the Fourth Preparatory—the limbo to which the debris ejected by the machine
> is relegated.[649]

Pearse intended to provide his pupils with a pantheon of Irish heroes to inspire the youth of twentieth-century Ireland to patriotic sacrifice.

> If our schools would set themselves that task, the task of fostering once again
> knightly courage and strength and truth—that type of efficiency rather than the
> peculiar type of efficiency demanded by the English Civil Service—we should
> have the beginnings of an educational system. And what an appeal an Irish school
> system might have! What a rallying cry an Irish Minister of Education might give

to young Ireland! When we were starting St Enda's I said to my boys: We must re-create and perpetuate in Ireland the knightly tradition of Cuchulainn, 'better is a short life with honour than a long life with dishonour'; 'I care not if I were to live my life but one day and one night, if only my fame and my deeds live after me'; the noble tradition of the Fianna, 'we, the Fianna, never told a lie, falsehood was never imputed to us'; 'strength in our hands, truth on our lips, and cleanness in our hearts'; the Christ-like tradition of Colmcille, 'if I die it shall be from the excess of love I bear the Gael'. And to that antique evangel should be added the evangels of later days: the stories of Red Hugh and Wolfe Tone and Robert Emmet and John Mitchel and O'Donovan Rossa and Eoghan O'Growney. I have seen Irish boys and girls moved inexpressibly by the story of Emmet or the story of Anne Devlin, and I have always felt it to be legitimate to make use for educational purposes of an exaltation so produced.[650]

Boys attending the school enjoyed a huge range of subjects, from tending the large gardens to Egyptology, and they had their own informal magazine, *An Scoláire* (The Scholar).[651] Among its teachers (full- or part-time) were Frank Burke,[652] Vincent Brien, William Carroll (physical education), Joseph Clarke, Con Colbert, Padraic Colum, Dr Patrick Doody (classics), John Henry, Owen Lloyd (music), Tomás MacDomhnaill (music), Thomas MacDonagh, Joe MacDonagh, Michael MacRuaidhri (gardening classes), Standish O'Grady, Margaret Pearse and Michael Smithwick (Smidic) (mathematics). Guest lecturers included Beatrice Elvery, Alice Stopford Green, Edward Martyn, Dr Douglas Hyde, Eoin MacNeill, Mary Hayden, Sarah Purser and W.B. Yeats. Among its students were Milo MacGarry,[653] James Larkin's sons Jim, Denis and Fintan, three sons and a nephew of Eoin MacNeill, two sons of Peter McGinley, a son of William Bulfin, and various relatives of Seán O'Casey, Padraic Colum and Agnes O'Farrelly.

Enrolment increased from 30 in 1908 to 130 in 1909–10, but shrank after that to 70 in 1910–11. After 1912 the numbers never reached 60, and in the final year before the Rising there were only 28 boys over fourteen who stayed for two terms.

Mrs Pearse willed a life estate to her daughter, Senator Margaret Pearse,[654] and it passed to the Irish state upon Margaret's death in 1969.[655] The Hermitage is now the Pearse Museum and its grounds form St Enda's Park, both under the Office of Public Works.[656]

Green Lane: Home of Patsy O'Toole. The arms dump for E Company, 4th Battalion (Rathfarnham Battalion).

Rathfarnham: Woodtown Park. Eoin MacNeill's home at the time of the Rising. (James MacNeill, Eoin's brother, acquired the house in 1915.) In the foothills of the

Dublin Mountains, it was here that in the early hours of Good Friday, 21 April, MacNeill was informed that the Rising was planned for Easter Sunday.[657] (See 53 Rathgar Road [Dublin 6].)

Some people reported that when the Rising went ahead despite his notice calling it off, MacNeill wanted to fight, and on Monday said: 'I will go home for my Volunteer uniform, and go out and fight! My friends and comrades are fighting and dying, and I must join them.' Others were not so complimentary: 'MacNeill could not make up his mind whether to fight in his uniform or in civilian clothes, and he racked himself so much with metaphysical speculations on these points that the Rising was over before he made up his mind'.[658] One of Tom Clarke's last comments to Kathleen was that MacNeill's role in the cancellation should never be forgotten or forgiven.[659]

St Mary's Terrace, Rathfarnham: Home of Capt. James (Séamus) and Rose Murphy, both of whom fought in the 1st Battalion during the Rising.[660]

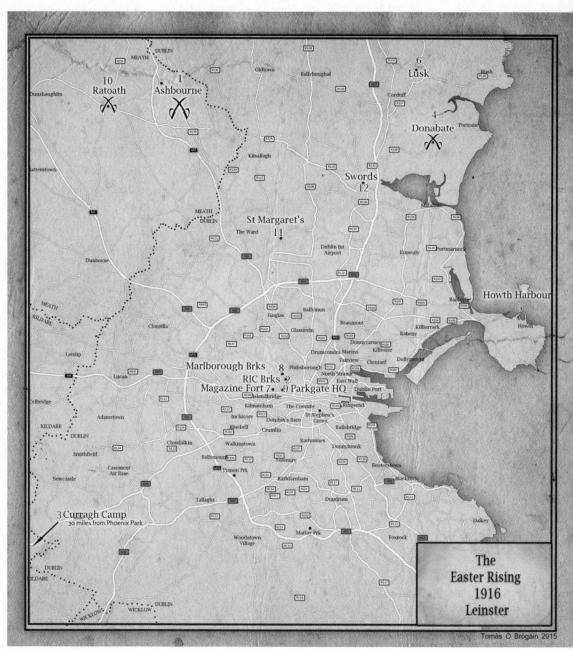

The
Easter Rising
1916
Leinster

Tomás Ó Brógáin 2015

1   Ashbourne, Co. Meath, Volunteer 5th Battalion
    mustered here and ran attacks on the area from here
2   RIC Barracks
3   Curragh British Army Camp, Co. Kildare
4   Donabate, Co. Dublin, 5th Battalion Volunteers
    attacked an RIC barracks here
5   Howth Harbour, Co. Dublin, Volunteers landed arms
    here on 26 July 1914
6   Lusk, Co. Dublin, a company of the 5th Battalion
    Volunteers was based here

7   Magazine Fort, Phoenix Park
8   Marlborough Barracks, Phoenix Park
9   Parkgate Barracks, Phoenix Park, British Military HQ
10 Ratoath (Rath's Cross), Co. Meath, 5th Battalion
    Volunteers attacked an RIC barracks here
11 St Margaret's, Co. Dublin, a company of the 5th
    Battalion Volunteers was based here
12 Swords, Co. Dublin, a company of the 5th Battalion
    Volunteers was based here

Ashbourne—Fingal Brigade
North County Dublin–County Meath

Key locations
Ashbourne
Rath Crossroads

T he 5th Battalion, under the command of Cmdt Thomas Ashe, carried out a series of raids and reconnaissance movements throughout north County Dublin from Easter Monday to Friday.[661] (After the Rising the unit became known as the 'Fingal Brigade', but it was not known as such at the time.) Volunteers came from companies in Lusk, Skerries and St Margaret's. The Swords and Lusk contingents were the largest, with about 30 men on their rolls who reported. James V. Lawless commanded the St Margaret's men, Dick Coleman commanded Swords, Edward Rooney commanded Lusk, and Joe Thornton and Jim McGuinness commanded Skerries.

'[Richard Mulcahy's] plan of attack was to make full use of the morale factor by driving home a vigorous assault with all possible force'
Col. J. V. Lawless

Ashe was a fine physical specimen of manhood—courageous and high-principled, something of a poet, painter and dreamer—and had been appointed O/C only a few weeks before the Rising. In military matters he was, however, somewhat impractical. Early in the week the north Dublin men were joined by a few stragglers from the city, amongst whom was Richard (Dick) Mulcahy. The other members of the staff knew Mulcahy already, and it was soon apparent that he had the mind necessary to plan and direct operations. Cool, clear-headed and practical, and with a personality and tact that enabled him to take virtual control of the situation without in any way undermining Ashe's prestige as commander, it was Mulcahy who was the commander of the Ashbourne Volunteers to all intents and purposes.

Like most Volunteer units, it was never near battalion strength; in fact, the area at that period was able to muster only one infantry company. Almost the entire roster mustered on Easter Sunday because the men were ready to mobilise then. They paraded at Saucerstown, each man bringing two days' rations, and then were allowed to go home that night. Frank Lawless and Richard Hayes travelled to Dublin and were told by Connolly that 'All was off for the moment, but hold in readiness to act at any time'. Owing to the confusion of the cancellation orders on Easter Sunday, however, little more than half the men who mobilised on Sunday answered the mobilisation call on the following day. On Monday the order came from Pearse—'Strike at one o'clock today'[662]—and the men mobilised again at Knockshedan Bridge, at the back of Swords Village near what is now Dublin Airport. Here the men of Swords joined up with the men of Lusk. Capt. Coleman paraded the 65 men for inspection and found one shouldering his cocked rifle. To demonstrate the danger of this, Coleman pressed the trigger and the rifle went off. The men later commented that it was 'the first shot' fired by the battalion in the Rising.

Most of the men who reported on Easter Monday did so on bicycles. The raids on RIC barracks and communications in the area were undertaken with the purposes of collecting arms, hampering enemy movements and drawing some enemy attention away from the Volunteers fighting in Dublin.

On Monday afternoon they moved off, under the command of Ashe, towards Finglas. The convoy consisted of one automobile (driven by Dr Dick Hayes), one motor-bike and one horse and cart. The battalion took up a position for the night at a farm where the Premier Dairies were later located. That night, on James Connolly's instructions, Coleman was sent with twenty men towards Blanchardstown to create a disturbance—to try and distract some of the military forces from Dublin.[663]

At 10 a.m. on Tuesday, Ashe received instructions from Connolly to send 40 men into Dublin, but Ashe decided to send only half that number. Having selected the men, he sent them into the city under the command of Capt. Coleman. Coleman, one of the few wearing uniform, entered the GPO with his men and reported to Connolly. They were given a meal and Fr Sheehan asked whether the men had been to Confession. He was assured that Fr Toher of Lusk had heard the men's confessions. The detachment of twenty men stopped only shortly at the GPO, and then some were redeployed by James Connolly to other city garrisons, many to the Mendicity Institute. The remainder of the Volunteers left in the north Dublin area were ordered by Connolly to engage in activities that would divert enemy attention and troops, if possible, from the city.[664]

On Wednesday Connolly sent about six Volunteers under the command of Paddy Houlihan to reinforce the battalion, and the column descended on Garristown, taking all its supplies and ammunition.[665] The Volunteers took over the village and forced the police to surrender. They remained there until Thursday morning, when they advanced about three miles to Newbarn. On Friday Ashe learned that the British were going to send troops from Athlone to Dublin, so he decided to cut the railway line at Batterstown about twelve miles from Newbarn; this would also give his men the opportunity to attack any British attempting to repair the lines. As they were about to depart, they remembered that they had not neutralised the RIC barracks at Ashbourne and determined to capture it, the RIC men there and all of their weapons before they cut the railway lines.

The attack on the RIC barracks at Ashbourne, Co. Meath, just over the county boundary, was the battalion's first really serious engagement.[666] The barracks was usually manned by a sergeant and four constables but, given the level of fighting in Dublin, reinforcements had been called in from surrounding barracks, and so on the day of the attack there were about 35 RIC men stationed there.[667]

Houlihan was to lead a section to dismount at a crossroads known locally as 'Rath Cross'. His Volunteers opened fire on the RIC men, who had taken cover behind a barricade in front of the barracks and soon retreated into the barracks itself. The Volunteers advanced on the barracks, disarming two RIC men who were setting up another barricade. With these two men disarmed and captured, Ashe called on the remaining officers to surrender, and immediately a siege situation turned into a shoot-out. There was little sign of capitulation among the RIC men in the barracks until the use of a home-made grenade resulted in their offering to surrender by waving a white handkerchief out of a window. But then one of the captive RIC men, Sergeant Brady, recognised one of the Volunteers holding him captive, Gerry Golden, and cried out: 'Golden, I'll get you before I die'. Golden and Brady ended up rolling on the ground before other Volunteers pulled them apart, but the other RIC captive escaped during the fight.[668] Those inside the barracks then decided that they wouldn't surrender after all, and Brady was taken at gunpoint to convince them to give up. When Brady reached the barracks, however, he leapt through a gap in the barricade and fled into the building.

Ashe then led his men further up the road to a better position and again called on the RIC to surrender, but he was met by rifle fire, and the shooting between the Volunteers and RIC became continuous. More grenades were thrown against the walls and finally broke the RIC's resistance, and they shouted 'We surrender' for a second time.

However, just as Ashe and Mulcahy were advancing into the yard to take their surrender and before the RIC men could emerge, the hoot of a car horn was heard to the north-west.[669] County Inspector Alexander Grey had received word of the siege, and he and District Inspector Henry Smyth assembled about 55 men at Slane in seventeen motorcars and rushed to Ashbourne to put down the uprising. Their arrival was completely unexpected because the scouts Ashe had placed on the road became so engrossed in the battle at the barracks, as if it were a football match, that they completely forgot to watch the road.

The Volunteers spread out and rushed along the Slane road to stop the convoy reaching Rath Cross. Ashe was going to order a withdrawal, but Mulcahy, realising that the RIC reinforcements were just as surprised as the Volunteers, ordered the Volunteers to attack.

> His plan of attack was to make full use of the morale factor by driving home a vigorous assault with all possible force from the vicinity of the crossroads and giving the enemy an impression of superior force on our side by fire from the rear.[670]

The RIC reinforcements took heavy fire from the Volunteers from all sides. The firefight lasted for many hours before Volunteer reinforcements arrived from Baldwinstown. The RIC eventually surrendered to the Volunteers but suffered nine fatalities and up to twenty other casualties.[671] Those killed were:

> County Inspector Alexander Gray
> District Inspector Henry Smyth
> Sgt John Shanagher
> Sgt John Young
> Const. James Clery
> Const. James Gormley
> Const. James Hickey
> Const. Richard McHale
> Albert George Keep (a chauffeur recruited to drive the police, who was shot and died later)

When all ammunition and equipment had been secured, and the wounded treated, Ashe ordered his men to carry the wounded to the cars and return to camp.[672]

While many consider the attacks as precursors of the 'flying column' tactics of the War of Independence, the victory at Ashbourne can really be attributed to Mulcahy's leadership. It was he who recognised that the British were as disoriented as the Volunteers, and reckoned that his forces were about equal in size to the RIC. He determined to take the battle to the British and rallied the Volunteers. Given that the uprising in Dublin had been put down, however, the Fingal Volunteers eventually gave themselves up two days later.[673]

Cmdt Thomas Ashe was sentenced to death for his part in the attack, but this was later commuted to penal servitude for life.

County Wicklow

Key location
Kilcoole

A rms were landed at Kilcoole for the Volunteers on 1 August 1914. These were part of the shipment that had been purchased in Munich, the majority of which were landed at Howth, Co. Dublin.[674] Sir Thomas Myles, a lifelong nationalist, took part in this gunrunning. He picked up 600 single-shot Mauser 71s, along with 20,000 rounds of ammunition, from Conor O'Brien's *Kelpie*, which had delivered them from Germany to the Welsh coast.[675] Myles, a Protestant, sailed them in his vessel, the *Chotah*, to Kilcoole. He was a temporary lieutenant-colonel in the Royal Army Medical Corps and honorary surgeon in Ireland to the king—two positions from which he would doubtless have been dismissed had the British known that he had just lent his yacht for the purpose of gunrunning. It was borrowed at the request of yet another Protestant conspirator, James Creed Meredith, who later became a member of the Supreme Court of the Irish Free State that he helped to create.

'...THE KEY FIGURES INVOLVED WERE MEMBERS OF THE CHURCH OF IRELAND. BUT WHY IS THE KILCOOLE GUNRUNNING LARGELY FORGOTTEN...?'
Revd Patrick Comerford

The *Chotah* met the *Kelpie* off the Llyn Peninsula of north central Wales. The *Kelpie*'s cargo was offloaded onto the larger yacht, allowing the *Kelpie* to sail on across the Irish Sea, providing a decoy for the *Asgard* and the *Chotah* against the prying eyes of the Coastguard. A week after the guns were landed at Howth, the *Chotah* approached the coast of Kilcoole and was met in the darkness south of the Kish lighthouse by the *Nugget*, a Howth-based trawler. The *Nugget* towed the yacht close to the Kilcoole shore, near today's train station, and a flotilla of smaller vessels went out to collect the guns. From the beach, the arms were loaded by Volunteers and their supporters onto vehicles and bicycles—and also, according to local folklore, into babies' prams—and taken away hurriedly.[676]

Dermot Coffey and Capt. Harvey de Montgomery of the British Army completed the crew.[677] (See Howth [Dublin 13].)

Notes

1   *Irish Times*, 25 April 1916.
2   *Irish Times*, 1 May 1916.
3   *Irish Times*, 8 May 1916.
4   Fitzgibbon, Seán: Witness Statement 130.
5   Ó Rahilly 1915a, 3.
6   O'Connor, Séamus: BMH Contemporary Documents 64, 107.
7   Ó Lochlainn, Colm: Witness Statement 751.
8   Hobson 1918, 17–18.
9   Martin, Éamon: Witness Statements 591, 592, 593.
10 Moore, Col. Maurice, 'The Rise of the Irish Volunteers', a serial in the *Irish Press*, 4 January–2 March 1938. (Apparently written in 1917; see National Library of Ireland ILB 94109.)
11 Ó Snodaigh 1998.
12 Bateson 2010, 200.
13 Carrigan, James: Witness Statement 613.
14 *Irish Independent*, 8 May 1916.
15 *Irish Independent*, 20 May 1916.
16 Larkin 2006.
17 *Sunday Independent*, 23 April 1916.
18 Colivet, Michael: BMH Contemporaneoous Document 145.
19 Martin 1963, 38.
20 Figgis 1924, 49–58.
21 *Report of the Royal Commission on the circumstances in connection with the landing of arms at Howth on 26th July 1914*, Parliamentary Papers, 1914–1916, xxiv, p. 805.
22 *Ibid.*, pp 824–89; Townshend 2005, 57.
23 *Report of the Royal Commission on the circumstances in connection with the landing of arms at Howth on 26th July 1914*, Parliamentary Papers, 1914–1916, xxiv, p. 805.
24 Yeates 2014.
25 Good, Joe: Witness Statement 388.
26 Bracken, Peadar: Witness Statements 12, 361.
27 N. O'Brien 1932; Bateson 2010, 180.
28 Martin 1967, 2–3.
29 O'Kelly, Seán T.: Witness Statements 611, 1765.
30 *Weekly Irish Times*, 29 April 1916.
31 Fox 1944 [2014 edn], 61ff.
32 J. White 1930 [2005], 157ff.
33 Doyle 2007.
34 *Evening Telegraph*, 5 May 1914.
35 O'Casey 1919 [1980], chapter VII.
36 Carpenter, Walter: Witness Statement 583.
37 McGowan, Séamus: Witness Statement 542.
38 Robbins, Frank: Witness Statement 585.
39 O'Casey 1919 [1980], chapter IX.
40 Robbins 1977, 201; MacDonnacha 2002.
41 *Workers' Republic*, 22 April 1916.
42 *Ibid.*
43 Letter from Clare Cowley, Molly O'Reilly's granddaughter.
44 *Unfurling the flag*, The Irish Republican Digest, Book 1 (pamphlet; Cork, 1956), 31–2.
45 *Workers' Republic*, 22 April 1916.
46 Bateson 2010, 25.
47 Robbins, Frank: Witness Statement 585.
48 Frank Robbins in *Irishman*, 19 May 1928, recorded his memory of Connolly's last speech at Liberty Hall, indicating that the 'Citizen Army would stand to arms until the Irish claim was heard'.
49 Brady, Christopher: Witness Statement 705.
50 Molloy, Michael: Witness Statement 716; Molloy 1966.

[51] O'Brien, Liam: Witness Statement 323.

[52] J. O'Connor 1986, 27ff.

[53] Brady, Christopher: Witness Statement 705.

[54] Hackett, Rose: Witness Statement 546. Taillon 1996, 6.

[55] Molony, Helena: Witness Statement 391. Donnelly, Charles: Witness Statement 824. 'While presenting printed copies of the Proclamation of 1916 to three members of the Dublin Typographical Society who set up the Proclamation of 1916 in Liberty Hall, Mr [Oscar] Traynor, Minister for Defence, stated he was aware that 2500 copies were printed and that probably they were intended for distribution throughout the country. He was in the GPO for the best part of the week and did not see the Proclamation. He did not see a copy afterwards except the one the President of Ireland had framed at present, and the time had come when someone more closely connected with this aspect of the Rising would have to fill the void. On Easter Monday evening 1916, while on a window barricade at the GPO, Commandant-General P.H. Pearse instructed me to hand bundles of the Proclamation to the newsboy for distribution through the city. I called a newsboy of about eighteen years of age whom I asked to have the Proclamation distributed. He took a large bundle of same and, in less than an hour, he came back holding his cap by the peak and the back, full of silver coins, mostly 2/- and 2/6d pieces. I refused the money, telling him he was told to give them out free. He said he thought we wanted the money to buy food for the garrison. I asked him who he had at home and he informed me he had a widowed mother and small brothers and sisters, so I told him to go and give the money, which he had got for the Proclamation, to his mother. (This I believe he did.) He came back again and collected the balance of the Proclamations, stating he would give them out without charge (which I believe he did).'

[56] Molony, Helena: Witness Statement 391.

[57] Oman, William: Witness Statement 421.

[58] McGowan, Séamus: Witness Statement 542.

[59] G.A. Hayes-McCoy, 'A military history of the Rising', in Nowlan 1969, 325; Joye 2010; Ireland 1966, 38–45. The *Muirchu* was built in Liffey Dockyard in 1908 as a fishery protection cruiser and was named *Helga II*. She was then under the control of the Department of Agriculture and Technical Instruction (Ireland) until she was taken over by the Admiralty in March 1915, when she was officially renamed as HMY *Helga*, an armed steam yacht. At this time the 'II' was dropped from her name and she served as an anti-submarine patrol vessel as well as undertaking escort duty in the Irish Sea. In April 1918 she was credited with the sinking of a submarine off the Isle of Man, and for the remainder of her career she carried a star on her funnel as an award for this achievement. In October of the same year the RMS *Leinster* was torpedoed off the Kish Bank and 600 passengers were lost. The *Helga* was fuelling in Dún Laoghaire at the time and managed to rescue 90 of the passengers. She was later used to transport Black and Tans around the coast when many of the roads in Ireland were rendered impassable by Irish forces in the War of Independence. Eventually the *Helga* was handed over to the Irish Free State in August 1923 and was renamed *Muirchu*. She thus became one of the first ships in the newly established Irish navy.

[60] Duffy 2013.

[61] Burke 2005.

[62] 'Seán Lemass killed baby brother in tragic accident', *Irish Mail on Sunday*, 21 July 2013.

[63] Duffy 2013.

[64] *Ibid.*

[65] See Irish Census of 1911 (http://www.census.nationalarchives.ie/reels/nai000119513/).

[66] De Burca 1958.

[67] Vincent Hearn, 'Origin of the Irish national anthem' (http://www.from-ireland.net/history/origin.htm).

[68] Brennan-Whitmore 1926.

[69] Kennerk 2013.

[70] Byrne, Seán: Witness Statement 579.

[71] Skinnider 1917, 50–1, 76–8.

[72] Perolz, Marie: Witness Statement 246.

[73] O'Doherty, Kitty: Witness Statement 355.

[74] Dolan, Edward: Witness Statement 1078.

[75] Ó Duigneain 1991.

[76] McGarry, Seán: Witness Statement 368.

[77] Bateson 2010, 173.

78 Duffy 2013.
79 Hobson 1918, 27–8.
80 Hobson 1931.
81 *Freeman's Journal*, 26 November 1913.
82 Ceannt, Áine B.E.: Witness Statement 264.
83 Macardle 1937 [1965], 96.
84 O'Higgins 1925, 40.
85 O'Farrell 1997, 21
86 Conlon, Mrs Martin: Witness Statement 419.
87 O'Mahony 1987 [1995], 64.
88 O'Farrell 1930 (26 April); McHugh 1966, 206ff.
89 Miss O'Farrell's account of her role in the surrender negotiations with the British is most
    completely given in *An t-Éireannach*, 12–29 Feabhra 1936, in two chapters of 'Cu Uladh's'
    Blaidhain na h-Aiserighe, a complete history of the Rising in Irish based on the original statements
    of the participants and translations of documents, and covering all the Volunteer positions
    throughout Dublin.
90 Ó Duigneain 1991.
91 'Patriot Priest', *An Phoblacht*, 1 May 1997.
92 See Irish Census of 1911 (http://www.census.nationalarchives.ie/reels/nai000119513/); Duffy
    2013.
93 Reilly 2005, 12ff.
94 Walker, Charles: Witness Statements 241, 266.
95 Source for occupants: Land Valuation Office, Dublin; Registry of Deeds, Dublin; and *Thom's
    Directories* (1900–20).
96 O'Higgins 1925, 37.
97 Duffy 2013.
98 Good, Joe: Witness Statement 388.
99 Henderson, Frank: Witness Statement 821.
100 Wyse-Power, Charles: Witness Statement 420.
101 Clarke 1997, 69.
102 Molloy, Michael: Witness Statement 716; Molloy 1966.
103 Dempsey 1993.
104 O'Neill 1991.
105 Ceannt, Áine B.E.: Witness Statement 264.
106 Wyse-Power, Nancy: Witness Statement 541.
107 Duffy 2013.
108 Reilly 2005.
109 Duffy 2013.
110 See Irish Census of 1911 (http://www.census.nationalarchives.ie/reels/nai000119513/).
111 Duffy 2013.
112 Source for occupants: Land Valuation Office, Dublin; Registry of Deeds, Dublin; and *Thom's
    Directories* (1900–20). See also Kennerk 2012.
113 Steinmeyer 1926.
114 Kennerk 2013.
115 See http://www.ireland.com/focus/easterrising/saturday/.
116 Elizabeth O'Farrell always wrote of this as the building in which the leaders met after breakfast
    on 29 April, and that 'after breakfast, Mr Connolly and the other wounded men were carried
    through the holes and all the others followed. Mr Connolly was put to bed in a back room in
    16 Moore Street. The members of the Provisional Government were in this room for a
    considerable length of time' (McHugh 1966, 207ff).
117 Kennerk 2013.
118 Doherty 1995.
119 Ryan 1949 [1957], 253.
120 O'Higgins 1925, 84.
121 McLoughlin, Seán: Witness Statement 290; McLoughlin 1948.
122 Bateson 2010, 221.
123 McGuire 2006.
124 Ó Dubghaill 1966, 266. Miss O'Farrell's account of the scene in 16 Moore Street and her role in
    the surrender negotiations with the British is most completely given in *An t-Éireannach*, 12–29

Feabhra 1936, in two chapters of 'Cu Uladh's' *Blaidhain na h-Aiserighe*, a complete history of the Rising in Irish based on the original statements of the participants and translations of documents, and covering all the Volunteer positions throughout Dublin. O'Farrell 1917.

125 Bateson 2010, 185.

126 MacThomais 2005; Woggan 2000a; 2000b.

127 Kennerk 2013.

128 See http://www.taoiseach.gov.ie/index.asp?locID=200anddocID=3087. 'Documents from this period now firmly establish that No. 16 Moore Street and the adjacent buildings at Nos 14, 15 and 17 are indeed the buildings occupied by the leaders retreating from the GPO at the end of Easter Week. The historical significance of this building is mostly [*sic*] vividly captured in the moving written account of the surrender given by Nurse Elizabeth O'Farrell, who was in 16 Moore Street with Padraic Pearse, the wounded James Connolly, Thomas Clarke, Joseph Plunkett and Seán Mac Dermott. Nurse O'Farrell's contemporaneous account included her witnessing Pearse comforting a wounded British prisoner in the house, before she took the white flag to the Crown forces at the top of Moore Street. She was the person who brought out the surrender communication ending the Rising to General Lowe, who was in operational control of the British forces. From a historical, social and political standpoint 16 Moore Street is of significant national importance. Last year, Dublin City Council [declared] that 16 Moore Street, the 1916 leaders' "last stand" headquarters, should be preserved and added to the Record of Protected Structures. It gives me great pleasure to announce today . . . to declare 16 Moore Street as a National Monument' (Taoiseach Bertie Ahern at the Annual Liam Mellows Commemoration, Castletown, Co. Wexford, 10 December 2006).

129 McHugh 1966, 206–19.

130 Kennerk 2013.

131 Burke 2005.

132 McGarry, Seán: Witness Statement 368.

133 Fitzgerald, Maurice: Witness Statement 326. Fitzgerald was the principal of the Wireless College.

134 Daly, Denis: Witness Statement 110.

135 Ó Lochlainn, Colm: Witness Statement 751.

136 Bateson 2010, 20.

137 *Ibid.*, 21.

138 *Ibid.*, 19.

139 Quilty, John J.: Witness Statement 516. (He was the owner of the car that drove off the pier.)

140 Craven, Thomas: BMH Contemporary Documents 141, 197.

141 Henderson, Frank: Witness Statement 821.

142 See Warwick-Haller and Warwick-Haller 1995.

143 Ni Chumnaill 1933; Conlon 1969.

144 Ceannt, Áine B.E.: Witness Statement 264.

145 Gavan-Duffy, Louise: Witness Statement 216.

146 O'Kelly, Seán T.: Witness Statements 611, 1765.

147 Ó Ceallaigh 1963.

148 Ó'Brien, William: Witness Statement 1766.

149 Lynch 1957, 30, and footnotes on pp 131–2.

150 *Ibid.*, 150–1.

151 O'Hegarty 1924 [1998], 3.

152 Ryan 1949 [1957], 9; Ryan, Desmond: Witness Statement 725.

153 McCullough, Denis: Witness Statements 914, 915; Coogan 1966, 10.

154 Bergin 1910.

155 Scollan, John J.: Witness Statements 318, 341. Kelly, Edward: Witness Statement 1094.

156 Traynor, Oscar: Witness Statement 340.

157 Ó Rahilly 1991.

158 Bateson 2010, 209.

159 Mitchell made the following statement: 'While driving through Moore St. to Jervis St. Hospital one afternoon towards the end of the week the sergeant drew my attention to the body of a man lying in the gutter in Moore Lane. He was dressed in a green uniform. I took the sergeant and two men with a stretcher and approached the body which appeared to be still alive. We were about to lift it up when a young English officer stepped out of a doorway and refused to allow us to touch it. I told him of my instructions from H.Q. but all to no avail. When back in the lorry I asked the sergeant what was the idea? His answer was—"he must be someone of importance

and the bastards are leaving him there to die of his wounds. It's the easiest way to get rid of him." We came back again about 9 o'clock that night. The body was still there and an officer guarding it, but this time I fancied I knew the officer—he was not the one I met before. I asked why I was not allowed to take the body and who was it? He replied that his life and job depended on it being left there. He would not say who it was. I never saw the body again but I was told by different people that it was The Ó Rahilly.' Mitchell began his recollections by reminding the questioner that it was more than 30 years after the event. Mitchell, Albert: Witness Statement 196.

160 McLoughlin 1948.
161 Ryan 1949 [1957], 253–4.
162 *Irish Times*, 30 April 1916.
163 O'Donoghue, Florence: Witness Statement 554.
164 *Irish Times*, 6 May 1916.
165 Matthews 2010a, 33.
166 Hally 1966–7, Part 1, 325.
167 Reilly 2005, 44ff.
168 *Ibid.*, 44–5.
169 Original's whereabouts are unknown. Printed by the *Irish War News* from O'Keefe's Printers on Halston Street by Joe Stanley at Pearse's direction. Later printed in the *Sinn Féin Rebellion Handbook* published by the *Irish Times* (1916), p. 47. A copy is in the Irish Volunteer papers, University College Dublin.
170 Steinmeyer 1926.
171 O'Higgins 1925, 36.
172 Robinson, Séamas: Witness Statements 156, 1721, 1722.
173 O'Kelly, Fergus: Witness Statement 351.
174 Eyewitness account of J.J. O'Leary in the *Dublin Saturday Post*, in an edition issued after the Rising (combining 29 April, 6 May and 13 May 1916).
175 O'Kelly, Fergus: Witness Statement 351.
176 O'Connor, John J. (Blimey): BMH Contemporaneous Document 152.
177 Saurin 1926.
178 Traynor, Oscar: Witness Statement 340.
179 Dillon, Geraldine Plunkett: Witness Statement 29.
180 Brennan-Whitmore 1996, 20ff.
181 *Ibid.*, 116ff.
182 Regarding the snipers in TCD, see 'Inside Trinity College', *Blackwood's Magazine*, July 1916.
183 Traynor, Oscar: Witness Statement 340; Saurin 1926.
184 Bateson 2010, 87.
185 Duffy 2013.
186 *Ibid.*
187 Bateson 2010, 30; see Irish Census of 1911 (http://www.census.nationalarchives.ie/reels/nai000119513/); Duffy 2013.
188 See Irish Census of 1911 (http://www.census.nationalarchives.ie/reels/nai000119513/); Duffy 2013.
189 Robbins 1977.
190 Bateson 2010, 144.
191 *Ibid.*, 146.
192 Bermingham, DMP Constable Patrick J.: Witness Statement 697.
193 Ó Maitiu 2001.
194 Ó Riain, Padraic: Witness Statement 98.
195 Lawlor 2009.
196 Bateson 2010, 45.
197 *Ibid.*, 266.
198 *Ibid.*, 50.
199 *Ibid.*, 73.
200 *Ibid.*, 15.
201 *Ibid.*, 110.
202 *Ibid.*, 99.
203 *Ibid.*, 199.
204 *Ibid.*, 195.
205 *Ibid.*, 80.

206 Gallagher 1953, 230.
207 Bateson 2010, 157.
208 Ryan 1949 [1957], 168.
209 Duffy 2013.
210 See Irish Census of 1911 (http://www.census.nationalarchives.ie/reels/nai000119513/).
211 Simon Donnelly, 'Thou shalt not pass—Ireland's challenge to the British forces at Mount Street Bridge, Easter 1916', IMA CD 62/3/7 (pamphlet).
212 Christian, William: Witness Statement 646.
213 Bateson 2010, 127.
214 *Ibid.*, 126.
215 Doyle, Séamus (James): Witness Statement 166.
216 T. Walsh 1966; Walsh, James and Thomas (joint): Witness Statement 198.
217 Simon Donnelly, 'Thou shalt not pass—Ireland's challenge to the British forces at Mount Street Bridge, Easter 1916', IMA CD 62/3/7 (pamphlet).
218 Oates 1920, 39.
219 T. Walsh 1966.
220 Ó hUid 1966.
221 Ceannt, Áine B.E.: Witness Statement 264.
222 See A.A. Luce papers, TCD MS 4874.
223 Elsie Mahaffy, daughter of the provost of Trinity College, left her memoirs and a diary of the events: TCD MS 2074. (See Richmond Barracks/Grangegorman Road Upper [Dublin 7].)
224 Andrews 1979, 83
225 Kennerk 2013.
226 *Ibid.*
227 Ó Snodaigh 1999.
228 Hally 1966–7, Part 2, 54–5.
229 Fox 1944 [2014], 172–4.
230 King, Martin: Witness Statement 543.
231 *Irish Volunteer*, 22 May 1915.
232 Martin 1961, 248.
233 *Irish Volunteer*, 22 April 1916.
234 *Irish Times Supplement*, 7–9 April 1966; *Sunday Press*, 10 April 1966; Foy and Barton 1999, 54–5; Townshend 2005, 110, 162–4.
235 'There was never any question of taking the Castle. The forces were too small for the Castle to be taken and held. It was hoped, however, that by holding the Guardroom and commanding the entrance from adjacent posts, the effectiveness of the Castle as an attacking base would be destroyed. Here, again, the plan was crippled by the small number taking part. But the success achieved by the audacious attack created panic on the other side.' Fox 1944 [2014], 149; Ryan 1949 [1957], 116–18.
236 *Irish War News*, 25 April 1916; *Irish Times, Sinn Féin Rebellion Handbook* (1916), 42.
237 Fox 1944 [2014], 146.
238 Béaslaí 1926, 97; Peadar Kearney, quoted in De Burca 1958, 116.
239 LeRoux 1932, 384; Macardle 1937 [1965], 169ff.
240 O'Connor, Joseph: Witness Statement 157.
241 Donnelly, Simon: Witness Statements 113, 433, 481.
242 Thornly 1966.
243 Duffy 2013.
244 Ceannt, Áine B.E.: Witness Statement 264.
245 Clarke 1997, 113ff.
246 Golden, Gerry: Witness Statement 522.
247 Novak 2008.
248 Wyse-Power, Dr Nancy: Witness Statement 587.
249 British PRO/CO904/100, Inspector General's Report (August 1916).
250 McCarthy 2007, 75–8.
251 Ceannt, Áine B.E.: Witness Statement 264.
252 O'Reilly, Eily O'Hanrahan: Witness Statements 270, 415.
253 Daly, Madge: Witness Statements 209, 855.
254 See Gallagher 1953.
255 Ó Briain, Liam: Witness Statements 3, 6, 7, 565, 784.

256 Little 1942, 454ff; O'Kelly, Séamus: Witness Statement 471.

257 Kelly 1942.

258 Duffy 2013.

259 Elsie Mahaffy, the daughter of J.P. Mahaffy, left her memoirs and a diary of the events: TCD MS 2074. (See Richmond Barracks/Grangegorman Road Upper [Dublin 7].)

260 O'Connor 1966; Joseph O'Connor, NLI MS 13735.

261 Byrne, Seán: Witness Statement 422.

262 Lyons 1926.

263 Ó Ruairc 2011, 73: 'De Valera's leadership of the Boland's Mills garrison during the Rising had been less than spectacular'.

264 Later the *Helga* was one of the boats that went to the assistance of the RMS *Leinster*, the Dublin–Holyhead mailboat that was torpedoed by a German submarine on 10 October 1918 with the loss of 501 lives. Following the Irish take-over of power after the Treaty, the *Helga* served in the Irish Fisheries Protection Service as the LE *Muirchu*.

265 Longford and O'Neill 1966.

266 Coogan 2001, 118.

267 Coogan 1990, 42.

268 Lyons 1926.

269 But see Pinkman 1998, 201: 'Suffering from battle hysteria, Cmdt de Valera had to be forcibly restrained by some of his men of the Boland's Mill garrison before the end of the Easter Week's fighting and removed to Sir Patrick Dun's Hospital. It was in a room of the hospital that de Valera made his formal surrender to Captain Hitzen of the 5th Lincolnshire Regiment at about 1 pm on Sunday, 30 April 1916.'

270 J. Pearse 1886; this was written in response to a pamphlet by Dr Thomas Maguire, professor of Moral Philosophy at Trinity College Dublin, which was an extreme piece of anti-Home Rule polemic.

271 Bateson 2010, 177.

272 *Ibid.*, 189.

273 Edwards 1977, 24

274 MacThomais 1965, 30.

275 Lyons 1926; Bateson 2010, 136.

276 Kavanagh, Séamus: Witness Statement 208.

277 Bateson 2010, 107; Duffy 2013.

278 Seán Ó Luing, 'Arthur Griffith and Sinn Féin', in Martin 1967, 2–3; Ó Luing 1953, 247–67.

279 Skinnider 1917, 9ff.

280 *Irish Times*, 25 April 1916.

281 Robbins, Frank: Witness Statement 585.

282 See Mitchell 1990.

283 'Gallantry of Red Cross Workers, St John Ambulance Brigade', *Irish Times 1916 Rebellion Handbook*, 232ff.

284 Duffy 2013.

285 Bulmer Hobson, 'Foundation and growth of the Irish Volunteers', in Martin 1963, 30–1.

286 Gogan, Liam: Witness Statement 799.

287 Lonergan, Michael: Witness Statement 140.

288 Martin, Éamon: Witness Statements 591, 592, 593.

289 Ó Lochlainn, Colm: Witness Statement 751.

290 Ó Riain, Padraic: Witness Statement 98.

291 As late as 1912, Pearse was still critical of the IRB as an 'association of talkers and old Fenians, past all capacity for action'; Desmond Ryan in the *Irish Press*, 7 December 1963. It has always been questioned exactly *when* Pearse joined the IRB. The most probable date is shortly *after* the foundation of the Volunteers. See Thornly 1966, 11. See also David Thornley, 'Patrick Pearse— the evolution of a republican', in Martin 1967, 157ff. See F.X. Martin, 'McCullough, Hobson, and republican Ulster', in Martin 1967, 103: 'In December [1913], Hobson took a further decisive step—he swore Pearse into the IRB'. However, see Ryan 1949 [1957], 11: 'He joined the IRB in 1913, five months before the Irish Volunteers began'. Pearse was also said to have been refused membership in the circle in the ordinary way and was 'co-opted' into the IRB at the end of 1913; LeRoux 1936, 127.

292 Burke 2005.

293 Bateson 2010, 266.

294 Walker 1916; Smith 1916; 'Gallantry of Red Cross workers, St John Ambulance Brigade', *Irish Times 1916 Rebellion Handbook*, 232ff.

295 Ó Snodaigh 2000; Ó hUid 1966.

296 O'Connor, Joseph: Witness Statement 157; O'Connor 1966; P. O'Brien 2007; Lyons 1926; Lennon 1948; Donnelly 1922; Donnelly 1917.

297 McGuigan 2005–6.

298 Pte J. Jameson, 2635/Sherwood Foresters: 'My experiences whilst in Ireland', Document Reference No. 999/519, National Archives, Dublin.

299 Edmunds 1960.

300 Hall 1920, 19.

301 Oates 1920, 34.

302 Caulfield 1995, 228ff.

303 McCann 1946, 46ff.

304 Hally 1966–7, Part 2, 50.

305 'The Robin Hoods', 1/7th, 2/7th and 3/7th Battalions. Oates 1920, 282.

306 Caulfield 1995, 208–28.

307 B.C. Webster, 'A few pages of a diary of an eyewitness of the Sinn Fein rebellion', in 'A diary of the rebellion in Ireland, Easter 1916', 2. Transcription by Cliff Housley. Original owned by the Sherwood Foresters Museum, Nottingham, England.

308 Doyle, Revd James: Witness Statement 311.

309 James Woods, 'Small town, great war', *Mansfield and North Notts. Advertiser*, 19 May 1916.

310 Ryan 1949 [1957], 162.

311 *Ibid.*, 187ff.

312 Edmunds 1960.

313 Reilly 2005.

314 Duffy 2013.

315 See Irish Census of 1911 (http://www.census.nationalarchives.ie/reels/nai000119513/).

316 Sheehy-Skeffington 1917.

317 Brennan-Whitmore 1996, 2.

318 McHugh 1966, 207ff.

319 Duffy 2013.

320 P. O'Brien 2013.

321 British PRO, WO35/69; Skinnider 1966.

322 See Mathews 2010b, 126–30, for a contrasting view of the countess's role at St Stephen's Green.

323 P. O'Brien 2013, 18.

324 Extract from the diary of Geraldine Fitzgerald, dated 24 April 1916. War Office Papers, WO 35/207/127.

325 This type of 7.63mm Mauser pistol converted into a rifle with a removable stock. It was nicknamed a 'Peter the Painter' after Peter Piaktow, a Latvian anarchist in London, a painter, who was sought but never caught following the 1911 London riots on Sidney Street.

326 Caulfield 1995, 97.

327 Hally 1966–7, Part 1, 321. There is a graphic account of events at St Stephen's Green in the memoirs of Breda Grace, Dr D.A. Courtney and Simon Donnelly, De Valera Papers, Killiney, MSS 94/385. See also the Easter Week diary of Douglas Hyde, who lived on Earlsfort Terrace: TCD MS 10343/7.

328 Ryan 1949 [1957], 121.

329 Bowen 1951; O'Sullivan and O'Neill 1999.

330 Ryan 1949 [1957], 121.

331 Duffy 2013.

332 MacThomais 1965, 37.

333 Grace, Séamas: Witness Statement 310.

334 Donnelly, Simon: Witness Statements 113, 433, 481.

335 McDowell 1967.

336 Figgis 1924, 15–21; O'Brennan 1922; T. Desmond Williams, 'Eoin MacNeill and the Irish Volunteers', in Martin 1967, 142ff.

337 Bulmer Hobson, 'Foundation and growth of the Irish Volunteers', in Martin 1963, 32.

338 Griffith and O'Grady 2002, 156.

339 Elsie Mahaffy, daughter of the provost of Trinity College, left her memoirs and a diary of the events: TCD MS 2074. She had no pity for the countess. (See Richmond

Barracks/Grangegorman Road Upper [Dublin 7].)
[340] Doherty 1995.
[341] See http://www.ireland.com/focus/easterrising/saturday/; O'Higgins 1925, 88.
[342] MacLochlainn 1971, 183.
[343] O'Farrell 1997, 39; Grenan 1917a
[344] Grenan 1917a.
[345] The original is in the possession of the MacDonagh family. MacLochlainn 1971, 63.
[346] Duffy 2013.
[347] Thornly 1966, 11.
[348] 'They were schoolboys—the Pearse brothers at the "Row"', *Christian Brothers Westland Row Centenary Record, 1864–1964*.
[349] MacThomais 1965, 29.
[350] Ceannt, Áine B.E.: Witness Statement 264.
[351] Duffy 2013.
[352] *Ibid.*
[353] White 1930 [2005], 157ff.
[354] Henderson, Frank: Witness Statements 249, 851.
[355] O'Reilly, Michael W.: Witness Statement 886.
[356] Ó Mahony 1987 [1995], 61ff.
[357] McGarry, Seán: Witness Statement 368.
[358] Clarke 1997, 71.
[359] Skinnider 1966.
[360] Skinnider 1917, 9–10.
[361] *Ibid.*, 9.
[362] Henderson, Frank: Witness Statements 249, 821.
[363] Hopkinson 1998.
[364] Ó Mahony 1987 [1995], 48, 54, 55, 60.
[365] Warwick-Haller and Warwick-Haller 1995, 13ff.
[366] *Weekly Irish Times, 1916 Rebellion Handbook*, 20, 107–10, 233–4.
[367] Heron, Áine: Witness Statement 293.
[368] Plunkett, John (Jack): Witness Statements 488, 865.
[369] Doyle, Revd James: Witness Statement 311.
[370] Duffy 2013.
[371] McGarry 2010, 184.
[372] Diary of Mrs Arthur Mitchell: National Library of Ireland MS 24553. See also J.J. O'Leary's day-by-day account in the *Dublin Saturday Post*, 29 April, 6 May and 13 May 1916. See also the diary of Mary Martin, which gives another view from a mother whose son was serving in the British army: http://dh.tcd.ie/martindiary/site/index.xml. Mary Martin, the author of the diary, was a wealthy Roman Catholic widow and mother of twelve children. In 1916, when the diary was written, she was living in Monkstown, an affluent and largely Protestant suburb of Dublin. Her son Charlie was a British soldier and at the time she started writing the diary he was missing in action on the Salonika front. Mary wrote the diary to Charlie as if it were an extended letter—in the hope that he would return soon and, by reading its pages, feel as though he hadn't missed anything while he was away.
[373] MacNeill, Agnes: Witness Statement 213.
[374] See Warwick-Haller and Warwick-Haller 1995.
[375] McCoole 2003, 196ff; The Ó Rahilly 1915b; 1915c.
[376] See Pinkman 1998, 201: 'Suffering from battle hysteria, Cmdt de Valera had to be forcibly restrained by some of his men of the Boland's Mill garrison before the end of the Easter Week's fighting and removed to Sir Patrick Dun's Hospital. It was in a room of the hospital that de Valera made his formal surrender to Captain Hitzen of the 5th Lincolnshire Regiment at about 1 pm on Sunday, 30 April 1916.'
[377] Comerford, Máire: BMH Contemporaneous Document 59. See Griffith and O'Grady 2002.
[378] On Tuesday morning James Doyle went to the school to collect ammunition and found the position abandoned. Those in the school had returned to the 3rd Battalion HQ. Ó hUid 1966.
[379] Christian, William: Witness Statement 646.
[380] Bateson 2010, 118.
[381] Grace, Séamas: Witness Statement 310.
[382] MacThomais 1965, 26.

383 Caulfield 1995, 133–5; Duff 1966, 132–3; Henry Hanna, a member of the GRs, gives an eyewitness account in TCD MS 10066/192.1.
384 British PRO WO141/6.
385 Caulfield 1995, 228ff.
386 McCann 1946, 46ff; Caulfield 1995, 208–28.
387 Bateson 2010, 274; Walker 1916.
388 Gerrard, Capt. E.: Witness Statement 348.
389 Henry Hanna, a member of the GRs, gives an eyewitness account in TCD MS 10066/192.1.
390 Smyth 1997.
391 Lynn, Dr Kathleen: Witness Statement 357.
392 Mulholland 2002.
393 Molony, Helena: Witness Statement 391.
394 Burke 2005.
395 A. Sheehy-Skeffington 1982.
396 Bateson 2010, 275.
397 Luddy 1995.
398 H. Sheehy-Skeffington 1902.
399 H. Sheehy-Skeffington 1917.
400 Philip Rooney, 'The Green Jacket: the story of the Countess', *Sunday Press*, 15, 18 and 25 September and 2 October 1960.
401 Rosemary Cullen Owens, 'Constance Markievicz's "Three Great Movements" and the 1916 Rising' (lecture given at a conference entitled 'The Long Revolution: 1916 in Context' at University College Cork, 27 January 2006); Brian Farrell, 'Markievicz and the women of the Revolution', in Martin 1967, 227ff.
402 *Workers' Republic*, 22 January 1916.
403 Hay 2005.
404 Bouchier-Hayes 2009.
405 Plunkett, Grace Gifford: Witness Statement 257.
406 McCoole 2003, 168.
407 Duffy 2013.
408 Ryan, Dr James: Witness Statement 70; Ryan 1942.
409 McCoole 2003, 206–8.
410 Mulcahy, Mary Josephine: Witness Statement 399.
411 *Ibid.*
412 Seán Ó Luing, 'Arthur Griffith and Sinn Féin', in Martin 1967, 2–3.
413 Fitzgibbon, Seán: Witness Statement 130; Fitzgibbon 1949.
414 Ó Briain, Liam: Witness Statement 6.
415 Dr Séamus Ó Cellaigh, *Gleanings from Ulster history* (Ballinascreen Historical Society, rev. edn 1994), 141–52.
416 Martin 1961.
417 *Sunday Independent*, 23 April 1916.
418 Molony, Helena: Witness Statement 391.
419 Original's whereabouts are unknown. Printed by the *Irish War News* from O'Keefe's Printers on Halston Street by Joe Stanley at Pearse's direction. Later printed in the *Sinn Féin Rebellion Handbook* published by the *Irish Times* (1916), 47. A copy is in the Irish Volunteer papers, University College Dublin.
420 D. FitzGerald 1966, 1.
421 Béaslaí 1926, 90.
422 Clarke 1997, 94.
423 Joyce 1966, 353. In his Witness Statement No. 729, Msgr Patrick Browne, who saw MacDermott the night before he was executed, wrote that MacDermott:
'... was rather severe against it, in his condemnation of McNeill [*sic*], because, he said, that in his opinion it would have been a really formidable Rising with a much better chance of world reverberation than that week's fighting in Dublin. I think he felt very bitter about the calling off. As a matter of fact, he was not wasting time talking about that. He said what a pity that it prevented the Rising being a respectable Rising, that it would have been over a considerable part of the country, employing a lot of British troops, and that, as far as the Germans were concerned, it would have been a more valuable thing than the mere flash in the pan it was. I don't think he even referred to McNeill as a person beyond the fact that he considered it a shocking

disappointment that it had not come off as a Rising.'

[424] Ó Conluain 1963, 165–6.

[425] Ceannt, Áine B.E.: Witness Statement 264.

[426] Talbot 1923, chapter 3.

[427] Gibbon 1966; 'Shooting of Three Men, Royal Commission of Inquiry', *Irish Times 1916 Rebellion Handbook*, 213ff; 'Courts-Martial at Richmond Barracks, The Shooting of Francis Sheehy Skefington', *Irish Times 1916 Rebellion Handbook*, 108ff.

[428] Foy and Barton 1999, 190.

[429] Hughes, Julia: Witness Statement 880.

[430] *Royal Commission on the Arrest and Subsequent Treatment of Mr Francis Sheehy Skeffington, Mr Thomas Dickson and Mr Patrick James McIntyre*, Cd. 8376, paras 11, 13, 17.

[431] Statement of 2Lt W.L.P. Dobbin, 3rd Irish Rifles, WO 35-67.

[432] *Royal Commission on the Arrest and Subsequent Treatment of Mr Francis Sheehy Skeffington, Mr Thomas Dickson and Mr Patrick James McIntyre*, Cd. 8376, para. 42.

[433] Townshend 2005, 193.

[434] *Royal Commission on the Arrest and Subsequent Treatment of Mr Francis Sheehy-Skeffington, Mr Thomas Dickson and Mr Patrick James McIntyre*, Cd. 8376, paras 7, 11, 13, 16; Luke 19: 27.

[435] Townshend 2005, 194. See 'A Pacifist Dies', a lecture delivered by Hanna Sheehy-Skeffington in 1917, quoted in McHugh 1966, 276–88. Hughes, Julia: Witness Statement 880.

[436] H. Sheehy-Skeffington 1917.

[437] *Hansard*, 1 August 1916.

[438] Vane 1929.

[439] O'Casey 1919 [1980], Afterword.

[440] Lynd 1917, 141ff.

[441] Diary of Mrs Augustine Henry, National Library of Ireland MS 7984; Cullen 2013, 144. See also J.J. O'Leary's day-by-day account in the *Dublin Saturday Post*, 29 April, 6 May and 13 May 1916.

[442] Matthews 2010a, 7ff.

[443] Nunan 1967.

[444] Dillon 2007, 151–2, 195. She describes route marches beginning in September 1914 and leaving from Larkfield, in which up to 6,000 Volunteers marched overnight into the Dublin Mountains.

[445] Matthews 2010a, 15.

[446] Agnew, Arthur: Witness Statement 152.

[447] Gleeson, Joseph: Witness Statement 367.

[448] Good, Joe: Witness Statement 388.

[449] O'Connor, John: BMH Contemporaneous Document 152.

[450] Robinson, Séamus: Witness Statements 156, 1721, 1722.

[451] Bracken, Peadar: Witness Statements 12, 361.

[452] Daly, Denis: Witness Statement 110. He worked in London for the British Post Office and joined the IRB in 1913; he was great friends with Michael Collins in London.

[453] Macardle 1937 [1965], 912.

[454] Ó Lochlainn, Colm: Witness Statement 751.

[455] Plunkett, John (Jack): Witness Statements 488, 865; Ryan 1949 [1957], 73.

[456] Plunkett, Grace Gifford: Witness Statement 257. 'I remember the document that was published because I wrote it out myself for Joe, sitting on his bed in Larkfield House. Joe did not do it in the nursing home . . . It did come out from the Castle, I know who brought it out. Donagh MacDonagh was married to a girl named Smith. It was her father that brought it out.' Smith, Eugene: Witness Statement 334; Hanna Sheehy-Skeffington, *Irish Press*, 4 January 1937; Geraldine Plunkett, *Irish Press*, 8 January 1937; O'Neill 2000, 34–5; Ryan 1949 [1957], 64–75; O'Hegarty 1952, 699–700; Brennan 1958; Townshend 2005, 125–36; Foy and Barton 1999, 34–45; but see 'The "Not-So-Bogus" Castle Document': Ó Dubghaill 1966, 196–203.

[457] Little 1942; Smith, Eugene: Witness Statement 334.

[458] Donagh MacDonagh, 'Plunkett and MacDonagh', in Martin 1967, 170–1.

[459] Ryan 1949 [1957], 68.

[460] Martin 1966a, 119–21; Browne, Msgr Patrick: Witness Statement 729.

[461] Ceannt, Áine B.E.: Witness Statement 264.

[462] Townshend 2005, 133.

[463] Townshend 2006.

[464] Gaskin, Frank: Witness Statement 386.

[465] Holohan, Garry: Witness Statement 328.

[466] Martin, Éamon: Witness Statements 591, 592, 593.

[467] Murphy, John J. (Seán): Witness Statement 204.

[468] Holohan, Garry: Witness Statement 328. Though Holohan and others identified the 'youth' as seventeen-year-old Gerald Playfair, in fact Gerald was not killed in the Rising. His older brother George (23) 'died from bullet wounds to the abdomen' in 1 Park Place, beside the Islandbridge Gate to Phoenix Park. See Duffy 2013.

[469] Dunleavy 2002; O'Donnell 1972.

[470] Doyle 1932; Igoe 2001.

[471] Soughley, Michael T.: Witness Statement 189.

[472] Hally 1966–7, Part 2, 53.

[473] Duffy 2013.

[474] See Irish Census of 1911 (http://www.census.nationalarchives.ie/reels/nai000119513/).

[475] Coady 1966.

[476] J.J. O'Leary, Dublin Saturday Post, combined editions of 29 April, 6 May and 13 May 1916.

[477] Bulmer Hobson, 'Foundation and growth of the Irish Volunteers', in Martin 1963, 42.

[478] Archer, Liam: Witness Statement 819.

[479] Ui Chonaill 1966, 184.

[480] Conlon, Martin: Witness Statement 798. See also the personal account of Bulmer Hobson in the Irish Times, 6 May 1961. Conlon, Mrs Martin: Witness Statement 419. Foy and Barton 1999, 131–2; Townshend 2005, 137.

[481] Ó Luing 1961.

[482] Ceannt, Áine B.E.: Witness Statement 264.

[483] O'Donovan, Con: Witness Statement 1750.

[484] Collins, Maurice: Witness Statement 550.

[485] Gavan-Duffy, Louise: Witness Statement 216. (Her statement is more reflective and politically aware than many of the others.)

[486] Caulfield 1995, 157.

[487] Lennon, Michael: BMH Contemporaneous Document 56.

[488] Thornton, Brigid Lyons: Witness Statement 259.

[489] Duffy 2013.

[490] P. O'Brien 2012, 3ff.

[491] O'Neill 2006.

[492] Aloysius, Revd: Witness Statement 200; Fr Aloysius 1942.

[493] Augustine, Revd: Witness Statement 920.

[494] Fr Albert 1966.

[495] MacLochlainn 1971, 111.

[496] Bateson 2010, 110.

[497] Augustine, Revd: Witness Statement 920.

[498] Fr Columbus's manuscript of his diary was discovered in the Capuchin Archives in Church Street. See Benedict Cullen, 'Echoes of the Rising's final shots', Irish Times (http://www.aohdiv7.org/hist_easter_aftermath.htm).

[499] Clarke 1997, 93.

[500] MacDonagh, Sr Francesca: Witness Statement 717.

[501] Collins, Con (Conor, Cornelius): Witness Statement 90. Quilty, John J.: Witness Statement 516 (he was the owner of the car that drove off the pier).

[502] Bateson 2010, 311.

[503] O'Reilly, Eily O'Hanrahan: Witness Statements 270, 415.

[504] Royal Commission on the Rebellion in Ireland, London, 18 May 1916.

[505] Duffy 2013.

[506] See Irish Census of 1911 (http://www.census.nationalarchives.ie/reels/nai000119513/).

[507] Reilly 2006.

[508] Molony, Helena: Witness Statement 391; Helena Molony, 'Women of the Rising', RTÉ Archive, 16 April 1963.

[509] McCoole 2003, 56.

[510] Kelly 1966.

[511] Duffy 2013.

[512] Shouldice, Jack (John F.): Witness Statement 162.

[513] MacThomais 1965, 25.

[514] Bateson 2010, 103; Flanagan, M.: Witness Statement 800.

[515] Duffy 2013.
[516] On 1 January 2001 the British War Office in London released papers detailing the atrocities (British PRO, Kew, London, WO 141.21 and WO 141.27).
[517] *Irish Catholic*, 20 May 1916.
[518] Coogan 2001, 147.
[519] *Ibid.*, 148.
[520] *Irish Times*, 1 January 2001.
[521] Caulfield 1995, 293.
[522] *Daily Mail*, 20 May 1916.
[523] Cowell 1997, 53.
[524] Duffy 2013.
[525] Reynolds 1919, 11–12.
[526] *Royal Commission on the Rebellion in Ireland*, Report (1916), Cd. 8279, Minutes of Evidence, Cd. 8311.
[527] Bateson 2010, 260.
[528] *Irish Catholic*, 20 May 1916.
[529] P. O'Brien 2012.
[530] O'Neill 2006.
[531] Liam Tobin, who served in C Company of the 1st Battalion, stated: 'I was struck by the small numbers who showed up . . . I had often seen our Company . . . muster a bigger number than the whole battalion did that morning' (Tobin, Liam: Witness Statement 1753).
[532] P. O'Brien 2012, 3ff.
[533] Hally 1966.
[534] O'Neill 2006; J. Reynolds 1926.
[535] *The War History of the 2/6th South Staffordshire Regiment* (London, 1924).
[536] Jamie 1931.
[537] Cowell 1997, 53.
[538] Clarke 1997, 128–9.
[539] Holohan, Garry: Witness Statement 328.
[540] Kelly, Patrick: Witness Statement 78.
[541] Bateson 2010, 307.
[542] Coogan 2001, 148.
[543] Byrne, Joseph: Witness Statement 461.
[544] Cuffe 1942.
[545] McHugh 1966, 320; Duffy 2013; Bateson 2010, 155.
[546] Duffy 2013.
[547] O'Carroll, Liam: Witness Statements 314, 594.
[548] Duffy 2013.
[549] *Ibid.*
[550] Béaslaí 1947.
[551] Bateson 2010, 45.
[552] Éamon Ceannt told his wife: 'We can't let the Citizen Army go out alone; if they go out, we must go with them' (Ceannt, Áine B.E.: Witness Statement 264).
[553] Rees 1998, 201.
[554] O'Hegarty, P.S.: Witness Statement 26.
[555] Béaslaí 1952a.
[556] Collins 2012, 259.
[557] Dillon 2007, 197–8.
[558] For a complete analysis and comparison of reports and theories see Ó Dubghaill 1966, 109–15: 'Connolly's "Three Days Incommunicado"'.
[559] Dore, Éamon: Witness Statement 392. 'We met, but sometime later Connolly went of his accord.'
[560] Hyland (1997, 48), however, claims that Connolly was 'detained in Chapelizod'. See Ryan 1949 [1957], 268: 'The house was near Chapelizod'. See also Fox 1944 [2014], 120: 'He was held in a house in the Lucan area'.
[561] Malony, Helena: Witness Statement 391.
[562] Ryan 1949 [1957], 61.
[563] Ceannt, Áine B.E.: Witness Statement 264.
[564] *Ibid.*
[565] McCoole 2003, 146–7.

566 Bateson 2010, 43.

567 MacThomais 1965, 31.

568 Browne, Msgr Patrick: Witness Statement 729.

569 Annan Dickson: 1916 Field Pocket Book of Captain A.A. Dickson. Transcription by Cliff Housley. Original owned by the Imperial War Museum, London, England.

570 Plunkett, Grace Gifford: Witness Statement 257.

571 P. O'Brien 2010.

572 Doolan 1918.

573 MacThomais 1965, 32.

574 Bateson 2010, 268.

575 Burgess, Alfred: Witness Statement 1634.

576 Plunkett, Grace Gifford: Witness Statement 257.

577 MacThomais 1965, 43; but Hyland (1997, 54) notes that Connolly 'was not strapped to a chair, but placed seated on a rough wooden box ... and then executed'.

578 Aloysius, Revd: Witness Statement 200.

579 Bateson 2010, 266.

580 Coughlan, James: Witness Statement 304.

581 Collins 1997, 10.

582 *Irish Times*, 28 April 1916.

583 O'Neill 1939, 65.

584 Hally 1966–7, Part 1, 319.

585 Cosgrave, William T.: Witness Statements 268, 449.

586 Nevin, Revd Eugene: Witness Statement 1605.

587 Murphy, Séamus: Witness Statement 1756.

588 McCarthy, Thomas: Witness Statement 307.

589 O'Flaherty, Liam: Witness Statement 248.

590 McCarthy, Thomas: Witness Statement 307.

591 Buckhill, Alfred: Witness Statement 1019; Barton 2002.

592 Elizabeth, Countess of Fingall, *Seventy years young* (Dublin, 1991 [1937]), 376.

593 Wylie, W.E.: Witness Statement 864. Wylie's 'statement' was actually the recording of an interview with him by Col. J.V. Joyce of the Bureau of Military History, who asked Wylie for his recollection of the trials. Wylie, though giving some few details, mostly indicated that he had written everything down, only to be published after his death.

'I approached The Hon. W.E. Wylie, Q.C., at the Curragh Races, yesterday, and had an interview lasting quite a considerable time with him. In previous interviews I had urged on him the necessity of his recording his experiences for the Bureau. He told me yesterday that he had now actually written his account of his experiences but that he had decided not to give it to anybody whosoever during his lifetime and he had made a proviso in his Will leaving it to his daughter after his death to use in her discretion.

I told him there were a few factual matters that we were particularly interested in at the moment relating to the courtsmartial following the 1916 Rising, and he told me that all these courtsmartial were drumhead courtsmartial in the early stages, and he appears to be quite satisfied that no records were made or kept of these courtsmartial. He stated that the three officers constituting the Court made occasional notes but that no official record was taken or kept. General Blackader presided at these drumhead courtsmartial, and Mr. Wylie stated that he himself was present at them all. [. . .]

Immediately following the Rising he was sent for by General Sir Joseph Byrne (afterwards Commissioner of the D.M.P.) and told that he was to prosecute at the forthcoming trials of the leaders of the insurrection. He asked General Byrne what they were to be charged with and was told that the charges were a matter for him to prepare; that that was his business. He told me that all this was included in his statement.

I might add that Mr Wylie was very friendly during this interview. He emphasised that his reason for keeping his statement completely to himself was that he did not want any living person to see it while he was still alive, because, he added, no matter however well disposed he might be, there was always the danger that he might allude to it in some way or another. Even giving it to us under seal, which I had mentioned previously to him, did not seem to satisfy him.'

594 Reports of the court martial proceedings of rebel leaders, British PRO WO 71/344/58.

595 Coogan 2001, 135–6.

596 Schmuhl 2013.

597 De Valera statement, 3 July 1969. Éamon de Valera Papers, University College Dublin.

598 Coogan 1993, 78. Wylie gave this account to David Gray, US Ambassador to Ireland, at a luncheon at the US Embassy on 21 May 1941.

599 Haverty 1988, 162.

600 Ó Broin 1989, 27. Ó Broin's account is drawn from the unpublished memoir of W.E. Wylie, prosecutor at Markievicz's trial. The memoir was written at least 23 years after the event, although rumours of the alleged breakdown did circulate in Dublin in May 1916. There is no reference to Markievicz's having begged for her life in any formal trial record, in which she was reported to have said, 'It doesn't matter what happens to me. I did what I thought was right and I stand by it.' It seems unlikely that the court would fabricate such defiant words if they had seen Markievicz beg for her life. It seems equally unlikely that a woman who had begged for her life would, in the same sitting, utter such defiant words. Thus the Wylie account seems somewhat suspect. See also Townshend 2005, 285–6. Townshend notes that Wylie's motive for any alleged fabrication on his part remains obscure. See also Barton 2002, 80.

601 Elsie Mahaffy, daughter of the provost of Trinity College, left her memoirs and a diary of the events (TCD MS 2074). Throughout her diary she had no pity for the countess.

602 Ó Broin 1989, 27.

603 Holland, Robert: Witness Statements 280, 371.

604 Duffy 2013.

605 *Ibid.*

606 Bateson 2010, 73.

607 Duffy 2013.

608 Connolly 1899.

609 Brennan 1966.

610 Heuston 1966, 34ff.

611 Balfe, Richard: Witness Statement 251.

612 Bateson 2010, 112.

613 Balfe, Richard: Witness Statement 251.

614 Bateson 2010, 308.

615 Brennan 1966.

616 Those marked with # came from the 5th Battalion in Ashbourne.

617 Duffy 2013.

618 Ó Mahony 1987 [1995], 46, 48, 49, 54.

619 Ceannt, Áine B.E.: Witness Statement 264.

620 J.J. O'Leary, *Dublin Saturday Post*, in an edition issued after the Rising (combining 29 April, 6 May and 13 May 1916).

621 Duffy 2013.

622 See Irish Census of 1911 (http://www.census.nationalarchives.ie/reels/nai000119513/).

623 O'Brennan 1922.

624 Ceannt, Áine B.E.: Witness Statement 264; BMH Contemporaneous Documents 94, 295.

625 O'Doherty, Kitty: Witness Statement 355.

626 *Ibid.*

627 Aan de Weil 2000; 2004–5.

628 MacThomais 2012.

629 Oman, William: Witness Statement 421. Thornton, Frank: Witness Statement 510.

630 O'Donovan Rossa 1872 [1991]; 1898 [1972].

631 McDonnell 1972, 37.

632 Ryan 1949 [1957], 57; McGarry, Seán: Witness Statement 368.

633 *Diarmuid Ó Donnabhain Rossa, 1831–1915: Souvenir of Public Funeral* (1915).

634 'Are women people?', *Irish Citizen*, 7 August 1915; McCallum 2005.

635 Many newspapers carried copies of the address, most completely in the *Irish Volunteer*. The original handwritten script is on display in the Pearse Museum, St Enda's, Rathfarnham, Dublin. See Joyce 2009.

636 T. Desmond Williams, 'Eoin MacNeill and the Irish Volunteers', in Martin 1967, 142ff.

637 Nelson 2014.

638 Figgis 1924, 15–21; O'Brennan 1922.

639 Bulmer Hobson, 'Foundation and growth of the Irish Volunteers', in Martin 1963, 32.

640 Nixon and Healy 2000.

641 Mary Spring-Rice wrote the most detailed diary of the voyage, from the time the arms were

transferred until their landing: Mary Spring-Rice, 'Diary of the *Asgard* 1–26 July 1914', in Martin 1964, 79, 80, 95. See 'The death of the Honorable Mary Ellen Spring-Rice', *Limerick Chronicle*, 4 December 1924.

642 Bulmer Hobson notes that 'a General Shepherd [*sic*], who was later killed in France', was a member of Childers's crew: Bulmer Hobson, 'Gunrunning at Howth and Kilcoole, July–August 1914', in Martin 1963, 42. See also Leslie 1924.

643 Figgis 1924, 40–58.

644 Bermingham, DMP Constable Patrick J.: Witness Statement 697. Rosney, Joseph: Witness Statement 112.

645 *Irish Freedom*, September 1914.

646 Canavan 2006.

647 M.M. Pearse 1942; St Enda's School Papers, University College Library (Dublin). See http://www.rte.ie/radio1/doconone/documentary-podcast-this-man-had-kept-a-school-bilingual-padraig-pearse-education.html.

648 *An Claidheamh Soluis*, 27 August 1904.

649 Pearse 1916.

650 *Ibid.*

651 Cooke 1986; Kilcullen 1967.

652 Burke, Fergus (Frank): Witness Statement 694.

653 MacGarry 1942.

654 Ryan 1942.

655 De Barra 1969.

656 Canavan 2006; M.M. Pearse 1942.

657 O'Kelly, Dr Séamus: Witness Statement 471; Martin 1961.

658 Ryan 1949 [1957], 119.

659 Clarke 1997, 75–7, 80, 94, 141.

660 Murphy, Séamus: Witness Statement 1756.

661 Coogan 2013; P. O'Brien 2012b.

662 Lawless, Joseph: Witness Statement 1043. Lawless's statement runs to 418 pages and provides a remarkably complete and detailed account of the Fingal Volunteers in the Ashbourne engagement and the north Dublin area from 1913 through the entire revolutionary period.

663 Crenigan, James: Witness Statements 148, 1395.

664 Lawless, Joseph: Witness Statement 1043.

665 Paddy Houlihan, 'The Battle of Ashbourne', NLI MS 18098.

666 'Graphic story of Ashbourne', *Gaelic American*, 23 September 1916; Laing *et al.* 2006.

667 Bratton, RIC Constable Eugene: Witness Statement 467.

668 Gerry Golden, 'The story of the fight at Rath Cross Roads or the Battle of Ashbourne', Allen Library, Dublin.

669 Austin, John: Witness Statement 904. Austin was the local postman and observed the battle from the side of a hill.

'At this time I worked in the Post Office in the village and delivered all telegrams and messages, and it was I who delivered any messages that came through to the police. When the Rebellion started in Dublin on Easter Monday, no attempt was made by the police to barricade or fortify the barracks . . .

On Friday morning some extra police arrived from Navan, Dunboyne and Slane to reinforce the garrison. At about 10.30 a.m. on that day I was standing at the Barracks, talking to the police and, on looking up towards the Cross of the Rath, I saw some of the rebels arriving there on bicycles, with guns on their shoulders. I said to Constable Tully, who was in the Barracks, that the rebels were coming. The police came out and put a barricade across the main road. This consisted of a ladder resting on two boxes. This would not stop anything except a motorcar or a cyclist. Constable Roche, who had come from Dunboyne, came out of the Barracks and proceeded towards the Cross where the rebels were, and started cutting the pole carrying the telephone wires with a saw. This was a junction pole and was situated at the crossroads. The rebels told him to stop and he then took his rifle from his shoulder, fired a shot in the air and made off towards Ratoath. He got under the bed in Byrne's house in Cookstown, some distance over the road. Some of the rebels followed him and fired at him. They pulled him from under the bed and made him a prisoner . . .

A few minutes later Tom Ashe came walking down the road and went to the Barracks, and asked the police to surrender. I knew Ashe from seeing him in charge of the Lusk Pipers Band formerly. The police refused to surrender. Ashe went back to his men, got them undercover, and the battle began in earnest. Sergeant Toomey was in charge of the Barracks at the time. I now went towards Ashbourne and had only gone a few hundred yards when the first volleys were fired. Some of the rebels got on to the footpath along the road, behind the fence in front of the Barracks and behind the fence on the opposite side of the road, while some others were on the north side of the Barracks. Some were behind a wall which was on the south-west side of the crossroads. Another party went up the road to Hamilton Hill and took up positions there: it was here that Volunteer Crinnigan was killed. Hamilton Hill is the elevated portion of the main road, just a couple of hundred yards north of the Cross of the Rath. Crinnigan tried to cross the road and one of the policemen shot him. Another man named Rafferty from Lusk was also shot and died subsequently . . .

During the time the fight was in progress, I was on Lime-kiln Hill, a small elevation near the village, and from which you had a good view of the road where the fighting was taking place . . . We could see the police reinforcements arriving, the police getting out of their cars and taking cover on the sides of the road. The leading cars drove almost up to the crossroads before stopping, and they were only a very short distance from where the rebels were behind the wall at the crossroads . . .

Stray bullets were reaching the hill on which we were, and one of them nearly got me. We could see the police jumping up and running to new positions along the road. When the firing died down and it was apparent that the battle was over, I went back to the scene. Someone—I can't now remember who it was—asked me to take the dead men off the road. I got a horse and cart and proceeded up the road . . .

Tom Ashe and his men were at the crossroads. They were very excited after their victory and were cheering, as men would after a football match. I told Ashe what I was going to do, and he told me to go ahead. Two of the policemen who had not been wounded helped me to collect the dead policemen into the cart. I had eight dead men in the cart when I had finished. Included in this number were Sergeant Shanagher from Navan and Sergeant Young. Two of the dead men were civilians whom I believe were drivers of cars. The bodies of the County Inspector of Police and the District Inspector had been taken away before I got on the scene, and the wounded men were also taken away . . .

The police had twenty-seven casualties all told. Sergeant Shanagher had been stationed in Ashbourne some years previous to this, and a right bad one he was. He would know the country around Ashbourne well and as such he was in one of the leading cars. He was shot right between the eyes as he left the car and slumped into a small depression on the side of the road . . .

The road that evening was a terrible sight with blood and bandages strewn on it.

Inspector McCormack of the R.I.C. wanted me to travel with my load of dead men to Slane. I refused to do this. He said he would give me a strong escort, and I said, "If we met the rebels on the way, what use would your escort be and where would I be?" We put the dead men in the washhouse at the end of the Barracks, and the following day coffins arrived for them and they were taken away in a lorry.

Tom Ashe and his men had left by this time and returned to their camp at Borranstown.

When things had quietened down, the surviving police came down to the village and bought themselves some drink and food. They had money as the rebels had not interfered with any of their personal belongings. They were very shaken and were shivering. One of them remarked to me that the rebels were great men, and I replied, "If you had won, I know what you would do". The surviving police stayed in the Barracks that night, and the following day they were all taken to Navan . . .

An inquest was held at Ashbourne and, although I was notified for the jury, I was not called. The rebels took their two men that were killed and wounded away with them that evening.'

670 Lawless 1966, 313.
671 Coogan 2013, 52–7.
672 O'Connor, James: Witness Statement 142.

'On Friday, after leaving a small party in the camp, we set out in the direction of Ashbourne. I understood our job was to destroy the railway line near Batterstown. We were on bicycles, and I was in the leading section. Charles Weston was in charge of this section. Near the cross of the Rath there was a barricade across the road leading to Garristown. That was the road we were on. Two policemen surrendered there without firing. After they had been disarmed we tied white handkerchiefs on their helmets and they were sent forward to the Barracks to tell their comrades that they were prisoners and to tell them to surrender. The police did not return. We had now taken cover on the side of the road. Tom Ashe came along and gave me a sledge and told me to go with him that I was to break in the barrack door. Just as we arrived at the barrack door, the R.I.C. opened fire from the upstairs windows. They were not firing at us, but at our comrades down on the Garristown Road. Ashe ordered me away from there and we had to turn down along the ditch to where we started from. Firing between the garrison, the barracks and our men was now general. Just then I noticed cars and lorries pulling up on the north side of the main road near the cross roads. R.I.C. were dismounting from them and were heavily engaged by our men who had rifles. I did not fire then as my shotgun had not sufficient range. I saw several of the R.I.C. fall as if they had been hit. Firing continued and some of our men got slight wounds. After some time Frank Lawless and the men who had been left in the camp joined us. Dick Mulcahy then came along and he brought us across the fields keeping under cover of the hedges and ditches on to the main road, on the north or Slane side of the place where the cars were halted. We moved up along the road firing at any R.I.C. man we could see. Just at that time D.I. Gray was shot by Frank Lawless. After that the remainder put up their hands and surrendered. There seemed to be a lot of them killed and wounded. We had one man killed and three or four wounded. I thought Dick Mulcahy was a very brave man as he went up the middle of the road disregarding any cover and firing at the R.I.C. as he went. He had a big pistol. The name of the man who was killed was John Crinnigan and Tom Rafferty died the following day from his wounds. After the surrender we took all the arms and ammunition belonging to the R.I.C. and packed it into the bread van which Frank Lawless had brought up. The R.I.C. in the barracks on seeing their comrades on the road surrender also surrendered and we collected their arms and equipment also and put them in the van. The van was now very heavily loaded. The wounded R.I.C. men were placed on a farm cart and brought to the barracks where they were attended to by Dr Hayes. The R.I.C., who were prisoners, were paraded by Tom Ashe and warned that they were not to fight again against the Irish people. Dr Hayes treated Tom Rafferty and he was left in a house nearby as he was too bad to move further. The remainder of our wounded were able to proceed back to camp with us. Two priests arrived shortly after the R.I.C. surrendered and attended to the dead and wounded. They were very hostile to us and called us "murderers". The Battn then proceeded back to camp where we had a good meal of meat, bread and tea. We were then issued with one of the rifles belonging to the R.I.C. and 50 rounds of .303. We were all in good humour and spirits after our victory at Ashbourne.

We now had plenty of rifles and ammunition and plenty of good food ...

A rumour spread around camp that evening that the British Cavalry were coming and that night we moved to a new camp at "New Barn" near Kilsallaghan. It was dark when we got there and we lay that night in the sheds on straw. Strong guards were mounted on the camp.

Saturday morning found everybody in good spirits and looking forward to further action. About 2 p.m. on that date Ashe told us that it was all over, that they had surrendered in Dublin and that it would be ridiculous for us to hold out. He seemed very disappointed and naturally we were very disappointed too. He told me to go home and make the best of it. A few others who were the youngest also went home.'

[673] Laing *et al.* 2006.
[674] Nelson 2014.
[675] 'The Kilcoole gunrunning', *An Phoblacht*, 3 August 2000.
[676] Murtagh 2014.
[677] Bulmer Hobson, 'Foundation and growth of the Irish Volunteers', in Martin 1963, 42; Rosney, Joseph: Witness Statement 112.

Bibliography

MANUSCRIPTS, NEWSPAPERS AND PRINTED PRIMARY SOURCES

1916 Papers, Box 5608, No. 5688, National Archives, Dublin.

An Claidheamh Soluis.

An tÓglach.

An Phoblacht.

Bean na hÉireann.

Piaras Béaslaí Papers, National Library of Ireland.

Augustine Birrell Papers, Trinity College Dublin.

British Parliamentary Archive Papers, 'The Irish Uprising, 1914–1921'.

Cathal Brugha Papers, University College Library.

Máire Ni Shuibhne Brugha Papers, University College Library.

The Capuchin Annual.

The Catholic Bulletin.

Daniel Cohalan Papers, National Library of Ireland.

Éamon de Valera Papers, University College Dublin.

John Devoy Papers, National Library of Ireland MS 18157.

Documents relative to the Sinn Féin movement (London, 1921, Cmd. 1108).

The Easter Commemoration Digest, 1964.

Forward.

The Freeman's Journal.

The Gaelic American.

Gerry Golden, 'The story of the fight at Rath Cross Roads or the Battle of Ashbourne', Allen Library.

The Harp.

Mary Hayden diaries, National Library of Ireland.

Mrs Augustine Henry diary, National Library of Ireland.

Bulmer Hobson Papers, National Library of Ireland.

Paddy Houlihan, 'The Battle of Ashbourne', National Library of Ireland MS 18098.

The Irish Catholic.

The Irish Citizen.

Irish Freedom.

The Irish Independent/Sunday Independent.

The Irish Independent, Golden Jubilee Supplement (1966)/*Sunday Independent,* Easter Rising Commemorative Supplement (1966).

Irish Republican Brotherhood Papers, University College Library.

The Irish Times.

The Irish Volunteer.

Irish Volunteers Papers, University College Library.

The Irish Worker.

Pte J. Jameson, 2635/Sherwood Foresters, 'My experiences whilst in Ireland', Document Reference No. 999/519, National Archives, Dublin.

Patrick Little Papers, University College Library.

Diarmuid Lynch, 'Recollections and comments on the IRB', National Library of Ireland MS. 11128.

Denis McCullough Papers, University College Library.

Joseph McGarrity Papers, National Library of Ireland.

Eoin MacNeill Papers, National Library of Ireland.

Mary Martin diary, Trinity College Library, http://dh.tcd.ie/martindiary/.

Military Archives of Ireland, Cathal Brugha Barracks, Dublin:

Introduction to the Bureau of Military History 1913–1921 (Defence Forces Printing Press, 2003).

Bureau of Military History Witness Statements:

Aghlas (Ashe), Nora: Statement 645.

Agnew, Arthur: Statement 152.

Aloysius, Revd, OFM Cap.: Statements 200, 207.

Archer, Liam: Statement 819.

Augustine, Revd, OFM Cap.: Statement 920.

Austin, John: Statement 904.

Balfe, Richard: Statement 251.

Béaslaí, Piaras: Statements 261, 675.

Beaumont, Mrs Seán (Maureen McGavock): Statement 385.

Golden, Gerry: Statements 177, 206, 521, 522.

Good, Joe: Statement 388.

Grace, Séamus: Statement 310.

Griffith, Maud: Statement 205.

Hackett, Rose: Statement 546.

Hales, Tom: Statement 20.

Handley, Sgt Edward: Statement 625.

Hayes, Michael: Statement 215.

Hayes, Dr Richard: Statements 97, 876.

Healy, Seán: Statements 686, 1479, 1643.

Hehir, Hugh: Statement 683.

Henderson, Frank: Statements 249, 821.

Heron, Áine: Statement 293.

Heron, Ina (née Connolly): Statement 919.

Hobson, Bulmer: Statements 30, 31, 50, 51, 52, 53, 81, 82, 83, 84, 85, 86, 87, 652, 1089, 1365.

Hobson, Claire (née Gregan): Statement 685.

Holland, Robert: Statements 280, 371.

Holohan, Garry: Statements 328, 336.

Hughes, Julia: Statement 880.

Hynes, James: Statement 867.

Hynes, Thomas: Statement 714.

Irvine, George: Statement 265.

Jackson, Valentine: Statement 409.

Joyce, Col. J.V.: Statement 1762.

Kavanagh, Séamus: Statements 208, 998.

Keating, Pauline: Statement 432.

Keegan, John: Statement 217.

Kelly, Edward: Statement 1094.

Kelly, Patrick: Statement 78.

Kennedy, Senator Margaret: Statement 185.

Kennedy, Patrick (Paddy): Statement 499.

Kennedy, Seán: Statements 842, 885.

Kenny, Lt James (Howth, Kilcoole): Statement 174.

Kenny, James (E Co., 4th Btn, 1916): Statement 141.

Kent, William: Statement 75.

Keogh, Margaret: Statement 273.

King, RIC Constable Frank: Statement 635.

King, Martin: Statement 543.

Laffan, Nicholas: Statements 201, 703.

Lalor, Mary (née Hyland): Statement 295.

Larkin, James: Statement 906.

Lavin, Revd Thomas: Statement 1407.

Lawless, Sr Eithne (Evelyn, Eibhlin): Statement 414.

Lawless, Col. Joseph V.: Statement 1043.

Leahy, Thomas: Statement 660.

Lonergan, Michael: Statement 140.

Lynch, Diarmuid: Statements 4, 120, 121, 364, 651.

Lynch, Fionan: Statement 192.

Lynn, Dr Kathleen: Statement 357.

Lynskey, William: Statement 1749.

McAllister, Michael: Statement 1494.

Macardle, Dorothy: Statement 457.

McBride, Maud Gonne: Statement 317.

McCartan, Patrick: Statements 99, 100, 766.

McCarthy, Cathleen: Statement 937.

McCarthy, Dan: Statement 722.

McCarthy, Thomas: Statement 307.

MacCarvill, Eileen: Statement 1752.

McCrea, Patrick: Statement 413.

McCullough, Denis: Statements 111, 636, 914, 915, 916.

MacDonagh, Sr Francesca: Statement 717.

MacDonagh, John: Statements 219, 532.

McDonnell, Andrew: Statement 1768.

McDonnell, Michael (Mick): Statement 225.

McDowell, Maeve (née Cavanagh): Statement 258.

McElligott, Patrick: Statement 1013.

McEllistrom, Thomas: Statement 275.

MacEntee, Margaret (née Browne): Statement 322.

MacEntee, Seán: Statement 1052.

McEoin, Capt. James: Statement 436.

McGaley, Jack: Statement 126.

MacGarry, Maeve: Statement 826.

MacGarry, Milo: Statement 356.

McGarry, Seán: Statement 368.

McGowan, Séamus: Statement 542.

McGuinness, Joseph: Statement 607.

McKenna, Kathleen (née Napoli): Statement 643.

McLoughlin, John (Seán): Statement 290.

McLoughlin, Mary: Statement 934.

McNamara, Rose: Statement 482.

MacNeill, Agnes: Statement 213.

MacNeill, Niall: Statement 69.

McWhinney, Linda (née Kearns): Statement 404.

Mallin, Thomas: Statement 382.

Malone, Bridget (née Walsh): Statement 617.

Martin, Brigid (née Foley): Statement 398.

Martin, Éamon: Statements 591, 592, 593.

Mernin, Lily: Statement 441.

Mitchell, Albert: Statement 196.

Molloy, Michael: Statement 716.

Ryan, Dr James: Statement 70.

Ryan, Máirín (née Cregan): Statement 416.

Saurin, Charles: Statement 288.

Saurin, Frank: Statement 715.

Scollan, John J.: Statements 318, 341.

Scully, Thomas: Statement 491.

Shelly, Charles: Statement 870.

Shouldice, Jack (John F.): Statement 162.

Slater, Thomas (Tom): Statement 263.

Slattery, James (Jim): Statement 445.

Smart, Thomas: Statement 255.

Smith, Eugene: Statement 334.

Smyth, Patrick: Statement 305.

Soughley, Michael T.: Statement 189.

Stack, Una: Statements 214, 418.

Stafford, Jack: Statement 818.

Staines, Michael: Statements 284, 943, 944.

Stapleton, William James (Bill): Statement 822.

Styles, John J.: Statement 175.

Tannam, Liam: Statement 242.

Thornton, Dr Brigid (née Lyons): Statement 259.

Thornton, Frank: Statements 510, 615.

Thornton, Nora: Statement 655.

Traynor, Oscar: Statement 340.

Twamley, John: Statement 629.

Ui Chonnaill, Eilis Bean (née Ryan): Statement 568.

Walker, Charles: Statements 241, 266.

Walker, Michael: Statement 139.

Walpole, R.H. (Harry): Statement 218.

Walsh, James and Thomas: Statement 198.

Ward, Patrick: Statement 1140.

Weston, Charles: Statement 149.

Whelan, William: Statement 369.

Woods, Mary (née Flannery): Statement 624.

Wylie, W.E.: Statement 864.

Wyse-Power, Charles: Statement 420.

Wyse-Power, Nancy: Statements 541, 587, 732.

Young, Thomas: Statement 531.

General Maxwell Report to Field Marshal, Commanding-in-Chief, Home Forces, 25 May 1916.

General Richard Mulcahy Papers, University College Dublin.

New Ireland.

Diarmuid Ó Donnabhain Rossa, 1831–1915: Souvenir of Public Funeral.

Florence O'Donoghue Papers, National Library of Ireland.

Agnes O'Farrelly Papers, University College Library.

The Ó Rahilly (Michael Joseph) Papers, University College Library.

James Pearse Papers, National Library of Ireland.

Patrick Pearse Papers, National Library of Ireland.

Count George Noble Plunkett Papers, National Library of Ireland.

Royal Commission on the Landing of Arms at Howth on 26th July 1914, Report (1914), Cd. 7631.

Royal Commission on the Rebellion in Ireland, Report (1916), Cd. 8279, Minutes of Evidence, Cd. 8311.

Royal Commission on the Arrest and Subsequent Treatment of Mr Francis Sheehy Skeffington, Mr Thomas Dickson and Mr Patrick James McIntyre, Report (29 September 1916), Cd. 8376.

Desmond Ryan Papers, University College Library.

Dr James Ryan Papers, University College Library.

St Enda's School Papers, University College Library.

Sinn Féin.

The Spark.

Austin Stack Papers, National Library of Ireland.

Thom's Irish Almanac and Official Directory.

Trinity College Library, Manuscript Department:

Henry Hanna, a member of the GRs, eyewitness account, MS 10066/192.1.

Elsie Mahaffy, 'Ireland in 1916: an account of the Rising in Dublin', MS 2074.

A.A. Luce Papers, MS 4874.

Peadar Ó Cearnaigh, 'Reminiscences of the Irish Republican Brotherhood and Easter Week 1916', MS 3560/1.

Peadar Ó Cearnaigh, 'Founding of the Irish Republican Brotherhood', MS 2560/2.

The Voice of Labour.

The Worker.

The Workers' Republic.

SECONDARY SOURCES

Aan de Weil, J. 2000 Archbishop Walsh and Mgr Curran's opposition to the British war effort in Dublin, 1914–1918. *Irish Sword* **22** (88).

Aan de Wiel, J. 2003 *The Catholic Church in Ireland 1914–1918*. Dublin.

Aan de Wiel, J. 2004–5 Easter Rising 1916: Count Plunkett's letter to Pope Benedict XV. *Irish Sword* **24**.

Adams, G. 2001 *Who fears to speak? The story of Belfast and the 1916 Rising*. Belfast.

Albert, Fr, OFM Cap. 1926 Seán Heuston's last moments. *Fianna* (May 1926).

Albert, Fr, OFM Cap. 1942 Seán Heuston: how Seán Heuston died. *Capuchin Annual* (1942).

Alberti, J. 1998 *Beyond suffrage: feminists in war and peace, 1914–1928*. Basingstoke.

Alderman, C.L. 1972 *The wearing of the green: the Irish Rebellion, 1916–1921*. New York.

Allen, K. 1990 *The politics of James Connolly*. London.

Aloysius, Fr, OFM Cap. 1942 Easter Week: personal recollections. *Capuchin Annual* (1942).

Andrews, C.S. 1979 *Dublin made me*. Cork.

Anon. 1917 *Arthur Griffith: a study of the founder of Sinn Féin*. Dublin.

Anderson, W. 1994 *James Connolly and the Irish Left*. Dublin.

'An Rathach' 1948 London Volunteers. *Irish Democrat* (April 1948).

Arthur, Sir G. 1932 *General Sir John Maxwell*. London.

Asquith, Lady C. 1968 *Diaries, 1915–1918*. London.

Bartlett, T. and Jeffrey, K. (eds) 1996 *A military history of Ireland*. Cambridge.

Barton, B. 2002 *From behind a closed door: secret court martial documents of the 1916 Rising*. Belfast.

Bateson, R. 2010 *They died by Pearse's side*. Dublin.

Béaslaí, P. 1926 *Michael Collins and the making of a new Ireland* (2 vols). Dublin.

Béaslaí, P. 1952a The Connolly 'kidnapping'. *Irish Independent*, 24 April 1952.

Béaslaí, P. 1952b The fixing of the date of the 1916 Rising. *Irish Independent*, 24 April 1952.

Béaslaí, P. 1953 The National Army is founded. *Irish Independent*, 5 January 1953.

Béaslaí, P. 1961–5 Moods and memories. *Irish Independent*, October 1961–June 1965.

Beckett, J.C. 1963 *The making of modern Ireland, 1603–1923*. New York.

Bergin, J.J. 1910 *History of the Ancient Order of Hibernians*. Dublin.

Bew, P. 1994 The real importance of Roger Casement. *History Ireland* **2** (2).

Bew, P. 1996 *John Redmond*. Dublin.

Bew, P. 2007 *Ireland: the politics of enmity, 1789–2006*. Oxford.

Birmingham, G.A. 1919 *An Irishman looks at his world*. London.

Birrell, A. 1937 *Things past redress*. London.

Boland, K. 1977 *Up Dev*. Dublin.

Bolger, D. (ed.) 1989 *16 on 16*. Dublin.

Bouch, J.J. 1933 Republican Proclamation of 1916. *Bibliographical Society of Ireland* **5** (3).

Bouchier-Hayes, F. 2008a An Irishman's Diary: Darrell Figgis. *Irish Times*, 21 April 2008.

Bouchier-Hayes, F. 2008b An Irishman's Diary: The Irish Republican Brotherhood. *Irish Times*, 4 August 2008.

Bouchier-Hayes, F. 2008c An Irishman's Diary: Cathal Brugha. *Irish Times*, 18 August 2008.

Bouchier-Hayes, F. 2009 An Irishman's Diary: Bulmer Hobson. *Irish Times*, 11 August 2009.

Bourke, M. 1967 *The Ó Rahilly*. Tralee.

Bourke, M. 1968 Thomas MacDonagh's role in the plans for the 1916 Rising. *Irish Sword* (1968).

Bowen, E. 1951 *The Shelbourne: a centre in Dublin life for more than a century*. London.

Bowman, T. 2002 The Ulster Volunteers 1913–1914: force or farce? *History Ireland* **10** (1).

Boyce, D.G. and Hazelhurst, C. 1977 The unknown chief secretary. *Irish Historical Studies* **20** (79).

Boyle, A. 1977 *The riddle of Erskine Childers*.

London.

Boyle, J.F. 1916 *The Irish rebellion of 1916.* London.

Boyle, J.W. 1967 Irish Labour and the Rising. *Éire-Ireland* **2**.

Boyle, J.W. 1986 *Leaders and workers.* Cork.

Bradbridge, Lt Col. E.U. 1928 *Fifty-ninth Division, 1915–1918, a compilation.* Chesterfield.

Brennan, J. 1958 The Castle Document. *Irish Times*, 28 March 1958.

Brennan, J. 1966 Mendicity Institution area. *Capuchin Annual* (1966).

Brennan, L.M. 1926 We surrender. *An tÓglach*, 12 June 1926.

Brennan-Whitmore, W.J. 1917 *With the Irish in Frongoch.* Dublin.

Brennan-Whitmore, W.J. 1926 The occupation of the North Earl Street area. *An tÓglach*, 30 January and 6 February 1926.

Brennan-Whitmore, W.J. 1953 The North Earl Street area. *Irish Weekly Independent*, August–September 1953.

Brennan-Whitmore, W.J. 1966 How long could they hold out? *Irish Independent*, 11 April 1966.

Brennan-Whitmore, W.J. 1996 *Dublin burning: the Easter Rising from behind the barricades.* Dublin.

Brewer, J.D. 1990 *The Royal Irish Constabulary: an oral history.* Belfast.

Briollay, S. [writing as Roger Chauvire] 1922 *Ireland in rebellion.* Dublin.

Browne, Revd P. (ed.) 1917 *Aftermath of Easter Week.*

Brugha, M. MacSwiney 2005 *History's daughter.* Dublin.

Burke, T. 2005 The other women of 1916. *20th Century Social Perspectives, 20th Century Contemporary History* **5**.

Butler, R.M. 1916 The reconstruction of O'Connell Street. *Studies: The Irish Jesuit Quarterly Review* **5**.

Callan, P. 1987 Recruiting for the British Army in Ireland during the First World War. *Irish Sword* **17** (66).

Callender, I. 1939 A diary of Easter Week. *Dublin Brigade Review* (1939).

Campbell, Cmdt L. 2006a A military analysis of the Rising. *An Cosantoir* (April/May 2006).

Campbell, Cmdt L. 2006b A tale of two soldiers. *An Cosantoir* (April/May 2006).

Canavan, T. 2006 Pearse Museum. *History Ireland* **14** (2).

Cardozo, N. 1979 *Maud Gonne.* London.

Carroll, F.M. 1978 *American opinion and the Irish question, 1910–1923.* Dublin.

Carty, J. 1951 *Ireland—from the Great Famine to the Treaty of 1921.* Dublin.

Carty, X. 1978 *In bloody protest: the tragedy of Patrick Pearse.* Dublin.

Casement, Sir R. 1914 *Ireland, Germany and the freedom of the seas.* New York.

Casement, Sir R. 1958 *The crime against Europe* (ed. H.O. Mackey). Dublin.

Caulfield, M. 1995 *The Easter Rebellion, Dublin 1916.* Dublin.

Ceannt, Á. 1946 Looking back to Easter Week. *The Leader*, 20 April 1946.

Ceannt, É. 1914 The founding of the Irish Volunteers. *Irish Volunteer*, 20 June 1914.

Chatterton, E.K. 1934 *Danger zone: the story of the Queenstown command.* London.

Clare, A. 2011 *Unlikely rebels: the Gifford girls and the fight for Irish freedom.* Cork.

Clarke, K. 1997 *Revolutionary woman. My fight for Ireland's freedom* (ed. H. Litton). Dublin.

Clarke, T. 1970 *Glimpses of an Irish felon's prison life* (with foreword by P.S. O'Hegarty). Cork.

Clery, A.E. 1917 Pearse, MacDonagh and Plunkett: an appreciation. *Studies: The Irish Jesuit Quarterly Review* **6**.

Clery, A.E. 1919 The Gaelic League, 1893–1919. *Studies: The Irish Jesuit Quarterly Review* **8**.

Clery, A.E. 1922 A review of Pearse's political writings and speeches. *Studies: The Irish Jesuit Quarterly Review* **11**.

Clifford, B. 1997 *War, insurrection and election in Ireland, 1914–21.* Belfast.

Clifford, B. 2002 *Casement as traitor patriot.* London.

Coady, S. 1966 Remembering St John's Convent. *Capuchin Annual* (1966).

Coakley, J. 1983 Patrick Pearse and the 'noble lie' of Irish nationalism. *Studies in Conflict and Violence* **62**.

Coates, T. (ed.) 2000 *The Irish uprising,*

1914–1921: papers from the British Parliamentary Archive. London.

Coffey, T.M. 1969 *Agony at Easter.* London.

'Coilin' 1917 *Patrick H. Pearse: a sketch of his life.* Dublin.

Collins, L. 2012 *16 Lives: James Connolly.* Dublin.

Collins, L., Kostick, C. and MacThomais, S. 2004 Tragedy in the Connolly family. *History Ireland* 12 (3).

Collins, S. 1997 *The Cosgrave legacy.* Dublin.

Colum, P. 1931 The career of Roger Casement. *Dublin Magazine* (October–December 1931).

Colum, P. 1959 *Arthur Griffith.* Dublin.

Comerford, A. 1969 *The Easter Rising, Dublin 1916.* New York.

Comerford, M. 1986 Women in struggle. In P. McGlynn (ed.), *Eiri amach na casca.* Dublin.

Conlon, L. 1969 *Cumann na mBan and the women of Ireland, 1913–1972.* Kilkenny.

Connell, J.E.A. Jnr 2006 *Where's where in Dublin: a directory of historic locations 1913–1923.* Dublin.

Connell, J.E.A. Jnr 2009 *Dublin in rebellion.* Dublin.

Connell, J.E.A. Jnr 2011a The Proclamation of the Irish Republic. *History Ireland* 19 (1).

Connell, J.E.A. Jnr 2011b Role of the GAA in formation of nationalism. *History Ireland* 19 (2).

Connell, J.E.A. Jnr 2011c St Enda's School/St Ita's School. *History Ireland* 19 (3).

Connell, J.E.A. Jnr 2011d The Irish Republican Brotherhood. *History Ireland* 19 (6).

Connell, J.E.A. Jnr 2012a Tom Clarke's return to Ireland. *History Ireland* 20 (1).

Connell, J.E.A. Jnr 2012b Home Rule rally on O'Connell Street, March 1912. *History Ireland* 20 (2).

Connell, J.E.A. Jnr 2012c Liberty Hall. *History Ireland* 20 (3).

Connell, J.E.A. Jnr 2012d Reaction to Home Rule in Ulster and the Ulster Covenant. *History Ireland* 20 (5).

Connell, J.E.A. Jnr 2012e Fianna na hÉireann. *History Ireland* 20 (6).

Connell, J.E.A. Jnr 2013a Irish Women's Franchise League/Irish Women's Workers' Union. *History Ireland* 21 (1).

Connell, J.E.A. Jnr 2013b 'A Soldier's Song'/*Amhrán na bhFiann. History Ireland* 21 (2).

Connell, J.E.A. Jnr 2013c Founding of Cumann na mBan. *History Ireland* 21 (3).

Connell, J.E.A. Jnr 2013d Founding of the Irish Citizen Army. *History Ireland* 21 (5).

Connell, J.E.A. Jnr 2013e Founding of the Irish Volunteers. *History Ireland* 21 (6).

Connell, J.E.A. Jnr 2014a Larne gunrunning. *History Ireland* 22 (2).

Connell, J.E.A. Jnr 2014b Howth/Kilcoole gunrunning. *History Ireland* 22 (3).

Connolly, J. 1898 *The workers' republic.* Dublin.

Connolly, J. [writing as 'Setanta'] 1899 The Mendicity and its guests. *Workers' Republic*, 27 August 1899.

Connolly, J. 1913 Arms and the man. *Irish Worker*, 13 December 1913.

Connolly, J. 1915 *The re-conquest of Ireland.* Dublin.

Connolly, J. 1916a The programme of Labour. *Workers' Republic*, 19 January 1916.

Connolly, J. 1916b Cannon fodder for British imperialism. *Workers' Republic*, 12 February 1916.

Connolly, J. 1916c We will rise again. *Workers' Republic*, 25 March 1916.

Connolly, J. 1916d The call to arms. *Workers' Republic*, 1 April 1916.

Connolly, J. 1916e The Irish flag. *Workers' Republic*, 8 April 1916.

Connolly, J. 1916f Labour and Ireland. *Workers' Republic*, 22 April 1916.

Connolly, J. and De Leon, D. (n.d.) *Connolly/De Leon Controversy on Wages, Marriage and the Church* (undated pamphlet).

Connolly, J. and Walker, W. (n.d.) *The Connolly/Walker Controversy on Socialist Unity in Ireland* (undated pamphlet). Cork.

Connolly, J. 1949 *Labour and Easter Week: a selection from the writings of James Connolly* (ed. D. Ryan). Dublin.

Connolly, L. 2002 [2003] *The Irish women's*

movement. New York [Dublin].

Connolly, M. 1952 James Connolly: socialist and patriot. *Studies: The Irish Jesuit Quarterly Review* **41**.

Connolly, M. 1966 City Hall area. *Capuchin Annual* (1966).

Connolly, N. 1918 *The Irish rebellion of 1916, or, The unbroken tradition.* New York.

Connolly, N. (O'Brien) 1975 *Portrait of a rebel father.* Dublin and London.

Connolly, N. (O'Brien) 1981 *We shall rise again.* London.

Connolly-Heron, I. 1966a James Connolly, the search for roots. *Liberty* (May 1966).

Connolly-Heron, I. 1966b James Connolly—a biography. *Liberty* (August 1966).

Conroy, J. 2005 The Plough and Stars: sixteen characters in search of analysis. *Red Banner* **21**.

Coogan, O. 2013 *Politics and war in Meath— 1913–1923.* Meath County Council.

Coogan, T.P. 1966 *Ireland since the Rising.* London.

Coogan, T.P. 1990 *Michael Collins.* London.

Coogan, T.P. 1993 *De Valera: Long Fellow, long shadow.* London.

Coogan, T.P. 2001 *1916: the Easter Rising.* London.

Cooke, P. 1986 *Scéal Scoil Éanna.* Dublin.

Cooney, A. 1930 The Marrowbone Lane Post. *An Phoblacht,* 26 May 1930.

Corkery, D. (n.d.) *What's this about the G.A.A.?* (undated pamphlet).

Cornish, V. 1916 The strategic geography of the British Empire. *Royal Colonial Institute Journal* (February 1916).

Costello, F. 2003 *The Irish Revolution and its aftermath, 1916–1923.* Dublin.

Cottrell, P. 2006 *The Anglo-Irish War: the Troubles of 1913–1922.* Oxford.

Coulter, C. 1993 *The hidden tradition: feminism, women, and nationalism in Ireland.* Cork.

Courtney, D.A. 1916 [1980] *Reminiscences of the Easter Rising.* Nenagh.

Cowell, J. 1997 *Dublin's famous people and where they lived.* Dublin.

Cowell, J. 2005 *A noontide blazing. Brigid Lyons Thornton: rebel, soldier, doctor.* Dublin.

Coxhead, E. 1965 *Daughters of Erin.* London.

Coyle, E. 1933 The History of Cumann na mBan. *An Phoblacht,* 8 April 1933.

Crawford, F. 1947 *Guns for Ulster.* Belfast.

Creel, G. 1919 *Ireland's fight for freedom.* New York.

Cronin, S. 1966 *Our own red blood: the story of the 1916 Rising.* Dublin.

Cronin, S. 1972 *The McGarrity Papers.* Tralee.

Cronin, S. 1978 *Young Connolly.* Dublin.

Cuffe, T.S. 1942 They lit a torch. *Capuchin Annual* (1942).

Cullen, C. (ed.) 2013 *The world upturning: Elsie Henry's Irish wartime diaries, 1913–1919.* Dublin.

Cullen, M. and Luddy, M. (eds) 1995 *Women, power and consciousness.* Dublin.

Cullen, M. and Luddy, M. 2001 *Female activists: Irish women and the change, 1900–1960.* Dublin.

Curran, C.P. 1966 Griffith, MacNeill and Pearse. *Studies: The Irish Jesuit Quarterly Review* (Spring 1966).

Curran, J. 1975 The decline and fall of the I.R.B. *Éire-Ireland* **10** (1).

Curry, C.E. 1922 *Sir Roger Casement's diaries.* Munich.

Czira, S.G. 1974 *The years flew by.* Dublin.

Dalton, C. 1929 *With the Dublin Brigade.* London.

Daly, D. 1974 *The young Douglas Hyde.* Dublin.

Daly, M.E. (ed.) 2006 *Roger Casement in Irish and world history.* Dublin.

Daly, M.E. and O'Callaghan, M. (eds) 2007 *1916 in 1966: commemorating the Easter Rising.* Dublin.

D'Arcy, W. 1947 *The Fenian Movement in the United States.* Washington, DC.

Dargan, P. 2005–6 The Fianna Eireann and the War of Independence—a personal experience. *Irish Sword* **25**.

Davison, J. 2005 Feature: Remembering James Connolly. *An Phoblacht,* 9 May 2005.

Deasy, J. 1963 [2004] *The fiery cross: the story of Jim Larkin.* Dublin.

De Barra, É. 1969 A valiant woman: Margaret Mary Pearse. *Capuchin Annual*

(1969).

De Blacam, A. 1918 *Towards the Republic*. Dublin.

De Blaghd, E. 1962 Ireland in 1915. *An tÓglach* 1 (5).

DeBurca, M. 1980 *The G.A.A.: a history of the Gaelic Athletic Association*. Dublin.

De Burca, S. 1958 *The Soldier's Song: the story of Peadar Kearney*. Dublin.

Deeney, A.T. 2001 What effects did Eoin MacNeill's Countermanding Order have on the Easter Rising in 1916? Unpublished MA thesis, University of Ulster.

Dempsey, J. 1993 Jennie Wyse Power, 1858–1941. Unpublished MA thesis, St Patrick's College, Maynooth.

Denieffe, J. 1906 [1969] *A personal narrative of the Fenian Brotherhood (Irish Republican Brotherhood)*. New York [Dublin].

Denman, T. 1994 'The Red Livery of Shame': the campaign against army recruitment in Ireland, 1899–1914. *Irish Historical Studies* 29 (114), 208–33.

De Paor, L. 1997 *On the Easter Proclamation and other declarations*. Dublin.

Depuis, N. 2009 *Mna na hÉireann: the women who shaped Ireland*. Cork.

Derwin, D. 2000 The taming of Jim Larkin. *Red Banner* 2.

Desmond, S. 1923 *The drama of Sinn Féin*. London.

Devine, F. (ed.) 2013 *A capital in conflict: Dublin City and the 1913 Lockout*. Dublin.

Devoy, J. 1929 *Recollections of an Irish rebel*. New York.

Dillon, G.P. 1936a Casement and Easter Week. *Irish Press*, 3 January 1936.

Dillon, G.P. 1936b 'How much did the Castle know? *Irish Press*, 14 January 1936.

Dillon, G.P. 1958 Joseph Plunkett: origin and background. *University Review* (1958).

Dillon, G.P. 1960 The Irish Republican Brotherhood. *University Review* 2 (9).

Dillon, G.P. 1968 Joseph Plunkett's diary of his journey to Germany. *University Review* (1968).

Dillon, G.P. 2007 *All in the blood: a memoir of the Plunkett family, the 1916 Rising, and the War of Independence* (ed. H. O'Brochlain). Dublin.

Doerries, R. 2000 *Prelude to the Easter Rising: Sir Roger Casement in Imperial Germany*. London.

Doherty, G. and Keogh, D. 2003 *De Valera's Ireland*. Cork.

Doherty, G. and Keogh, D. (eds) 2007 *1916. The long revolution*. Cork.

Doherty, S. 1995 Elizabeth O'Farrell and the women of 1916. Unpublished MA thesis, National University of Ireland.

Doherty, S. 1998 Will the real James Connolly please stand up? *International Socialism* 80.

Donnelly, N. 1930 With the Citizen's Army in Stephen's Green. *An Phoblacht*, 19 April 1930.

Donnelly, S. 1917 Mount Street Bridge. *Catholic Bulletin* (October, 1917).

Donnelly, S. 1922 With the 3rd Battalion. *Poblacht na hÉireann*, 20 April 1922.

Doolan, J. 1918 The South Dublin Union [a four-part account]. *Catholic Bulletin* (March, April, May and June 1918).

Dooley, P. 1944 *Under the banner of Connolly*. London.

Dore, É. 1968 Seán MacDermott as I knew him. *Leitrim Guardian*, Christmas 1968.

[Douglas, Harry] 2005–6 The 1916 diary of 2nd Lieutenant Harry Douglas, Sherwood Foresters. *Irish Sword* 25.

Doyle, J., Clarke, F., Connaughton, E. and Somerville, O. 2002 *An introduction to the Bureau of Military History, 1913–1921*. Dublin.

Doyle, K. 2007 A revolutionary misfit: Jack White. *Red Banner* 24.

Doyle, S. 1932 With Pearse in Arbour Hill. *Irish Press*, 3 May 1932.

Duff, C. 1966 *Six days to shake an empire*. London.

Duff, D. 1934 *Sword for hire*. London.

Duff, D. 1940 *The rough with the smooth*. London.

Duffy, J. 2013 Children of the Revolution. *History Ireland* 21 (3).

Duggan, J.P. 1966 Asserting it in arms. *An Cosantoir* 26.

Duggan, J.P. 1970 German arms and the

1916 Rising. *An Cosantoir* 30.

Duggan, J.P. 1995 Poltergeist pistol. *History Ireland* 3.

Dunleavy, M. 2002 *Dublin barracks*. Dublin.

Dunsany, Lord 1939 Recollections of 1916. *Irish Digest* (April 1939).

Durney, J. 2004 *The Volunteer: uniforms, weapons, and history of the Irish Republican Army, 1913–1917*. Naas.

Dwane, D.T. 1922 *The early life of Éamon de Valera*. Dublin.

Dwyer, T.R. 1980 *Éamon de Valera*. Dublin.

Dwyer, T.R. 2014 *Thomas MacDonagh*. Dublin.

Ebenezer, L. 2006 *Fron-Goch and the birth of the IRA*. Llanrwst.

Edmunds, Capt. G.J. 1960 *The 2/6th Battalion: the Sherwood Foresters, 1914–1918*. Chesterfield.

Edwards, O.D. 1987 *Éamon de Valera*. Cardiff.

Edwards, O.D. and Pyle, F. (eds) 1968 *1916: the Easter Rising*. London.

Edwards, O.D. and Ransom, B. (eds) 1973 *James Connolly: selected political writings*. London.

Edwards, R.D. 1977 *Patrick Pearse: the triumph of failure*. London.

Edwards, R.D. 1981 *James Connolly*. Dublin.

Ellis, P.B. (ed.) 1973 *James Connolly: selected writings*. Harmondsworth.

Ervine, St J. 1917 The story of the Irish rebellion. *Century Magazine* (1917).

Fallon, L. 2013 *Dublin Fire Brigade and the Irish Revolution*. Dublin.

Fanning, R. 2013 *Fatal path: British government and Irish revolution 1910–1922*. London.

Feeney, B. 2014 *Seán MacDiarmada*. Dublin.

Feeney, T. 2008 *Seán MacEntee: a political life*. Dublin.

Figgis, D. 1917 *A chronicle of jails*. Dublin.

Figgis, D. 1924 *Recollections of the Irish war*. London.

Fingall, Elizabeth, Countess of 1937 [1991] *Seventy years young*. London [Dublin].

Finnan, J.P. 2004 *John Redmond and Irish unity, 1912–1918*. Syracuse, NY.

Fitzgerald, D. 1939 *Prelude to statecraft*. London.

Fitzgerald, D. 1966 Inside the GPO. *Irish Times Supplement*, 7 April 1966.

Fitzgerald, D. 1968 *Desmond's Rising*. Dublin.

Fitzgerald, G. 1966 The significance of 1916. *Studies: The Irish Jesuit Quarterly Review* (Spring 1966).

Fitzgerald, W.D. (ed.) (n.d.) The historic Rising of Easter Week, 1916. *The Voice of Ireland* (undated).

Fitzgibbon, C. 2004a Easter 1916, Part I. *An Phoblacht*, 5 April 2004.

Fitzgibbon, C. 2004b Easter 1916, Part II. *An Phoblacht*, 7 April 2004.

Fitzgibbon, S. 1949 The Easter Rising from the inside. *Irish Times*, 18–21 April 1949.

Fitzhenry, E.C. 1935 *Nineteen sixteen—an anthology*. Dublin.

Fitzpatrick, D. 1986 *Ireland and the First World War*. Dublin.

Fitzpatrick, D. 2002 'Decidedly a personality': de Valera's performance as a convict, 1916–1917. *History Ireland* 10 (2).

Flanagan, Fr J. 1918 The General Post Office area. *Catholic Bulletin* (August 1918).

Fox, R.M. 1935 *Rebel Irishwomen*. Dublin and Cork.

Fox, R.M. 1938 *Green banners: the story of the Irish struggle*. London.

Fox, R.M. 1944 [2014] *History of the Irish Citizen Army*. Dublin.

Fox, R.M. 1946 *James Connolly, the forerunner*. Tralee.

Fox, R.M. 1947 How the women helped. In The Kerryman, *Dublin's fighting story 1916–1921, told by the men who made it*. Tralee.

Foy, M.T. and Barton, B. 1999 *The Easter Rising*. Stroud.

French, G. 1931 *The life of Field Marshal Sir John French*. London.

Gallagher, F. [writing as David Hogan] 1953 *The four glorious years*. Dublin.

Gallagher, M. 2014 *Éamonn Ceannt*. Dublin.

Garnham, N. 2004 Accounting for the early success of the Gaelic Athletic Association. *Irish Historical Studies* 34 (133).

Garvin, T. 1986 The anatomy of a nationalist revolution: Ireland,

1858–1928. *Contemporary Studies in Society and History* (July 1986).

Gaughan, J.A. 1977 *Austin Stack: portrait of a separatist*. Dublin.

Gerson, G. 1995 Cultural subversion and the background of the Irish 'Easter Poets'. *Journal of Contemporary History* **30** (2).

Gibbon, M. 1966 Murder in Portobello Barracks. *Dublin Magazine* **5**.

Gibney, J. 2013 *Seán Heuston*. Dublin.

Gilley, S. 1986 Pearse's sacrifice: Christ and Cuchulainn crucified and risen in the Easter Rising, 1916. In Y. Alexander and A. O'Day (eds), *Ireland's terrorist dilemma*. Dortrecht.

Gillis, E. 2013 *Revolution in Dublin: a photographic history 1913–1923*. Cork.

Gilmore, G. (n.d.) *The relevance of James Connolly in Ireland today*. Dublin.

Ginnell, L. 1918 *D.O.R.A. at Westminster*. Dublin.

Githens-Mazer, J. 2006 *Myths and memories of the Easter Rising: cultural and political nationalism in Ireland*. Dublin.

Goldring, D. [writing as 'An Englishman'] 1917 *Dublin explorations and reflections*. Dublin.

Golway, T. 1998 *Irish rebel: John Devoy and America's fight for Irish freedom*. New York.

Good, J. 1996 *Enchanted by dreams: the journal of a revolutionary* (ed. M. Good). Tralee.

Gray, B. [E.] 1948 A memory of Easter Week. *Capuchin Annual* (1948).

Greaves, C.D. 1961 *The life and times of James Connolly*. London.

Greaves, C.D. 1968 James Connolly, Marxist. *Marxism Today* (June 1968).

Greaves, C.D. 1982 *The Irish Transport and General Workers' Union: the formative years: 1909–1923*. Dublin.

Greaves, C.D. 1991 *1916 as history: the myth of the blood sacrifice*. Dublin.

Green, A.S. 1922 Arthur Griffith. *Studies: The Irish Jesuit Quarterly Review* **11**.

Gregory, P. 1917 Poets of the insurrection: John F. MacEntee. *Studies: The Irish Jesuit Quarterly Review* **6**.

Grenan, J. 1916 After the surrender. *Wolfe Tone Annual*, Special 1916 Edition.

Grenan, J. 1917a Events of Easter Week. *Catholic Bulletin* (June 1917).

Grenan, J. 1917b Story of the surrender. *Catholic Bulletin* (June 1917).

Griffith, A. 1904 *The resurrection of Hungary: a parallel for Ireland*. Dublin.

Griffith, K. and O'Grady, T. (eds) 2002 *Ireland's unfinished revolution: an oral history*. Boulder, CO. [First published as *Curious journey: an oral history of Ireland's unfinished revolution* (London, 1982).]

Grob-Fitzgibbon, B. 2008 *Turning points of the Irish Revolution: the British government, intelligence and the cost of indifference, 1912–1921*. Dublin.

Gunther, J. 1936 Inside de Valera. *Harper's Magazine* (August 1936).

Gwynn, D. 1923 Patrick Pearse. *Dublin Review* (January–March 1923).

Gwynn, D. 1931 *The life and death of Roger Casement*. London.

Gwynn, D. 1932 *The life of John Redmond*. London.

Gwynn, D. 1933 *De Valera*. London.

Gwynn, D. 1948 *Young Ireland*. Cork.

Gwynn, D. 1950 *The history of Partition, 1912–1925*. Dublin.

Hadden, P. 1986 *Divide and rule*. London and Dublin.

Hall, W.G. 1920 *The Green Triangle: being the history of the 2/5th Battalion The Sherwood Foresters (Notts & Derby Regiment) in the Great European War, 1914–1918*. Garden City.

Hally, Col. P.J. 1966 The Easter Rising in Dublin: a military evaluation of Easter Week. *An Cosantoir* **7** (29).

Hally, Gen. P.J. 1966–7 The Easter Rising in Dublin, the military aspects (Parts 1 and 2). *Irish Sword* **7** (29) (1966), and **8** (30) (1967).

Hartnett, S. 1971 Comradeship Kilmainham. *Irish Press*, 30 December 1971.

Haswell, J. 1973 *Citizen armies*. London.

Haverty, A. 1988 *Countess Markievicz: an independent life*. London.

Hay, M. 2005 Bulmer Hobson: the rise and fall of an Irish nationalist, 1900–16. Unpublished Ph.D thesis, University College Dublin.

Hay, M. 2009 *Bulmer Hobson and the nationalist movement in twentieth-century Ireland*. Manchester.

Haydon, A. 1976 *Sir Matthew Nathan*. Queensland.

Hayes, A. (ed.) 2000 *The years flew by: recollections of Madame Sydney Gifford Czira*. Galway.

Hayes, A. and Urquhart, D. 2001 *The Irish women's history reader*. London.

Hayes, J. 1919 *Patrick H. Pearse: storyteller*. Dublin.

Hayes-McCoy, G.A. (ed.) 1964 *The Irish at war*. Cork.

Headlam, M. 1947 *Irish reminiscences*. London.

Hearn, D. 1992 The *Irish Citizen, 1914–1916: nationalism, feminism, militarism. Canadian Journal of Irish Studies* **18** (1).

Hegarty, P. 2010 *The Easter Rising: a momentous week in Irish history seen through the eyes of a young boy*. Dublin.

Hegarty, S. and O'Toole, F. 2006 *The* Irish Times *Book of the 1916 Rising*. Dublin.

Helferty, S. 2006 1916 in the de Valera Papers. *History Ireland* **14** (2).

Henry, R.M. 1922 Arthur Griffith. *Studies: The Irish Jesuit Quarterly Review* **11**.

Henry, W. 2005 *Supreme sacrifice: the story of Éamonn Ceannt, 1881–1916*. Cork.

Henry, W. 2014 *John MacBride*. Dublin.

Hepburn, A.C. 1998 *Ireland, 1905–1925. Volume II*. Newtownards.

Herlihy, J. 1997 *The Royal Irish Constabulary*. Dublin.

Herlihy, J. 2001 *The Dublin Metropolitan Police: a complete alphabetical list of officers and men, 1836–1925*. Dublin.

Heuston, J.M. 1966 *Headquarters Battalion, Army of the Irish Republic, Easter Week 1916*. Carlow.

Higgins, R. 2013 *Transforming 1916: meaning, memory and lore of the fiftieth anniversary of the Easter rising*. Cork.

Higgins, R. and Ui Chollatain, R. (eds) 2009 *The life and after-life of P.H. Pearse*. Dublin.

Higgins, R., Holohan, C. and O'Donnell, C. 2006 1966 and all that. *History Ireland* **14** (2).

Hill, M. 2003 *Women in Ireland*. Belfast.

Hobson, B. 1918 *A short history of the Irish Volunteers, 1913–1916*. Dublin.

Hobson, B. 1931 The origin of Oglaigh na hÉireann. *An tÓglach* (June 1931).

Hobson, B. 1968 *Ireland, yesterday and tomorrow*. Tralee.

Hoff, J. and Coulter, M. (eds) 1995 Irish women's voices: past and present. *Journal of Women's History* **6** (4) and **7** (1).

Hoff, M. 2006 The foundations of the Fenian uprising. Senior thesis, United States Military Academy.

Hoff, M. 2007 A successful failure: the catalyst of the 1916 Easter Rising. MA thesis, United States Military Academy.

Holohan, P. 1942 Four Courts area. *Capuchin Annual* (1966).

Holt, E. 1960 *Protest in arms: the Irish Troubles, 1916–1923*. London.

Hopkinson, M. (ed.) 1998 *Frank Henderson's Easter Rising: recollections of a Dublin Volunteer*. Cork.

Horgan, J.J. 1948 *Parnell to Pearse*. Dublin.

Horgan, J.J. 1997 *Lemass*. Dublin.

Hourihane, A.M. 2014 Children of the Revolution. *Irish Times*, 21 March 2014.

Hoy, H.C. 1932 *40 O.B.* or *How the war was won*. London.

Hughes, B. 2012 *Michael Mallin*. Dublin.

Humphreys, R. 1966 A rebel's diary. *The Belvederian* (Belvedere College Annual) **25** (2).

Hunt, G. 2009 *Blood upon the rose. Easter 1916: the rebellion that set Ireland free*. Dublin.

Hyland, J.L. 1997 *Life and times of James Connolly*. Dundalk.

Igoe, V. 2001 *Dublin burial grounds and graveyards*. Dublin.

Ireland, J. de Courcy 1966 *The sea and the 1916 Rising*. Dublin.

Irish Life 1916 The record of the Irish rebellion of 1916 [pamphlet].

Irish Republican Digest 1965 *Irish Republican Digest, featuring the Rising of 1916, Book 1*. National Publications Committee, Cork.

Irish Times 1917 [1998] *1916 Rebellion handbook*. Dublin.

Jackson, A. 1993 Larne gunrunning, 1914.

History Ireland **1** (1).

Jackson, A. 2004 *Home Rule, an Irish history 1800–2000*. Oxford.

James, L. 1994 *The rise and fall of the British Empire*. London.

James, W. 1956 *The code breakers of Room 40: the story of Admiral Sir William Hall, genius of British counter-intelligence*. New York.

Jamie, Lt Col. J.P.W. 1931 *The 177th Brigade, 1914–1918*. Leicester.

Jeffery, K. 1994 Irish culture and the Great War. *Bullan* (1994).

Jeffery, K. (ed.) 1999 *The Sinn Féin Rising as they saw it* [incorporating *The Sinn Féin Rising as I saw it* by M. Norway and *Experiences in war* by A. Hamilton Norway]. Dublin.

Jeffrey, K. 2000 *Ireland and the Great War*. Cambridge.

Jenkins, R. 1964 *Asquith*. London.

Johnson, T. 1918 *A handbook for rebels: a guide to successful defiance of the British government*. Dublin.

Johnston, A., Larragy, J. and McWilliams, E. 1990 *Connolly: a Marxist analysis*. Dublin.

Jones, F.P. 1917 *History of the Sinn Féin movement and the Irish rebellion of 1916*. New York.

Jones, M. 1988 *These obstreperous lassies: a history of the Irish Women Workers' Union*. Dublin.

Jordan, A. 1991 *Major John MacBride: MacDonagh and MacBride, Connolly and Pearse*. Westport.

Joy, M. (ed.) 1916 [2007] *The Irish rebellion of 1916 and its martyrs: Erin's tragic Easter*. New York.

Joyce, J. 2009 June 30th, 1915: O'Donovan Rossa's death famous for oratory at grave. *Irish Times*, 29 June 2009.

Joyce, M. 1966 The story of Limerick and Kerry in 1916. *Capuchin Annual* (1966).

Joyce, T. 1996 The American Civil War and Irish nationalism. *History Ireland* **4** (2).

Joye, L. 2010 TSS *Helga*. *History Ireland* **18** (2).

Joye, L. and Malone, B. 2006 The Roll of Honour of 1916. *History Ireland* **14** (2).

Kain, R. 1980 A diary of Easter Week: one Dubliner's experience. *Irish University Review* **10**.

Kavanaugh, Sub-Lt P. 1966 John Mitchel's place in Irish military thinking. *An Cosantoir* **26**.

Kautt, W.H. 1999 *The Anglo-Irish War, 1916–1921*. Westport, CT, and London.

Kearns, L. 1922 *In times of peril*. Dublin.

Kee, R. 1972 *The green flag* [combining three separate volumes entitled *The most distressful country*, *The bold Fenian men* and *Ourselves alone*]. London.

Keith, J. 2006 *The GPO and the Easter Rising*. Dublin.

Kelly, M. 2006 *The Fenian ideal and Irish nationalism, 1882–1916*. Dublin.

Kelly, M. 2008 Nationalism's pilot light? *History Ireland* **16** (6).

Kelly, P. 1966 The women of Easter Week: Helena Molony. *Evening Herald*, 31 March 1966.

Kelly, S. [published anonymously] 1916 *Pictorial review of 1916*. Dublin.

Kelly, T. 1942 I remember. *Capuchin Annual* (1942).

Kendall, T. 2013 Lost memoir tells how James Connolly returned to his faith before execution. *Irish Independent*, 25 May 2013.

Kennedy, C.M. 2003 Genesis of the rising, 1912–1916: a transformation of nationalist opinion? Unpublished Ph.D thesis, University College Cork.

Kennerk, B. 2012 *Moore Street—the story of Dublin's market district*. Cork.

Kennerk, B. 2013 Compensating for the Rising. *History Ireland* **21** (2).

Kenny, M. 1993 *The road to freedom: photographs and memorabilia from the 1916 Rising and afterwards*. Dublin.

Keny, C. 2012 Face of hope for all that might have been. *Sunday Independent*, 8 January 2012.

Keogh, D. 1978 William Martin Murphy and the origins of the 1913 Lockout. *Saothar* **4**.

Kerryman, The 1947 *Dublin's fighting story, 1916–1921: told by the men who made it*. Tralee.

Kilcullen, J. 1967 Appreciation: Headmaster of St Enda's. *Éire-Ireland* (Summer 1967).

Killeen, R. 1995 *The Easter Rising*. Hove.

Kostick, C. 2013 James Connolly in the Bureau of Military History. *Irish Marxist Review* **1** (5).

Kostick, C. 2014 *Michael O'Hanrahan.* Dublin.

Kostick, C. and Collins, L. 2000 *The Easter Rising: a guide to Dublin in 1916.* Dublin.

Laing, Cmdt V., Donovan, Sgt C. and Manning, Pte A. 2006 The Ashbourne engagement. *An Cosantoir* (April/May 2006).

Larkin, E. 1965 *James Larkin: Irish Labour, 1876–1947.* London.

Larkin, F.M. 2006 A great daily organ: *The Freeman's Journal*, 1763–1924. *History Ireland* **14** (3).

Larkin, J. Jnr (n.d.) *In the footsteps of Big Jim: a family biography.* Dublin.

Lawless, Cmdt F. 2006 Personal recollections: Ashbourne. *An Cosantoir* (April/May 2006).

Lawless, Col. J.V. 1926 Ashbourne. *An tÓglach*, 31 July 1926.

Lawless, Col. J.V. 1941 Ashbourne. *An Cosantoir* (April 1941).

Lawless, Col. J.V. 1946 Thomas Ashe. *An Cosantoir* (November 1946).

Lawless, Col. J.V. 1966 The fight at Ashbourne. *Capuchin Annual* (1966).

Lawless, Col. J.V. 2006 From the archives: a contemporary view. *An Cosantoir* (April/May 2006).

Lawlor, B. 1991 *The ultimate Dublin guide.* Dublin.

Lawlor, D. 2009 *Na Fianna Éireann and the Irish Revolution—1909 to 1923.* Dublin.

Lee, J.J. 2006 1916 as virtual history. *History Ireland* **14** (2).

Leiberson, G. (ed.) 1966 *The Irish uprising, 1916–1922.* New York.

Lemass, S. 1966 I remember 1916. *Studies: The Irish Jesuit Quarterly Review* (Spring 1966).

Lennon, M.J. 1922 A retrospect. *Banba* (April 1922).

Lennon, M.J. 1948 Easter Week diary. *Irish Times*, 29 March–3 April 1948.

Lennon, M.J. 1949 'The Easter Rising from the inside': the account of Seán Fitzgibbon. *Irish Times*, 18–22 April 1949.

LeRoux, L.N. 1932 *Patrick H. Pearse* (trans. D. Ryan). Dublin.

LeRoux, L.N. 1936 *Tom Clarke and the Irish freedom movement.* Dublin.

Leslie, S. (ed.) 1924 *Memoirs of Brigadier-General Gordon Shephard.* Privately printed.

Leslie, S. (n.d.) *The Irish tangle for English readers.* London.

Levenson, L. 1983 *With wooden sword: a portrait of Francis Sheehy Skeffington.* Boston, MA.

Levenson, L. and Natterstad, J. 1986 *Hanna Sheehy Skeffington: Irish feminist.* Syracuse, NY.

Levenson, S. 1973 *James Connolly: a biography.* London.

Levenson, S. 1977 *Maud Gonne.* London.

Limond, D. 2006 A work for other hands. *History Ireland* **14** (2).

Little, P.J. 1942 A 1916 document. *Capuchin Annual* (1942).

Litton, H. 2013 *Edward Daly.* Dublin.

Litton, H. 2014 *Thomas James Clarke.* Dublin.

Longford, Lord and O'Neill, T.P. 1966 De Valera in the Easter Rising. *Sunday Telegraph*, 27 March 1966.

Luddy, M. 1995 *Hanna Sheehy Skeffington.* Dundalk.

Luddy, M. 1999 *Women in Ireland 1800–1918: a documentary history.* Cork.

Luddy, M. 2012 Ireland Rising. *History Today* **62** (9).

Luddy, M. and Murphy, C. 1990 *Women surviving: studies in Irish women's history in the 19th and 20th centuries.* Dublin.

Lynch, B. 2006 Through the eyes of 1916. *History Ireland* **14** (2).

Lynch, D. 1957 *The I.R.B. and the 1916 insurrection* (ed. F. O'Donoghue). Cork.

Lynch, D. 1966 The countermanding orders of Holy Week, 1916. *An Cosantoir* **26**.

Lynd, R. 1917 *If the Germans conquered England, and other essays.* Dublin.

Lynd, R. 1919 *Who began it?* (Pamphlet issued by the Peace in Ireland Council.)

Lyons, F.S.L. 1971 *Ireland since the Famine.* London.

Lyons, F.S.L. 1981 De Valera revisited. *Magill* (March 1981).

Lyons, G. 1926 Occupation of the Ringsend area. *An tOglach*, 10, 17 and 24 April 1926.

Lysaght, D.R. O'Connor 2003 The rhetoric of Redmondism, 1914–16. *History Ireland* 11 (1).

MacAnBheatha, P. 1981 *James Connolly and the workers' republic*. Dublin.

MacAonghusa, P. (ed.) 1979 *Quotations from P.H. Pearse*. Cork.

MacAonghusa, P. (ed.) 1983 *Quotations from Éamon de Valera*. Dublin.

MacAonghusa, P. (ed.) 1995 *What Connolly said*. Dublin.

Macardle, D. 1937 [1965] *The Irish Republic*. New York.

MacAtasney, G. 2005 *Seán MacDiarmada, the mind of the revolution*. Dublin.

MacAtasney, G. 2013 *Tom Clarke: life, liberty, revolution*. Dublin.

MacBride, M.G. 1950 *Servant of the queen*. Dublin.

McCallum, C. 2005 *And they'll march with their brothers to freedom—Cumann na mBan, nationalism, and women's rights in Ireland, 1900–1923*. Dublin.

McCann, B.P. 1996–7 The diary of 2nd Lieutenant A.V.G. Killingley, Easter Week, 1916. *Irish Sword* 20.

McCann, J. 1946 *War by the Irish*. Tralee.

McCarthy, Cal 2007 *Cumann na mBan and the Irish Revolution*. Cork.

McCarthy, M. 2013 *Ireland's 1916 Rising: explorations of history-making, commemorations and history in modern times*. Ashgate.

McCay, H. 1966 *Padraic Pearse: a new biography*. Cork.

McCoole, S. 1997 *Guns and chiffon*. Dublin.

McCoole, S. 2003 *No ordinary women: Irish female activists in the revolutionary years*. Dublin.

McCormack, W.J. 2012 *Dublin 1916 and the French connection*. Dublin.

McCullough, D. 1966 The events in Belfast. *Capuchin Annual* (1966).

MacCurtain, F. 2006 *Remember, it's for Ireland*. Cork.

MacCurtain, M. and O'Corrain, D. (eds) 1978 *Women, the vote and revolution. Women in Irish society: the historical

dimension. Dublin.

McDermott, N. 2005 Jim Larkin: a man on a mission. *Red Banner* 20.

McDermott, P. 2006 Brothers in arms. *Irish Echo*, 19–25 April 2006.

McDermott, P. 2006b One family's Rising. *Irish Echo*, 3–9 May 2006.

MacDonagh, D. 1945a Patrick Pearse. *An Cosantair* (August 1945).

MacDonagh, D. 1945b Joseph Plunkett. *An Cosantoir* (November 1945).

MacDonagh, D. 1946 Éamonn Ceannt. *An Cosantoir* (October 1946).

MacDonagh, M. 1916 *The Irish at the Front*. London.

McDonagh, M. 2009 Call for memorial to be put up to citizens of Dublin killed in Rising. *Irish Times*, 22 June 2009.

MacDonnacha, M. 2002 Deserting the Starry Plough. *An Phoblacht*, 19 December 2002.

MacDonnell, J.M. (n.d.) *The story of Irish Labour*. Cork.

McDonnell, K.K. 1972 *There is a bridge at Bandon*. Cork.

McDowell, R.B. 1967 *Alice Stopford Green: a passionate historian*. Dublin.

McEneany, K.T. (ed.) 1982 *Pearse and Rossa*. New York.

MacEntee, S. 1966 *Episode at Easter*. Dublin.

MacEoin, U. (ed.) 1980 *Survivors*. Dublin.

McGahern, J. 1991 *Amongst women*. New York.

McGarry, F. 2006 Keeping an eye on the usual suspects: Dublin Castle's 'Personality Files', 1899–1921. *History Ireland* 14 (6).

McGarry, F. 2010 *The Rising: Easter 1916*. Oxford.

McGarry, F. 2011 *Rebels: voices from the Easter Rising*. Dublin.

MacGarry, M. 1942 Memories of Scoil Eanna. *Capuchin Annual* (1942).

McGee, O. 2005 *The I.R.B.: the Irish Republican Brotherhood from the Land League to Sinn Féin*. Dublin.

McGill, P.J. 1966 Padraic Pearse in Donegal. *Donegal Annual* (1966).

MacGiolla, C.B. (ed.) 1966 *Intelligence notes 1913–1916, preserved in the State Paper Office*. Baile Átha Cliath.

McGough, E. 2013 *Diarmuid Lynch: a forgotten Irish patriot*. Cork.

McGowan, J. 2005 *Countess Markievicz: the people's countess*. Sligo.

McGuigan, J. 2005–6 A duty to execute: the 1916 pocket book of Captain Annan Dickson of the Sherwood Foresters. *Irish Sword* **25**.

McGuire, C. 2006 Seán McLoughlin: the boy commandant of 1916. *History Ireland* **14** (2).

McGuire, C. 2011 *Seán McLoughlin: Ireland's forgotten revolutionary*. Dublin.

McHugh, R. (ed.) 1966 *Dublin, 1916*. London.

McInerney, M. 1967 James Ryan. *Irish Times*, 15–17 March 1967.

McInerney, M. 1968 Gerald Boland's story. *Irish Times*, 8–19 October 1968.

McInerney, M. 1971 *The riddle of Erskine Childers*. Dublin.

McInerney, M. 1974 Seán MacEntee. *Irish Times*, 22–25 July 1974.

McIntosh, G. and Urquhart, D. 2010 *Irish women at war: the twentieth century*. Dublin.

McKay, F. 1966 Clann na nGaedheal Girl Scouts. *Irish Press*, 3 May 1966.

McKenna, L. 1920 [1991] *The social teachings of James Connolly*. Dublin.

MacKenna, S. [writing as Martin Daly] 1917 *Memories of the dead*. Dublin.

McKenzie, F.A. 1916 *The Irish Rebellion: what happened and why*. London.

McKeown, E. 1966 A family in the Rising. *Electricity Supply Board Journal* (1966).

McKillen, B. 1982 Irish feminism and national separatism. *Éire-Ireland* **17**.

McKittrick, D. 1991 Rebels of 1916 leave mixed legacy. *Irish Independent*, 12 March 1991.

McLaughlin, T. 2006 The aftermath. *An Cosantóir* (April/May 2006).

MacLochlainn, P. 1971 *Last words, letters and statements of the leaders executed after the Rising at Easter, 1916*. Dublin.

McLoughlin, S. 1948 Memories of the Easter Rising. *Camillian Post* (Spring 1948).

MacManus, M.J. 1944 *Éamon de Valera*. Dublin.

McManus, R. 2002 *Dublin 1910–1940: shaping the city and suburbs*. Dublin.

MacManus, S. 1921 [1978] *The story of the Irish race*. Dublin [Old Greenwich, CT].

McNally, F. 2009 An Irishman's Diary: Dublin in rebellion. *Irish Times*, 12 June 2009.

MacNeill, E. 1913 The North began. *An Claidheamh Soluis*, 1 November 1913.

MacNeill, E. 1915 Ireland for the Irish nation. *Irish Volunteer*, 20 February 1915.

MacNeill, E. 1919 Recollections of Pearse. *New Ireland*, 14 June 1919.

MacNeill, E. 1937 *Phases of Irish history*. Dublin.

MacSwiney, T. 1921 [1936] *Principles of freedom*. Dublin.

MacThomais, É. 1965 *Down Dublin streets, 1916*. Dublin.

MacThomais, S. 2005 The historical significance of 16 Moore Street. *An Phoblacht*, 1 September 2005.

MacThomais, S. 2012 *Dead interesting: stories from the graveyards*. Dublin.

McVeigh, J. 1998 Constance Markievicz: aiming for the stars. *An Phoblacht*, 17 September 1998.

Maher, J. 1998 *Harry Boland: a biography*. Cork.

Malins, E. 1965 *Yeats and the Easter Rising*. Dublin.

Mandle, W. 1977 The IRB and the beginning of the Gaelic Athletic Association. *Irish Historical Studies* **20** (80).

Mandle, W. 1979 Sport as politics: the Gaelic Athletic Association 1884–1924. In R. Cashman and M. McKernan (eds), *Sport in history*. Queensland.

Mandle, W. 1987 *The Gaelic Athletic Association and Irish nationalist politics, 1884–1924*. Dublin.

Mansergh, N. 1966 *The Irish Question, 1840–1921*. Toronto.

Mansergh, N. 1991 *The unresolved question: the Anglo-Irish Settlement and its undoing, 1912–1972*. London.

Mansergh, N. 1997 *Nationalism and independence: selected Irish papers*. Cork.

Manzor, P.J. 2002 The impact of the American Civil War on the emergence of Irish-American nationalism. Unpublished

MA thesis, NUI Galway.

Marcus, L. 1964 The G.A.A. and the Castle. *Irish Independent*, 9–10 July 1964.

Markievicz, Countess C. 1909 *Women, ideals and the nation* [pamphlet, reissued 1918]. Dublin.

Markievicz, Countess C. 1918 *A call to the women of Ireland*. Dublin.

Markievicz, Countess C. 1923 *What Irish republicans stand for*. Glasgow.

Markievicz, Countess C. 1926 Cumann na mBan. *Cumann na mBan* **11** (10).

Markievicz, Countess C. 1987 *Prison letters of Countess Markievicz*. London.

Marreco, A. 1967 *The rebel countess: the life and times of Constance Markievicz*. London.

Martin, A.E. 1966 To make a right rose tree. *Studies: The Irish Jesuit Quarterly Review* **55**.

Martin, F.X. 1961 Eoin MacNeill on the 1916 Rising. *Irish Historical Studies* **12**.

Martin, F.X. (ed.) 1963 *The Irish Volunteers, 1913–1915*. Dublin.

Martin, F.X. 1964 *The Howth gunrunning and the Kilcoole gunrunning*. Dublin.

Martin, F.X. 1966a 1916—myth, fact and mystery. *Studia Hibernica* **7**.

Martin, F.X. (ed.) 1966b The McCartan Documents, 1916. *Clogher Record* (1966).

Martin, F.X. (ed.) 1966c *The Easter Rising, 1916, and University College, Dublin*. Dublin.

Martin, F.X. (ed.) 1967 *Leaders and men of the Easter Rising*. London.

Martin, F.X. 1968 The 1916 Rising—a *coup d'état* or a 'bloody protest'? *Studia Hibernica* **8**.

Martin, F.X. and Byrne, J.F. (eds) 1973 *The scholar revolutionary: Eoin MacNeill*. Shannon.

Martin, H. 1921 *Ireland in insurrection*. London.

Matthews, A. 2007a Citizen Army women in the GPO in 1916. *Red Banner* **28**.

Matthews, A. 2007b Rebel women in prison in 1916. *Red Banner* **29**.

Matthews, A. 2008 Vanguard of the Revolution. In R. O'Donnell (ed.), *The impact of the 1916 Rising among the nations*. Dublin.

Matthews, A. 2010a *The Kimmage garrison, 1916: making billy-can bombs at Larkfield*. Dublin.

Matthews, A. 2010b *Renegades: Irish republican women 1900–1922*. Dublin.

Matthews, A. 2010c Cumann na mBan and the Red Cross. In J. Kelly and R.V. Comerford (eds), *Associated culture in Ireland and abroad*. Dublin.

Matthews, M.E. 2002 Women activists in Irish republican politics, 1900–1941. Unpublished Ph.D thesis, NUI Maynooth.

Maume, P. 1994 Lilly Connolly's conversion. *History Ireland* **2** (3).

Maume, P. 1995a *D.P. Moran*. Dundalk.

Maume, P. 1995b Parnell and the I.R.B. oath. *Irish Historical Studies* **29** (115).

Maume, P. 1999 *The long gestation: Irish nationalist life, 1892–1921*. Dublin.

Maume, P. 2001 From deference to citizenship: Irish republicanism, 1870–1923. *The Republic* **2**.

Maume, P. 2006 The man with thirty lives? *History Ireland* **14** (2).

Maye, B. 1997 *Arthur Griffith*. Dublin.

Mayhew, G. 1963 A corrected typescript of Yeats' 'Easter 1916'. *Huntington Library Quarterly* **27**.

Meakin, Lt W. 1920 *The 5th North Staffords and the North Midland Territorials, 1914–1919*. Longton.

Meleady, D. 2014 *John Redmond: the national leader*. Dublin.

Mellows, L. 1946 An account of the Irish rebellion [partial reprint]. *Wolfe Tone Annual* (1946).

Mitchell, A. 1997 Casement's Black Diaries: closed books reopened. *History Ireland* **5** (3).

Mitchell, A. 2001 The Casement 'Black Diaries' debate: the story so far. *History Ireland* **9** (2).

Mitchell, A. 2003 Robert Emmet and 1916. *History Ireland* **11** (3).

Mitchell, A. 2014 *Roger Casement*. Dublin.

Mitchell, A. and Ó Snodaigh, P. 1985 *Irish political documents, 1916–1949*. Dublin.

Mitchell, D. 1990 *A 'peculiar' place: the Adelaide Hospital, Dublin, 1839–1989*. Dublin.

Molloy, M.J. 1966 He helped to print the proclamation. *Evening Herald*, 4 April 1966.

Monteith, R. 1953 *Casement's last adventure*. Dublin.

Mooney, J.E. 1991 Varieties of Irish republican womanhood: San Francisco lectures during their United States tours: 1916–1925. Unpublished MA thesis, San José State University, California.

Moore, Col. M. 1938 The rise of the Irish Volunteers [serial]. *Irish Press*, 4 January–2 March 1938. [Apparently written in 1917. See National Library of Ireland ILB 94109.]

Moran, B. 1978 Jim Larkin and the British Labour Movement. *Saothar* 4.

Moran, M. 2010 *Executed for Ireland*. Dublin.

Moran, S.F. 1989a Patrick Pearse and the European revolt against reason. *Journal of the History of Ideas* 50 (4).

Moran, S.F. 1989b Patrick Pearse, the Easter Rising and Irish history. *Graduate Review* (Summer 1989).

Moran, S.F. 1994 *Patrick Pearse and the politics of redemption*. Washington, DC.

Morgan, A. 1988 *James Connolly: a political biography*. Manchester.

Mulcahy, Gen. R. 1980 The development of the Irish Volunteers, 1916–1922. *An Cosantoir* 40.

Mulcahy, R. 1999 *Richard Mulcahy (1886–1971): a family memoir*. Dublin.

Mulcahy, R. 2003 The Mulcahy Tapes and Papers. *History Ireland* 8 (1).

Mulcahy, R. 2009 *My father, the general, and the military history of the revolution*. Dublin.

Mulholland, M. 2002 *The politics and relationships of Kathleen Lynn*. Dublin.

Mulqueen, J. and Wren, J. 1989 *De Valera: an illustrated life*. Dublin.

Munck, R. 1985 *Ireland: nation, state and class struggle*. Boulder, CO.

Murphy, B.P. 1991 *Patrick Pearse and the lost republican ideal*. Dublin.

Murphy, C. 1989 *The women's suffrage movement and Irish society in the early twentieth century*. London.

Murphy, Major H.L. 1996 Countess Markievicz. *An Cosantoir* (June 1946).

Murray, J. 1996 *Erskine Childers*. London.

Murray, M. 1922 A girl's experience in the GPO. *Poblacht na hÉireann*, 20 April 1922.

Murray, R.H. 1916 The Sinn Féin rebellion. *The Nineteenth Century and After* (June 1916).

Murtagh, P. 2014 Equally audacious: the Kilcoole gun-running. *Irish Times*, 17 July 2014.

Myers, K. 1991 The glory that was hijacked. *Guardian*, 30 March 1991.

Neeson, E. 2007 *Myths from Easter 1916*. Aubane.

Nelson, C. 2014 Murderous renegade or agent of the crown? The riddle of Erskine Childers. *History Ireland* 22 (3).

Nevin, D. (ed.) 1964 *1913: Jim Larkin and the 1913 Lockout*. Dublin.

Nevin, D. 1968 *Connolly bibliography*. Dublin.

Nevin, D. (ed.) 1978 [1998] *James Larkin: lion in the fold*. Dublin.

Nevin, D. 2005 *James Connolly: a full life*. Dublin.

Nevin, D. (ed.) 2008 *Between friends: James Connolly letters and correspondence, 1889–1916*. Dublin.

Newsinger, J. 1979 Revolution and Catholicism in Ireland, 1848–1923. *European Studies Review* 9.

Newsinger, J. 1986 James Connolly, the German Empire, and the Great War. *Irish Sword* 16 (65).

Newsinger, J. 1993 The Devil it was who sent Larkin to Ireland: the Liberator, Larkinism, and the Dublin Lockout of 1913. *Saothar* 18.

Newsinger, J. 2002 Irish Labour in a time of revolution. *Socialist History* 22.

Ní Chorra, E. 1936 A rebel remembers. *Capuchin Annual* (1936).

Ní Chumnaill, E. 1933 The history of Cumann na mBan. *An Phoblacht*, 8 April 1933.

Ní Dhonnchadha, M. and Durgan, T. (eds) 1991 *Revising the Rising*. Derry.

Ní Dhuibhne, E. 2002 Family values: the Sheehy Skeffington Papers in the National Library of Ireland. *History Ireland* 10 (1).

Ní Ghairbhi, R. 2014 *William Pearse.* Dublin.

Níc Shiubhlaigh, M. 1955 *The splendid years* (as told to E. Kenny). Dublin.

Nixon, W. and Healy, E. 2000 *Asgard.* Dublin.

Nolan, L. and Nolan, J.E. 2009 *Ireland and the war at sea, 1914–1918.* Cork.

Norman, D. 1988 *Terrible beauty: a life of Constance Markievicz.* London.

Norman, E.R. 1965 *The Catholic Church and Ireland in the age of rebellion.* Ithaca, NY.

Norstedt, J.A. 1980 *Thomas MacDonagh: a critical biography.* Charlottesville, VA.

Norway, M. 1916 *The Sinn Féin rebellion as I saw it.* London.

Novak, R. 2008 Keepers of important secrets: the Ladies Committee of the IRB. *History Ireland* **16** (6).

Nowlan, K. (ed.) 1969 *The making of 1916: studies in the history of the Rising.* Dublin.

Nunan, E. 1966 The Irish Volunteers in London. *An tÓglach* (Autumn 1966).

Nunan, E. 1967 The Kimmage Garrison. *An tÓglach* (Winter 1967).

Oates, Lt Col. W.C. 1920 *The Sherwood Foresters in the Great War, 1914–1919.* Nottingham.

Ó Braonain, C. 1916 Poets of the insurrection II—Patrick H. Pearse. *Studies: The Irish Jesuit Quarterly Review* **5**.

O'Brennan, L. 1922 Letter to the Editor: An appreciation of Erskine Childers. *Irish Independent,* 21 November 1922.

O'Brennan, L.M. 1936 The dawning of the day. *Capuchin Annual* (1936).

O'Brennan, L.M. 1947 We surrender. *An Cosantoir* (June 1947). [Reprinted in *An Cosantoir* (April/May 2006).]

Ó Briain, L. 1923 *The historic Rising of Easter Week, 1916.* Dublin.

Ó Briain, L. 1966 Saint Stephen's Green area. *Capuchin Annual* (1966).

O'Brien, N. Connolly 1932 Women in Ireland, their part in the revolutionary struggle. *An Phoblacht,* 25 June 1932.

O'Brien, P. 2007 *Blood on the streets: 1916 and the battle of Mount Street Bridge.* Cork.

O'Brien, P. 2010 *Uncommon valour: 1916 and the battle for the South Dublin Union.* Cork.

O'Brien, P. 2012a *Crossfire—the battle of the Four Courts.* Dublin.

O'Brien, P. 2012b *Field of fire—the battle of Ashbourne.* Dublin.

O'Brien, P. 2013 *Shootout: the battle for St Stephen's Green, 1916.* Dublin.

O'Brien, W. 1916 An Irish soldier and the rebellion. *Irish Times,* 9 May 1916.

O'Brien, W. 1936 Was the date changed? *Irish Press,* 25 January 1936.

O'Brien, W. 1959 *Fifty years of Liberty Hall.* Dublin.

O'Brien, W. 1969 *Forth the banners go* (ed. E. MacLysaght). Dublin.

O'Brien, W. and Ryan, D. 1953 *Devoy's postbag, 1871–1928.* Dublin.

Ó Brochláin, H. 2012 *Joseph Plunkett.* Dublin.

Ó Broin, L. 1966 *Dublin Castle and the 1916 Rising.* London.

Ó Broin, L. 1969 *The chief secretary: Augustine Birrell in Ireland.* London.

Ó Broin, L. 1976 *Revolutionary underground: the story of the I.R.B., 1858–1924.* Dublin.

Ó Broin, L. 1989 *W.E. Wylie and the Irish Revolution, 1916–1921.* Dublin.

Ó Buachalla, S. (ed.) 1980a *The letters of P.H. Pearse.* London.

Ó Buachalla, S. (ed.) 1980b *A significant educationalist: the educational writings of P.H. Pearse.* Dublin.

O'Callaghan, J. 2014 *Con Colbert.* Dublin.

O'Callaghan, S. 1956 *The Easter lily.* London.

O'Callaghan, S. 1974 *Execution.* London.

O'Carroll, J.P. and Murphy, J.A. (eds) 1983 *De Valera and his times.* Cork.

O'Casey, S. [writing as P. Ó Cathasaigh] 1919 [1980] *The story of the Irish Citizen Army.* Dublin and London [London].

Ó Cathasaigh, A. (ed.) 1997 *James Connolly, the lost writings.* Harmondsworth.

Ó Ceallaigh, P. 1966 Jacob's Factory area. *Capuchin Annual* (1966).

Ó Ceallaigh, S.T. 1936 The founding of the Irish Volunteers. *An Phoblacht,* 30 April 1936.

Ó Ceallaigh, S.T. 1961 Memoirs. *Irish Press,*

3 July–9 August 1961.

Ó Ceallaigh, S.T. 1963 The founding of the Irish Volunteers. *Capuchin Annual* (1963).

Ó Ceallaigh, S.T. (n.d.) *A trinity of martyrs.* Dublin.

O'Ceirin, K. and O'Ceirin, C. 1996 *Women of Ireland.* Galway.

Ó Clerigh, G. 2008 John Redmond and 1916 [letter]. *Irish Times*, 7 April 2008.

Ó Conluain, P. (ed.) 1963 *Seán T.* Dublin.

O'Connor, E. 1988 *Syndicalism in Ireland, 1917–1923.* Cork.

O'Connor, E. 1992 *A labour history of Ireland, 1824–1960.* Dublin.

O'Connor, J. 1966 Boland's Mill area. *Capuchin Annual* (1966).

O'Connor, J. 1986 *The 1916 Proclamation.* Dublin.

O'Connor, U. 1975 *A terrible beauty is born: the Irish Troubles, 1912–1922.* London.

O'Connor Lysaght, D.R. 2006 The Irish Citizen Army, 1913–16. *History Ireland* **14** (2).

O'Daly, N. 1926 The women of Easter Week: Cumann na mBan in Stephen's Green and the College of Surgeons. *An tÓglach*, 3 April 1926.

O'Day, A. 1998 *Irish Home Rule, 1867–1921.* Manchester.

O'Doherty, L. 1970 Dublin, 1920. *Capuchin Annual* (1970).

O'Donnell, J. 1990–1 Recollections based on the diary of an Irish Volunteer. *Cathair na Mart* **10** (1) (1990); **11** (1991).

O'Donnell, P.D. 1972 Dublin military barracks. *Dublin Historical Record* **25** (4).

O'Donnell, R. (ed.) 2008 *The impact of the 1916 Rising among the nations.* Dublin.

O'Donnell, R. 2014 *Patrick Pearse.* Dublin.

O'Donoghue, F. 1949 A review of the 1916 Rising. *Irish Historical Studies* (September 1949).

O'Donoghue, F. 1955 A review of *Casement's last adventure. Irish Historical Studies* (March 1955).

O'Donoghue, F. 1963 Plans for the 1916 Rising. *University Review* **3**.

O'Donoghue, F. 1966 The failure of the German arms landing at Easter 1916. *Journal of the Cork Historical and Archaeological Society* **71**, 49–61.

O'Donovan Rossa, D. 1898 [1972] *Rossa's recollections, 1838–1898* (introduction by S. Ó Luing). New York [Shannon].

O'Donovan Rossa, J. 1872 [1991] *Irish rebels in English prisons.* New York [Dingle].

Ó Dubghaill, M. 1966 *Insurrection fires at Eastertide.* Cork.

Ó Duigneain, P. 1991 Linda Kearns—the Sligo nurse in the 1916 Rising. *Sligo Champion*, 5 April 1991.

Ó Duigneain, P. 2002 *Linda Kearns.* Manorhamilton.

Ó Dulaing, D. 1984 *Voices of Ireland.* Dublin.

O'Dwyer, R. 2010 *The Bastille of Ireland: Kilmainham Gaol, from ruin to restoration.* Dublin.

Ó Faolain, S. 1933 *The life of de Valera.* Dublin.

Ó Faolain, S. 1934 *Constance Markievicz.* London.

Ó Faolain, S. 1939 *De Valera.* London.

O'Farrell, E. 1917 Events of Easter Week. *Catholic Bulletin* (May 1917).

O'Farrell, E. 1930 Recollections. *An Phoblacht*, 26 April and 10 May 1930.

O'Farrell, M. 1999 *A walk through rebel Dublin, 1916.* Cork.

O'Farrell, P. 1997 *Who's who in the Irish War of Independence and Civil War.* Dublin.

O'Hanrahan, M. 1917 *Irish heroines.* Cumann na mBan pamphlet.

O'Hegarty, P.S. 1918 *An indestructible nation.* Dublin.

O'Hegarty, P.S. 1919a *Sinn Féin: an illumination.* Dublin and London.

O'Hegarty, P.S. 1919b P.H. Pearse. *Irish Commonwealth* (St Patrick's Day issue).

O'Hegarty, P.S. 1924 [1998] *The victory of Sinn Féin.* Dublin.

O'Hegarty, P.S. 1931 Patrick Pearse. *Dublin Magazine* (July–September 1931).

O'Hegarty, P.S. 1952 *A history of Ireland under the Act of Union.* London.

O'Higgins, B. 1925 *The soldier's story of Easter Week.* Dublin.

O'Higgins, B. 1935 The soldier's story of Easter Week. *Wolfe Tone Annual* (1935).

O'Keefe, J. 1932 Easter Week and Connolly. *Workers' Voice*, 14 May 1932.

O'Kelly, S. 1996 *The glorious seven*. Dublin.

O'Leary, J. 1896 *Recollections of Fenians and Fenianism*. London.

Ó Luing, S. 1953 *Art Ó Griofa*. Dublin.

Ó Luing, S. 1961 Talking to Bulmer Hobson. *Irish Times*, 6 May 1961.

Ó Luing, S. 1968 Thomas Ashe. *Capuchin Annual* (1968).

Ó Luing, S. 1970 *I die in a good cause: a study of Thomas Ashe, idealist and revolutionary*. Tralee.

O'Mahony, S. 1987 [1995] *Frongoch, university of revolution*. Killiney.

Ó Maitiu, S. 2001 *W & R Jacob: celebrating 150 years of Irish biscuit-making*. Dublin.

O'Neill, B. 1939 *Easter Week*. New York.

O'Neill, Cmdt D. 2006 The Four Courts: Easter 1916. *An Cosantoir* (April/May 2006).

O'Neill, Col. E. 1966 The Battle of Dublin, 1916. *An Cosantoir* **26**.

O'Neill, É. 1935 Patrick Pearse, some other memories. *Capuchin Annual* (1935).

O'Neill, M. 1991 *From Parnell to de Valera: a biography of Jennie Wyse-Power, 1858–1941*. Dublin.

O'Neill, M. 2000 *Grace Gifford Plunkett and Irish freedom: tragic bride of 1916*. Dublin.

Ó Neill, T. and Ó Fiannachta, P. 1968–70 *De Valera* (2 vols). Dublin.

Ó hÓgartaigh, M. 2005 *Kathleen Lynn, patriot doctor*. Dublin.

Ó Rahilly, A. 1991 *Winding the clock: The Ó Rahilly and the 1916 Rising*. Dublin.

Ó Rahilly, M.J. (The) 1915a *The secret history of the Irish Volunteers*. Dublin.

Ó Rahilly, The 1915b The history of the Irish Volunteers. *Gaelic American*, 2 January 1915.

Ó Rahilly, The 1915c The Volunteer colours: flags for the regiments. *Irish Volunteer*, 23 May 1915.

Oram, H. 1983 *The newspaper book*. Dublin.

O'Riordan, M. 1979 *The Connolly Column*. Dublin.

Ó Ruairc, P. Óg 2011 *Revolution*. Cork.

O'Shannon, C. (ed.) 1959 *Fifty years of Liberty Hall, 1909–1959*. Dublin.

O'Shea, Cmdt B. and White, CQMS G. 2006 The Volunteer uniform. *An Cosantoir* (April/May 2006).

Ó Siochain, S. 2007 *Roger Casement: imperialist, rebel, revolutionary*. Dublin.

Ó Snodaigh, A. 1997 Arming the Volunteers. *An Phoblacht*, 20 June 1997.

Ó Snodaigh, A. 1998 The Irish Volunteers founded. *An Phoblacht*, 26 November 1998.

Ó Snodaigh, A. 1999 The first 1916 Rising casualty. *An Phoblacht*, 1 April 1999.

Ó Snodaigh, A. 2000 Remembering the past: the Battle of Mount Street Bridge. *An Phoblacht*, 20 April 2000.

O'Sullivan, M. 1994 *Seán Lemass*. Dublin.

O'Sullivan, M. and O'Neill, B. 1999 *The Shelbourne and its people*. Dublin.

O'Sullivan, N. 2007 *Every dark hour: a history of Kilmainham Jail*. Dublin.

O'Sullivan, N. 2009 *Written in stone: the graffiti in Kilmainham Jail*. Dublin.

O'Sullivan, T.F. 1916 *The story of the G.A.A.* Dublin.

O'Toole, F. 1999 *The* Irish Times *book of the century*. Dublin.

Ó Tuile, P. (n.d.) *Life and times of Brian O'Higgins*. Navan.

Ó hUid, Ceannaire T.C. 1966 The Mount Street action, April 26, 1916. *An Cosantoir* **26**.

Owens, R.C. 1984a *Did your granny have a hammer?* Dublin.

Owens, R.C. 1984b *Smashing times: a history of the Irish women's suffrage movement, 1889–1922*. Dublin.

Parks, E.W. and Parks, A.W. 1967 *Thomas MacDonagh: the man, the patriot, the writer*. Athens, GA.

Paseta, S. 1999 *Before the revolution: nationalism, social change and Ireland's Catholic elite, 1879–1922*. Cork.

Paseta, S. 2014 *Irish nationalist women, 1900–1918*. Cambridge.

Pearse, J. 1886 *England's duty to Ireland as plain to a loyal Irish Roman Catholic*. Dublin.

Pearse, M.B. (ed.) 1934 *The home life of Padraig Pearse*. Dublin.

Pearse, M.M. 1942 St Enda's. *Capuchin Annual* (1942).

Pearse, M.M. 1943 Patrick and Willie Pearse. *Capuchin Annual* (1943).

Pearse, P. 1913 The coming revolution. *An*

Claidheamh Soluis, 8 November 1913.

Pearse, P.H. 1914 At last—an Irish army! *Irish Volunteer*, 4 July 1914.

Pearse, P.H. 1915 Why we want recruits. *Irish Volunteer*, 22 May 1915.

Pearse, P.H. 1915 The Irish flag. *Irish Volunteer*, 20 March 1915.

Pearse, P.H. 1916 *The murder machine.* Dublin.

Pearse, P.H. 1918 *The Singer and other plays.* Dublin.

Pearse, P.H. 1922 *Collected works of Padraic H. Pearse. Political writings and speeches.* Dublin.

Pearson, P. 2000 *The heart of Dublin.* Dublin.

Phillips, W.A. 1923 *The revolution in Ireland, 1906–1923.* London.

Pinkman, J.A. 1998 *In the legion of the vanguard* (ed. F.E. Maguire). Dublin.

Plunkett, G. 1958 Joseph Plunkett: origin and background. *University Review* (1958).

Plunkett, G. 1968 Joseph Plunkett's diary of his journey to Germany. *University Review* (1968).

Plunkett, G. Gifford 1922 The white flag of 1916. *Phoblacht na h-Éireann* **1** (12).

Poets of the insurrection 1918 [Essays originally published in *Studies: The Irish Jesuit Quarterly Review*.] Dublin and London.

Pollard, H.B.C. 1922 *The secret societies of Ireland: their rise and progress.* London.

Porter, R. 1973 *P.H. Pearse.* New York.

Prunty, J. 1998 *Dublin slums, 1800–1925.* Dublin.

Reddin, K. 1943 A man called Pearse. *Studies: The Irish Jesuit Quarterly Review* (June 1943).

Redmond, J. 1916 *The Rising.* London.

Redmond-Howard, L.G. 1916 *Six days of the Irish Republic.* Dublin.

Rees, R. 1998 *Ireland, 1905–1925*, Vol. 1. Newtownards.

Reeve, C. and Barton, A. 1978 *James Connolly and the United States: the road to the 1916 Irish rebellion.* Atlantic Highlands, NJ.

Reid, B.L. 1976 *The lives of Roger Casement.* New Haven, CT.

Reilly, J. 2006 Mater nuns supported Rising, R.I.C. files claim. *Irish Independent*, 2 April 2006.

Reilly, T. 2005 *Joe Stanley, printer to the Rising.* Dingle.

Reynolds, J.J. 1919 *A fragment of 1916 history.* Dublin.

Reynolds, J.J. 1926 The Four Courts and North King Street in 1916. *An tÓglach*, 15, 22 and 29 May 1926.

Reynolds, M. 1926 Cumann na mBan in the GPO. *An tÓglach*, 27 March 1926.

Ring, J. 1996 *Erskine Childers.* London.

Robbins, F. 1928 The Citizen Army and Easter Week. *Irishman*, 19 May 1928.

Robbins, F. 1977 *Under the Starry Plough: recollections of the Irish Citizen Army.* Dublin.

Robertson, N. 1960 *Crowned harp: memories of the last years of the crown in Ireland.* Dublin.

Roche, A.J. (ed.) 2000 *A family in revolution.* Dublin.

Roper, E. (ed.) 1934 *Prison letters of Countess Markievicz.* London.

Rowbotham, S. 1997 *A century of women.* New York and London.

Ruane, M. 1991 *Ten Dublin women.* Dublin.

Ryan, A. 2005 *Witnesses: inside the Easter Rising.* Dublin.

Ryan, A. 2007 *Comrades: inside the War of Independence.* Dublin.

Ryan, D. (ed.) 1917 *The story of a success by P.H. Pearse, being a record of St Enda's College, September 1908 to Easter 1916.* Dublin.

Ryan, D. 1919 *The man called Pearse.* Dublin.

Ryan, D. 1924 *James Connolly and his life.* Dublin.

Ryan, D. 1934 *Remembering Sion: a chronicle of storm and quiet.* London.

Ryan, D. 1936 *Unique dictator: a study of Éamon de Valera.* London.

Ryan, D. 1937 *The phoenix flame.* London.

Ryan, D. 1942 Margaret Pearse. *Capuchin Annual* (1942).

Ryan, D. 1948 *Socialism and nationalism: a collection of the writings of James Connolly.* Dublin.

Ryan, D. 1949 [1957] *The Rising: the*

complete story of Easter Week. Dublin.

Ryan, D. 1957 Pearse, St Enda's, and the Hound of Ulster. *Threshold* (1957).

Ryan, D. 1958 St Enda's—fifty years after. *University Review* (1958).

Ryan, D. 1961 The Easter Rising. *Irish Press*, 24–29 April 1961.

Ryan, D. (ed.) 1963 [1995] *The 1916 poets*. Dublin.

Ryan, D. (ed.) (n.d.) *Collected works of Padraic H. Pearse: St Enda's and its founder.* Dublin.

Ryan, J.T. 1931 The origin of the *Aud* expedition. *An Phoblacht*, 25 April 1931.

Ryan, Dr J. 1942 The General Post Office area. *Capuchin Annual* (1942).

Ryan, L. 1992 The *Irish Citizen*, 1912–1920. *Saothar* 17.

Ryan, L. 1994 Women without votes: the political strategies of the Irish suffrage movement. *Irish Political Studies* 9.

Ryan, L. 1996 *Irish feminism and the vote: an anthology of the* Irish Citizen *newspaper, 1912–1920*. Dublin.

Ryan, L. and Ward, M. (eds) 2004 *Irish women and nationalism: soldiers, new women and wicked hags*. Dublin.

Ryan, M. 2014 *Thomas Kent*. Dublin.

Ryan, M., Browne, S. and Gilmour, K. (eds) 1995 *No shoes in summer: days to remember*. Dublin.

Salmon, L.M. 1923 *The newspaper and the historian*. New York.

Saurin, C. 1926 Hotel Metropole Garrison. *An tÓglach*, 13 and 20 March 1926.

Sawyer, R. 1993 *'We are but women': women in Ireland's history*. London.

Sceilg [J.J. O'Kelly] (n.d.) *Stepping stones* (undated pamphlet). Irish Book Bureau, Dublin.

Sceilg (J.J. O'Kelly) (n.d.) *A trinity of martyrs* (undated pamphlet). Irish Book Bureau, Dublin.

Schuller, G. 1986 *James Connolly and Irish freedom: a Marxist analysis*. Cork.

Schmuhl, R. 2013 Ambiguous reprieve: Dev and America. *History Ireland* 21 (3).

Severn, B. 1971 *Irish statesman and rebel: the two lives of Éamon de Valera*. Folkstone.

Sexton, S. 1994 *Ireland: photographs, 1840–1930*. London.

Shaw, Revd F. 1972 The canon of Irish history: a challenge. *Studies: The Irish Jesuit Quarterly Review* (Summer 1972).

Sheehy, J. 1980 *The rediscovery of Ireland's past: the Celtic Revival, 1830–1930*. London.

Sheehy-Skeffington, A.D. 1982 The Hatter and the Crank. *Irish Times*, 5 February 1982.

Sheehy-Skeffington, A. and Owens, R. (eds) 1975 *Votes for women: Irish women's struggle for the vote*. Dublin.

Sheehy-Skeffington, F. 1914 *War and feminism*. Dublin.

Sheehy-Skeffington, H. 1902 Women and the university question. *New Ireland Review* 17.

Sheehy-Skeffington, H. 1912 The women's movement—Ireland. *Irish Review* (July 1912).

Sheehy-Skeffington, H. 1917 *British militarism as I have known it*. New York.

Sheehy-Skeffington, H. 1919 *Impressions of Sinn Féin in America*. Dublin.

Sheehy-Skeffington, H. 1928 Constance Markievicz in 1916. *An Phoblacht*, 14 April 1928.

Sheehy-Skeffington, H. 1943 Women in politics. *The Bell* 7 (2).

SIPTU 1997 *Tribute to Lames Larkin, orator, agitator, revolutionary, trade union leader.* Services, Industrial, Professional and Technical Union publication. Dublin.

Sissen, E. 2004 *Pearse's patriots*. Cork.

Skinnider, M. 1917 *Doing my bit for Ireland*. New York.

Skinnider, M. 1966 In Stephen's Green. *Irish Press* Supplement, 9 April 1966.

Small, S. 1998 *An Irish century, 1845–1945*. Dublin.

Smith, N.C. 2008 *A 'manly study'? Irish women historians, 1868–1949*. Dublin.

Smith, W.G. 1916 *Report of work done by St John's Ambulance Brigade during the Sinn Féin rebellion, April–May 1916*. Dublin.

Smyth, H.P. 1997 Kathleen Lynn, MD, FRCSI (1874–1955). *Dublin Historical Record* 30.

Spindler, K. 1931 *The mystery of the Casement ship*. Berlin.

Staines, M. and O'Reilly, M. 1926 The

defence of the GPO. *An tÓglach*, 23 January 1926.

Stanley, D. 1999 *Images of Ireland: central Dublin*. Dublin.

Steele, K. 2007 *Women, press and politics during the Irish Revival*. Syracuse, NY.

Steinmeyer, C. 1926 The evacuation of the GPO. *An tÓglach*, 27 February 1926.

Stephens, J. 1916 [1978] *The insurrection in Dublin*. Gerrard's Cross.

Stephens, J. 1922a *Arthur Griffith, journalist and statesman*. Dublin.

Stephens, J. 1922b Arthur Griffith. *Studies: The Irish Jesuit Quarterly Review* 11.

Stephenson, J. 2005 *Patrick Joseph Stephenson: 'Paddy Joe'*. Dingle.

Stephenson, P.J. 1966 *Heuston's fort: a participant's account of the fight by the Mendicity Institute Garrison in Dublin, Easter Week 1916*. Whitegate.

Taillon, R. 1996 *When history was made: the women of 1916*. Belfast.

Talbot, H. 1923 *Michael Collins' own story*. London.

Tansill, C.C. 1957 *America and the fight for Irish freedom, 1866–1922*. New York.

Tarpey, Sr M.V. 1970 The role of Joseph McGarrity in the struggle for Irish independence. Unpublished MA thesis, University of Michigan.

Thompson, W.I. 1967 *The imagination of an insurrection. Dublin, Easter 1916: a study of an ideological movement*. London.

Thornly, D. 1966 Patrick Pearse. *Studies: The Irish Jesuit Quarterly Review* (Spring 1966).

Thornly, D. 1971 Patrick Pearse and the Pearse family. *Studies: The Irish Jesuit Quarterly Review* (Autumn/Winter 1971).

Thornton, Cmdt B.L. 1975 Women and the Army. *An Cosantoir* (November 1975).

Throne, J. 1976 Easter Rising—1916: 60 years after, what are the lessons? *Militant Irish Monthly* 43.

Tierney, M. 1964a *Bibliographical memoir of Eoin MacNeill*. Dublin.

Tierney, M. 1964b Eoin MacNeill: a biographical study. *Saint Patrick* (1964).

Tierney, M. 1980 *Eoin MacNeill, scholar and man of action, 1867–1945*. Oxford.

Tobin, F. 2013 *The Irish Revolution, 1912–1925: an illustrated history*. Dublin.

Toby, T. 1997 *Exemplary violence used in British colonial policy: one explanation for General John Maxwell's violent reaction to the Easter Rising of 1916*. Boston, MA.

Toibin, C. 1966 Playboys of the GPO. *London Review of Books*, 18 April 1966.

Townshend, C. 1979 Martial Law: legal and administrative problems of civil emergency in Britain and the Empire, 1800–1940. *Historical Journal* 25.

Townshend, C. 1983 *Political violence in Ireland: government and resistance since 1848*. Oxford.

Townshend, C. 1989 Military force and civil authority in the United Kingdom, 1914–1921. *Journal of British Studies* 28.

Townshend, C. 1993 Militarism and modern society. *Wilson Quarterly* (Winter 1993).

Townshend, C. 1994 The suppression of the Easter Rising. *Bullán* 1 (1).

Townshend, C. 2005 *Easter 1916: the Irish rebellion*. London.

Townshend, C. 2006 Making sense of Easter 1916. *History Ireland* 14 (2).

Travers, C. 1966a *Seán MacDiarmada (1883–1916)*. Dublin.

Travers, C. 1966b Seán MacDiarmada, 1883–1916. *Breifne* (1966).

Travers, P. 1994 *Éamon de Valera*. Dublin.

Trimble, D. 1992 *The Easter Rebellion of 1916*. Belfast.

Ui Chonaill, E. Bean 1966 A Cumann na mBan recalls Easter Week. *Capuchin Annual* (1966).

Ui Dhonnachadha, S. Bean 1986 Memories of Easter Week. *An Phoblacht*, 27 March 1986.

Valiulis, M.G. 1992 *Portrait of a revolutionary: General Richard Mulcahy and the founding of the Irish Free State*. Blackrock.

Valiulis, M.G. 2008 *Gender and power in Irish history*. Dublin.

Van Voris, J. 1967 *Constance de Markievicz: in the cause of Ireland*. Amherst, MA.

Vane, Sir F. 1929 *Agin the government*. London.

'Volunteer, A' 1966 South Dublin Union area. *Capuchin Annual* (1966).

Walker, J. Crampton 1916 Red Cross work

and stretcher bearing during the Irish Republic. *Irish Life*, 26 May 1916.

Walsh, B. 2013 *Boy republic: Patrick Pearse and radical education*. Dublin.

Walsh, L.J. 1921 *On my keeping and in theirs*. Dublin and London.

Walsh, L.J. 1934 *Old friends: being memories of men and places*. Dundalk.

Walsh, M. 2008 *The news from Ireland: foreign correspondents and the Irish Revolution*. Dublin.

Walsh, O. 2002 *Ireland's independence, 1880–1923*. London.

Walsh, P. 1928 *William J. Walsh, archbishop of Dublin*. London.

Walsh, P. and Malcomson, A.P.W. 2010 *The Connolly archive*. Dublin.

Walsh, S.P. 1979 *Free and Gaelic: Pearse's idea of a national culture*. Dublin.

Walsh, T. 1966 The epic of Mount Street Bridge. *Irish Press* Supplement, April 1966.

Ward, A.J. 1980 *The Easter Rising: revolution and Irish nationalism*. Arlington Heights, IL.

Ward, M. 1983 *Unmanageable revolutionaries: women and Irish nationalism*. Dingle.

Ward, M. 1994 The missing sex: putting women into Irish history. In A. Smythe (ed.), *A dozen lips*. Dublin.

Ward, M. (ed.) 1995 [2001] *In their own voice*. Dublin.

Ward, M. 1997 *Hanna Sheehy Skeffington: a life*. Cork.

Warwick-Haller, A. and Warwick-Haller, S. (eds) 1995 *Letters from Dublin, Easter 1916: Alfred Fannin's diary of the Rising*. Dublin.

Wells, W.B. 1917 *An Irish apologia. Some thoughts on Anglo-Irish relations and the war*. Dublin.

Wells, W.B. 1919 *John Redmond: a biography*. London.

Wells, W.B. and Marlowe, N. 1916 *A history of the Irish rebellion of 1916*. Dublin.

West, N. 1981 *MI-5: British Secret Service operations, 1900–1945*. London.

Whearity, P.F. 2013 *The Easter Rising of 1916 in north County Dublin: a Skerries perspective*. Dublin.

Whelan, G. 1996 *The guns of Easter*. Dublin.

White, G. and O'Shea, B. 2003 *Irish Volunteer soldier, 1913–1923*. Northants.

White, J. 1919 *The significance of Sinn Féin*. Dublin.

White, J. 1930 [2005] *Misfit: a revolutionary life*. Dublin.

White, V. (ed.) 2009 *Cullenswood House: old ghosts and new dreams*. Dublin.

Wilkinson, B. 1974 *The zeal of the convert: the life of Erskine Childers*. Washington, DC.

Williams, D.T. (ed.) 1966 *The Irish struggle, 1916–1921*. London.

Williams, D.T. (ed.) 1973 *Secret societies in Ireland*. Dublin.

Wills, C. 2009 *Dublin 1916: the siege of the GPO*. London.

Woggan, H. 2000a *Silent radical: Winifred Carney 1887–1943. A reconstruction of her biography*. Dublin.

Woggon, H. 2000b The silent radical: Winifred Carney, 1887–1943. *Studies in Irish Labour* 6.

Wohl, R. 1979 *The generation of 1914*. Cambridge, MA.

Wrench, J.E. 1935 *Struggle, 1914–1920*. London.

Wright, A. 1914 *Disturbed Dublin: the story of the great strike of 1913–1914*. London.

Yeates, P. 2000 *Lockout: Dublin 1913*. Dublin.

Yeates, P. 2001 The Dublin Lockout, 1913. *History Ireland* 9 (2).

Yeates, P. 2011 *A city in wartime*. Dublin.

Yeates, P. 2014 How a Volunteer's role in Howth gun-running created an irreparable family breach. *Irish Times*, 17 July 2014.

Young, Capt. T. 1926 Fighting in South Dublin: with the garrison in Marrowbone Lane during Easter Week,

Index